D0228713

HD9999. C9472 NEG
2011.
Sociology &
Culture

Negotiating Values in the Creative Industries

Fairs, festivals and competitive events play a crucial role in the creative industries; yet their significance has been largely overlooked. This book explores the role of such events through a series of studies that include some of the most iconic fairs and festivals in the world. It brings together a team of distinguished scholars to examine art fairs, *biennales*, auctions, book fairs, television programming markets, film festivals, animation film festivals, country music festivals, fashion weeks, wine classifications and wine-tasting events. This diverse set of studies shows that such events serve a variety of purposes: as field-configuring events (FCEs), as a way of ritualizing industry practices, and as 'tournaments of values' where participants negotiate different cultural values to resolve economic issues. Suitable for academics and practitioners, this book presents a fascinating new perspective on the role and importance of fairs, festivals and competitive events in the creative industries.

BRIAN MOERAN is Professor of Business Anthropology and Director of the ©*reative Encounters* research programme at the Copenhagen Business School.

JESPER STRANDGAARD PEDERSEN is Professor of Organization Theory and Director of *Imagine..*, the Creative Industries Research Centre, at the Copenhagen Business School.

Negotiating Values in the Creative Industries

Fairs, Festivals and Competitive Events

Edited by
BRIAN MOERAN AND
JESPER STRANDGAARD PEDERSEN

CAMBRIDGE
UNIVERSITY PRESS

CAMBRIDGE UNIVERSITY PRESS
Cambridge, New York, Melbourne, Madrid, Cape Town,
Singapore, São Paulo, Delhi, Tokyo, Mexico City

Cambridge University Press
The Edinburgh Building, Cambridge CB2 8RU, UK

Published in the United States of America by Cambridge University Press, New York

www.cambridge.org
Information on this title: www.cambridge.org/9781107004504

© Brian Moeran and Jesper Strandgaard Pedersen 2011

This publication is in copyright. Subject to statutory exception
and to the provisions of relevant collective licensing agreements,
no reproduction of any part may take place without the written
permission of Cambridge University Press.

First published 2011

Printed in the United Kingdom at the University Press, Cambridge

A catalogue record for this publication is available from the British Library

Library of Congress Cataloging-in-Publication Data
Negotiating values in the creative industries : fairs, festivals and competitive
events / edited by Brian Moeran and Jesper Strandgaard Pedersen.
    p.   cm.
Includes index.
ISBN 978-1-107-00450-4
1. Cultural industries.   2. Value.   3. Creative ability – Economic aspects.
4. Fairs – Economic aspects.   5. Festivals – Economic aspects.
I. Moeran, Brian, 1944–   II. Pedersen, Jesper S. (Jesper Strandgaard), 1959–
HD9999.C9472N44   2011
381′.18–dc22

                                                                    2010041739

ISBN 978-1-107-00450-4 Hardback

Cambridge University Press has no responsibility for the persistence or
accuracy of URLs for external or third-party Internet websites referred to
in this publication, and does not guarantee that any content on such
websites is, or will remain, accurate or appropriate.

Contents

Figures

Tables

Contributors

N. Anand is Professor of Organisational Behaviour at IMD Lausanne. Anand's research, much of it set in the culture industries, focuses on the role of rituals and classifications in structuring fields, and has been published in distinguished journals such as *Academy of Management Journal, Annual Review of Sociology, Journal of Management Studies* and *Organization Science*.

Grégoire Croidieu is an assistant professor at Grenoble Ecole de Management. He earned a Ph.D. in management at EMLYON Business School in 2009. His research focuses on the emergence, stabilization and decline of institutions and the diffusion of cultural innovations. His chapter in this book is part of a larger research project that he is conducting on the evolution of the Bordeaux wine region (1700–2007). His research has been published in *Research in the Sociology of Work*.

Hélène Delacour is an associate professor in strategy at Institut d'Administration des Enterprises (IAE) of Toulouse, University of Toulouse Capitole. She holds a Ph.D. from the IAE of Paris, University of Paris 1 Pantheon-Sorbonne. Her research interests in creative activities relate to the evolution of the art market.

Joanne Entwistle is a senior lecturer at the Centre for Culture, Media and Creative Industries, Kings College, University of London. Her research interests are in the areas of fashion, economic sociology and the body. She is author of *The Fashioned Body: Fashion, Dress and Modern Social Theory* (2000) and *The Aesthetic Economy of Fashion: Markets and Value in Clothing and Modelling* (2009), along with numerous articles on fashion buyers and models. She is currently editing *Fashioning Models* (with Elizabeth Wissinger, forthcoming).

Timothy Havens is an associate professor of television and media studies in the Department of Communication Studies and the Program in African-American Studies at the University of Iowa. His research explores the intersections between cultural and economic practices in media globalization, particularly the ways in which racial and ethnic differences shape cultural flows. He is the author of *Black Television Travels: Media Globalization and Contemporary Racial Discourse* (forthcoming) and *Global Television Marketplace* (2006); author, with Amanda D. Lotz, of *Understanding Media Industries* (2011) and a former Senior Fulbright Scholar to Hungary. His research has also appeared in *Communication, Culture & Critique*; *Critical Studies in Media Communication*; *The Journal of Broadcasting & Electronic Media*; *International Communication Gazette* and *Global Media Journal* as well as in several anthologies on media globalization and television studies.

Ji-hyun (Jason) Kim is a Ph.D. student at the Stern School of Business, New York University. His research interests include modelling emergence of categorical structures, tradeoffs between exploration and exploitation in multi-nested systems and influence of political behaviour on organizational learning outcomes.

Joseph Lampel is Professor of Strategy at Cass Business School, City University, London, where he is also Director of Film, Media and Entertainment Research. He is co-editor, with Jamal Shamsie and Theresa Lant, of *The Business of Culture: Emerging Perspectives in Media and Entertainment* (2005), and has published in *Strategic Management Journal, Organization Science, Journal of Management Studies and Sloan Management Review*, among others. Joseph Lampel does research on the film, fashion, music and fragrance industries.

Bernard Leca is an associate professor in strategy at Rouen Business School. He holds a Ph.D. from the University of Lille 1. His research interests in creative activities relate to the movie industry and the evolution of the art market. Recent publications include *Institutional Work. Actors and Agency in Institutional Studies of Organizations*, co-edited with Thomas Lawrence and Roy Suddaby (2009).

Jennifer C. Lena is an assistant professor of sociology at Vanderbilt University in Nashville, Tennessee. She holds a Ph.D. in sociology from Columbia University. Her research focuses on innovation within the creative industries, particularly in music. Her work has been published in *American Sociological Review, Social Forces, American Behavioral*

Scientist and *Communication in Critical/Cultural Studies*, among others. Her book on music genres as classificatory schemes is to be published by Princeton University Press later in 2011.

Carmelo Mazza is a professor at Instituto de Empresa Business School in Madrid where he teaches organizational behaviour and organization theory. He was previously an assistant professor at Copenhagen Business School and an affiliate professor at Grenoble Ecole de Management. His research focuses on the application of new institutional theory to the domain of organizational transformation. Professor Mazza has studied the processes of institutionalization and transformation in the business media field, in the film industry and in the MBA field. He has analyzed the processes of institutionalization of practices, focusing on creative fields like haute cuisine and filmmaking as well as on the production of management knowledge. Recently he has studied the reform of universities as part of his research agenda on the institutionalization and transformation of organizational fields. His research has been published in top-rated international journals, as well as in edited volumes.

Janne Meier is a social anthropologist and Ph.D. fellow at ©*reative Encounters*, Copenhagen Business School. Her doctoral research is based on multi-sited fieldwork in the fashion industry in India, and at industry events, fairs and festivals in northern Europe. This comparative study traces the ways in which 'ethical' values are categorized and appropriated in the production, staging and consumption of fashion.

Stephen J. Mezias is the Abu Dhabi Commercial Bank Chair in International Management, Professor in Entrepreneurship and Family Enterprise and Academic Director of INSEAD's Middle East Campus. His current research focuses on cognitive and social aspects of institutional processes, especially as they relate to legal environments, the emergence of new industries, the production of culture, organizational learning processes, and cultural differences and similarities in performance evaluation. He is an active leader at the Academy of Management, where he has served as both Division Chair and representative-at-large for two divisions. He is a member of the editorial boards of *Organization Science* and *Strategic Management Journal*. He has previously served as an associate editor at *Management Science* and on the editorial boards of *Journal of Management* and *Administrative Science*

Quarterly. His publications have appeared in or are forthcoming in *Management Science, Organization Science, Administrative Science Quarterly* and *Strategic Management Journal*, as well as numerous other journals.

Brian Moeran is Professor of Business Anthropology in the Department of Intercultural Communication and Management at the Copenhagen Business School, and Director of ©*reative Encounters*, a research programme dedicated to the study of the socio-economic organization of creative industries. A social anthropologist by training, he has conducted extensive fieldwork on ceramics, art marketing, advertising, women's fashion magazines, incense production and the publishing industry, primarily in Japan. His books include *A Japanese Advertising Agency* (1996), *Folk Art Potters of Japan* (1997), *The Business of Ethnography* (2005) and *Ethnography at Work* (2006).

Jesper Strandgaard Pedersen is Professor of Organization Theory and Director of *Imagine..*, the Creative Industries Research Centre, at the Copenhagen Business School. His research focuses on the processes of identity creation and legitimation in knowledge intensive firms, strategies for organizing and managing creative enterprises, organization and transformation in the film and media field with a recent focus on the role of international film festivals as field-configuring events. His research has appeared in such journals as *Organization Studies, Organization, Journal of Creativity and Innovation Management, Scandinavian Journal of Management, Journal of Management Learning*, and *American Behavioral Scientist*.

Agnès Rocamora is a senior research fellow and senior lecturer in cultural and historical studies at the London College of Fashion, University of the Arts, London. Her current research interest is in the area of fashion and new media. She is the author of *Fashioning the City: Paris, Fashion and the Media* (2009) and of numerous articles on the fashion media.

Charles-Clemens Rüling is an associate professor of organization theory and coordinator of the creative industries research group at Grenoble Ecole de Management. His main research interests are in industry events and professional life trajectories in the animation and graphic design industries, as well as in bricolage in organizations. His research has appeared in such journals as *Organization Studies*, *Scandinavian Journal of Management* and *Journal of Information Technology*.

Lise Skov is an associate professor of creative industries at the Copenhagen Business School. She has done extensive research on fashion and other creative industries in Asia and Europe, and has published in a variety of academic journals and books. She is the editor of the West Europe volume in the *Berg Encyclopedia of World Dress and Fashion*, and co-editor (with Patrik Aspers) of *Encounters in the Global Fashion Business*, a themed issue of *Current Sociology*, which includes her article 'The role of trade fairs in the global fashion business'.

Charles W. Smith is Professor Emeritus of Sociology at Queens College and the Graduate Schools of City University New York (CUNY). For forty-five years he has studied how social practices and ideations mutually structure each other, particularly in auction markets of varying sorts including financial markets. He is the author of *The Mind of the Market* (1981), *Auctions: The Social Construction of Value* (1989), *Success and Survival on Wall Street* (1999) and *Market Values in American Higher Education* (2000). He has also written numerous articles and chapters including most recently 'Markets as definitional practices', *Canadian Journal of Sociology* (2007); 'Financial edgework: trading in market currents', *Edgework: The Sociology of Risk Taking* (2005) edited by Steven Lyng; 'Auctions', *Encyclopedia of Economic Sociology* (2005); and 'Globalization, higher education and markets', *Globalization and Higher Education* (2004). Since 1983 he has been editor of *The Journal for the Theory of Social Behaviour*.

Silviya Svejenova is an associate professor of strategy and entrepreneurship in the Business Policy Department at the Escuela Superior de Administrmarióry Dirección Empresas (ESADE) Business School, Ramon Llull University, Spain. Her research examines emergence, novelty, organizing and business models in creative industries, as well as the work and careers of executives. Her work has been published in *Academy of Management Perspectives*, *Journal of International Business Studies*, *Journal of Management Studies*, *Journal of Organizational Behavior*, *Long Range Planning*, *Organization* and *Sloan Management Review*. She has served on the board of the European Group for Organizational Studies (EGOS) since 2004, and her book, *Sharing Executive Power*

(2005), was an Academy of Management Terry Book Award finalist for best management book in 2007.

Jeannine Tang is an art historian and critic, and has written for publications such as *Journal of Visual Culture* and *Theory, Culture and Society*'s *Annual Review*. She is currently preparing an essay on collection and post-conceptualism entitled 'Future circulations: on the work of Hans Haacke and Maria Eichhorn' for an edited anthology on provenance forthcoming from the Getty Research Institute. A doctoral candidate at the Courtauld Institute of Art, she is currently completing a dissertation on conceptualism, media and the Cold War. She was previously a fellow at the Smithsonian American Art Museum and a critical studies participant at the Whitney independent study program.

Don Thompson is Nabisco Brands Chair Emeritus and Senior Scholar at the Schulich School of Business, York University, Toronto. He has taught at Harvard University, and held visiting positions at University College London, London School of Economics, University of Toronto, Macquarie University in Sydney, Australia and Singapore. Most recently he was visiting professor at the Faculty of Business Administration, Bilkent University in Ankara, Turkey. He is author of *The $12 Million Stuffed Shark: The Curious Economics of Contemporary Art* (2008), which has been published in ten languages.

Acknowledgements

This edited volume is the result of an intensive workshop organized by Brian Moeran and Jesper Strandgaard Pedersen in September 2009 under the title of *Industry Encounters: Fairs and Festivals*. This was one of a number of similar workshops taking place under the auspices of ©*reative Encounters*, an interdisciplinary research programme focusing on the socio-economic organization of creative industries. It is funded by the Strategic Research Council of Denmark (2007–11), and based at the Copenhagen Business School. We are very grateful to both organizations for enabling us to engage in such exciting research.

As organizers, we would like to thank Carsten Yssing, programme administrator of ©*reative Encounters*, Sarah Netter and Jane Deters for all the cheerful hard work that they put in to make the workshop so successful. We are also very grateful to Asaf Darr for his invaluable contribution to our discussions and to Grégoire Croidieu for providing a wine tasting event that quickly had all participants engaged in enthusiastic, intellectual and exhilarated (we dare not say inebriated!) exchanges at the end of a long day.

As editors, we wish to extend our gratitude to Paula Parish at Cambridge University Press for nursing this manuscript to book form, and to Frederik Larsen for his unstinting attention to detail and standardization in preparation of the manuscript.

If we were ourselves members of the creative industries that our authors describe in the pages that follow, we would at this stage start thanking our children, colleagues, designers, guinea pigs, managers, mothers-in-law, producers, publishers, wives, etcetera, etcetera, for this or that, but we aren't, so we won't.

Brian Moeran
Jesper Strandgaard Pedersen

Introduction

BRIAN MOERAN AND JESPER
STRANDGAARD PEDERSEN

This book is about how those working in the creative industries take into account, negotiate and try to use to their advantage different kinds of values when participating in fairs, festivals and competitive events. It addresses three broad themes that cover the production, exchange and consumption of cultural or creative products. One concerns the nature of creative industries themselves and their production processes; another the role of fairs and festivals as institutions of economic and cultural exchange in the creative industries; and the third the ways in which different fields of cultural production are constituted and evolve through negotiation of the various values that different actors bring to bear on, and that ultimately extend to the consumption of, cultural products.

Creative industries

The – seemingly oxymoronic – notion of a 'creative industry' is an amalgam of two older terms that can be traced back to two separate sources. The first is 'creative arts', which derived from the philosophy of civic humanism espoused by the Earl of Shaftesbury and Sir Joshua Reynolds in England during the eighteenth century, and which came to be associated with an intellectual ideology of 'public art' (Hartley, 2005: 6–7). The second is 'culture industry', a term coined in 1947 by two members of the Frankfurt School, Max Horkheimer and Theodor Adorno, in their influential book, *Dialectic of Enlightenment*, to describe the role of media in contemporary society. This phrase was preferred to that of 'mass culture' because the authors wished to argue against the then prevalent idea that culture arose spontaneously from the masses themselves. Instead, they suggested that cultural products were carefully tailored for consumption by the masses and were thus manufactured more or less according to plan (Adorno, 1991: 85). For this reason, Adorno later explained, the expression 'industry' was not intended to be taken too literally. It did not refer strictly to production processes, but to the standardization of cultural products, as well as to the rationalization of techniques relating to their distribution (Adorno, 1991: 87). Both these terms, in their separate ways, were originally advocated in opposition to the commercial exploitation of creativity.

In spite of Adorno's clarification, it was production processes that were taken up in ensuing research on what, in an attempt to avoid the monolithic determinism of Horkheimer and Adorno, have since been called the 'cultural industries'. Scholars such as Paul Hirsch, Howard Becker and Richard Peterson have all in their various ways advocated what has been called a 'production of culture' perspective – either by analysing the role of gatekeepers and distributor organizations (brokers, distributors, media outlets) as a crucial means of linking creative people to their audiences (Hirsch, 1972; 2000); or by showing how creative people do not work in aetherial isolation, but make use of networks to produce works that are very much a result of co-operative endeavour (Becker, 1974; 1982); or by focusing on 'how the symbolic elements of culture are shaped by the systems in which they are created, distributed, evaluated, taught and observed' (Peterson and Anand, 2004: 311; Peterson, 1976). Gary Fine (1992) has added his own nuance to this approach by looking at the aesthetic choices and constraints facing creative people (in his case professional cooks) in what he refers to as 'the culture of production'.

'Cultural industries' were – provisionally, at least – overtaken by the term 'creative industries', which came into policy and education discourses in Australia and the UK in the mid-1990s initially, before spreading to other parts of Europe, Asia and the Americas, as creativity was, and still is, openly exploited for political and commercial ends. It is national and local governments in particular, rather than the industries themselves, that have identified which industries are 'creative' and which, by implication, are not in the so-called 'new economy', where value arises out of processing information and creating experiences rather than products *per se*. And yet, as John Hartley (2005: 26–30) further argues, creative industries cannot be identified at the levels of either industry or organization since creativity is, unlike an automobile or sheet of aluminium, an input, not an output. Moreover, the creative industries have not developed common interest associations that might exploit their 'creativity', partly because creative workers are for the most part employed on a casual, part-time, freelance basis and thus develop 'portfolio' rather than organization-based careers.

Perhaps because of the sheer variety of ways in which they can be examined, creative industries are now variously referred to as copyright and (digital) content, as well as creative and cultural industries, depending on whether assets, technology, industrial production, labour inputs or public policy funding are the focus of attention (Hartley, 2005: 30).[1] Whichever of these terms is adopted, what is at issue is the extent to which such industries can, or cannot, be explained by economics. In a seminal work, the economist Richard Caves (2000) uses the theory of contracts to ask why self-interested parties in the creative industries structure their work in the ways that they do. He assumes that creative workers do not differ from others in that they are purposive and 'intendedly rational' in what they do. However, their preferences or tastes, together with production processes and the goods and services that they produce, differ in substantial and systematic ways from those of people working in other parts of the economy where creativity is not an issue. From this Caves (2000: 3–10) argues that there are certain 'bedrock properties' – which include the infinite variety of creative products, together with an accompanying uncertainty of demand; a need for close temporal and social co-ordination in production because of timing and the diverse skills required to complete creative works; the care that creative people bring to their work, which is itself qualitatively differentiated in terms of their rank; and intellectual property rights with their durable rents – that distinguish creative industries from other sectors of the economy.

Contributors to this edited volume have been trained in various different social sciences, though not in economics. Their focus, therefore, is more on the symbolic practices and organizational forms characterizing different forms of cultural production such as animation, art, book publishing, fashion, film, music, television and wine, than on economics *per se*. What interests them all is the ways in which various aspects of what might be broadly construed as 'culture' interact with, affect and are themselves affected by the economy of fairs, festivals and other competitive events including wine contests, art biennales and auctions.

Fairs and festivals

In spite of their obviousness and the fact that they have been increasing in number very rapidly over the past two decades (for example, currently more than 3,500 film festivals take place worldwide [see Mazza and Strandgaard Pedersen, 2008]), trade fairs and festivals have, until recently, largely been ignored by scholars working in such disciplinary fields as sociology, anthropology, strategy and management, as well as economics, although – as we shall here see – not by geographers or historians.[2] In hindsight this is surprising. After all, historically, fairs have been the essential tools of long-distance trade since medieval times and, some would aver, from much, much earlier. The fairs of Troyes, for example, are alleged to date back to Roman times, and those of Lyon to AD 172 (Braudel, 1992: 82). Whether such allegations are true may be of doubt, but from medieval times fairs, like those of Champagne (Face, 1958), were extremely important elements in what was an international economy. They functioned to break the usual cycle of trade and 'interrupt the tight circle of everyday exchanges' (Braudel, 1992: 82) – a function still performed, as we shall later see, by such creative industry events as the Venice Biennale (Tang, Chapter 3), London Fashion Week (Entwistle and Rocamora, Chapter 10), and Fan Fair country music festival in Nashville (Lena, Chapter 9).

Although the present-day 'sample' fair is in many ways different from the 'commodity' fair of old (Allix, 1922: 557–60), a number of historical parallels between the two should be noted. Firstly, fairs have always taken on the appearance of *temporary townships* or cities (Skov, 2006; see also Skov and Meier, Chapter 11). Either they have been incorporated in a fixed town (like Leipzig), taking over everything in it and itself 'becoming' the town – something we see in the Cannes Film Festival (Mezias *et al.*, Chapter 7) or the Documenta art exhibition held every five years in the German city of Kassel – or they are held in juxtaposition to a town, outside its limits, and becoming thereby an extension of the town, like the Frankfurt Book Fair held in the city's Messe (Allix, 1922: 542–4; Braudel, 1992: 82–4). Occasionally, an event may move from the centre of a town to its edge (Moeran, Chapter 5), or from the edge to its very centre (Lena), or from one city to another and back again (Skov and Meier).

Secondly, unlike markets which are held on regular days of a week or month to enable immediate exchange, fairs were instituted to enable periodic forms of exchange for large-scale, especially international, commerce. This periodicity existed in terms of both the frequency and length of time with which fairs were held, and depended originally upon the itinerancy of traders and their merchandise (Allix, 1922: 540).

Precisely because merchants needed time to travel from town to town with their packhorses, carts and goods, fairs were timed to accommodate their movement. In this respect they formed *networks of fairs* – or, in the current terminology of economic geographers, 'cyclical clusters' (Power and Jansson, 2008) – that were mutually dependent and communicated with one another. This kind of *perpetuum mobile* is still true of industry fairs and art biennales (Thompson, Chapter 2; Tang) today – so much so that a fair will create its own network if none at first exists (Rüling, Chapter 8). Just as a merchant used to travel to the fairs centred on Linz along the Danube – from Krems to Vienna, and thence to Freistadt, Graz, Salzburg and Bolzano, before heading back to Krems (Braudel, 1992: 92) – so nowadays does a book publisher move (albeit by somewhat swifter means of transport) from Abu Dhabi to, in quick succession, the Leipzig Book Fair, Bologna Children's Book Fair and Salon du Livre in Paris in March, before travelling on to the great spring fair in London in mid-April, and thence, if so inclined, to the Thessaloniki Book Fair at the end of the same month, and the Tehran International Book Fair and Book Expo America in May.[3] There is a hierarchy of fairs in each network (Power and Jansson, 2008: 439; see also Thompson; Moeran; and Mezias *et al.* in this volume) and clashes of fair schedules that might upset this hierarchy – as when Frankfurt decided to hold its fair at the same time as Leipzig's in the early 1700s (Beachy, 1999: 437–38) – are frowned upon. This explains why a lesser fair, like the Tokyo International Book Fair, for example, had to adjust its timetable by rescheduling from April to July when the London Book Fair shifted *its* dates from March to April in 2005 because of a move to a new location (Moeran, 2009: 3–4).

Thirdly, fairs are not simply places in which to conduct business. They have always 'meant noise, tumult, music, popular rejoicing, the world turned upside down' (Braudel, 1992: 85) and were often centres of popular entertainment (Isherwood, 1981) where celebration could become contestation (Rearick, 1977: 437; (Delacour and Leca, Chapter 1). Fair time, in other words, was like *carnival time* (Thompson). It was also spectacle time with its processions, competitions, bonfires, fireworks, juggling, miracle cures and tooth-pulling. Nowadays, perhaps, we may prefer to have our teeth examined (at worst, pulled) in the private comfort of a dentist's chair, but creative industry fairs and festivals today still provide an entertaining array of spectacles for participants – from boozy book fair parties to topless would-be actresses on the beach at Cannes, by way of the red carpet approach to the Academy Awards venue. It is in their concentrations of goods (books, films, music, fashion, wine), people and entertainment that fairs and festivals retain their importance and make their mark.

Finally, fairs have several *symbolic functions*. Fairs and festivals distinguish between 'insiders' and 'outsiders', between the more and the less privileged (Thompson; Havens, Chapter 6; Entwistle and Rocamora). In the past this was revealed in clothing and accessories distinguishing buyers from sellers, as well as different professional specializations (Gueusquin-Barbichon, 1980: 328), although nowadays such distinctions are made most obviously in the different colours and kinds of badges worn by participants, as well as in more general styles of dress (Smith, Chapter 4). It is also revealed in terms of the disposition of space – of who is placed where in an exhibition hall (Moeran), and of who may go where, when and for what purpose (Gueusquin-Barbichon, 1980; see also Havens). The medieval 'passport', or 'conduct of the fair', which assured travelling merchants of free passage to a fair on certain defined routes during a prescribed time is also replicated in the accreditation badges that not only permit entry to contemporary fairs and festivals (Entwistle and Rocamora), but also give special advantages (like free travel on city transport) for their duration (Allix, 1922: 540, 560).

More generally, the symbolic function of fairs is to be seen in activities that are carried on *outside* the normal course of trade exchange. Food and drink are shared, parties held, relationships between male and female participants formed and occasionally cemented, and all the time information is exchanged. In contemporary as in traditional town fairs, it is in the cafés and 'watering holes' surrounding the marketplace of commodities that the main exchanges often occur. In the old days, everything from the trade of goods to the arrangement of marriages took place there, so that the fair has been an opportunity for the renewal of social communion among participants, and an occasion to reinforce in-group boundaries (Maho, 1980: 66).

Given these historical continuities between medieval and contemporary fairs, we should note that fairs and festivals, though not exactly the same, share a number of common features. Firstly, they are *spatially bounded*: usually stage-set in, and framed by, a particular location – whether an indoor exhibition hall, park, around a town or city, or a combination thereof. Such settings are often set apart from their surroundings, thereby reflecting the liminal nature of the events that they house (Skov, 2006: 768). Spatial boundedness may also be found in the display of cultural products themselves (Delacour and Leca).

Secondly, they are *temporarily bounded* in terms of both duration and regularity. Fairs are short-term events in which all related activities take place over a period of from three days to three weeks, although some festivals – especially those with artistic content – tend to go on considerably longer (in some special cases up to three months). They are also usually held at regular intervals – normally once a year, but sometimes, as with fashion weeks, more frequently (Entwistle and Rocamora; Skov and Meier) and occasionally much less so, as with art biennales which are held every two, five or ten years (Tang). Temporality also asserts itself in other ways. For instance, it is crucial for collectors that they get access to art works displayed in art fairs before their competitors since prized pieces sell very quickly; for this they are prepared to pay premium admission prices. Also, both fashion shows and auctions are marked by a temporal flow in which selected cultural products are exhibited and sold. Finally, temporality occurs as a means of creating, sustaining or subverting a fair or festival's hier-archical structure, as the chapters on a wine classificatory system and competition by Croidieu (Chapter 12) and Anand (Chapter 13) attest.

Thirdly, fairs and festivals are *socially bounded* in that they bring together a large and diverse number of participants – industry manu-facturers, distributors, wholesalers and retailers – who are closely involved in the production and distribution of the products and services being exhibited. As such, in their composition, they closely approximate DiMaggio and Powell's (1983: 143) definition of an organizational field as: 'those organizations that, in the aggregate, constitute a recognized area of institutional life: key suppliers, resource and product consumers, regulatory agencies, and other organizations that produce similar services and products'. Such organizations structure a field as 'a configuration of objective relations between positions' (Bourdieu and Wacquant, 1992: 97) and as 'a socially structured space in which agents struggle' (Wacquant, 1992: 17). Such social boundedness means that end-users tend to be marginal.

Finally, fairs and festivals are also *functionally unbounded*. By this we mean that they serve multiple purposes – purposes that are often tightly related to the actors and agents participating in these events, since both fairs and festivals bring together a large and diverse group of

participants who also happen to have diverse agendas and reasons for
going to such events (Moeran; Skov and Meier). Some may come to
trade (to buy or to sell products exhibited); others to obtain financial
support for projects; some to build or maintain social relations and
networks; others to engage in some form of reputation-management by
promoting a product, a company, themselves, or some kind of political
agenda. Fairs and festivals also attract other kinds of participants who
are not closely linked to the industry concerned: for example, media
organizations gather at such events in order to get or create a good story
(Reff Pedersen and Strandgaard Pedersen, 2008). Indeed, formal and
informal talk and opinion, information exchanges, and story-telling are
an inherent aspect of fairs and festivals (Delacour and Leca; Smith;
Moeran; Entwistle and Rocamora), during the course of which certain
discourses emerge and the meanings of symbolic keywords are contested and negotiated (Rüling; Skov and Meier; Croidieu).

This leads us to the following definition, where we ourselves rephrase
André Allix's modification (1922: 568) of his own earlier definition of
fairs (Allix, 1914): *a fair or festival is a temporary township, superimposed at intervals upon a permanent town or city, which in important, though not regularly defined, social and symbolic ways contributes
to the global needs of a particular industry and those who work therein.*

What is interesting about fairs and festivals, then, together with
awards, prizes, auctions, exhibitions and other related phenomena, is
the intersection of institutions and individuals, on the one hand, and of
economic, social and symbolic activities, on the other. Overtly, trade
fairs are about exhibiting 'the new', be it an idea in its initial state or a
finalized product, showing one's capabilities, and trading in a particular
commodity (that can range from aerospace to art, by way of electrical
engineering, energy, food and restaurants, hardware, health, information technology (IT) and telecoms, jewellery, leisure boats, optics, packaging, pharmaceuticals, security, toys and travel, to keep the list fairly
short). They provide opportunities for participants to enter into business negotiations with long-term partners, to gain knowledge through
market information exchanges and to initiate and sustain social relations (Anand and Watson, 2004; Skov, 2006; Lampel and Meyer,
2008). Fairs also let participants observe competitors' exhibits. They
may lead to vertical integration along an industry's supply and value
chains, as well as to horizontal interaction among competing firms
therein (Maskell *et al.*, 2006: 1,001–2). But, contrary to the claim

made by Maskell and his co-authors, actual trade itself is *not* necessarily marginal (Skov, 2006: 770), even though trade fairs (and festivals) are largely about social relationships, symbolic hierarchies and cultural capital prized by the institutions and individuals attending them. One indication of the economic importance of fairs is a participant's expenditure and income. Booths at the Maastricht Art Fair, for example, may cost as much as €50,000, with total costs for a dealer wishing to exhibit there (including shipping, travel, accommodation, food and entertainment) reaching €80,000. In 2007, sales arranged at this venue for the 219 participating dealers had a value of €790 million, with dealers claiming that 40–70 per cent of their annual sales were made during the eleven days of the fair (Thompson, 2008: 188–9).

Values

The research carried out on fairs and festivals so far shares at least one concern: the extent to which what might be broadly termed 'cultural phenomena' inflect economic practices and vice-versa, as different values are brought to bear by the different actors involved (Throsby, 2001).[4] This concern may be traced back to anthropological approaches to the study of so-called 'primitive economies' (Sahlins, 1965; Firth, 1967), but the study of values has always been central to explanations of the political economy.

Economists regard the notion of 'value' (utility, price and worth) as the origin of, and motivation for, all forms of economic behaviour (Throsby, 2001: 19). In its singular form, value has been examined principally as a means towards equating the 'inherent' qualities of commodities with their quantitative worth. As Karl Marx (1976: 138) noted long ago: 'they are only commodities because they have a dual nature, because they are at the same time objects of utility and bearers of value'. Many other social scientists, however, adopt a very different approach and regard economists' notion of value as at best problematic. But there is little coherence among the different disciplinary approaches in their conceptualization and measurement of such values (Hitlin and Piliavin, 2004: 359–60). For sociologists, for example, values tend to be abstract ideals – as opposed to norms which are 'definitive principles or rules which people are expected to observe' (Giddens, 1993: 31) – and refer to the taken-for-granted processes by which social structures regulate individual actions. For linguists, however, values indicate

'meaningful differences' in language, where 'the value of any one element depends on the simultaneous coexistence of the others' (de
Saussure, 1983: 113). For their part, economists have built theories of
value around the concept of a price system (e.g., Debreu, 1987). It is the
idea that, like fairs themselves, values are meaningful only in so far as
they form a system of complementary differences that this introduction
develops.

Values are the criteria by which people judge what is legitimate
(Suchman, 1995: 574) and worthwhile in their everyday lives
(Graeber, 2001: 3). They are concepts or beliefs about desirable end
states or behaviours. They transcend specific situations, and tend to
guide evaluations of behaviour and events. They are also usually
ordered by relative importance (Schwartz and Bilsky, 1987: 551). It is
the patterns of values held by different professional groups occupying
different social structural positions in different creative industries; the
ways in which such values are negotiated (by whom, with whom, when,
where, for what ends, and so on); and how they motivate social behaviour that are of interest here. Such patterns also affect cultural products
themselves, and the (re)valuation – or 'consecration' (Bourdieu, 1993) –
of art works, books, fashions, films, music and so on 'is one of the
central processes in the cultural industries' (Lampel and Nadavulakere,
2009: 239).

Fairs, festivals and competitive events provide a venue for the
(re)enactment of institutional arrangements in a particular industry's
field and for the negotiation and affirmation of the different values that
underpin them. Thus, while the function of economic exchange may be
to create value, all sorts of other, different kinds of – material, social,
temporal, spatial, appreciative and other – values are introduced and
promoted as part of the negotiation of the economic worth of an art
work, fashion collection, book, film, television programme, or other
creative product. In this respect, fairs and festivals epitomize Simmel's
argument that value is never an inherent property of objects, but arises
from a judgement made about those objects by people whose whole
lives 'consist in experiencing and judging values'. In other words, the
conceptual meaning of value or valuation is not itself part of the world,
but 'the whole world viewed from a particular vantage point' (Simmel,
1978: 60). For this very reason, values become what might broadly be
called 'cultural'. This book explains how particular professional
worlds, bounded in space and time, are viewed from the vantage points

of different participants for whom the values they hold form a comprehensive part of their world views and are thus a counterpart to their very being.

The question then arises: why continue to use the term 'value' in the singular? One possible answer, perhaps, is to be found in the overwhelming dominance of economics in contemporary societies. It was only economics among the social sciences that did not explicitly focus on the study of values in the 1960s (Hitlin and Paliavin, 2004: 362). Certainly, neo-classical economists are dismissive of cultural economists who do try to adopt a broader view of cultural phenomena (Throsby, 2001: xii), and find it difficult to comprehend patterns of values held by members of different cultural groups who occupy different social structural positions.[5] After all, the process of evaluation is always contingent on who is evaluating what for whom, when, where, how, why, and in what context. In other words, value is 'neither a fixed attribute, an inherent quality, nor an objective property of things but, rather, an effect of multiple, continuously changing, and continuously interacting variables or, to put this another way, the product of a system, specifically an *economic* system' (Herrnstein-Smith, 1988: 30).

Another answer may lie in the very diversity and variability of values themselves, which can be used to refer to anything from the aesthetic, spiritual, social, historical, symbolic and authenticity values found in art works (Throsby, 2001: 28–9) to the ten value-types of hedonism, power, achievement, stimulation, self-direction, universalism, benevolence, conformity, tradition and security analysed for seventy different cultures around the world (Schwartz, 1994). Alternatively, they may include the 'non-user values' of option, existence, bequest, prestige and innovative values discussed by Frey (2003), as well as 'interests, pleasures, likes, preferences, duties, moral obligations, desires, wants, goals, needs, aversions and attractions, and many other kinds of selective orientations' (Williams, 1979: 16). Given the broad range of enumerated values and the variety of applications to which they are put (some psychological, others social), is it possible, or even advisable, to try to synthesize these different emphases on the concept of value?

Our concern here is with the production, negotiation, and transaction of various kinds of values in the context of fairs and festivals transacting *commodities* (in this instance, cultural products): animation, art works, books, fashion items, music, films, television programmes, wine, and so on. It is these that make Value (with, if we are to singularize it, a capital V). Following earlier work by Brian Moeran (1997; 2004), we wish to suggest that what constitutes Value in the kinds of cultural *products* (as opposed to agents or social processes) that are the focus of trade fairs and festivals are technical/material, social, situational, appreciative and utility or use values which, together, create a symbolic exchange value. It is this qualitative symbolic value that is then exchanged for a quantitative economic value, or what we prefer to call commodity exchange value.

What exactly are these different kinds of values and how can we see them at work in the production, distribution and exchange of creative goods at fairs, festivals and similar forms of competitive events?

Firstly, let us take *technical/material* values. These stem, on the one hand, from the materials that creative personnel use during the course of designing and making cultural products and, on the other, from the specialized professional knowledge and techniques that they bring to bear on those materials. For example, a fashion designer will select a material (wool, fur, cotton, muslin and so on) for an item of clothing in terms of its suitability of purpose, and then design it according to the way in which that particular material is amenable to the forms that they wish to wring therefrom, or hangs from the body, and so on. Similarly, a photographer will pay close attention to camera type, shutter speed, focus, lighting, background and so forth during the course of setting up a shot; while a potter will explain in some detail the difficulties involved in forming pots with a certain kind of clay, as well as what he can and cannot do with particular glazes when finished forms are placed in different parts of a wood-fired kiln (and what effects wood – as opposed to electricity or gas – might produce during the course of firing). These kinds of technical values are based on the craft knowledge and skills developed by a professional during the course of his work, and are not necessarily known or shared by others involved. Sometimes, as in the case of recipes for incense production, for instance, they are closely-guarded secrets handed down from one generation of blenders to another.

Secondly, *social* values: here we find that almost all cultural products are affected by social relations of one sort or another, some of them at the level of the individual, others at that of organizational, interaction. A fashion designer will choose a particular photographer because of previous experiences of working together or because of a recommendation by someone else whom they know and respect. The photographer in turn will select a particular model not simply for the appropriateness of her 'look' *vis-à-vis* the task in hand, but also because they may be distantly related to a minor 'royal' and have appeared on the front cover of *Vogue*, whose fashion editor the photographer also knows. A gallerist will back up his claim to a 'discerning eye' by means of his 'stable' of artists and ability to gather around him name collectors prepared to pay for the art works on display. Similarly, a designer will proclaim their 'provenance' by making continued reference to the fashion school from which they graduated and fashion houses for which they have worked. In this way, institutional affiliations, as well as individual social contacts and networks of one sort or another, are used to give or enhance the perceived value of a cultural product (fashion item, photograph, or art work). Such social values tend to incorporate notions of status and prestige: witness the importance attributed to a particular dress or piece of jewellery worn by a particular film star at the Academy Awards, and the attention paid to the clothing of celebrities in fashion magazines. There is a continuous two-way slippage between persons and things in the construction and maintenance of social values.

Thirdly, *situational* values: the values accruing to an item because of its use in a particular situation which may be temporal or spatial, and often embracing notions of rarity and authenticity. Examples of situational values can be found in the white glove worn by Michael Jackson at his 1983 performance of *Billie Jean* at the Motown 25 television special where he performed the moonwalk for the first time, and which was auctioned in November 2009 for $350,000; and in the thirteenth-century ash-glazed jar unearthed by a bulldozer in rural Japan which was first authenticated and then designated an important intangible cultural property by the country's Agency for Cultural Affairs, before not one but two well-known contemporary Japanese potters claimed that they had themselves made, glazed and fired it!

As can be seen from these examples, situational values are closely related to social values in that history itself focuses on the exploits of famous individuals. However, more specifically situational values may be seen in the world premiering of films (discussed by Mezias *et al.*), the temporal ordering of fashion clothes worn by models in a catwalk show (with later items often being seen as 'more important' than earlier ones), or in the spatial arrangement of art works in a gallery (or jewellery items in a store). The space between exhibited items, their positioning at the 'front' or in the 'depth' of a gallery, and their placement on a plinth, behind glass or other protective element, setting the object symbolically aside from its audience, all reveal and affect their perceived commodity-exchange value.

Fourthly, *appreciative* values: primarily, but not exclusively, aesthetic (focusing on such concepts as taste, harmony, creativity, form, style, and so on) and emerging from the ways in which cultural products are praised or damned by critics in media reviews (as in 'his style is superbly musical and allusive, but the content is vague'). Certain kinds of aesthetic language come to be used for certain kinds of cultural products (think fashion, food, film, or wine), and can even be used to make distinctions within categories. The language used to appraise traditional craft pottery, for instance ('pregnant beauty', 'rounded form'), differs radically from that used to describe less functional sculptural forms ('dynamic masculinity', 'vertical upward thrust'). At the same time, however, such language is not necessarily strictly aesthetic, since product advertising, for example, can make use of a different kind of appreciative language designed to attract consumers to buy the product in question and, ideally, convert it into a 'brand' (think *Guinness is good for you* or L'Oréal's *Because you're worth it*). Appreciative values also include legal evaluations (affecting, for instance, copyright in some creative products), so that they are in many respects ideological values which impact upon the perceived Value of a cultural product.

Finally *utility* or use values: the intended function of a cultural product and the uses to which it is actually put. Generally speaking, clothes are worn, photographs are looked at, and pots are eaten out of, or used for decorative purposes. However, a stocking can serve as an elongated container for Christmas presents or as a bank robber's mask; magazine photographs can be used as wrapping paper; and a plate as an ashtray. Most times such uses are temporary, but they can become more permanent, as when a number of photographs are put together as wallpaper, or a jar originally designed to pickle onions and to be placed in an earth-floored farmhouse storeroom is used as a decorative vase in the sacred *tokonoma* raised dais of a Japanese home (Moeran, 1997: 199). It is the uses to which we wish to put a cultural product, and the potential functions that that product possesses, that influence our decision about whether or not to purchase it. It can be seen that utility is very often valued by consumers, but utility values also come into play in cultural production. A hair stylist can suddenly improvise with a pair of chopsticks to hold up a model's hair, for instance, or a potter use a shaving brush to achieve a particular design effect with slip clay and iron oxide.

Together, these different values constitute different criteria for valuation and form a field that influences our selection of various cultural products. Sometimes we are influenced by the beauty of an object, at other times by its utility, craftsmanship, or brand association. We weigh up the different aspects of technical/material, social, situational, appreciative and utility or use values in every cultural product, and try to calculate their combined *symbolic-exchange* value, which we then test against an economic criterion – money or price. Does this piece of sculpture that we like have one too many zeros on its price tag? Does that dress that first attracted us on the clothes rack turn out to be 'cheap and nasty'? If the price established for a product meets our symbolic exchange evaluation, and we decide to purchase a little black dress by Chanel, a photographic print by Helmut Newton, or a dish by Lucie Rie, then we have engaged in what might be termed *commodity-exchange* value. Although some values may be given more emphasis than others (a fashion model's social recommendations rather than her appreciated beauty *per se*, or the technical skills achieved by an artist or potter rather than the finished work that each produces), it is here that quality meets quantity, culture meets economy, and values are converted into Value.

One advantage of the approach to the study of values of cultural products outlined here is that it accounts for their ongoing social construction and negotiation as people go about their everyday lives. Another is that it links the evaluation of commodities with more general evaluative practices in social worlds, or fields, and thereby complements previous theorizing of values in terms of *social relations*. For instance, Pierre Bourdieu (1993: 30) has argued that all kinds of different interests are at stake in every field, and that participants invest in these and often compete for control of the resources of the field in which they operate. Such resources are sometimes material, sometimes social, sometimes ideological or symbolic, and the way that they are distributed defines each field.

Bourdieu developed the concept of 'capital' to describe these resources, and analysed the various forms of economic, educational, cultural, social and symbolic capital that *people* try to build up, before converting it into another form that they lack, as part of their struggle for power in a particular field – something to which we will return below. Thus a designer who has graduated from a prestigious fashion school can use her educational capital to obtain a job with a well-known fashion house and thereby convert her educational into social and cultural, and thence economic, capital. A fashion model who appears on the cover of *Vogue* (for little more than $200) can use the symbolic capital accrued to immediately double her rates for other magazine fashion shoots or an advertising campaign. Similarly, a traditional potter who is designated the holder of an 'important intangible cultural property' by Japan's Ministry of Culture can convert this newly acquired symbolic capital into economic capital by raising his prices three- or four-fold overnight. In other words, people are trying to capitalize on a particular situation and turn it to their advantage, depending on their position in a particular field of cultural production. The conversion of different forms of capital is made possible by the different values that different people bring to bear on their activities depending on their positions within a particular field or social world.

The approach to the study of values proposed here examines the *things* produced by people making use of different forms of capital. It suggests that a designer dress, fashion model, or stoneware pot is 'beautiful' not in itself, but because of the different technical, social, situational, appreciative, utility or use, symbolic and commodity exchange values that are brought to bear in its aesthetic and commercial judgement. Such an approach stresses their ongoing social construction and negotiation as we go about our everyday lives.[6] Different people in a social world will tend to stress different kinds of values: a seamstress is likely to be more focused on technical/material, and a fashion designer on aesthetic, values than – say – a fashion model for whom social networks are more important, while for the consumer the wearability of a garment is probably a decisive factor in the symbolic-commodity exchange equation. Similar considerations come into play in the art, film, music and other creative worlds, and they tend to take centre stage in events like art fairs and exhibitions, film festivals and so on, where cultural products are on display and transformations of symbolic values regularly take place (Anand and Jones, 2008: 1049–51).

Tournament fields

Mention of symbolic values brings us to the final part of our theoretical discussion, and to the issue of how best to theorize the role of fairs and festivals in the creative industries. In the introduction to an influential edited volume, *The Social Life of Things*, anthropologist Arjun Appadurai takes issue with the standard argument put forward by political economists that 'commodities are special kinds of manufactured goods (or services), which are associated only with capitalist modes of production and are thus to be found only where capitalism has penetrated' (Appadurai, 1986: 7). He argues, instead, that all commodities have their social lives; that they are things with a particular kind of social potential, in some ways and from certain points of view distinguishable from objects, artefacts, products and goods; and that they circulate in different regimes of value in both space and time (Appadurai, 1986: 3–6). If, he continues, one accepts that a commodity is '*any thing intended for exchange*', then the question arises: 'What sort of exchange is commodity exchange?' (Appadurai, 1986: 9).

Such a question necessarily implies a cultural framework within which exchange becomes possible because, at a certain phase in its social life (or career) and in a particular context, a commodity elicits some measure of shared cultural assumptions (Appadurai, 1986: 15–16). Commodities are not mechanically governed by laws of supply and demand; rather, they have their 'paths' and 'diversions'; in any given situation the flow of commodities is 'a shifting compromise between socially regulated paths and competitively inspired diversions' (Appadurai, 1986: 17).

The example that Appadurai uses to illustrate his argument is that of the celebrated *kula* exchange – an extremely complex system devised for the circulation of certain kinds of valuables among men of reputation in the Massim group of islands in the Western Pacific (see Malinowski, 1922). Precisely because the large-scale exchanges of shells define the value of the men who value and exchange them, the paths and diversions taken by such shells become very important to the politics of reputation.

It is here that the *kula* ring becomes a paradigm for what Appadurai calls *tournaments of value*. These, he says, are:

Complex periodic events that are removed in some culturally defined way from the routine of everyday economic life. Participation in them is ... both a privilege for those in power and an instrument of status contests between them. The currency of such tournaments is also ... set apart through well understood cultural diacritics ... What is at issue ... is not just status, rank, fame, or reputation of actors, but the disposition of the central tokens of value in the society in question. Finally, though such tournaments of value occur in special times and places, their forms and outcomes are always consequential for the more mundane realities of power and value in ordinary life. (Appadurai (1986: 21))

Appadurai clearly recognized that 'an agonistic, romantic, individual-istic, and gamelike ethos that stands in contrast to the ethos of everyday economic behavior' (Appadurai, 1986: 50) is to be found in contempo-rary industrialized societies – something we have ourselves noted above in our discussion of the historical features of fairs. In answer to his call for 'a fuller examination of the modes of articulation of these "tourna-ment" economies' (*Ibid.*), Brian Moeran went on to argue in his dis-cussion of competitive presentations in the Japanese advertising industry that tournaments of value also included:

The various *haute couture* and *prêt-à-porter* fashion shows held in Paris, London, Milan, New York and Tokyo; certain types of auction put on with accompanying publicity by Sotheby's, Christie's and other art auctioneers; annual media events such as the Miss World and Miss Universe beauty competitions, the Eurovision Song Contest, the Grammy awards for music, the Oscar awards for those working in the film industry; some art exhibitions and film festivals themselves (in Cannes, Venice and so on); and, of course, the Nobel prizes. (Moeran (1993: 93))

This suggestion lay dormant for more than a decade until Anand and Watson (2004), referring once again to Appadurai, drew on perspec-tives from ritual theory to show how ceremonies such as the Grammy awards were 'an important institutional mechanism for shaping organ-izational fields' referring to such events as 'tournament rituals'. Publication of this article coincided more or less with developments in the fields of management and organization studies where a number of scholars were engaged in research on conferences, ceremonies and trade shows, and had begun to discuss their analyses in terms of 'field-configuring events', or FCEs (Meyer *et al.*, 2005; Lampel and Meyer, 2008: 1025–6). It is the latter term that now dominates the management and organization studies literature, where different aspects of creative industries are also discussed (e.g., Watson and Anand, 2006; Anand and Jones, 2008; Glynn, 2008). Once again, we find ourselves faced with an issue of terminology: are we to think of fairs, festivals and other competitive events as 'tournaments' of some kind, or as 'field-configuring events' (FCEs), or as somehow forming an interlocking relationship?

The idea of fairs as tournaments in fact goes back a long way. Appadurai himself notes that he has drawn on an earlier work by Mariott (1968), who referred to 'tournaments of rank' in his analysis of Indian caste food transactions, while almost two decades before that Merle Curti (1950: 833) described late-nineteenth century world fairs as 'tournaments of industry'. If, once again, we turn to history, we note that the comparison is not without foundation in terms of timing, layout, and 'currency'. In medieval times, tournaments and round tables were periodically held for a limited length of time, in (often circular) fields outside castles or towns, around which participants' tents and pavilions were set up for the duration of the event in a form of 'medieval court' (Cline, 1945: 211; Entwistle and Rocamora). Some knights formed retinues under leading earls, who were themselves ranked in what Caves (2000: 7) would refer to as *A List/B List* (for instance, the Earls of Lancaster and Gloucester, or Warenne and Arundel), in much the same way as nowadays, for example, publishing companies are grouped together under the name of their owners (Hachette or Bloomsbury); while other 'knights of the commune' attend singly (independent publishers like Earthscan or Cambridge University Press) (Tomkinson, 1959: 78–9). Both tournaments and round tables had as their currency a lady as a prize, and the noble who held the *fête* feasted all participants at their end (Cline, 1945: 209, 204).

In many ways, to judge from how they have so far been defined, FCEs hardly differ from tournaments. The editors of a special edition of the *Journal of Management Studies* devoted to FCEs (Lampel and Meyer, 2008) say that the latter firstly, 'assemble in one location actors from diverse professional, organizational and geographical backgrounds' – something we have noted of both tournaments and fairs in medieval times. Similarly, secondly, their 'duration is limited, normally running from a few hours to a few days'. Thirdly, they 'provide unstructured opportunities for face-to-face social interaction'.[7] Fourthly, they 'include ceremonial or dramaturgical activities' – in other words, rituals of the kind noted by Anand and Watson (2004). Fifthly, like regional town fairs in France (Maho, 1980), they 'are occasions for information exchange and collective sense-making'. And finally, they 'generate social and reputational resources that can be deployed elsewhere and for other purposes' (Lampel and Meyer, 2008: 1,027) – as was clearly the case for some knights who made strategic alliances at tournaments (Tomkinson, 1959: 86–7).

If, so far, we seem to be covering already trodden ground, in their article in the same issue of the journal, Anand and Jones (2008) make a case for a distinction between tournament rituals and field configuring events, although Anand also recognizes in his chapter in this volume that the former can be used to serve the interests of the latter. For a field to be 'configured' four mechanisms need to be deployed. Firstly, participants in a field must be able to increase their interaction and communication in some way. Secondly, they must also be made to feel that they are interested in a common issue, or set of issues, by means of some kind of category (like the Booker Prize or the Grammy awards). The latter, thirdly, is itself imbued with power and agency and thus facilitates structures of domination. As a result, fourthly, it becomes possible for participants to transform one kind of capital (say, symbolic) into another one (say, economic), so that transformations of different kinds of capital can take place more generally within a field. In these respects, 'tournament rituals are but one interesting event through which fields are configured ... [They] are political symbols that are fabricated and controlled by interested and motivated actors or ritual entrepreneurs whose aim is to influence field configuration' (Anand and Jones, 2008: 1,057).

Configuring the volume

Whether contributors to this volume follow to the letter Anand and Jones's argument is a moot point. Anand himself, in his chapter on a wine tasting competition, uses the phrase 'tournament ritual'. Thompson, Smith, Moeran and Havens all talk of 'tournaments of values' or value. Rüling, Skov and Meier and Mezias and his co-authors prefer field-configuring events. Delacour and Leca, as well as Lena, combine the two, while Skov and Meier introduce the concept of 'figured world'. Tang ignores them all in favour of broader ideological questions relating to politico-economic concerns, and Entwistle and Rocamora frame their discussion in terms of Bourdieu's analysis of fields of cultural production.

The sheer variety of topics and disciplines represented in the following chapters is daunting: art fairs, salons and biennales; auctions; book and television fairs; (ethical) fashion shows; (animated) film and music festivals; and wine classifications, written about by scholars of art history, business administration, communications, marketing, organizational behaviour, social anthropology, (institutional) sociology and strategic management. We will, however, now attempt to summarize each of the chapters in this book.

In Chapter 1, Hélène Delacour and Bernard Leca provide a historical analysis of the *Salon de Peinture*, the most prominent event in the field of contemporary art in France during the eighteenth and nineteenth centuries. In tracing its development, they show how established power relations in the Academy were twice contested – firstly by an emergent player in the field, the art critic, who challenged the worth of certain works selected for exhibition and who was instrumental in linking aesthetic debates with larger social and political discourses in French society; and secondly by a group of painters who rejected the conservatism of the Academy and the 'high' historical genre favoured by the Salon jury and – dejected at being unable to exhibit, gain public recognition, or gain access to the art market – eventually organized a regular series of parallel exhibitions for their own work (which came to be labelled 'impressionism').

Delacour and Leca theorize their material along two lines. Firstly, they argue, so long as the Academy and its jury were able to establish hegemony in the field of art, the salon was a tournament of value. However, once this hegemony was contested and alternative views arose, the salon became a tournament of values (Moeran) in which aesthetic battles could take place. Both were in their own ways FCEs. The former, though, merely reinforced aesthetic and social hierarchies within a particular segment of the field, whereas the latter enabled reconfiguration of the field as a whole through contestation and the successful promulgation of alternative aesthetic philosophies. In both cases, however, it was individual actors – critics, painters and members of the Academy – who developed and acted upon well-defined strategies as they tried to make sense of the field.

Don Thompson continues the theme of art in Chapter 2 by examining art fairs – industry trade shows where dealers and collectors gather for several days at a time to offer and buy art works, while also often engaging in carnivalesque activities with partying, celebrities and conspicuous consumption. Like book fairs, discussed in a later chapter, art fairs have a long history in which the distinction between exhibitions, biennales and fairs is often blurred. Like book and other trade fairs, art fairs take place in different parts of the world throughout the year, with some – Maastricht, Art Basel, Miami Basel and London's

SAID BUSINESS SCHOOL EXECUTIVE EDUCATION LIBRARY

Frieze – occupying pride of place over others, whose total number tends to fluctuate wildly according to the general state of the world economy.

Thompson argues that dealers have used art fairs as a weapon with which to strengthen their position in an ongoing battle with auction houses. In this way, they have reconfigured the field. Art fairs have become important because a lot more works are on offer than at an auction. Collectors find them a convenient means to do 'comparison shopping', and dealers benefit from collectors' impulsive buying on the basis of 'herd behaviour'. However, fairs are time-consuming and expensive for dealers and offer a poor physical environment in which to view art works – something deplored by artists themselves, although they are flattered to have their work shown and make use of such occasions to enhance their reputation. In buying and selling art works in such quantities at different art fairs, therefore, members of the contemporary art world negotiate different values as they validate, create an aura around and 'brand' art works and artists in what is essentially a tournament of values.

In Chapter 3, Jeannine Tang, who is an art historian working at the intersection of post-war art and politics, asks what ideological interests art biennales serve. The target of her critique is, therefore, not the individual biennale, nor the individual actors who constitute the field of art, but 'the interests we are made to serve without our consent and against our well-being'. She notes a parallel development between the *system* of biennales, or what she calls the 'biennalization of the artworld', and the push towards creative industries by governments worldwide, each coinciding with the rise of economic neo-liberalism, and asks whether this overall embrace of culture as a 'creative industry' is a healthy development for the arts and their workers.

While there are a number of quantitatively based similarities between biennales and the art fairs discussed by Thompson in the previous chapter, Tang highlights certain qualitative differences that separate the two. Biennales are curated exhibitions, which propose themed ideas as their *raison d'être* and remain more or less autonomous of, or at least play down, commercial interests, while using the occasion to attract nationalist publicity and tourism. It is thus *political* interests that become highly visible in the organization of biennales as different states and nations compete with one another for attention, while simultaneously championing with true neo-liberalist rhetoric the international identity of participating artists. Here lies the rub. Cultural policy seeks to co-ordinate the creativity of both business and the state with social cohesion. The state, argues Tang, uses the ideology of creativity to abdicate from its social responsibilities towards an exploited class of creative workers, while the creative economy rhetoric neatly folds its exploitation of creative labour into an aestheticization of the economy. Biennales, therefore, should never be assumed to represent community, ethics, difference and democracy in the way that they are so idealized.

In Chapter 4, we move to the topic of auctions which Charles Smith sees as 'tournaments of value', in which public and open contestations of both prices and ownership take place. This leads to their being staged as dramaturgical performances, both in the management of their spatial (front stage/back stage) and temporal boundaries, and in the establishment of various ritualistic and behavioural practices connected with dress codes, setting and appropriate audience behaviour. Just as a curator performs an art exhibition, an auctioneer orchestrates the rhythm of an auction, managing participants and establishing a sense of community and trust. It is the opportunity to belong to such a creative community that attracts buyers and sellers alike and encourages them to engage in various forms of (not always ethically acceptable) team play.

The aim of such practices is to generate particular meanings, values and expectations that reflect back on both participants and goods being auctioned. Auctions thus become processes that deal with ambiguity and uncertainty by generating prices that are socially legitimated and goods that are socially defined. In other words, although auction prices almost always have an impact on other prices, auctions themselves also 'tell us where and why different factors have greater and lesser impact in the way social meanings and values are established'. Auction values, Smith argues, are largely shaped by the meanings associated with their physical settings: that is to say, by their situational values.

One of the points made by Smith concerns the way in which some participants – in particular, the audience – is made invisible during a performance. This issue of in/visibility comes to the fore in Chapter 5 where Brian Moeran analyses book fairs (where new titles may also be auctioned off to the highest bidding publisher). Basing his research on participant observation at the London, Frankfurt and Tokyo International Book Fairs, he reveals the broad variety of issues – from selling translation rights and developing a digital platform to finding a new sales rep in South-east Asia or broaching the possibility of a corporate merger or takeover – with which publishers may have to deal in their daily activities at a book fair. It is during the course of such activities, he argues, that all kinds of technical, literary (appreciative), social and commodity considerations are weighed and negotiated in what – developing the original idea of Arjun Appadurai – he calls a 'tournament of values'.

It is the theme of in/visibility, however, which emerges most strongly in this chapter and which foreshadows similar discussions in following chapters on television markets and fashion weeks. In most book fairs, who has a stand where in the exhibition hall is extremely important. Location and the accompanying trappings of every stand in a fair signify each publisher's visible status in the publishing industry's hierarchy – a status which can be reinforced by means of daily media news, gossip and more or less lavish parties. In all this activity, however, one person crucial to the definition of publishing as a 'creative' industry is invisible: the author. Yet it is authors who lease the inalienable rights that form the central focus – the 'currency' – of the book fair as a tournament of values. Moeran notes the irony of a situation whereby the fair is designed to make visible the book as a commodity and to make invisible the given-while-kept inalienability of the book as a gift. It is in the shadow of the gift, he argues, that the commodity of the book is produced, distributed, sold and read.

In the global television markets described in Chapter 6, however, Timothy Havens notes that television is a largely authorless medium, and yet the trade in rights is still uniquely dependent on the cultivation of relationships. Although taking place in 'markets' rather than 'fairs' or 'festivals' as such, the trade in television rights sales exhibits many of the characteristics of other competitive events discussed in this volume: restricted access and promotional extravagance as indicators of prestige, intelligence gathering and buzz.

Havens argues that television markets permit multiple levels of participation and, in so doing, function as several distinct, though overlapping, tournament economies designed to make possible the world trade in television programming. Because of the unpredictability of audience tastes, a feature of creative industries in general, television rights are high-risk commodities, a fact which makes importers rely on their 'gut instincts' when deciding whether or not to purchase a programme. This instinct is nurtured, on the one hand, by networks and relationships and, on the other, by distributors' ability to create an impression that their programming has a universal appeal that goes beyond cultural particularities. This impression is achieved by means of multiple levels of exclusivity and extravagance in distributors' stands, access to which is seen by participants to confer them with social capital, as well as 'social' and 'situational' values on the programmes that are on offer there. Havens argues that distributors use restricted access and promotional extravagance for multiple self-serving purposes: to make a strong statement about the economic value of their programming; to establish their credibility as interpreters of global cultural tastes, rather than as purveyors of culturally specific programmes; to consecrate certain programmes as having 'universal' appeal; and to create the impression that such programmes are in scarce supply. These are what make television markets 'tournaments of values'.

Chapter 7 brings us to film festivals. Steve Mezias, Jesper Strandgaard Pedersen and their co-authors are concerned with the role of film festivals as FCEs and in particular to untangle their relative prestige and ability to translate artistic recognition into commercial success. The empirical setting for this study is a sample of films produced across the globe and premiered at one of the three major European film festivals: Berlin, Cannes and Venice. The study reports findings from a comparative study of data covering more than 600 films over a ten-year time frame from 1996–2005, with comparable award and performance statistics. These data are supplemented by on-site field observations generated through participation in the film festivals concerned.

The results from the study show that there is considerably greater audience interest in films nominated at Cannes than in those nominated at Berlin or Venice. Not only this, but by winning a prize a film significantly increases the size of the audience that goes to see it. Furthermore, the results show that films that win one of the best picture prizes experience a significantly greater increase in audience than films that win other prizes. These results lead Mezias and his co-authors to conclude that a status ordering can be observed at two levels. Firstly, the three European film festivals themselves are ordered by status, with Cannes providing the most valuable endorsement for films and being the most prestigious among the film festivals. And secondly, a status ordering is found among the various competitive arenas, with best picture being the most prestigious prize.

Chapter 8 continues the theme of film as Charles-Clemens Rüling examines event institutionalization and maintenance in his study of the annual Annecy International Animation Film Festival. The chapter presents a historical analysis of the Annecy festival which he sees as taking place in three stages: firstly, there is its early development and institutionalization, when Annecy was thought of as a community event (1956–82); secondly, there was a stage of growth, market creation and annualization when it became more of a showcase event (1983–2003); and thirdly, it went through a period of renewal, transaction and broker-age, as Annecy developed into an industry event (2003 to present day).

In his analysis of this international animation film festival, Rüling proposes four avenues along which to explore successful event institu-tionalization and maintenance. Firstly, event institutionalization occurs through several stages of historical development, in which events are related to community building and community sustaining processes – including ecological learning, attribution of status and economic trans-action. Secondly, the institutional maintenance of events depends on their ability to manage critical transitions in the co-evolution of an event and its environment. Thirdly, he suggests that symbolic-discursive insti-tutional work plays a particularly important role in the institutional maintenance of events in creative industries in general. Finally, Rüling suggests that institutional maintenance is related to an event's role in functioning as a boundary organization.

In Chapter 9, Jennifer Lena gives us an in-depth account of a country music festival in Nashville, Tennessee. Such festivals, she says, have the potential to create or rearrange symbolic and economic configurations in fundamental ways – a point that she proceeds to illustrate in her discussion of Fan Fair's physical relocation in 2001 from outlying fair-grounds to downtown Nashville in order to act as a 'signature event' in the city's rebranding as 'Music City, USA'.

The constellation of values that crystallized in the relocation of Fan Fair had a major impact on its production. Firstly, the move transformed the old downtown area, as 'meaningful' spaces were created out of 'empty' ones and a new heritage space was redefined to fit the festival. Second, the necessity for simultaneous performances in multiple venues (rather than consecutive performances at a single venue as previously) affected the kind of music played. Festival organizers dispensed with seasoned per-formers in the canon of country music and heritage acts in favour of new country performers singing highly produced pop- and rock-influenced songs. Thirdly, this market-driven scheduling, which prioritized chart performance over other determinants of value, appealed more to younger middle-class white women than to country music's typical rural, working class audience. Fan Fair's audience began to change radically, with a high proportion of women attending. Finally, these new attendees not only defined the genre's core values through their musical taste; they also appealed to new corporate sponsors because of their purchasing power. The move downtown thus produced alliances between country music and a hitherto largely absent universe of consumer goods and services. In these ways, the 2001 Fan Fair festival produced a newly configured community of new country singers and consumers.

Joanne Entwistle and Agnès Rocamora continue the discussion of the audience's role in events in Chapter 10, as they show how London Fashion Week maps out in spatial terms all the key agents and institutions within the field of fashion – producing, reproducing and legitimating the field of fashion and different players' positions therein. Fashion weeks constitute a network of global industry fairs in which the clear distinction between the business and art of fashion made by field participants is reflected in the spatial separation of the exhibition hall from the catwalk theatre in the fair.

Following analyses made in earlier chapters of this volume, Entwistle and Rocamora highlight two features of London Fashion Week: boundaries and access; and visibility – or, in their phrase, 'seeing and being seen'. Initial access marks a distinction between insiders and outsiders, but insiders then face further boundaries within boundaries as they try to gain access to catwalk theatre shows and private 'after show' parties in what Havens earlier describes as 'multiple levels of access'. Here, as in global television markets, what counts is social and symbolic capital, to use Bourdieu's felicitous phrase.

Participants' field positions are marked out and reproduced most obviously, firstly, in whether they have sitting or standing tickets for a fashion show, and secondly, in where they sit around the catwalk itself. It is here that visibility becomes an all-important sign of membership of the fashion world, as spatial arrangements map out power relations among participants, while also encouraging a shared sense of belonging to a fashion 'community'. As in Smith's discussion of auctions, we here find that dramaturgical performance – in particular, bodily poise and gestures – is paramount. It is participants' bodies that articulate fashion capital and their position and status in the field.

The theme of fashion is continued in Chapter 11 by Lise Skov and Janne Meier, who analyse how European fashion companies represent, reflect upon and commit themselves to the principle of sustainability in an industry that systematically advocates planned obsolescence in its biannual launching of new collections of clothes. Basing their analysis on fieldwork at the Berlin and Copenhagen Fashion Weeks in the summer of 2009, the authors suggest that the very vagueness (or semantic density) of the word 'sustainability' enables fashion companies to pursue one of three ethical strategies, each appealing to a different segment of the market. Firstly, there is a very large 'soft green' segment, consisting of brands that mainly use conventional materials and production methods, but which devote a small part of their collection to ethical initiatives. Secondly, there is the 'hardcore green' segment where environmental and social responsibility is an integral part of brand identity, associated more with politically committed consumers than with the fashion industry *per se*. And thirdly, a sub-field of 'green luxury' has emerged, aiming at the high end of the market and valuing quality and style (in the form of exclusive natural materials and craft-based manufacturing methods) over fast fashion.

Skov and Meier argue that fashion week is an FCE, but that *configuration* needs to be seen in the context of a *figured* world. While the former refers to 'outer forms constituting the whole', the latter 'signifies imagination or calculation in an informal everyday sort of way'. Making use of rich fieldwork data, they demonstrate that the sustainable fashion discourse is indeed having a tangible effect upon the external planned structure of the fashion industry, reconfiguring the field of fashion while maintaining its stability. But, at the same time, because fashion weeks offer participants the opportunity to engage in internalized and reflexive activities in the figured world of fashion, the multi-perspective sense-making and negotiations of meanings that emerge create fluidity in the field. Fashion weeks thus contribute to both stabilization and flux.

From fashion, we move to wine. In Chapter 12, Grégoire Croidieu takes us back in time to the emergence of the 1855 wine classification system established at the Paris Universal Exhibition that year. This classification has, for more than 150 years, remained remarkably stable and unchanged in the Médoc wine region in France, so that retrospectively the Paris Universal Exhibition can be seen as an FCE which resulted in the clear domination of an unambiguous hierarchy within the field of wine, headed by the brokers, not the producers. Croidieu notes that neo-institutional accounts of cultural field domination would predict that, over the kind of time span covered by the 1855 classification, we would see little contention among field participants, but instead a convergence of collective, as well as individual, discourses around a rationalized myth.

However, this is not what happens in the case of 1855. Through careful and diligent use of archival materials, Croidieu is able to depict how different actors – some in favour of, others against, the classification – have at various points in time commented on, contested and challenged the classification in various ways. During this process, there is an intriguing shift of emphasis whereby the original evaluation of wine according to market price (commodity exchange value) is taken over by other views that argue for soil (material value), or taste (appreciative value) as *the* criterion of quality. None of these different evaluations of Médoc wine wins out, however, so that the 1855 classification has continued as an 'inconvenient truce' in the midst of cultural domination.

In Chapter 13, Narasimhan Anand continues the discussion of wine by analysing the so-called 'Judgement of Paris' blind tasting event in 1976, from which Californian wines emerged as surprising winners over French wines. Anand shows how this single 'tournament ritual' was co-opted retrospectively by various players in the wine industry in order to reconfigure the field by marking a shift in the balance of power from old to new worlds in both production and critical appreciation. What makes the case particularly interesting is that, in sharp contrast to almost all other periodically enacted events discussed in this volume, the 'Judgement of Paris' was a one-off ritual, frozen in time, which was used retrospectively to shape the collective memory of the field in order to suit future interests.

Anand argues that the ways in which this ritual has been commemorated have had a significant impact on reconfiguration of the global wine field. Specifically, this particular form of social remembering has, firstly, enabled disparate producers in a nascent industry to come together and develop a collective social identity that stands in contradistinction to French wine producers. Secondly, it has been used to mark the displacement of France from the centre of the global wine trade – a displacement that was already set in motion, though not officially recognized, in diminishing wine consumption in France and in the transfer of technical processes of production from California to France. Thirdly, it challenged the continuing validity of the *grand cru* classification system discussed by Croidieu in the previous chapter by showing that great wine could be made outside French *terroir* and not necessarily by adhering to long-standing tradition. In these ways, the 'Judgement of Paris' highlights the importance of social remembering in field formation, while demonstrating how a one-off ritual can be used retrospectively to serve the interests of field configuring forces. It also reveals how social, appreciative and technical values can be renegotiated as a result of such a tournament ritual.

Finally, in an Afterword, Joseph Lampel outlines his thoughts based on the chapters described above, as well as on his active participation in the ©*reative Encounters* workshop at which most of the contributors participated. Fairs and festivals, he says, are interesting because of two distinguishing features. They are contexts where, firstly, 'all resources relevant to the field's strategies are valued in relation to each other' and, secondly, 'actors use resources entrepreneurially to create and obtain other resources that further these strategies'. It is from the standpoint of resources, Lampel argues, that we should look at the kinds of values and valuations discussed in this volume.

Lampel sees the key distinction here as being the one made by Moeran in his chapter on book fairs between 'attached' and 'alienable' resources. Attached resources are those that cannot be separated from the identity of those who hold them, while alienable resources can have their control or ownership transferred to others. Fairs and festivals allow field participants to resolve two basic problems in creative industries: how to value products (like books or music) that are alienable; and how to value resources like reputation or social connections that are attached to creative products (as, for example, in art, films and fashion). It is precisely because fairs, festivals and competitive events are sites where the values of resources are established that value is not absolute, but relative to the position occupied by the event *vis-à-vis* its competitors.

It is the boundedness of fairs and festivals mentioned earlier in this introduction that Lampel sees as ideally suited for the valuation of attached and alienable resources. He notes how the various boundaries established by events are extremely important to participants, who then negotiate both the value of their attached resources from that of competitors, as well as that of their alienable resources, and who strategize to convert the one into the other and *vice versa*. In so doing, they must distance themselves from the prevailing *habitus* that they have internalized at a particular fair or festival in order to act strategically. Fairs and festivals, therefore, do not merely reproduce a field, but 'interrupt the tight circle of everyday exchange' (Braudel, 1992: 82). In so doing, they enable the evaluation and conversion of resources. It is this 'predictable unpredictability' that makes fairs, festivals and other competitive events such a rich field of research.

Notes

1. What might now be called 'creative occupations' were half a decade ago referred to as 'service occupations' (see Becker, 1951).
2. Allix (1922: 545) points out that the effect of fixing commerce in a permanent location was 'not to diminish the *number* of fairs. On the contrary, as their importance declines their number increases'.
3. See Power and Jansson (2008: 439) for an annual schedule of the twenty largest furniture trade fairs in the world.
4. In this respect, 'the culturalization of economic life' (Flew, 2005: 349) is characteristic of not just creative industries and cultural production generally, but of many other sectors of advanced capitalist economies (Lash and Urry, 1994).
5. Indeed, even a cultural economist who simultaneously recognizes and espouses the plurality of values, while acknowledging the shortcomings of price as a measure of economic value and the multiple and shifting nature of cultural value within a single domain, cannot get away from a 'theory of value' (Throsby, 2001: 19, 24, 28).
6. The disadvantage, perhaps, is that it ignores individual or affective values (stemming from what Bourdieu would term *habitus*), although it could be argued that the latter are in fact socially constructed and therefore an integral part of social values.
7. We would here note that such opportunities, though unplanned, are in fact structured, in the sense of enabled, by the very existence of a fair or festival.

References

Adorno, T. W. 1991. *The Culture Industry*. Edited and with an Introduction by J. M. Bernstein. London: Routledge.

Allix, A. 1914. 'La foire de Goncelin', *Receuil des Travails de l'Institute de Géographie Alpine* 2, 299–334.

    1922. 'The geography of fairs: illustrated by Old World examples', *Geographical Review* 12:4, 532–69.

Anand, N. and Jones, B. 2008. 'Tournament rituals, category dynamics, and field configuration: the case of the Booker Prize', *Journal of Management Studies* 45:6, 1,036–60.

Anand, N. and Watson, M. 2004. 'Tournament rituals in the evolution of fields: the case of the Grammy Awards', *Academy of Management Journal* 47, 59–80.

Appadurai, A. 1986. 'Commodities and the politics of value', in A. Appadurai (ed.), *The Social Life of Things: Commodities in Cultural Perspective*. Cambridge University Press, pp. 3–63.

Beachy, R. 1999. 'Reforming interregional commerce: the Leipzig Trade Fair and Saxony's recovery from the Thirty Years' War', *Central European History* 32:4, 431–52.

Becker, H. 1951. 'The professional dance musician and his audience', *The American Journal of Sociology* 57:2, 136–44.

1974. 'Art as collective action', *American Sociological Review* 39, 767–76.

1982. *Art Worlds*. Berkeley and Los Angeles: University of California Press.

Bourdieu, P. 1993. *The Field of Cultural Production: Essays on Art and Literature*. Cambridge: Polity.

Bourdieu, P. and Wacquant, L. J. D. 1992. 'The purpose of reflexive sociology (The Chicago Workshop)', in P. Bourdieu and L. J. D. Wacquant (eds.), *An Invitation to Reflexive Sociology*. Cambridge: Polity Press, pp. 61–215.

Braudel, F. 1992. *The Wheels of Commerce*. Berkeley and Los Angeles: University of California Press.

Caves, R. 2000. *Creative Industries: Contracts Between Art and Commerce*. Cambridge, MA: Harvard University Press.

Cline, R. H. 1945. 'The influence of romances on tournaments of the Middle Ages', *Speculum* 20:2, 204–11.

Curti, M. 1950. 'America at the World Fairs, 1851–1893', *The American Historical Review* 55:4, 833–56.

Debreu, G. 1987 (1959). *A Theory of Value: an Axiomatic Analysis of Economic Equilibrium*. New Haven and London: Yale University Press.

DiMaggio, P. and Powell, W. 1983. 'The iron cage revisited: institutional isomorphism and collective rationality in organizational fields', *American Sociological Review* 48, 147–60.

Face, R. D. 1958. 'Techniques of business in the trade between the fairs of Champagne and the south of Europe in the twelfth and thirteenth centuries', *The Economic History Review* 10:3, 427–38.

Fine, G. 1992. 'The culture of production: aesthetic choices and constraints in culinary work', *American Journal of Sociology* 97:5, 1,268–94.

Firth, R. 1967. 'Themes in economic anthropology: a general comment', in R. Firth (ed.), *Themes in Economic Anthropology*, A.S.A. Monographs 6. London: Tavistock, pp. 1–28.

Flew, T. 2005. 'Creative economy', in J. Hartley (ed.), *Creative Industries*. Oxford: Blackwell, pp. 344–60.

Frey, B. S. 2003. *Art & Economics: Analysis & Cultural Policy*. Second edition. Berlin: Springer.

Giddens, A. 1993. *Sociology*. Second edition. Cambridge: Polity.

Glynn, M. A. 2008. 'Configuring the field of play: how hosting the Olympic games impacts civic community', *Journal of Management Studies* 45:6, 1,117–46.

Graeber, D. 2001. *Toward an Anthropological Theory of Value*. New York: Palgrave.

Gueusquin-Barbichon, M. 1980. 'Différenciation et espace sexuels dans les foires et marchés à Corbigny (Nièvre)', *Études rurales* 78/80, 327–30.

Hartley, J. 2005. 'Creative industries', in J. Hartley (ed.), *Creative Industries*. Oxford: Blackwell, pp. 1–40.

Herrnstein-Smith, B. 1988. *Contingencies of Value: Alternative Perspectives for Critical Theory*. Cambridge, MA: Harvard University Press.

Hirsch, P. M. 1972. 'Processing fads and fashions: an organization-set analysis of cultural industry system', *American Journal of Sociology* 77, 639–59.
2000. 'Cultural industries revisited', *Organization Science* 11:3, 356–61.

Hitlin, S. and Piliavin, J. A. 2004. 'Values: reviving a dormant concept', *Annual Review of Sociology* 30, 359–93.

Isherwood, R. 1981. 'Entertainment in the Parisian fairs in the eighteenth century', *The Journal of Modern History* 53:1, 24–48.

Lampel, J. and Meyer, A. D. 2008. 'Field-configuring events as structuring mechanisms: how conferences, ceremonies, and trade shows constitute new technologies, industries, and markets', *Journal of Management Studies* 45:6, 1,025–35.

Lampel, J. and Nadavulakere, S. S. 2009. 'Classics foretold? Contemporaneous and retrospective consecration in the UK film industry', *Cultural Trends* 18:3, 239–48.

Lash, S. and Urry, J. 1994. *Economies of Signs and Space*. London: Sage.

Maho, J. 1980. 'Les aspects non économiques des foires et marchés', *Études rurales* 78/80, 65–8.

Malinowski, B. 1922. *Argonauts of the Western Pacific*. London: Routledge.

Marriott, M. 1968. 'Caste-ranking and food transactions: a matrix analysis', in M. Singer and B. S. Cohn (eds.), *Structure and Change in Indian Society*. Chicago: Aldine, pp. 133–71.

Marx, K. 1976. *Capital: a Critique of Political Economy*. Volume 1. Harmondsworth: Penguin.

Maskell, P., Bathelt, H. and Malmberg, A. 2006. 'Building global knowledge pipelines: the role of temporary clusters', *European Planning Studies* 14:8, 997–1,013.

Mazza, C. and Strandgaard Pedersen, J. 2008. 'Who's last? Challenges and advantages for late adopters in the international film festival field', ©*reative Encounters* Working Paper 16, Copenhagen Business School.

Meyer, A. D., Gaba, V. and Colwell, K. 2005. 'Organizing far from equilibrium: non-linear change in organizational fields', *Organizational Science* 16, 456–73.

Moeran, B. 1993. 'A tournament of value: strategies of presentation in Japanese advertising', *Ethnos* 58: 1–2, 73–94.

1997. *Folk Art Potters of Japan*. Richmond: Curzon.

2004. 'Women's fashion magazines: people, things, and values,' in C. Werner and D. Bell (eds.), *Values and Valuables: From the Sacred to the Symbolic*. Walnut Creek, CA: Altamira, pp. 257–81.

2009. 'The field of Japanese publishing' ©*reative Encounters* Working Paper 46, Copenhagen Business School.

Peterson, R. A. 1976. 'The production of culture: a prolegomenon', in R. A. Peterson (ed.), *The Production of Culture*. Beverly Hills, CA: Sage, pp. 7–22.

Peterson, R. A. and Anand, N. 2004. 'The production of culture perspective', *Annual Review of Sociology* 30, 311–34.

Power, D. and Jansson, J. 2008. 'Cyclical clusters in global circuits: overlapping spaces in furniture trade fairs', *Economic Geography* 84:4, 423–48.

Rearick, C. 1977. 'Festivals in modern France: the experience of the Third Republic', *Journal of Contemporary History* 12:3, 435–60.

Reff Pedersen, A. and Strandgaard Pedersen, J. 2008. 'The role of the media in the co-production of identities in a filmmaking company', *Tamara Journal* 7, 91–108.

Sahlins, M. 1965. 'On the sociology of primitive exchange', in M. Banton (ed.), *The Relevance of Models for Social Anthropology*, A.S.A. Monographs 1. London: Tavistock, pp. 139–236.

de Saussure, F. 1983. *Course in General Linguistics*. London: Duckworth.

Schwartz, S. H. 1994. 'Are there universal aspects in the structure and content of human values?', *Journal of Social Issues* 50, 19–45.

Schwartz, S. H. and Bilsky, W. 1987. 'Towards a psychological structure of human values', *Journal of Personal Social Psychology* 53, 550–62.

Simmel, G. 1978. *The Philosophy of Money*. London: Routledge and Kegan Paul.

Skov, L. 2006. 'The role of trade fairs in the global fashion business', *Current Sociology* 54:5, 764–83.

Suchman, M. C. 1995. 'Managing legitimacy: strategic and institutional approaches', *Academy of Management Review* 20:3, 571–610.

Thompson, D. 2008. *The $12 Million Stuffed Shark: the Curious Economics of Contemporary Art and Auction Houses*. London: Aurum.

Throsby, D. 2001. *Economics and Culture*. Cambridge: Cambridge University Press.

Tomkinson, A. 1959. 'Retinues at the tournament of Dunstable, 1309', *The English Historical Review* 74, 70–89.

Wacquant, L. J. D. 1992. 'Towards a social praxeology: the structure and logic of Bourdieu's sociology,' in P. Bourdieu and L. J. D. Waquant (eds.), *An Invitation to Reflexive Sociology*. Cambridge: Polity Press, pp.1–59.

Watson, M. and Anand, N. 2006. 'Award ceremony as an arbiter of commerce and canon in the popular music industry', *Popular Music* 25:1, 41–56.

Williams, R. M. Jr 1979. 'Change and stability in values and value systems: a sociological perspective', in M. Rokeach (ed.), *Understanding Human Values: Individual and Societal*. New York: Free Press, pp. 15–46.

1 | A Salon's life: field-configuring event, power and contestation in a creative field

HÉLÈNE DELACOUR AND BERNARD LECA*

Research on field-configuring events (FCEs) is still at an early stage, but existing research suggests that such events as art fairs and biennales, film and music festivals are especially important within creative fields (e.g., Anand and Jones, 2008; Entwistle and Rocamora, 2006; Tang, Chapter 3). This might relate to the regular need to evaluate what should be considered as art, an uncertain and temporary notion, the shared understanding of which is the very basis of any 'artworld' (Danto, 1964). Hence, the stakes for participants are high. Galleries, for instance, struggle to obtain a booth at the main art fairs where millions of dollars worth of transactions are made (Thornton, 2008), and art fairs and biennales have risen to such a central position in the art market that they are now an industry in themselves – as the chapters by Don Thompson (Chapter 2) and Jeannine Tang (Chapter 3) in this volume show.

While FCEs are mostly considered as co-ordination mechanisms in the existing literature (Lampel and Meyer, 2008), research also suggests that in creative fields they operate as important mechanisms whereby the dominant group in the field is allowed to wield symbolic power (Anand and Watson, 2004). As such, a central FCE is a typical feature of a centralized field ruled by a dominant group. Referring to Appadurai's notion of a 'tournament of value' (Appadurai, 1986), N. Anand and his co-authors Mary Watson (2004) and Brittany Jones (2008) show that the FCE operates as a 'tournament of value' where the dominant view of value is enforced and that of creativity promoted as it rejects competing approaches (Peterson and Anand, 2004). Yet, Brian Moeran and Jesper Strandgaard Pedersen's notion of a 'tournament of values' outlined in the introduction, and developed further by Moeran in his chapter on book fairs (Chapter 5), opens up an alternative perspective to this approach by suggesting that FCEs might be events where dominant values are contested instead of being reinforced. Such a situation can be found in many FCEs where intense discussions, debates and disagreements take place around what should, and what should not, be considered as 'worthy', and 'unworthy', art, with or without 'value'.

Our intention in this paper is to explore the circumstances under which FCEs are 'tournaments of value' in the singular, and so contribute to the centralization of power within a field, and when they are 'tournaments of values' in the plural, where contestation takes place. To do so, we look at the French *Salon de Peinture*, which was founded in 1663, and became the dominant FCE in the field of fine arts from the 1740s and remained so until the end of the nineteenth century. Crow (2000: 1) has indicated that 'after 1737... [the Salon's] status was never in question, and its effects on the artistic life of Paris were immediate and dramatic'. The Salon was the place where artists wanted to have their works of art displayed and where artistic reputations were made and broken. In this respect, the Salon can be considered as the prototype of an FCE in a creative field in the modern age. Within the period studied, we distinguish two sub-periods: the first from 1737 to 1830, when what went on in the Salon was unchallenged; and the second from 1830 to 1881, when certain voices started to criticize the Salon's system of jurying, and artists themselves developed alternative venues in which to exhibit. During these two periods, we focus on the power plays between the dominant coalition in the Salon and other members in the field around it.

This case study suggests that the circumstances under which an FCE is a tournament of value or of values depend upon the kinds of power relations at play between the FCE's gatekeepers and the other members of the field. When competing views exist in the field, they are represented in an FCE, so that it is difficult for gatekeepers to impose a unique sense of worth, unless they are able to secure the support of a critical mass of field members. The case study also suggests that some level of contestation, and possibly scandal, within an FCE might be a useful means of ensuring that it remains prominent in the field. If gatekeepers impose a unique sense of worth or value in the field through an FCE, they will inevitably overlook innovation, contribute to the emergence of competing FCEs, and reduce the attractiveness of their own FCE. We suggest some extensions to these findings by drawing from examples in the contemporary art and film festival fields.

In the following section we will review existing theoretical insights into power and contestation in FCEs, before introducing the empirical setting and presenting the method that we have chosen to follow. We will then develop an analysis of the Salon and the creative field of contemporary art in France from 1737 to 1881, focusing on power and contestation within the field during this period. In the final section, we will discuss our insights and the limitations of our chapter, together with the potential that we envisage for further research.

Power and contestation over values in creative FCEs

FCEs are temporary social organizations where 'people from diverse social organizations assemble temporarily, with the conscious, collective intent to construct an organizational field' (Meyer *et al.*, 2005: 467) and 'to promote ideas about the way work in the field ought to be done' (Oliver and Montgomery, 2008: 1,048). Lampel and Meyer (2008) distinguish two kinds of FCE. The first consists of distinct, single FCEs – such as standard setting conferences – during which specific technical features are discussed and possibly agreed upon (e.g., Garud, 2008); the second consists of repetitive or periodical FCEs, such as award ceremonies (e.g., Anand and Watson, 2004) or art fairs, at which the field is periodically reassessed by participant members.

Studies of creative fields have, like our own, tended to concentrate in particular on the latter (e.g., Anand and Jones, 2008). In fact, they insist that these periodical events not only set standards and define categories, but also contribute to the ongoing reproduction and reassessment of creative activities, and what should be valued as art works. Periodical FCEs in creative fields have been considered as places and moments where those in control of the FCE reproduce and reactivate the dominating structure of the field. Referring to Lukes (1974), Anand and Watson (2004) apply the phrase 'agnostic thesis' to these FCEs, in that rituals not only help groups within a social system to exert control through processes of mystification, but also give rise to the taken-for-granted sanctioning of ritually endowed power that comes from patterning and repetition. As such FCEs can operate as rituals of ratification for the existing structure of domination (DiMaggio and Mullen, 2000). One powerful way to do this is through the distribution of symbolic power. FCEs, like award ceremonies, are rituals where the worth of art works is put to the test. To be awarded a prize, or even to be short-listed for one, implies that those in charge of the selection recognize and value the submitted work. As such, these gatekeepers have the power to impose their view on what 'art' should be in this field and are allowed to dispense symbolic power to the winners (Anand and Watson, 2004; Anand and Jones, 2008). It is likely that actors who do not share the aesthetic view (or 'appreciative value') of those in charge of the FCE will be rejected and marginalized.

Yet other research on FCEs suggests that contestation can and does take place within an FCE as different actors supporting different views struggle to achieve domination by one means or another (Garud, 2008; Oliver and Montgomery, 2008). Such studies tend to focus not on repetitive events like the ones we have discussed so far, but on one-off FCEs, such as those where a specific standard is being decided for the whole industry (Garud, 2008; Oliver and Montgomery, 2008). However, this dimension of contestation has largely been ignored in the existing research on FCEs in the so-called creative industries. What is important, therefore, is to evaluate the extent to which a periodical FCE either is a mechanism that contributes to the reproduction of domination within a field, or is a place for debate and contradiction. We may also need to evaluate the circumstances in which these two contradictory directions articulate themselves. But to do this we need to consider the organizational fields in which FCEs take place, both as hierarchical structures and as arenas of conflict.

Hierarchy and conflict over values in creative fields

Creative fields are organizational fields in which actors interact around a common purpose related to some kind of creative activity, such as film making, music, book publishing, and so on. However, creative fields cannot be reduced to creative industries, markets or populations, for they include not just the suppliers of creative goods and their buyers, but also all sorts of other kinds of actors – like critics, juries, professional bodies and patrons – who, in the aggregate, constitute a recognized area of creativity.

Organizational fields are hierarchical ensembles characterized by a structure of power. Dominant actors are able to impose their visions on others in the field, and then structure and eventually stabilize it (DiMaggio, 1983). Professional associations are typically part of the structure of domination (Greenwood *et al.*, 2002), in that they diffuse knowledge and norms in the field and influence other actors. By so doing, they also diffuse a specific view of how activities should be performed, leading to mimetic behaviour. Eventually there emerges a collective rationality that corresponds to the dominant view of the creative activity concerned (DiMaggio and Powell, 1983).

One way to enforce this dominant view is through periodical FCEs, which some authors (e.g., Anand and Watson, 2004; Anand and Jones, 2008; see also Moeran, 1993), taking up a felicitous phrase used by the anthropologist Arjun Appadurai, call 'tournaments of value'. Although not concerned with FCEs as such, Appadurai defines tournaments of value as complex periodic events, where actors compete for status, rank, fame or reputation. To develop this notion, he drew on material from the case of the Melanesian Kula where reputation and fame are gained through the giving, receiving and exchange of decorated necklaces and armshells. Just like these Kula exchanges, contemporary 'tournaments of value' have an impact beyond the specific place and time in which they occur, since 'their forms and outcomes are always consequential for the more mundane realities of power and value in ordinary life' (Appadurai, 1986: 21). During these 'tournaments of value', the worth of what field actors do is evaluated on the basis of the overall view of value shared in the field. Some works are rewarded and their creators then gain symbolic power. Film crew members can receive Academy Awards or Oscars (Baumann, 2001), musicians Grammy awards (Anand and Watson, 2004) and writers literary prizes (Anand and Jones, 2008) that are all recognition of the value of their work. As such these periodic rituals are moments where the established order is reenacted and the gatekeepers of a particular FCE are able to impose their view of what is valuable and to hand out rewards to those who comply with it. In this way FCEs like these contribute to a top down structure of the field (Peterson and Anand, 2004) where those who oppose the dominant view are marginalized or excluded (White and White, 1993).

Yet, an organizational field is not just a hierarchical structure where the many comply with an established order imposed by the few. Authors have moved beyond this arguably consensual view of the field, and now also account for it as an arena of strategy and conflict, as well as of negotiation and dialogue (DiMaggio, 1983; Hoffman, 1999). In particular, they show how participants argue about the sense they want to give to their activity, and how best to do so. This seems particularly relevant for creative organizations like fashion houses and film studios where discussions frequently take place about a particular activity and how it should be performed. Indeed, endless debates about creative activities are endemic to these fields, from the contradiction between the different, and apparently opposing, logics of commerce and aesthetics, on the one hand, to disagreement on fundamental definitions of what constitutes creativity or art, on the other. Differences of opinion about the very nature of aesthetics are also very important. For example, in painting, there is an historical debate between those who are convinced that drawing is more important than colour, and those who support the opposite view. How these different views can be expressed in an FCE where the worth of works is evaluated remains unclear. Yet, in their introduction to this volume, Moeran and Strandgaard Pedersen open up a new avenue for research by insisting on the plurality of values in contemporary societies. Accordingly, they suggest that another form of tournament might exist in creative fields: that of a 'tournament of values' – that is, a tournament where several competing values are involved and in constant negotiation. The notion of a 'tournament of values' is an invitation to us to consider the plurality of values at stake in an FCE. This includes tournaments where opposition to what should be the dominant set of values takes place, and as such maps out an important direction for us to better understand those FCEs where contestation over these dominant values takes place.

Our intention in the remainder of this chapter is to build on the distinction between 'tournament of value', on the one hand, and 'tournament of values', on the other. Our aim is to explore under which circumstances an FCE in a creative field can be called a 'tournament of values', where contestation takes place, and under what other circumstances it is a 'tournament of value', where consensus over value is reenacted and domination maintained. In order to focus on circumstances and reduce the risk of other explanations that might relate to the specificities of different FCEs, we here develop a longitudinal study of a single FCE, the annual *Salon de Peinture*, which was first a 'tournament of values' before becoming a 'tournament of value'.

Empirical setting and method

Our analysis outlines the influence of the *Salon de Peinture* (the Salon) on power and contestation within the field of French contemporary art from 1737 to 1881. By taking such a long period into consideration, we are able to document different points at which power relations within the field of art came to vary. The decades on which we focus correspond to a period during which French contemporary art rose to become prominent in Europe. While such prominence cannot be attributed only to the Salon, its importance as an FCE increased accordingly. This may be seen, perhaps, in the fact that during the nineteenth century artists, collectors and patrons would gather from all over Europe, as well as from parts of Asia and North and South America, to join the Salon, which as a result came to be seen as *the* major event of Parisian artistic life.

To go about this case study, we have used a historiographic method that links longitudinal and qualitative approaches (Ventresca and Mohr, 2002), and which seems particularly well suited to report on the complexity of institutional processes and major transformations taking place within an organizational field. In addition, this method permits an analysis that takes into account the actors in a field over a long time and allows an exploratory process facilitated by a qualitative approach. We have privileged contemporary sources where possible, and have made use of the archival resources of the National Institute of Art History (*Institut National d'Histoire de l'Art, INHA*) and the French National Library (*Bibliothèque Nationale de France, BNF*), both located in Paris. We have also collected data from contemporary sources like the notebooks of the Salon, correspondence between art traders and artists and articles written by the critics in specialist publications like *L'Artiste*, *La Chronique des Beaux Arts et de la Curiosité* and *Le Mercure de France*. To validate these archival data, we crosschecked and then enriched our information by drawing on secondary sources which included biographies of painters and art traders (e.g., Assouline, 2002), as well as analyses of artistic movements (e.g., Rewald, 1986), artistic life (e.g., Crow, 2000; Vaisse, 1995; White and White, 1993) and the Salon itself (e.g., Mainardi, 1993).

In our analysis of all these data, we drew on narrative technique as one way to realize a longitudinal analysis (Langley, 1999). Narrative techniques are particularly well suited to 'organizing data when time plays an important role and where a single case provides rich and varied incidents' (Chiles *et al.*, 2004: 505). We were thus able to confront the analyses of historians with the other analyses that we came across and thus moved closer to a more meditative view of our historic data, which we then organized into intermediate formats like tables to highlight the most interesting elements. Through this process approach, we were able to observe not only how the context evolved and how certain tendencies became more marked (Langley, 1999), but also how the positions of members of the field with regard to the Salon evolved. In other words, we engaged in a progressive layering of meaning onto the texts at our disposal in order to produce a theoretical narrative that answered our research question (Auerbach and Silverstein, 2003).

The Salon: 1737 to the 1840s

An analysis of power relations and contestation at work in the French contemporary art field suggests that we distinguish between two periods. In the first, lasting from 1737 to the 1840s, the main contestations and aesthetic battles taking place at the Salon may be classified as a 'tournament of values', in which amateurs, artists and critics disputed and renegotiated the accepted values of the Academy. After this, in the second period, contestation within the Salon seems to have become more difficult and to have moved to other venues, so that during this period the Salon can be viewed as a 'tournament of value'.

While the Salon was officially founded in 1667 as the place where members of the Academy (*Académie Royale de Peinture et de Sculpture*) could regularly show their work to the public, it actually became a periodical event only in 1737. Prior to this artists worked mainly at the command of their patrons and collectors, but from the fourth decade of the eighteenth century the Salon created a public space in which the greater public outside the art world could gather, look at and comment on contemporary paintings.

The official gatekeeper of the power of the Salon was the Academy, which was founded in 1648 under the protection of the King, with its main purpose being to elevate the fine arts and make them distinct from commercial craftsmanship. Central to this project was the training of artists, and the codification of the existing, mostly empirical, knowledge of painting (Sciulli, 2007). This strategy proved extremely successful. While during previous centuries France had arguably been a peripheral place for art compared with Italy, its importance increased along with the role of the Academy. Central to the codification that it oversaw was the establishment of a hierarchy of 'genres' – that is, it created an ideal according to which some styles of paintings were seen to be more valuable than others. This valuation was related to the capacity of a genre to embody the high ideal of art supported by the Academy and the expectation that painters become 'artists' who were not just craftsmen but individuals of 'genius' who could demonstrate their culture and imagination. This they were expected to do in particular in historical and religious paintings, which therefore came to be considered as the highest genres. Such paintings were also meant to educate their viewers, both aesthetically and morally. Landscapes and still life, on the other hand, together with paintings that depicted scenes from everyday life were considered to be 'minor' because they were mere reproductions of what an artist saw. Related to this hierarchy was also an emphasis on what Moeran and Strandgaard Pedersen refer to as 'technical' values. Painters were expected to be experts at drawing, in particular with regard to the anatomy and perspective. Drawing was considered to be a 'proper' activity for an educated man, while putting colours on a canvas was considered to involve more 'manual' work and as a result came to be valued less.

The Academy tried to enforce this hierarchy of genres and expected the Salon to be the place to do so. As the works on show began to be criticized by critics, who were emerging as a specialist group at this time, a commission was created in 1748 to examine all works in order to control their morality and protect the tradition of the 'great painting'. According to Crow (2000), the main purpose of this commission was to limit access for mediocre works and thus to reduce the possibility for critics to make negative comments about each year's Salon. This move was not entirely successful. While the creation of this jury led to a restriction in the number of works exhibited, their action did not have the impact intended upon the critics, who became the first source of contestation. As an anonymous critic complained in 1749, the Academy operated as an authority which was:

... wielded in the manner of those conquerors who distribute among their captains the lands which surrender to them, without bothering themselves over whether the people are left with the means to live. As long as this evil persists, one sees only discouragement in the latter and vain glory of the former. Cited in Crow (2000: 126)

This roused the wrath of the first secretary of the Academy, Mr Cochin, who demanded that critics should submit their work to censorship before publication and that it should not be allowed to be anonymous. He also teamed up with the chief of police to seize and destroy the work of all the 'unofficial critics' during the 1760s and 1770s.

In spite of all this, the Salon, like other FCEs, was not isolated from all that was going on in society at large – as Lise Skov and Janne Meier make clear in Chapter 11 in this book. It was these debates that influenced the kinds of discussions, as well as the evolution, taking place in the field of art. In this respect, critics were instrumental in linking the aesthetic debates in the field with the larger political and social debates in French society.

The notion of an art critic, and the profession associated with it, first emerged with the Salon (Wrigley, 1993). As the first Salons took place, comments appeared in booklets, journal articles and confidential letters. Unofficial critics became increasingly influential despite efforts to censor them. They supported painters of minor genres such as Vernet, Chardin and Greuze who enjoyed huge success among the bourgeoisie and the greater public, who learned about their works through reproductions. Greuze was the main figure (Crow, 2000), with his celebrated paintings representing moral scenes portraying humble people. Their quality challenged the hierarchy of genres and they were used by critics to diffuse their aesthetic, as well as political, opinions. Diderot, often regarded as the author who established a base line for the style of the Salon critic (Wrigley, 1993), insisted on bringing in moral and political dimensions. Challenging the hierarchy of the genre was one way to challenge the Academy, and beyond that the hereditary class society on which the monarchy was based. The popularity of Greuze's paintings contrasted with the lack of interest in historical paintings, considered by critics and the public alike to be boring.

What is of interest here is that the work of painters like Greuze came to be accepted at the Salon, which in itself enabled the critics to develop their comments and expect the public to go to these exhibitions, see the paintings on display, and share their views. For its part, the Academy tried to integrate these painters first by accepting their work at the Salon and then by encouraging them to become members of the Academy itself. Greuze, for example, had his first submission selected in 1755 and his work thereafter was never rejected until 1765. Two years later, however, he was told that his paintings would not be accepted for the Salon again until he submitted work to become a member of the Academy.[1]

During the following decades, the number of critics increased – as did the divorce of taste between the public and the Academy. Some suggested that the decline of the arts, a recurrent theme, was due to the Academy and its corporatism (Carmontelle, 1779), but the gap was eventually reduced once a new administration of fine arts took over. Reflecting the

values of the Enlightenment, this administration ordered historical paintings displaying a morality closer to that of the bourgeoisie. Eventually a
new school emerged in the 1780s – neo-classicism – which was able to
obtain the support of the Academy, critics and the general public. While
this school ruled the artistic field for a few decades, its domination was
challenged in the 1830s – not by critics so much as by artists themselves.

In 1791, during the French Revolution, the Salon jury was suppressed,
only for it to be reestablished in 1798 following numerous complaints
by both artists and officials. While still dominated by the Academy, the
new jury tolerated the exhibition of works that did not slavishly respect
the academic tradition and it was at the Salon that the next artistic battle
was to be fought: the one over romanticism.

Emerging by the beginning of the 1820s, romanticism opposed the
dominant neo-classical orientation of the Academy. The 'Raft of the
Medusa' (*Le radeau de la Méduse*) presented at the Salon by Guéricault
in 1819, and the 'Death of Sardanapalus' (*La mort de Sardanapale*)
exhibited by Delacroix in 1827, provoked an outcry because they
emphasized colour over drawing, and used loose brushwork and strong
colours or exotic settings. In these paintings, both artists referred to
historical painting in ways that were totally inappropriate for the tenets
of the Academic style. Guéricault used a large format and heroic style
which hitherto had been limited to historical painting that treated
contemporary events.[2] For its part, Delacroix's Sardanapalus had nothing to do with Western history, the traditional setting of historical art
works, and did not offer any moral conclusion. In both cases, the
paintings were accepted for the Salon, before being attacked by adher-
ents to the academic style, and defended by critics who happened to be
prominent romantic authors. The Salon thus became the place where
artistic battles were fought. Delacroix, the head of the romantic revolution, had all his submitted paintings accepted by the jury, with a rare
exception being the Salon of 1836 where his painting was rejected,
creating a scandal.[3] After many years of battle against the neo-classical
style, a compromise was finally reached and Delacroix was elected a
member of the Academy in 1857 at his seventh attempt.[4]

The second period: the 1840s to 1881

While the number of paintings accepted at the Salon every year increased,
so did the rejection rate, which seems to have been around a quarter of all

submitted works in the 1820s (28 per cent in 1833, 26 per cent in 1834), but more than half in the 1840s (57 per cent in 1840, 59 per cent in 1843). At the same time, the academic style became more specific and more popular. Starting in the 1770s, neo-classical painters led by David were able to secure the support of both the Academy and the public, and their influence on the Academy and the jury remained dominant. In the meantime, acceptance of work to be exhibited at the Salon became more and more difficult, in particular for those opposing the academic style. As a result, contestation developed outside the Salon.

A new genre of paintings, realism, emerged in the 1840s as a direct attack on the 'high' historical genre acclaimed by the Academy. Realism rejected all idealized forms of painting. Courbet, its main proponent, famously said: 'Show me an Angel and I'll paint you one'. Not surprisingly perhaps, his paintings were rejected by the Salon jury several times. Following the rejection of all the paintings he submitted in 1847, he observed:

It is bias on the part of the gentlemen of the jury: They refuse all those who do not belong to their school, except for one or two, against whom they can no longer fight, such as Messrs Delacroix, Decamps, Diaz, but all those who are not as well known by the public are sent away without a word. That does not bother me in the least, from the point of view of their judgment, but to make a name for oneself one must exhibit, and, unfortunately, that is the only exhibition there is. Cited in Galenson and Jensen (2002: 8)

Yet, while Courbet was periodically rejected from the Salon, he was in fact able to keep on exhibiting regularly elsewhere. In 1855, he even set up a pavilion in front of the Salon to show some of his paintings that had been rejected. Eventually, he and the Academy agreed on a truce and he became an accepted and well recognized painter in the 1870s.

Edouard Manet met with the same problems. When he submitted his first works to the Salon in 1859, a member of the Academy, Thomas Couture, wrote: 'Does anyone paint something so ugly?' (Blunden and Blunden, 1973). Manet firmly believed that the Salon was the place where innovators had to go in order to challenge the academic order. Yet his submissions were regularly rejected (in 1863, 1866, 1867 and even 1877) and, even when some of his work was passed by the jury, his style was still severely criticized both by the Academy and the critics and their public.

The jury and the Academy did not control just access to the Salon, but they were also in charge of the hanging of works, and thus of how each artist's work should be distributed in the space available in the galleries – a variation on the kind of 'situational value' that we will also see in later chapters by Timothy Havens (Chapter 6) and Brian Moeran (Chapter 5). The Academy's members in charge of this task made sure that the most interesting paintings – that is, those more likely to question the authority of the jury – would be difficult to see. In this way, together with the jury, they were able to limit access of the public to innovative artists.

In fact, the public and majority of the critics enjoyed the academic style. Indeed, the artists who practised this style had adapted to the need to make their work more interesting and so appeal to the public. Paintings in the academic style offered nicely brushed representations of moral scenes. Artists like Meissonier, Cabanel and Bouguereau who adhered to this style not only received official support and orders from patrons, but also enjoyed popular success.

On the other hand, both the general public and the critics found it hard to understand the work of the innovators. When admitted to the Salon, Courbet's and Manet's paintings repeatedly created scandals. In 1865, Manet had a nude painting accepted, 'Olympia', where a naked woman was portrayed in realistic style – in sharp contrast to the idealized nudes that were common in academic painting. The scandal surrounding the painting and the reaction of the public were such that the organizers had to remove the painting to a small remote room. The critic Paul de Saint Victor wrote that 'art sunk so low doesn't even deserve reproach' (cited in Hamilton, 1954), while Charles Blanc, who did regular Salon critiques from 1840 to 1880 and was very influential, always supported spiritualism and idealism in art (that is to say, paintings with a moral and some socially contextualized ideas) and opposed materialism (in other words, paintings mostly concerned with the reproduction of reality and art for its own sake). In his view, realists and impressionists were materialists whose work lacked a higher message (Flax, 1998). While there were a few critics who engaged in supporting the realists and impressionists, their audience remained limited.

Collectors further contributed to the enforcement of this domination by refusing to buy works that did not accord with the academic style. Paul Durand-Ruel, a prominent art dealer of the time and one of the few to support the impressionists, wrote in his memoirs:

Prince de Joinville, among others, told me pleasantly that he had been scolded one day by King Louis Philippe for having bought for my father a painting by Marilhat that had just been refused at the Salon. It was, so to speak, a crime in the eyes of many people. Venturi (1939: 150)

With the beginning of the Second Empire in 1852, the administration of the Salon and its jury entered a period of aesthetic conservatism. The Salon was to reflect the style of the Empire and celebrate the *status quo*. A-E Nieuwerkerke, the Superintendant for Fine Arts, headed the jury of the Salon from 1852 to 1870 and was opposed to innovation. He considered Courbet's painting style to be not 'the sort that the government should encourage' (Roos, 1996: 69). Then in 1872 the system for electing members of the jury changed, so that only those who had received medals and awards were allowed to select who should participate. Not surprisingly, these artists were the most conservative by temperament and had a strong interest in electing juries that would share their views and favour the acceptance of their own work in the Salon, rather than that of innovative artists (Roos, 1996).

Although those artists whose work was rejected regularly signed petitions to protest against the high rejection rate and the lack of openness of the jury, these had little effect upon the jury's practices. However, some critics supported the innovators. When reviewing the Salon of 1868, Emile Zola (1868), a supporter of Manet and the impressionists, wrote:

The Salon is opening today. I did not step in the exhibition rooms, and I already know what the long queues of paintings hanging on the walls look like. Our artists did not use us to expect any surprise, each year the same mediocrities are there with the same stubbornness.

Yet, the audience for such critics remained very limited and the Salon was extremely popular during this period. Between 200,000 and 450,000 visitors would come to the exhibition every year during the 1860s (Vaisse, 1995) and collectors offered to buy academic paintings for large sums of money.

The situation did not improve at the beginning of the 1870s when the Empire came to an end. Philippe de Chennevières, the new Director of Fine Arts who oversaw the Salon, revered only tradition. He dismissed new tendencies like 'democratic painting', which expressed a political tendency that he openly disliked. Commenting on 'A burial at Ornans' (*Un enterrement à Ornans*) by Courbet, one of the artist's most important (and controversial) paintings, Chennevières wrote:

If democratic painting is to be found in the dirtiest and most common tones modelling the most hideous forms of the ugliest choice, I certainly cannot deny that M. Courbet is a democratic painter. Cited in Lemaire (2004: 196)

Because the selection of works for the Salon was increasingly conservative, it became very difficult for innovative painters to obtain public recognition and access to the art market. One of them was Claude Monet who wrote to one of his sponsors in 1861:

That fatal rejection [from the Salon] has almost taken the bread out of my mouth; in spite of my not at all high prices, dealers and collectors turn their backs on me. Above all, it is saddening to see how little interest there is in a piece of art that has no list price. Rewald (1986: 225)

As they were regularly rejected (Table 1.1), a group of artists close to Manet decided to organize themselves and created an association – eventually becoming known as the 'impressionists' – whose purpose was to put on regularly a series of exhibitions parallel to the Salon (Galenson and Jensen, 2002). Those who wanted to take part in this exhibition were not allowed to submit to the Salon. The first exhibition took place in 1874 and was a modest critical success that attracted some attention even though it was a financial failure. Manet himself always refused to exhibit with them, arguing that the battle had to be fought at the Salon. Yet, the impressionists, along with their allies, started to develop an alternative to the Salon.

    While sceptical about the sort of art exhibited, critics supported the idea of holding and being able to view regular exhibitions outside the Salon. Increasingly a network of support was built to provide alternatives to the Salon. Art dealers extended their activities, with some trying to offer for sale those art works that had been rejected by the Salon. Paul Durand-Ruel (1831–1922), the 'art dealer of the impressionists', is considered by art historians as the symbol of this new type of actor in the art world (Green, 1987; Jensen, 1988; Moulin, 1987; Whiteley, 1979; White and White, 1993). His gallery was active in buying impressionist paintings from the 1870s and became increasingly successful as the monotony of the Salon became obvious to both critics and collectors. The former increasingly felt that academic art lacked some artistic genius, a new David or Ingres, who could give it a new start.

    As a result, Monneret (1999) suggests that, during the 1880s, two distinct systems emerged involving two types of artists, reputation

Table 1.1 *Participations in the Salon and in the impressionists exhibitions (1859–81)*

	Manet	Degas	Pissarro	Cézanne	Monet	Renoir	Sisley	Morisot
1859	R							
1860								
1861	A							
1862			R					
1863	Salon of refused works – included works by Manet, Pissarro, Cézanne							
1864	A		A	R				A
1865	A	A	A		A	A		A
1866	R	A	A	R	A	R	A	A
1867	A/R	A	A/R	R	A/R	A/R	A/R	A
1868	A	A	A	R	A/R	A	A	A
1869	A	A/R	A	R	R	A	R	
1870	A		A		R	A	A	A
1872	A	D	D	D	D	R	D	A
1873	A		D		D	R	D	A
1874	R/A	First exhibition by the impressionists						
1875	A (scandal)							
1876	R	Second impressionists exhibition	R					
1877	A/R	Third impressionists exhibition						
1878						A		
1879	A	Fourth impressionists exhibition		R		R	R	
1880		Fifth impressionists exhibition		R	A/R	A		
1881	A	Sixth impressionists exhibition		A				

A= Accepted; R= Reject; D= Decide not to submit

In grey are those artists who participated in the impressionists exhibition that year and did not submit their works to the Salon's jury.

Source: Rewald (1986).

mechanisms, art dealers and collectors. One type was the traditional Salon system; the other was a new art system organized around art dealers' galleries, and supported by critics. This alliance gave rise to the 'dealer-critic system' (White and White, 1993), and led to the formation of a new market. Within the Salon system, the situation worsened and the tension between the Academy and the newly established French Republic increased. Art dealers and critics, on the other hand, began to develop a sustainable alternative to the Salon with the express intention of promoting innovative painters.

Discussion and conclusion

In this chapter, our initial intention was to highlight circumstances in which an FCE either favours the reproduction of domination or allows contestation within a creative field. A historical analysis of the Salon from 1737 to 1881 allowed us to contrast two main periods in order to address this issue. In the first period, contestation took place within the Salon, making it a 'tournament of values', while in the second, the Salon became an event in which domination was reproduced in a 'tournament of value', where a consistent set of technical and aesthetic values held sway and other spaces outside the Salon had to be created for contestation to express itself.

This leads us to suggest that circumstances under which FCEs are 'tournaments of value' or 'tournament of values' relate to power relations and contestation within the field. An FCE can be a 'tournament of value' so long as its gatekeepers are willing to enforce a consistent set of valuation principles and receive the support of a critical mass of members of the field. This is what happened at the Salon from the 1840s to 1881, where the Academy and the jury were able to achieve hegemony in the field. Jury, critics, public, the state and collectors shared the same view of what constituted value in art and supported this dominant view. Building such a consensus was made possible by popular artists who were able to meet the expectations of both the Academy and the general public, as well as by critics who spread the view of value promoted by the Academy among the public. When the second condition, the support of a critical mass, and more particularly critical support, are absent, an FCE can become a 'tournament of values' so long as the gatekeepers are willing to accept contradictions within it. This is what happened from 1737 to the 1840s, when the dominant view was opposed by a critical mass of both critics and the public, leading to limitations on the power of the jury. As a result, the interests and values of the public had to be resolved, and the evaluations of both critics and the jury reconciled. In this respect, the Salon became a space of freedom where discussion and aesthetic battles could take place.

Finally, the results of this case study suggest a third point. An FCE can be a 'tournament of value' even if it lacks the support of a critical mass of field members. This is arguably what happened from 1881 onward, as the jury kept enforcing a single view of aesthetic value while a critical mass of collectors, critics and eventually officials were looking for more diversity and different forms of appreciation. In this case, the 'tournament of value' became increasingly marginalized and arguably was no longer an event that 'configured the field' because a critical mass of field members rejected it and walked away. As a result, the Salon did not reflect the field any more. This result suggests that whether an FCE is or is not a 'tournament of value' eventually coincides not only with decisions made by that event's gatekeepers, but also with overall power relations within the field as a whole.

These results highlight the fact that unless there is a high level of consensus in the field over the values held by its members, some level of contestation within an FCE might be necessary in creative fields for it to remain dominant. Contestation within the Salon, for example, reduced the power of the dominant faction, as well as their capacity to control the field. It also allows a debate about values to take place during the FCE concerned. As a tournament of values, a creative FCE like the Salon is a place where participants debate the meanings of those values and possibly go about renegotiating them. This diversity also attracts the attention of the public at large, which can enjoy the debates and occasional scandals that take place within the FCE. When the Salon became too restrictive, it shifted from being a 'tournament of values' to become an event where the gatekeepers would celebrate only their power and views, insisting on the number of art works that were exhibited, and seemingly ignoring the critics who insisted that these numerous works had little or no artistic value. In this way, the Academy gatekeepers rejected contestation. As diversity declined, the Salon became closed to innovation and lost its ability to be the kind of FCE where values of the creative field were debated, which in turn meant that it was then unable to provide an accurate picture of the field as a whole. Generally speaking, then, if debates take place outside an FCE, then that FCE cannot be a place where actors can make sense of the field. This restriction favours the emergence of other FCEs created by innovators who are excluded from the dominant FCE, thus leading to competition between old and new FCEs and the potential decline of the dominant one. It also reduces the attractiveness of the dominant FCE and increases the likelihood that field members will participate in other events that begin to reconfigure the field.

This suggests that an FCE should account for the different tendencies of the field and be the place where 'things happen', and where some scandal (or, in the terminology of some other contributors to this book, 'buzz') is at least made possible. If we look at the contemporary art fairs discussed by Don Thompson in Chapter 2, for example, we can see how much effort fair organizers put into making sure that all the various art tendencies are properly represented. Committees to select artists and special exhibitions rooms for *avant-garde* art are all features that allow an art fair to remain prominent.[5] In this respect, it might even be interesting to see the extent to which scandals, provocations and contestation within an FCE positively contribute to its overall reputation both in the contemporary art field and in other creative fields such as fashion and film. For example, the London-based Frieze Art Fair, arguably Europe's fastest growing art fair, benefited from events such as the Chapman brothers doodling obscene drawings on bank notes during its 2007 edition. The Cannes Film Festival, discussed by Steve Mezias and his colleagues (Chapter 7) is another example. The opening movie at the 2009 festival was 'Up', a US animated movie targeted at a broad, family-based audience – not exactly the sort of audience that might be anticipated for the winner of the Golden Palm award that year, which was Michael Haneke's 'The White Ribbon', a story built around strange events in a small Lutheran village which seem to involve some sort of ritual punishment involving the abused and suppressed children of the villagers. In the same year, the official selection included the much-discussed movie from Lars von Trier, 'Antichrist', which provoked a lot of debate and argument. What is at stake for the festival is for it to find a balance between more mainstream movies like Hollywood blockbusters, confidential art movies and movies that are potential sources of scandal, to attract attention and generate debates.

This chapter opens up avenues for future research. In particular, more attention could be paid to individual participants' strategies before, during and after an FCE. The decision to participate, or not, in an FCE can be considered as a strategic move, in that participation implies the acceptation of the event's underlying principles, while refusing to take part is a statement made by the actor concerned. FCEs can also be used as places to demonstrate and protest against the dominant view, a dimension that has not been explored so far. As such, FCEs are interesting settings to analyse the articulation between the institutionalized order, and the way actors are supposed to behave, and individual agency, and how actors can depart from expected behaviour and challenge the existing order. Further research could also help reduce the limitations of this chapter's findings. What appears as crucial in the case of the Salon is the role of the public, so that in those FCEs (like London Fashion Week or the Frankfurt Book Fair) to which the public has no, or limited, access, it may be possible to exert greater control within the professional field.

Notes

* The authors would like to thank for their help Dominique Lobstein of the Musée d'Orsay, Catherine Coudert, Jesper Strandgaard Pedersen, Brian Moeran, Grégoire Croidieu, Steve Mezias, Charles-Clemens Rüling, Jeannine Tang and all the participants in the ©reative Encounters workshop on fairs and festivals at which an early draft of this paper was first presented.

1. Despite his efforts to be accepted as a painter of history, Greuze was eventually received as a minor genre painter.
2. The wrecking of the boat Medusa happened some months before the painting was done. The tragedy occurred because of the incompetence of the captain, an aristocrat who had just returned from exile to be put in charge of the boat and did not listen to the advice of more experienced sailors who were of lower rank. Thus, the wrecking became a public scandal and the symbol for Republicans of the incompetence of the aristocrats who were back in power. As such the painting could also be considered as a critique of the restoration of the monarchy.
3. Two paintings by Delacroix were also rejected in 1845, although two others were accepted in the same year.
4. After the French Revolution, the Academy became known as the 'Institut'. For ease of comprehension, we use the term 'the Academy' throughout this chapter.
5. See, for example, Thornton (2008) on Art Basel.

References

Anand, N. and Jones, B. C. 2008. 'Tournament rituals, category dynamics, and field configuration: the case of the Booker Prize', *Journal of Management Studies* 45:6, 1,036–60.

Anand, N. and Watson, M. R. 2004. 'Tournament rituals in the evolution of fields: the case of the Grammy Awards', *Academy of Management Journal* 47:1, 59–80.

Appadurai, A. 1986. *The Social Life of Things: Commodities in Cultural Perspective*. Cambridge University Press.

Assouline, P. 2002. *Grâces lui Soient Rendues: Paul Durand-Ruel, le Marchand des Impressionnistes*. Paris: Gallimard.

Auerbach, C. F. and Silverstein, L. B. 2003. *Qualitative Data: an Introduction to Coding and Analysis*. New York University Press.

Baumann, S. 2001. 'Intellectualization and art world development: film in the United States', *American Sociological Review* 66, 404–26.

Blunden, M. and Blunden, G. 1973. *Journal de l'Impressionnisme*. Genève: Skira.

Carmontelle, M. 1779. *Coup de Patte sur le Salon de 1779. Dialogue Précédé et Suivi de Réflexions sur la Peinture*. Paris: Mimeo.

Chiles, T. H., Meyer, A. D. and Hench, T. J. 2004. 'Organizational emergence: the origin and transformation of Branson, Missouri's musical theatres', *Organization Science* 15:5, 499–519.

Crow, T. E. 2000. *Painters and Public Life in Eighteenth-century Paris*. New Haven and London: Yale University Press.

Danto, A. 1964. 'The artworld', *The Journal of Philosophy* 61:19, 571–84.

DiMaggio, P. J. 1983. 'State expansion and organizational fields', in R. H. Hall and R. E. Quinn (eds.), *Organizational Theory and Public Policy*. Beverly Hills, CA: Sage, 147–61.

DiMaggio, P. J. and Mullen, A. L. 2000. 'Enacting community in progressive America: civic rituals in national music week, 1924', *Poetics* 27:2–3, 135–62.

DiMaggio, P. J. and Powell, W. W. 1983. 'The iron cage revisited. Institutional isomorphism and collective rationality in organizational fields', *American Sociological Review* 48:2, 147–60.

Entwistle, J. and Rocamora, A. 2006. 'The field of fashion materialized: a study of London Fashion Week', *Sociology* 40, 735–51.

Flax, N. M. 1998. 'Charles Blanc: le moderniste malgrè lui', in J.-P. Bouillon (ed.), *La Critique d'Art en France, 1850–1900. Actes du Colloque de Clermont Ferrand des 25, 26 et 27 Mai 1987*. Publications de l'Université de Saint Etienne, 95–103.

Galenson, D. W. and Jensen, R. 2002. *Careers and Canvases: the Rise of the Market for Modern Art in the Nineteenth Century*, Working Paper 9,123, Cambridge, MA.

Garud, R. 2008. 'Conferences as venues for the configuration of emerging organizational fields: the case of cochlear implants', *Journal of Management Studies* 45:6, 1,061–88.

Green, N. 1987. 'Dealing in temperaments: economic transformation of the artistic field in France during the second half of the nineteenth century', *Art History* 10:1, 59–78.

Greenwood, R., Suddaby, R. and Hinings, C. R. 2002. 'Theorizing change: the role of professional associations in the transformation of institutionalized fields', *Academy of Management Journal* 45:1, 58–80.

Hamilton, G. H. 1954. *Manet and his Critics*. New Haven: Yale University Press.

Hoffman, A. J. 1999. 'Institutional evolution and change: environmentalism and the US chemical industry', *Academy of Management Journal* 42, 351–71.

Jensen, R. 1988. 'The avant-garde and the trade in art', *Art Journal* 47:4, 360–7.

Lampel, J. and Meyer, A. D. 2008. 'Field-configuring events as structuring mechanisms: how conferences, ceremonies, and trade shows constitute new technologies, industries, and markets', *Journal of Management Studies* 45:6, 1,025–35.

Langley, A. 1999. 'Strategies for theorizing from process data', *Academy of Management Review* 24:4, 691–710.

Lemaire, G. -G. 2004. *Histoire du Salon de Peinture*. Langres: Klincksieck.

Mainardi, P. 1993. *The End of the Salon: Art and the State in the Early Third Republic*. Cambridge University Press.

Lukes, S. 1974. *Power: a Radical View*. London: Palgrave.

Meyer, A. D., Gaba, V. and Colwell, K. A. 2005. 'Organizing far from equilibrium: non-linear change in organizational fields', *Organization Science* 16, 465–73.

Moeran, B. 1993. 'A tournament of value: strategies of presentation in Japanese advertising', *Ethnos* 58:1–2, 73–94.

Monneret, J. 1999. *Catalogue Raisonné du Salon des Indépendants, 1884–2000*. Le Plessis Robinson: E. Koehler.

Moulin, R. 1987. *Le Marché de la Peinture en France*. Paris: Editions de Minuit.

Oliver, A. L. and Montgomery, K. 2008. 'Using field-configuring events for sense-making: cognitive network approach', *Journal of Management Studies*. 45:6, 1,147–67.

Peterson, R. A. and Anand, A. 2004. 'The production of culture perspective', *Annual Review of Sociology* 30:1, 311–34.

Rewald, J. 1986. *Histoire de l'Impressionnisme*. Paris: Albin Michel.

Roos, J. M. 1996. *Early Impressionism and the French State (1866–1874)*. Cambridge University Press.

Sciulli, D. 2007. 'Paris Visual Académie as first prototype profession. Rethinking the sociology of professions', *Theory, Culture and Society* 24:1, 35–59.

Thornton, S. 2008. *Seven Days in the Art World*. London: Granta.

Vaisse, P. 1995. *La Troisième République et les Peintres*. Paris: Flammarion.

Ventresca, M. J. and Mohr, J. 2002. 'Archival research methods', in J. A. C. Baum (ed.), *Companion to Organizations*. Oxford: Blackwell, 805–28.

Venturi, L. 1939. *Les Archives de l'Impressionnisme*, vol. I, Paris and New York: Durand-Ruel Editeurs.

White, H. C. and White, C. A. 1993. *Canvases and Careers. Institutional Change in the French Painting World*. Second edition. University of Chicago Press.

Whiteley, L. 1979. 'Accounting for tastes', *Oxford Art Journal* 2, 25–8.

Wrigley, R. 1993. *The Origins of French Art Criticism from the Ancien Regime to the Restoration*. Oxford University Press.

Zola, E. 1868. 'Salon de 1868', in *L'Evénement Illustré*. Available at: www. cahiers-naturalistes.com/Salons/02–05-68.html.

2 | *Art fairs: the market as medium*

DON THOMPSON*

Art fairs are industry trade shows where dealers come together for several days to offer specialized work. Souren Melikian, a distinguished art writer and critic, says that art fairs have surpassed auctions as the premier events for buyers in the upper tiers of the market. Other critics have a more jaded view. New York art critic Jerry Saltz calls art fairs '... adrenaline-addled spectacles for a kind of buying and selling where intimacy, conviction, patience and focused looking, not to mention looking again, are essentially nonexistent'.

The work offered at the best fairs certainly equals in quality and quantity that offered by an auction house over an entire selling season. Art dealers are engaged in an ongoing battle with the branding, money and private dealing of auction houses Christie's and Sotheby's. Dealers needed a slingshot to combat Goliath. They needed to find some relative competitive advantage. They found it, not in mergers or blockbuster gallery shows but with branded and heavily marketed art fairs. In this respect, dealers were able to reconfigure the field of art by creating an event, or 'tournament of values', that enabled major players in the art world – dealers, collectors, art advisors, curators, museum directors, artists and journalists – to come together in new ways. The start of the twenty-first century was the decade of the art fair, of the market being the medium.

Commercial art fairs have existed for a long time. The earliest may have been Pand in Antwerp, in the mid-fifteenth century. This took place in the cloisters of the local cathedral over a six-week period. There were stalls for picture-sellers, frame-makers and colour-grinders. Four hundred years later, at the end of the nineteenth century, Paris had the Grand Exposition. The Royal Academy in London had a fair where artists exhibited their best work. The first major twentieth century art fair was the 1913 Armory exhibition in New York City, open to 'progressive painters usually neglected'; it included Braque, Duchamp and Kandinsky. Various art biennales served as covert art fairs; open marketing of the art exhibited at the Venice Biennale took place until 1968.

In 2009 a collector could still 'reserve' a work shown at Venice, but the words 'purchase' or 'price' were never to be uttered (see Chapter 3 by Tang in this volume).

Today there are four international fairs whose branding is such that they add provenance and value to works of modern and contemporary art sold there. They are to art what Cannes is to movie festivals (Chapter 7 by Mezias and his co-authors). One is The European Fine Art Foundation (TEFAF) fair, held in the Netherlands each March and known in the trade and in the press by its location, Maastricht. Another is Art Basel, held in that Swiss city each June. A third is an Art Basel spin-off, Art Basel Miami Beach, known as Miami Basel. Held each December, Miami Basel is famous for its blend of art, money and fashion. A fourth, the most recent addition, is London's Frieze, held each October.

The art fair season actually runs year round, and thus forms a 'network of fairs', as discussed by the editors in the Introduction to this book. There are several hundred lesser international fairs; mixed in are art biennales and hotel fairs. At the peak of art fair mania in 2007 there were eight art fairs held in New York City alone during February. At the bottom of the recession in 2009 there were four. The epidemic of fairs creates the malady of 'fair fatigue'; Munichis Michaela Neumeister, a partner in Phillips de Pury, says: 'Whenever I hear about a new art fair starting, it is almost physically painful to me. The art world has become a gypsy circus.'

Maastricht, the two Basel fairs and Frieze are 'must-sees', where dealers match auction houses in quality, speed of sale and payment. These attract consignments that might have gone to the fabled evening sales at Christie's or Sotheby's. They feature superstar dealers who come because the best fairs draw the most desirable collectors. These ultra-high-net-worth (UHNW) individuals come because superstar dealers are showing. It is what economists call a virtuous circle or network effect; it leads to a self-perpetuating oligopoly among a few top fairs. Each of the four fairs attracts the same group of dealers, art advisors, curators, museum directors and artists, with accompanying public relations advisors and journalists, each asking the other which artist is hot.

Below these four are twenty 'nice-to-see' fairs, mostly utilized by mainstream dealers. Below those are more minor fairs which feature new galleries showing local artists, or mid-level galleries showing work that has spent time in the dealer's storeroom.

The nice-to-see fairs understand the distinction. One Chicago fair official said they must 'stop chasing jet-setters and concentrate on the pool of collectors closer to home, those who spend $5,000 to $50,000 at a time ... every fair needs to know what its niche is'.

Collectors love fairs because they are convenient. The UHNW individuals beloved by the art world are time-poor. They like to consolidate research, search and purchase in a single location. Fairs offer comparison shopping; a single dealer might with difficulty, assemble three Gerhard Richters paintings at the gallery to show a client. Dealers at Art Basel will collectively offer ten to fifteen.

Fairs represent a culture change in the process of art buying. Quiet discussions held in a gallery are replaced with an experience akin to that of a high-end shopping arcade. There is a blend of art, status and socializing in one place. Collectors become shoppers who acquire impulsively, often purchasing only one work by an artist. The collector may never visit the gallery of the dealer from whom they purchase at a fair. With each fair and each purchase, collectors become more accustomed to buying art in a mall-like setting.

Fairs offer collectors a higher level of comfort than does a gallery. Just as the presence of underbidders reassures an auction bidder that he is not bidding foolishly, the number of people and 'sold' stickers at a fair alleviates the collector's uncertainty. The psychology at a fair is referred to as herding: when a buyer does not have sufficient information to make a reasoned decision, there is reassurance in following the behaviour of the herd.

Dealers reap favourable media coverage with proper handling of their appearance. A gallery may bring one or two good works that have already been sold, or have been borrowed for the occasion, to impress collectors and to gain media coverage. The featured works are placed at the front of the booth, drawing collectors to see lesser works that are actually available. The featured works sprout 'sold' stickers within five minutes of the opening.

Fairs allow a dealer with limited capital to compete for top-quality consignments, because the work is expected to resell quickly. A collector who wants to sell a painting might have the promise of a guarantee and advance from an auction house, but confirmation is slow if the terms have to be approved by a committee of the auction house's board. Final payment comes sixty days or more after the auction. A dealer offers the consignor immediate payment; the dealer can finance this with bank credit, against the expectation of reselling at a fair within weeks.

The downside for the dealer is that attending fairs is time-consuming and expensive. A dealer who goes to five fairs a year – the top four plus one in their home city – will spend seven or eight weeks away from the gallery, including travel, set-up and take-down time. The month before a major fair consists of phone and internet-based pre-fair discussions: dealers contact collectors, and collectors and their advisors check in with dealers. Five fairs will cost the dealer £200,000–300,000 – often more than the annual rent on her home gallery. Booths at Maastricht range up to €50,000; the total cost of an average 80 square metre booth, including shipping, accommodation, food and entertainment, reaches €80,000, but dealers queue to take part, because superstar dealers do. One dealer described his thinking, 'If I don't go, people will think the fair would not accept me.' For the gallery to be perceived as important, it is necessary to attend at least one branded fair. Attendance is also necessary to appease gallery artists who expect international exposure.

Fairs present a terrible physical environment in which to view art; they have been described as 'the best example of seeing art in the worst way'. The work is random and juxtaposed, with no sense of curatorial involvement. The setting and crowds are not conducive to evaluation. The lighting is always excessively bright, to appease safety concerns rather than to aid viewing. But every gallery shows with the same conditions – collectors accept them because they get to see so many new artists, and because at least once every fair, they hope to round a corner and spot a powerful work by someone previously unknown to them.

The Maastricht fair is held in southern Holland on the river Meuse. Maastricht is a sleepy Dutch city, thought to be the oldest city in the Netherlands. It may seem an odd place for one of the world's major fairs – why not Amsterdam? But the location seems to work in the fair's favour. Collectors find few other distractions. They eat, sleep and discuss art, and having travelled that far, are unsatisfied to return home empty handed. In 2009, 590 dealers applied to show and 239 were accepted. No important art dealer, curator or collector wants to miss Maastricht.

Contemporary art is a relatively new offering at Maastricht. The fair first specialized in Dutch and Flemish art, and evolved to sell modern art, Asian and Russian fine arts, silver and porcelain. Maastricht is important as the best strategic example of dealers banding together to compete with auction houses. Around €1.25 million are spent advertising Maastricht; it attracts 80,000 visitors to a city with a population of 120,000.

At the best fairs, and particularly at Maastricht, both dealers and the work to be shown are vetted in advance and again at the opening of the fair. Two days before the opening, dealers leave their stands as the vettors inspect each object. The important factors in assessing historical art are quality, scarcity and value. For contemporary art it is 'show worthiness', which involves the status and quality of the artist and the gallery rather than the work itself. Vetting adds value in the same way as expert appraisal and acceptance by a major auction house.

Vettors at Maastricht can be staff, dealers, auction house specialists or academics. There are concerns over using dealers, that competitiveness may lead to a rival's good pieces being 'vetted off', or that friendships may result in items of lesser quality being accepted. Three out of four members of the vetting committee must agree before a work is removed. The process is time-consuming and rigorous, but it gives a collector the confidence to purchase, and later to boast 'I bought this at Maastricht', as he might say 'at Christie's' or 'from the dealer Gagosian'.

In 2009, sales arranged at Maastricht had a value of about €750 million. Some exhibiting dealers claim that 40 per cent of their annual sales are made in the eleven days of Maastricht; a few claim up to 70 per cent. Because of high Dutch taxes, including 17.5 per cent value-added tax (VAT) and *droit de suite* (a European Union levy on art sales, paid to a living artist or estate), few sales are actually finalized at the fair. Price is agreed on. The dealer returns to an office in a more friendly tax environment – often the US, Canada or Switzerland, or in a true tax haven like Liechtenstein – where the sale is completed and the art shipped from Maastricht to a location of the buyer's choice. This migration happens at other fairs. ShContemporary, an important Shanghai fair held each September, operates with a 34 per cent luxury tax. Many of its art deals are later finalized in Hong Kong.

At the opening of a fair the competitive atmosphere is more like an auction – or 'tournament of values' (see Chapter 4 by Smith) – than a gallery. In the overheated art market of the years up to 2007, half the most important works were sold in the first hour, half of those in the first fifteen minutes. Buyers raced from booth to booth, committing to a purchase or asking for a 'hold' – and the dealer might say 'Ten minutes only, and give me your mobile number'. There was none of the gallery approach of: 'I will come back and look on the weekend', or 'Can I hang it in my home for thirty days?' In the recession years of 2008 and 2009, collectors at art fairs behaved less impulsively. Few deals were done in the first hour. Prospective buyers put works on reserve, promising to make a decision after a day or two of seeing other works and thinking about it.

Until 2007, the opening period of the fair was so critical that most fairs exploited it with tiered ticket pricing. The Armory Show in New York was the most extreme; tickets to enter the show at 5pm cost $1,000. This decreased to $500 at 5:30pm and $250 at 7pm. You got less than you might have thought for $1,000, because dealers could invite their own clients in at noon. The most desirable work had been sold or placed on reserve long before the $1,000 ticket holders arrived. On opening day at London's Frieze Art Fair, very important persons (VIPs) are allowed in at 2pm and very ordinary persons (VOPs) at 5pm. The very, very important persons (VVIPs), invited by sponsor Deutsche Bank, gain entry at 11am to check out the best work. And yes, dealers and auction houses both have been known to use the term very ordinary people. (See Chapter 6 by Timothy Havens for further discussion of the gradations of insiders.)

Maastricht, the two Basel fairs and Frieze have a different impact on the collector than an auction showroom or a gallery. When an auction specialist talks to collectors before an evening auction, he emphasizes the uniqueness and rarity of what is on offer. A gallery does this too, though the absence of other collectors removes the element of now-or-never found with the auction process. In contrast, walking through Maastricht with hundreds of dealers and thousands of art works offers the perception of abundance, but crowds also produce a 'last chance' atmosphere. One dealer says, 'With crowds like this, I can present work to a collector with the unspoken admonition that if they don't grab it, that guy over there, the one looking this way, might beat him out'.

During good economic times, the prices achieved for top quality work at a fair are remarkable. A work might be offered at 50 per cent more than what the dealer paid at public auction a few months earlier – and sell in the first half hour.

Art Basel is held each June in the medieval city on the Rhine. In 2007, 900 galleries from 28 countries applied for 290 spaces. Over €2 million was spent on advertising, and 50,000 people attended. In 2009, 550 galleries applied and 61,000 people attended; collectors love to shop in a down-market. Dealer fees for the smallest stand start at €17,000, with total costs about €40,000. NetJets, a shared-ownership jet aircraft company, provides more flights to Basel (175 in 2009) than they do to the Wimbledon tennis tournament.

Unlike the *Salon de Peinture* described and analysed in Chapter 1 by Hélène Delacour and Bernard Leca, where the jury consisted of fellow artists, at Art Basel the vetting committee is made up of art dealers and academics. Galleries that are rejected go to an appeal process with a separate jury. Those accepted keep their best work for the fair, as they do for Maastricht. Around 5–10 per cent of galleries are dropped each year, usually for not showing work of high enough quality.

By way of comparison with the works at a major auction, in 2007 New York's Tony Shafrazi Gallery offered five paintings at Art Basel with a total asking price of just under $100 million: two Francis Bacons at $25 million each; two Jean-Michel Basquiats at $20 million and $15 million; and an Ed Ruscha at $13 million. All sold.

Art Basel offers examples of frantic competition for more cutting edge work. In the excitement of the first ten minutes of opening night at the 2006 fair, a home improvement retailer from Manchester, UK, named Frank Cohen, got into a bidding war with British advertising legend and collector Charles Saatchi and French business magnate Bernard Arnault. The object of their lust was a sculpture by Canadian artist Terence Koh. Koh became a hot artist when Saatchi promised to feature him in the 2007 contemporary art show *USA Today* at London's prestigious Royal Academy. The Koh installation at Basel consisted of several glass boxes containing bronze casts of human excrement covered in 24-carat gold. Arnault said he wanted it, and Saatchi raised his bid. Cohen upped his bid to £68,000 and the others withdrew. Javier Peres, the American dealer who displayed the work at Art Basel, described the sculpture as 'an anti-consumerist statement'.

Only exhibitors can enter Art Basel's exhibition area before the fair's opening at 11am on the first day. An exception seems to exist for super-collectors like Eli Broad and Charles Saatchi, who are permitted to wander around earlier but not to purchase until opening. It is commonly believed that other collectors sneak in, disguised as workers. In 2005, a French dealer was caught doing this and banned from the 2006 fair. Apparently, he acquired a new disguise and attended anyway.

Miami Basel is the largest contemporary art fair in the world – a five-day bacchanal each December of Red Bull and vodka, partying, celebrities and conspicuous consumption – offering some similarity to the carnival-like medieval fairs discussed in the Introduction. Miami Basel promises its exhibitors that it will attract 'two thousand Very High Net Worth individuals' – and in good economic times it does.

Columnists call this the 'all singing, all dancing art fair'. It is the best example of market as medium. At one Miami Basel promotion, artist Joseph Beuys got into a cage with a live coyote; at another, artist Chris Burden arranged to have himself shot. The most publicized promotion saw fetish supermodel Dita von Teese take the stage at a dealer-sponsored party, strip to a G-string and pink panties, then ride a giant lipstick that bucked like a mechanical bull. In an example of the cross-platform marketing that pervades the fair, Ms. Von Teese's performance art was co-sponsored by MAC cosmetics. The intended message? Lipstick is sexy!

This is the fair where anti-establishment, monstrously proportioned art is featured. In 2007, collectors raced in at the opening to purchase Merlin Carpenter's text painting *Die Collector Scum*, and a Richard Prince tyre planter. Miami Basel was the first fair to show an art category called – I'm not kidding – 'Self loathing neon art'. Artist Dan Attoe offered 'We're all here because we were too afraid to deal with problems in our real lives', and Peter Liversidge added 'Miami Beach is where neon goes to die'. Both sold.

Miami Basel began in 2002. It now accepts 240 exhibitors from 800 applicants. The all-in cost of mounting an 80 square metre booth is about $110,000. The media campaign for the fair only mentions the names of star artists being shown, not the galleries exhibiting them. Miami Basel was created to provide access to North and South American wealth, money not being tapped by other fairs. The principal sponsor, Swiss bank UBS, ranks the fair equal in sponsorship importance to the America's Cup yacht race. It is the only sponsorship event UBS undertakes that is so obviously beneficial that it does not have to be approved at the bank's board level.

Art fairs have provided sponsors with opportunities to take up rival positions in the field of art. UBS has been so successful in using contemporary art to lure rich clients that one of its competitor banks, HSBC, responded by hosting a huge refreshment tent behind a Miami hotel. Deutsche Bank, another competitor, responded by sponsoring the Frieze and Cologne fairs. ING Bank then sponsored Art Brussels. The other sponsors of Miami Basel include Swarovski crystal, BMW, which offers chauffeured 7-Series cars to VIPs, and NetJets, which provides about 200 flights to Miami for each year's fair. That number exceeds what the company provides for American football's Super Bowl, and is second only to the 240–50 flights it sends to each year's Academy

Awards. Curators moan about how much sponsorship money is spent by UBS and others, and fantasize about the shows their museum could mount if only they were given the same resources.

To accommodate some of the hundreds of galleries unable to gain entry to Miami Basel there are nine satellite fairs. These were originally situated in warehouses and boutique hotels, and in a temporarily converted gym called World Class Boxing, but are now consolidated under one roof. They have names like Pulse, Flow, Aqua, Nada and Scope. These satellite fairs feature young artists, digital and video art, prints and photography. Many dealers come to the satellite fairs not just to sell, but to be able to return home and tell their collectors 'We showed at Miami Basel.'

In an average year, seventy-five museums – including New York Museum of Modern Art (MoMA), the Guggenheim, Tate Modern, the Reina Sofia and Sao Paulo MoMA – organize trips to Miami Basel for their trustees and patrons. The hope is that some of the art purchased will eventually be donated to their museum.

The remaining must-attend fair is Frieze, held in London each October, and quickly gaining a place equal with the first three. Begun in 2003, the fair was created by Matthew Slotover and Amanda Sharp, founders of the art magazine of the same name. The name came from searching a thesaurus for synonyms for 'art'; a frieze is a horizontal band of carved reliefs. In 2009, 390 galleries from Europe, the US, Russia and Japan applied for 152 spots at the fair.

Frieze best illustrates the divide between art industry insiders and outsiders, of the sort discussed in several other chapters of this book. Favoured collectors and agents get in early, eat and drink free in sponsored VIP lounges, and have dealers whisper, 'For you, my friend, a special price.' VOPs wearing sneakers queue two hours for the opening, drink £7 white wine from plastic glasses, and if they manage to corner a dealer, ask, 'Please, if it is permissible to ask – and please tell me if it isn't – how much is this painting?' Often they learn it is not permissible, usually by being told the work is 'not available'.

During the 2007–9 recession, the number of significant fairs around the world dropped from about 425 to about 225. Fairs that toppled and died ranged from New York's International Asian Art Fair to the Moscow Contemporary Art Fair. Fairs that survived featured more conservative and moderately priced art that would attract older buyers (and older money). Superstar galleries would still bring one or two museum-quality feature works to a major fair, but the rest of the booth was occupied by art at lower price points, closer to $50,000 than a million.

Those dealers who showed only one artist in their booth tended to reverse the well-known John Baldessari axiom. Baldessari, a British artist in his late seventies, was famous for telling students that they had to make dramatic new work in order to sell their older work. During the recession, galleries often featured older work at the fair booth, hoping that would add depth and perspective to the artist's new work. The art shown was also smaller, with little evidence of the huge sculptures and canvases that characterized boom times.

Many galleries showed emerging (thus less expensive) artists rather than established ones. 'Emerging' is one of those interesting art world terms that contributes to the appreciative value of a work; it is intended to mean 'young', or 'new to the gallery', but it describes where an artist is coming from, not where they are headed. Frieze introduced a new section called Frame, where galleries in existence less than six years – which would otherwise not have qualified for Frieze – showed solo (and non-juried shows) of emerging artists.

Some art offered at a fair may be there not just to highlight a dealer's booth, but as a way to evade restrictions on dealer pricing. The underlying problem is that gallery prices for successive shows of a hot artist never increase as fast as demand for the work would suggest. A collector who covets the artist's work may be denied the opportunity to acquire, because there is a long waiting list and a pecking order that favours museums, important collectors, and the gallery's best customers.

One solution is for a speculator to buy and immediately offer the work for resale at a higher price, usually at auction. Artists resent the huge profits that a lucky collector can earn by reselling their work at auction. Artists in Europe benefit from such a resale only through a tiny 'droit de suite'; artists in America and elsewhere get nothing.

Dealers discourage speculative resale by invoices or resale contracts specifying that any purchaser who resells the work must offer it first to the gallery, presumably at the purchase price. Some dealers inform clients that if they consign a work from the gallery to an auction house without checking with the dealer first, the gallery will never do business with them again. Other dealers say they would go further and circulate a blacklist.

But flipping does happen. An extreme case, described in my book *The $12 Million Stuffed Shark* (2008), involved German contemporary artist Matthias Weischer. In 2004, Weischer's large paintings were priced at €22,000–€25,000. His new work *Ohne Titel* was purchased that year by a private collector who had made it to the top of Weischer's waiting list. The buyer almost immediately consigned it to Christie's London for an October 2005 auction. The oil on canvas view of a room interior was estimated by Christie's at £18,000–£22,000, equal to its gallery pricing. After frantic bidding by two German collectors, it sold for £210,000, ten times the dealer's selling price.

What should Weischer's Berlin dealer Gert Lybke then have done? If he increased prices to match the auction market there would be very few collectors willing to purchase, because collectors expect small-step price increases, never 1,000 per cent jumps. But a dealer offering work for a fraction of what it might bring at auction has a very unhappy artist on his hands, and has issued an open invitation to speculators to buy and immediately consign the work.

One way Lybke could cut Weischer in on higher prices would be to give another dealer one or more new Weischer works to offer at an art fair at well above gallery prices. Wealthy collectors on the original waiting list would then be quietly informed that the works are available; they might bid up the high asking price even further. The selling dealer at the fair would get a sought-after work to feature, and would earn a small commission on its sale. The regular dealer earns his normal commission based on the gallery selling price, and the artist gets double or triple his normal proceeds from the sale. No one else on the waiting list is angered.

Artists have a mixed view of fairs. They are flattered to be shown and want their work exposed to foreign collectors, but they hate the way work is selected and presented. Only the top fairs show much work that challenges the artistic and economic *status quo*. Most mid-level fairs focus on conventional art by established artists. This is what artists call 'a mall for condo art', it is the art world equivalent of buying a high-end BMW to show in the driveway.

Dealer Roland Augustine of New York gallery Luhring & Augustine points out another problem. When a gallery sells at four fairs in three months, artists who sell are inevitably required to churn out repetitive work. Major gallery shows for an artist normally come at intervals of eighteen to twenty-four months, because it takes that long for the artist to develop the next stage in his body of work. With a demand for new work every few months, the evolution stops; the work remains cookie-cutter.

Augustine asks how much of 'turn out more this month' can possibly be first rate, and how much is 'same-as' previous work?

The best art fairs contribute to an artist's worth beyond just producing sales. The way that artists accrue value is sometimes unrelated to the quality of their work. It is a complex process that the art world calls validation, and the business world calls branding, and which the editors of this book call 'symbolic exchange' and 'commodity exchange' values. The hurdles in artist branding are first to find representation by a mainstream dealer, then to gain international exposure by the dealer taking your work to major international fairs. The next step is to have your work purchased by well respected, 'branded' collectors, and then to have your work donated to – and accepted by – a major, branded museum.

Gaining representation by a superstar gallery may follow as a fifth step in the process. For a few artists it may come as stage three or four. Being shown to an international audience at a major art fair is the second most important part of this process – after the critical first step of finding a mainstream dealer.

An artist's chances of having their work acquired by a branded collector go up exponentially if it is shown at a major fair. The ideal purchaser is a branded museum – if not MoMA or the Tate or the Centre Pompidou, at least a major museum in a major city. The next best purchaser is a well-known collector with a private foundation: Francois Pinalt (Paris and Venice), Bernard Arnault in Paris, Dakis Joannou in Athens, Don and Mera Rubel in Miami, Glenn Fuhrman in New York or Charles Saatchi in London are good examples.

Can a commercial art fair fill yet another role, as a culture platform for a city and worthy of substantial government subsidies? In 2007, the Art Paris fair, in conjunction with the Emirate of Abu Dhabi, launched Abu Dhabi Art. This was a fair for modern and contemporary art; it was intended to establish the capital of the United Arab Emirates (UAE) as the art centre of the Middle East, and one that might one day rank as a cultural destination alongside London and New York. Abu Dhabi has the highest per capita gross domestic product (GDP) in the world, but no tradition of collecting Western art.

In 2008, in the midst of the global financial meltdown, Abu Dhabi Art had such poor attendance and sales that the French partners withdrew their sponsorship of the 2009 show. On learning of this, the Abu Dhabi Tourism Investment Company (TDIC) and Abu Dhabi Authority for

Culture and Heritage (ADACH) declared that the fair was 'too important a cultural platform to be allowed to fail'.

The two agencies jumped in to provide financing so that the December 2009 fair could take place. When dealer interest seemed to waver, ADACH reportedly offered subsidies to several branded galleries to take part – White Cube, L&M Arts, Gagosian and Aquavella were mentioned as recipients. It was further rumoured that dealers who said they would bring museum quality art to Abu Dhabi were quietly assured of making a sale to the ADACH or to the ruling al-Nahyan family.

ADACH also funded panel discussions and design workshops held in conjunction with the fair. Total subsidies, including purchase premiums, were probably in the $10 million range. TDIC and ADACH said the fair will come to be considered one of the majors, and that they were prepared to subsidize it for a decade to ensure that happens. The Emirate of Abu Dhabi is already more heavily invested in art as a cultural and tourist-attracting entity than any other developing country in the world. ADACH is one of the financing sources for the $27 billion Guggenheim Abu Dhabi and Louvre Abu Dhabi museums, under construction at the Saadiyat Island cultural complex.

So, in the context of the theoretical argument developed in the Introduction to this book, what do we learn from this discussion of contemporary art fairs? Firstly, in their very establishment, dealers have used art fairs as a weapon with which to fight an ongoing battle with auction houses. In this respect, they have sought, to use the current jargon, to 'reconfigure' the field of art. At the same time, secondly, art fairs are 'tournaments of values' in which various participants in the contemporary art world come together to buy and sell art works, and in the process to negotiate their value. As this chapter makes abundantly clear, value, in the sense that economists use the word, is far more than a price tag or red dot signifying 'sold'. It is, rather, an amalgam of other values, some of them social, some situational, a few aesthetic, that together create an 'aura' around a work or artist and enable this symbolic value to be exchanged for money.

Note

* Don Thompson is Nabisco Brands Chair Emeritus and Senior Scholar at the Schulich School of Business, York University, Toronto. He is author of

the 2008 book *The $12 Million Stuffed Shark: The Curious Economics of Contemporary Art*, published in the UK by Aurum Press and in the US by Palgrave Macmillan. Some material in this chapter appeared in that book.

Reference

Thompson, D. 2008. *The $12 Million Stuffed Shark: The Curious Economics of Contemporary Art*. London: Aurum and New York: Palgrave Macmillan.

3 | Biennalization and its discontents

JEANNINE TANG

Introduction

While most chapters in this volume use the examples of different forms of fairs or festivals to theorize the field-configuring (FCE) event from the standpoints of organizational sociology and anthropology, this essay derives from another kind of disciplinary apparatus. As an art historian who works at the intersection of post-war art and politics, and whose language and methods draw from the arts and humanities' arsenal of aesthetics, theories of post-structuralism, politics and globalization, my tools bring me to another kind of analysis. In considering biennales, a type of art exhibition – characteristically large-scale, international and recurring – this chapter does not use the language of the FCE, because the temporality of these exhibitions exceeds the singularity of *an event*; it refuses the entitlement of biennales to configure the field of art; and forsakes an analysis of the micropolitics of bartering of power between the agents at biennales' physical sites, for the broader ideological questions of how these events and positions figure current conditions of political economy.

Pierre Bourdieu's notion of a field of production – wherein agents struggle for power and consequently define a field – has been taken up frequently to map the contingent exchanges of power between agents. However, the demystification of power's protocols is not Bourdieu's sole point, nor is it, in the strategic manoeuvring within a field, his ultimate concern. As his interlocutor, artist Andrea Fraser (2005: 57) notes, 'The critique of the art object's autonomy in this sense was less a rejection of artistic autonomy than a critique of the uses to which art works are put: the economic and political interests they *serve*'. If biennales are now increasingly part of the culture industry – this chapter asks, what interests do they serve? In writing an art history, one lends weight to one's objects, and in describing a field, one attributes power to the movement of objects within it, and attempts to redirect their course.

One step towards this lies in articulating the object of critique. Thus, my target of critique is not the individual biennale, nor its individual artists, critics and curators – who occasionally resist precisely what I critique – but the interests we are made to serve without our consent, and against our well being. Consequently, I consider a broad typology of *biennalization* (Nadarajan, 2006) – to refuse the animation and anthropomorphism of *a* single biennale, and the endowing of its invisible hand with independent life, when in reality it is saturated with and instrumentalized by the political.[1] This chapter will consider biennales in the age of capital's globalization, whose logic is both neo-liberal and nationalist. I consider the new subjectivity proposed by biennalization, whose erasure of cultural difference dovetails the rhetoric of the creative industries' 'creative worker' exemplified by biennales' transnational rhetoric. From the early 1990s onwards, the 'biennalization' of the art world progressed – particularly in developing nations – alongside the push towards the creative industries by governments worldwide, and coinciding with the rise of economic neo-liberalism. I argue that facets of this broader embrace of culture as a 'creative industry', of which biennalization is symptomatic, may be ultimately detrimental to the continued health of the arts and culture, and their workers.

The biennale industry

Biennales are a broad category for large-scale, spectacular exhibitions of contemporary art (generally defined as art after 1960 leading into the present day), where works of art and numbers of artists often run into the hundreds, mounted through high budgets ranking in the millions. At present, twenty to thirty-five biennales take place each year, and out of over thirty biennales in 2008, eleven took place in Asia between September and October alone.[2] The bulk of these exhibitions receive public funding, while exhibition organizers also solicit extensive private – frequently corporate – support in excess of what a large museum show commands. Biennales typically recur at a minimum rate of two years apart, sometimes operating in three- (the Auckland and Guangzhou Triennials), five- (Documenta), or ten- (Münster) year cycles. While biennales have existed since the beginning of the twentieth century, figures demonstrate that they mushroomed during the 1990s, a phenomenon that historians often correlate to the intensification of capital's globalization after the fall of the Berlin wall and the decline of communism

(Tang, 2007: 259). On the surface, a biennale's fundamental parameters of scale, independence from a single gallery or institution, transience and changes in leadership are valuable elements, as risky, ambitious curatorial projects may be executed, without being beholden to the singularity of an institution's branding or direction, with the added frisson of an auteur curator's intellectual weight and discursive contribution.[3]

The exhibition value, of biennales, is something I wish to expand upon here, as it hinges on the fundamental exhibition value of art.[4] According to Pierre Bourdieu in *The Field of Cultural Production* (1993a), the work of art requires the misrecognition – often through active suppression – of its material and financial value, for it to attain symbolic value *as art*, before this can be rendered as financial value in the long term. The literary or fine work of art must initiate itself as anti-economic for it to be valued as a unique, auratic object or gesture, apparently divorced from crude forces of instrumentalization and mass culture (Bourdieu, 1993a: 40). Such symbolic capital, or symbolic exchange value, is operative: produced through a 'field' of cultural production comprised of different positions, of which critics, exhibitions and galleries are agents whose various forms of work attach different kinds of value to the work of art (Bourdieu, 1993: 71, 81). Within this field, the exhibition of a work of art is one such enabler of symbolic value – the more prestigious the exhibition, curator and institution, the greater the credibility of the artist and the work in question, and *vice versa*. With the rise of the auteur curator in the 1960s and 1970s – often an independent practitioner organizing large experimental exhibitions – the attribution of social value to the work of art by its collection by a museum, or art historian, has since migrated to find value and endorsement through other channels, specifically that of display's discursive value, and the curator's organization of artwork.[5] While biennales are frequently spoken of – in the same disparaging sentence – as art fairs, I want to outline a few crucial differences between them, that are significant for biennales' rearticulation in national and economic terms. However, first I will sketch their apparent similarities.

Biennales and art fairs are both culturally legitimating events, sometimes co-ordinated together, and in such cases, their cross-marketing allowing people to speak of them in the same breath. This includes the tongue-in-cheek 2007 Grand Tour of the Venice Biennale, Documenta and Münster also included the art fair Art Basel as its final leg; in 2010, the Sharjah Biennale coincided with the fair Art Dubai. Art fairs have sought greater credibility in the past decade, while primarily operating as temporary venues for the trading, marketing and acquisition of art, fairs now also *produce* contemporary art, as Frieze, Art Basel and Shanghai Contemporary regularly commission performance, installation and films by important artists. Fairs, at times, play host to and attempt to foster dialogues and discussions – sometimes on related and self-reflexive subjects such as the relationship between art and commerce, in addition to more theoretical subjects such as the future of political practice in the terrain of the aesthetic. For the latter, they are presently able to command the participation of speakers, including the likes of philosopher Jacques Ranciere (cf. Bankowsky, 2005). That such intellectual engagement lengthens the marketing reach of art fairs is clear. Yet the presumed collapse of biennales and art fairs rests chiefly on quantitative terms – their internationalization of site, audience, mutual festivity and growing interest in becoming platforms for intellectual thought. Yet it is important to recall their qualitative and ideological differences: the terms on which they are organized and their attachments; the terms on which art itself is shown and the kinds of art works exhibited; their engagement with the theoretical interests of the moment and the scale and actual theoretical contribution of that theory. Biennales are ostensibly *curated exhibitions* – a curator selects and installs series of works, creating various kinds of narratives through their organization. Artworks from all over the world are included, drawn from the representation of numerous galleries and those artists unrepresented, showing them together with a theme, a purpose and a politics imagined by the curator. Art fairs are not curated in this respect – and those who choose to ignore this criterion forget that the actual objects of art, their modes of display, their ideological attachments and discursive field remain important points of engagement. Art fairs are, on the other hand, organized around the inclusion of galleries who show work by their own stable of artists, in order to sell their stable of artists at a rate that exceeds that of ordinary gallery sales.

While both biennales and art fairs attract international audiences and appear in many cities, it is important that the biennale's selection is by an independent curator, who travels the world conducting studio visits as a surveyor of currents and trends, lending the event a cultural prestige, legitimacy and even nationalism, as a country centrifugally draws towards itself the highlights of global thought, playing intercultural host via absorption. Such autonomy is not a presumption in a fair.[6] Art fairs are not, on the other hand, themed, they do not *propose* ideas as their *raison d'être*, and they are usually organized around a gallery's size and importance within the gallery system (for instance, in London, the more established blue-chip galleries show at Frieze, and the small up-and-coming ones show at the Zoo Art Fair). And while Frieze invites Jacques Ranciere to speak, this hardly constitutes a theoretical programme if the effects are not taken seriously beyond the borders of the fair itself. Moreover, the fact that Ranciere delivers a twenty-minute talk may lend lustre to the Frieze, but it is ultimately an anomaly amid the rampant sales taking place at the fair. Contrast this with Okwui Enwezor's Documenta 11, where the exhibition was co-ordinated with a symposium series taking place in various different countries, and featuring theorists such as Homi Bhabha, Immanuel Wallerstein and Chantal Mouffe, while constellating issues such as the fate of political democracy in an internationalized frame, the creolization of critical theory and the regional politics of the African sub-continent. The many hours of symposia complemented the exhibition themes, and the major product was not gallery accounts of sales, but several large volumes of critical essays that remain on course bibliographies of art and globalization, even today. There is no such equivalent for a fair. As Isabelle Graw notes, both biennales and art fairs are markets, but develop different criteria and standards for evaluation, solicit and affect different kinds of art production, depending on whether they operate 'in the knowledge market or whether one is trying to sell paintings directly through a gallery' (Graw, 2010: 33). However, Graw also notes that the 'commercial market regularly, and with astonishing purposefulness, steers a course towards those segments of the market associated with "knowledge," "market critique," or even "resistance."'

The aestheticization of commerce, its appropriation of knowledge, and the injection of the symbolic into the field of the fair to further supplement its importance, would apparently find its twin reflection in the growing commercialization of the exhibition space, particularly in biennales, given their high degree of private sponsorship. Biennales are underwritten by the joint efforts and relationships between collectors, gallerists and curators. However, the *visibility* of this network remains determinedly understated. Overt selling appears gauche, and while galleries frequently absorb the cost of a biennale artist's travel, works' fabrication and/or production costs, and informally tour collectors through the premises, no biennale will countenance red stickers marking a work as 'sold' on its wall labels, nor can gallerists claim booths with portfolios of artists and price lists – the very structure around which a fair is organized. Selling and its corollaries, at the biennale, are informal and discreet and do not intrude into official visibility; or, they take place under the artist's hand, as a quixotic rather than revelatory financial gesture.[7] Unlike the fair, the primary product of a biennale is *symbolic* capital, with its necessary suppression of economic capital, to maintain a myth of neutral exhibition space objectively according value to a disinterested work of art. Unlike the *kunsthaus*' securing of permanent value through a concentration on collections, biennales are more akin to the *kunsthalle* model of temporary exhibitions organized around ideas, but on a far more ambitious scale. While most biennales are involved in degrees of national representation, unlike both *kunsthalle/kunsthaus* forms of museum spaces, they are not charged with the responsibility of acting as more permanent or everyday institutions of the public sphere, even though they might temporarily inhabit them as physical venues.

Consequently, their commitment to the public in terms of education, history and social responsibility excludes biennales from the expectations accorded to public institutions, while their promotion is shot through with cultural nationalism.[8] While biennales such as Venice, Documenta and Kwangju began as a response to specific local political conditions, the bulk of biennales arise in search of nationalist publicity and tourism, using the *occasion* of the biennale to lure visitors to the city. Unlike art fairs, biennales are able to command important and multiple venues scattered across a city, so that one sees as much of the city as one does of art.[9] Through a biennale's occupation – and sometimes creation – of large spaces, installation work at biennales finds greater success through exclusive commissions, which, as critics have noted, necessitates the travel of others to the biennale site, as biennales become useful stimuli for gentrification, tourism and leisure industries. The pretence of a symbolic field that – however tenuously – distinguishes biennales from fairs, lends their appropriation a distinction privileged by certain forms of cultural nationalism, which a primary event cannot command.[10]

The acculturation of difference

The political interests of biennales are, however, highly visible, and these are frequently nationalist in publicity, and transnational in economic, political and cultural aspiration. Biennales are often attended by the rhetoric of post-nationalism – critic and historian Arthur Danto proclaiming them 'a glimpse of a transnational utopia' (Basualdo, 1999). In a less hyperbolic vein, historian Rachel Weiss claims them as 'an opportunity to redraw the global map with the centre newly located. As new areas log on to the global contemporary circuit, a biennale can magnetize a location, drawing in attention, ideas and works from faraway places and aligning them with the local reality. A biennale can also serve the parallel function of directing local attention (of both artists and public) outward, towards those places, trends and individuals with strongest relevance to the interests of the biennale epicentre' (Weiss, 1997). The rhetoric of biennalization invokes fantasies of realigning global economic and power imbalances; however, unlike earlier instances of large-scale international exhibitions such as 'Magiciens de la terre' at the Pompidou (1989) that represented early attempts to show non-Western art, albeit in extremely problematic ways, representations of the colonized 'other' are not scarce in present public culture, as Martha Rosler notes (Griffin, 2003).[11] And as biennales normalize as exhibition venues where one sees the most recent art, Rosler rightly observes that 'The global exhibitions serve as grand collectors and translators of subjectivities under the latest phase of globalization'.[12] Within this global perspective, biennales are largely nationalist enterprises engaged in cultural competition. Often titled after their nations or states (for example, the Sharjah Biennale, the Yokohama Triennial, far more infrequent are independent biennales such as Performa or Manifesta) biennales compete with one another, and the largest of all, the Venice Biennale, consisting of two curated sections at the Arsenale and Giardini in addition to national pavilions, is often joked about by the press as the Olympics of the art world: seventy-seven countries participated in pavilions in 2009, in unspoken competition with each other.

Hosting a biennale or taking a pavilion is also tantamount to a declaration of having arrived at a certain level of cultural power, or at least, of harbouring an ambition towards such an arrival; and for those who assume first world status, the elongation of reach is assiduously maintained – at the 2009 Venice Biennale, the US' pavilion extended across three sites – while other pavilions generally contain themselves to a single site (Higgins, 2009; Moss, 2009). The liberalism used to champion biennales also lends itself to revising the national image of the repressive or totalitarian states as, for instance, in the case of the Havana Biennale (Stallabrass, 2004: 37).[13] At the 2009 Venice Biennale, at the Mexican pavilion, in '¿De qué otra cosa podríamos hablar?' (What else could we talk about?), Teresa Margolles hung a flag on the building's façade, the flag dyed with the blood of over 5,000 people put to death for drug-related crimes on the northern border of Mexico in 2008. Inside the venue, jewellery was shown, made with glass fragments from shattered window shields, and women embroidering blood-steeped clothes left behind at the execution site with messages left by drug lords after their score-settlings in the north of Mexico.[14] These reams of cloth were hung near the entrance of the US pavilion, alluding to the drug trade between the US and north Mexico border. While Margolles' work was evidently critical of both Mexico and the US, the work nonetheless drew recognition of and praise for the Mexican pavilion itself. On the other hand, some biennales have taken issue with the positive face of multi-nationalism: for instance, Julian Stallabrass' Brighton Photo Biennale 'Memory of Fire: the War of Images and the Images of War' (2008), which showed the photojournalism and photographic apparatus of the twentieth and twenty-first centuries' armed conflicts, including a comparison of the Vietnam and Iraq wars, reportage from Afghanistan, as well as historical photography from the first world war, and the civil insurrections in Latin America in the 1960s and 1970s. It used the scale of the event to present a politically invested survey of global warfare, in part as an indictment of Britain's participation in the war on terror. More conservatively, curating the region may substitute regional loyalties for internationalism: for instance, the Dak'art Biennale, which restricts its choice of artists for a pan-African show. Some biennales have focused on the immediate regions as a matter of practicality: for instance, the second Singapore Biennale of 2008, the funding of which was reduced by at least 60 per cent after its first incarnation, intended to welcome the IMF–World Bank meeting held in Singapore in 2006.

Yet these are exceptions rather than the norm. Biennales generally show art and artists from as many continents as possible, employing networking curators in the Americas, Eastern and Western Europe, South, Southeast and East Asia, Australia and Africa, whose suggestions are then taken up by the artistic directors. The post-cold war dissolution of nation-states, the fall of communism and the triumph of advanced capitalism, the erasure of differences between city centres and peripheries and sponsorship of cutting-edge art forms of new media in an increasingly networked globe, are consequently invoked in praise of the biennale industry. At biennales, a complex navigation of race and citizenship for the sake of nationalism and sovereignty ensues: who does the biennale represent, and *through whom*? The identification of exhibition, state and subject is necessarily complicated by the rhetoric of globalization, as the transnationalization of capital sees nations and states claiming symbolic power as concentrators of diversity and aggregators of multi-culturalism (Chang, 2009: 14–17).[15] Such an unmooring of national subjectivities emerged, with controversy, at the 2009 Venice Biennale, when curator Nicolaus Schafhausen invited Liam Gillick, a British citizen and resident in London, to represent the German pavilion.[16] However, this was not the first time such an incident emerged, as Nam June Paik, a Korean artist resident in New York, also represented the German Pavilion with German-born artist Hans Haacke in 1993. If the enrichment and differential capacity of the state advances, so does its opposite – the fantasy of the state's dissolution of sovereignty.[17] The material vectors of immigration puncture both ends of this rhetoric, according to Chin-Tao Wu's figures taking Documenta as a case study. Wu researched 'not only where the artists come from, but also, in the case of those who move or emigrate, which places they choose to emigrate to – the *direction* of the cultural flows they personify' such a distribution of cultural power is clearly more rhetoric than fact (Wu, 2009). According to Wu's statistics on artists represented at Documenta, after Okwui Enwezor's Documenta 11 (2002) the number of artists from the US and Europe fell from over 90 per cent to 60 per cent; of the artists born in other countries increasingly represented at biennales, the majority are now resident in London, New York, Paris and Berlin, while denizens of these latter cities rarely relocate to the allegedly equal margins of the world (Wu, 2009: 110–11). As artists are largely identified in press material by their place of birth rather than that of residence, this arguably allows biennale marketing to exploit their identities as representatives of developing or third world countries, when in actuality the identifications of these artists may well accord more with geographical and intellectual communities in the traditionally dominant metropolises of culture.[18] The model of international identity championed by biennalization parallels what Saskia Sassen (1998a: xxiii–xxx) refers to in her work on global cities, as a transnationalization of capital that requires a simultaneous transnationalization of subjectivity, denationalization of space and state – which in fact produces new forms of centralization and control, rather than an actual dispersion of power.

Such an *acculturation of difference* persists under the multi-cultural alibi of transnational exchange. Rather than actually redrawing the lines of power between centres and peripheries, or interrogating their cases of production, power may instead be further centralized by incorporating the rhetoric of difference and claiming its dissolution, concealing the historical geopolitics that intensify rather than expunge financial and political debts. The title of the 2008 Guangzhou Triennial, 'Farewell to Post-colonialism', curated by Gao Shiming, Sarat Maharaj and Johnson Chang Tsong-zung, is one such instance. Their rhetoric claimed not an outright rejection of histories of colonialism, but an interest in 'how do we establish an "ethics of difference" within the framework of difference in cultural production? How do we prevent a "tyranny of the 'other'" without sacrificing the grounds already gained against the power status quo?' To this end, the curators attempted to formulate a new foundation for the discussion of transcultural difference forty years after 1968, by shifting it away from 'an all pervasive socio-political discourse'.[19] Oddly enough, Chang situates the biennale in 'pre-modern Chinese "global" spirit of *tian-xia* ("under-heaven"), which sees the world as abundance; each new possibility needs to be understood and dealt with, on its own terms and from one's own position, so as to use it properly. The spirit of Confucian "rites" summarizes this attitude; it also lies at the heart of traditional aesthetics'.[20] Allying the global to a political, aesthetic and social Confucianism is a fundamentally conservative operation, as Confucianism politics are based on the patriarchal family structure with the Chinese State as its divine head, and assumes an archaic Chinese essence to be drawn from unproblematically – which has itself been mobilized for much of Chinese nationalism that emerges in racial conflicts and border disputes.[21]

Co-curator Sarat Majaraj claimed the exhibition was to 'sound the emerging knowledge economy, how it was shaping new, global conditions of creativity' (Maharaj, 2008: 6). Artist and catalogue contributor Simon Leung remarked how 'similar this utopian proposition is to the newer, more sensitive language of global capitalist expansion, unrestrained by national boundaries and ever optimistic', and drew upon his own experience as an artist exhibiting in biennales as 'the role of this international exhibiting artist, following the flows of capital and seizing trans-national opportunities, as a highly privileged but nevertheless itinerant "guest worker"' (Leung, 2008: 44–5). Leung's contribution

to the biennale, the short film *Squatting/Guangzhou*, depicted the physical act of squatting and aligned the physical gesture with the politics of
bodies seizing urban habitation, in a two-channel video whose aural,
visual and textual translations in Mandarin, Cantonese and English
transmit discordantly together, their tensions apparent. Leung's catalogue text observes that the curators' presumption of a break with post-
coloniality signalled 'the point that China's desire to go beyond
post-colonial a refraction of the fact that China is also a coloniser?'
(Leung, 2008: 45). Leung's critique of power that – often violently –
constitutes common language, belonging, residence, citizenship is crucial,
as the danger of such an acculturation is its failure to recognize the cost of
its cosmopolitanism. For those who receive such entitlements, there are
increasing numbers of workers and subjects whose classes and identities –
for instance the foreign blue-collar labourers at the heart of many global
cities – become ever more impenetrable and immobile. Sassen (1998b:
82) notes 'a narrative of eviction' as the procedures of globalization's
fantasies which 'excludes a whole range of workers, firms, and sectors
that do not fit the prevalent image of international relations'. In Sassen's
feminist analysis, the 'unbundling' of territoriality opens space for non-
governmentality and non-state actors and subjects to intervene – for
instance with regards to human rights and international civil society,
themselves not unproblematic, yet nonetheless a counternarrative less
frequently taken up in biennale festivities (Sassen, 1998b: 92).

Creativity and its discontents

The avoidance of more difficult politics is perhaps unsurprising, as the
rhetoric of neo-liberalism hinges on the terms afforded by a specific
notion of aesthetic practice: the flexibility, deregulation and unblocking
of trade barriers for the ease and speed of finance's flows are the
mainstays of neo-liberalism. These coincide with ideals championed
for contemporary art, particularly the positioning of the art world as
a 'zone of freedom' as described by Stallabrass (2004: 6).[22] The idealized subject of this world is imagined in the cosmos of culture, and its
chief representative is what Charlotte Bydler (2004) refers to as 'the
so-called global or nomad artists [...] the professional cultural broker'
at home in 'many places at the same time, ideally mobile and unimpeded
by strings or liabilities to anyone but the smooth operations of social
networks', exemplary of both late liberal calls for individual rights and

capitalism's global net (Bydler, 2004). For Andrea Fraser, this idealized border-crossing artist is a worker free of place, government or national obligations – a poster child of globalization's virtues.[23]

However, the rhetoric of the artist as neo-liberalism's ideal subject sees its set of contradictions in cultural policy. At the Singapore Biennale's inception, the chairman of the National Arts Council, Lee Hsuan Hiang, noted that the state's sponsorship of the biennale targeted three concerns: the flourishing of a notion of 'art for art's sake' – the autonomous freedom spoken of by Stallabrass and Bourdieu; 'art for business' sake' as the arts were positioned as a catalyst for business innovation in the knowledge economy; and art for the community, strengthening state-sanctioned concepts of national identity and history. The biennale – and its artist – was positioned at the co-ordination of these three ambitions: the creativity of business, the creativity of the state and the social cohesion.

The remainder of this chapter will pursue the contradictions latent in such a formulation, where art's economic advantage may in fact be pursued at the expense of art's existence. Fundamentally, asking the arts to behave like the corporate sector in fact erodes a difference crucial to the existence of art as a separate category on which business may draw as catalyst and as inspiration. David Harvey (2006) notes: 'some way has to be found to keep some commodities or places unique and particular enough [. . .] to maintain a monopolistic edge in an otherwise commodified and often fiercely competitive economy.' And as Bourdieu (2005: xv) reminds us, 'sponsors do not in fact threaten the autonomy of artistic production but rather demand it, to the detriment of the reassuring atmosphere of a business held together by "corporate culture", because they have grasped that it is essential to the image of the philanthropist – at once disinterested and avant-gardist – that they want to construct for themselves'. Art for art's sake, and art for business' sake, are in fact operations that *negate* one another. The third term, a policy directive of 'art for community' may in fact conceal the tensions, poverty and class relations that constitute the social – an art for community, at the *expense* of community. As Andrew Ross (2007: 24) also notes, within the creative economy championed by Tony Blair and New Labour in the 1990s – now taken up in numerous developing countries – artists were pushed to be social in 'passive and complicit ways, and to eschew any real opposition to the state', as projects were solicited for artists to play pre-determined roles in society towards the 'improvement of public health, race relations, urban blight, special education [...] and, of course, economic development'. Such a pre-determination of art that also occludes its assumed autonomy and capacity for being a catalyst, and the self-defining right of communities to produce its own demands; moreover, demanding that art practices be affirmative, rather than critical of current social policy in order to be sponsored, drastically reduces the function of art practice to an undemocratic form of instrumentalization.[24]

While artists are asked to serve the social needs of the state, what about the social needs of the artists themselves – and the materiality of the category they constitute? Mark Stern and Susan Steifert (2008: 1) have noted that creative economy rhetoric 'misperceives culture and creativity as a product of individual genius rather than collective activity' and therefore fails to produce social structures in which creativity may flourish; they also criticize such policy's 'willingness to tolerate social dislocation in exchange for urban vitality or competitive advantage', modeling a creative society as fundamentally *anti-social*. Andrew Ross has also noted that the positioning of the artist as the creative industries' ideal avatar, as opposed to its colleagues in theatre, journalism, music and the performing arts, is in fact the creative industries' most economically insecure and vulnerable category of actors. If we consider the actual conditions of most artists: irregular working hours, the retention of multiple jobs out of necessity and, in the US and many parts of Asia, constant eviction due to the forces of gentrification and the inability to access or afford basic healthcare – we would observe an impoverished class of creative workers, their conditions fundamentally incompatible with the rhetoric of the transnational artistic class invoked by the biennale's temporary glory. Questioning the actual effects of work flexibility espoused by the creative industries, Ross (2007: 21) observes that:

The non-commercial arts have long been a domain of insecurity, underpayment, and disposability, interrupted only by those few who can break through into an often lucrative circuit of fame. Maps of the 'creative industries', as pioneered by the British Department for Culture, Media and Sport (DCMS), include the traditionally unionised commercial sectors, but the entrepreneurial paradigm touted by the policy-makers defiantly points away from the fair standards commonly associated with a union job. The preferred labour profile is more typical of the eponymous struggling artist, whose long-abiding vulnerability to occupational neglect is now magically transformed, under the new order of creativity, into a model of enterprising, risk-tolerant pluck. So, too, the quirky, nonconformist qualities once cultivated by artists as a guarantee of quasi-autonomy from market dictates are now celebrated as the key for creative souls with portfolio careers to integrate into the global value chains that are central to the new topography of creative markets export.

This is no mere fantasy of leftist cultural critics: such policy incorporating a flexible, artist-based model of labour as viable for development has been taken up in countries such as Russia, Singapore and China – countries which, at the same time, have embraced the biennale model of showing art – as the notion of the creative industries appears to be a motor propelling such countries into more advanced stages of development, so that they might compete with the megalopolises of the world, in the production of knowledge and innovation's constant cycle. For them, the concept of 'the creative industries' unfortunately yield uncertain results. Ross (2007: 25) also notes that 'it was yet to be shown that the nature of the enterprise produces good work, *never mind good jobs*' (my emphasis) as productivity statistics never attempt to measure these things. Ross continues, arguing that as the economy becomes feelgood and free, it certainly does not become any more just, and that attention to creative work often leaves out how very precarious such work is, the sacrificial cost of creative work (longer hours, price discounts, disposability that comes along with mobility and autonomy) frequently neglected in the literature on creative industries policy-making. In fact, Ross argues, for the creative economies to flourish, there should be provisions for income stability, as well as the continued persistence of the very existence of the creative class – health insurance, affording housing, civil rights to freedom of expression, civil rights of kinship and affiliation – that allow such a class to even exist. The 'creative industries' threat is dual: the actual productive value of creative industries' rhetoric remains unproven; and its purported accumulations of prestige come at an extraordinary expense of cultural workers' dispossession.[25]

The triad of creativity – that the arts enact a pre-determined form of social responsibility; that the arts become autonomous; that art courts business and that business courts art – also suggests an abdication of the state from its responsibility towards social necessities, and its responsibility towards art, leaving the arts to stand in for the social, and redirecting the lifeline of the arts towards business privatization. New Labour, as Ross observes, in fact withdrew from its support of the arts through creative industries rhetoric. And writing from this moment of economic recession, business support for the arts is far from a secure source of funding. On the other hand, this is also indicative of what Jaime Stapleton (2005: 137–8) describes as the ideology of the creative economy which:

economic and political theory has tended to present such creative labour as an *ideal organising principle* of the dematerialized economy as a whole. What could be regarded as simple self-interest at the level of business, fits comfortably with a long, though contested, tendency (in economic and political theory) to see aesthetics as a key tool in economic and political management. A central feature of the knowledge economy then is the folding together of attempts to maximize the *production of creative labour* with a more general tendency to *view the economy in aesthetic terms*.

After the bursting of the dot-com bubble in which creative economy rhetoric was forged, we now experience the fallout of ideas of creative destruction, the aestheticization of derivative models of finance, creativity and innovative competition – in this climate, state regulation of corporate culture and a demand for economic practices' accountability, is perhaps more necessary than preaching its rampant creativity, the effects of the latter felt painfully in both the US and the UK – which developing countries unfortunately seek to emulate. Finally, currently creative industries policy may well drain the life of the very class it purports to champion, when the state refuses to sponsor its existence, or sponsors it on such contradictory terms.

As one who has previously written about biennales in both art magazines and journals, I think it necessary to move away from their privileging, as *the* site of investment, display and production in art, and to contest the rhetoric that these events should be a primary inspiration and instigator of sustainable networks, education, commissions, infrastructure and exchange. It is necessary to contest the assumptions that biennales in and of themselves necessarily represent community, ethics, difference and democracy, and their justification as an exceptional state that facilitates these values. Because networks, infrastructure, populations, education, commissions and exchange, and a commitment to ethics, difference and democracy, should exist in the state's everyday support of art and social life, rather than the sponsorship of temporary events as an excuse for short-term instantiations of these. If the state abdicates responsibility towards the foundations of what its identity and people depend on – healthcare, social services, civil rights, the right to a just and dignified life and the cultural–aesthetic space to express and define what these mean – and outsources these responsibilities to a deregulated transnational market logic (whose overvalorized superprofit-making has demonstrated with its ineptitude at governance) – it may force the arts and social life into decline. Privatizing the arts in lockstep with a neo-liberal order, and biennializing its 'creativity' is in many ways a false solution, and risks becoming exemplary of advanced capitalism's high cost.

Notes

1. Nadarajan uses the term 'biennalization' to describe the global proliferation of biennales, and notes the attempt of most biennales to stage the global, or curate the world, as 'the general thrust of most biennales has been to exemplify a particular notion/reading of "global" arts practices where the curatorial formula seems to be creating a cumulative and representative list of all the countries/cultures one could possibly represent within the budgetary, temporal and spatial constraints of that event [...] it is not surprising that some of the countries that have been historically marginalized by these events would embark on "their own" biennales [...] an attempt by these countries to strategically position themselves, their artists and concerns in a contemporary art world that would otherwise remain oblivious and even resistant to them' (Nadarajan 2006). Elsewhere, Carlos Jiménez notes Gerhard Haupt as first using the term (Jiménez, 2004).
2. The *Universes in Universes* biennale calendar maintains a comprehensive – although not exhaustive – account of biennale activity worldwide. See www.universes-in-universe.de/car/e-calendar.htm (last retrieved 25 August 2009).
3. Biennales, however, may also be identified with the celebrity of certain curators, and the branding of the event is associated with the artistic director. For instance, the Venice Biennales and Documentas are characterized as frequently by their year as by their curator, e.g., Harald Szeeman's 49th Venice Biennale; Hans Ulrich Obrist's 50th Venice Biennale; Catherine David's Documenta 10; Okwui Enwezor's Documenta 11.
4. For a longer history of biennales and their function as exhibitions in the earlier twentieth century, see Altshuler *et al.* (2008).
5. For instance, the Venice Biennales and Documentas are characterized as frequently by their year as by their curator, e.g., Harald Szeeman's 49th Venice Biennale (2001), Hans Ulrich Obrist's 50th Venice Biennale (2003), Catherine David's Documenta 10 (1994) and Okwui Enwezor's Documenta 11 (2002).

6. Critic Jerry Saltz (2005) has bemoaned this, praising the egalitarian nature of fairs for not being curated by a single curatorial voice (quite forgetting that the wealth of the collectors attending the fairs renders them a singularly unegalitarian enterprise to begin with). However, Saltz also rightly admits that mushrooming of fairs forces gallerists to commission more and more work suited to the fair format, which is not in the interests of the artists or of the work, and reduces their subsequent critical or curatorial interest: 'Now, there are so many of them that critic Brian Sholis is right to call them "cookie-cutter corporate fairs". A downside to the cookie cutters is that artists are asked to churn out work for fairs. They do; the work is sold; and they're asked to do it again when the next fair comes around. How much of this art is first-rate is debatable. It's a vicious cycle, and it's accelerating.'

7. At the Venice Biennale in 2009, at the People's Republic of China pavilion, artist Liu Ding set up an online store from which people could purchase a number of objects at varying prices: for instance a painting signed by the artist was offered at RMB1,500, whereas a cabinet of curiosities entitled 'A container of experience' retailed for over RMB741,093 (Liu Ding's Store, 2009).

8. Admittedly the status of museums as public institutions is one also contested, as many are now privately funded (in the US this has been the case for the large part of the twentieth century) and those publicly funded have embraced corporate models of governance, operation and marketing, in the 'Bilbao' Guggenheim operational model of franchising.

9. As curator Catherine David notes, 'In times of global cultural tourism, I find it interesting that you can go to a place just for a specific exhibition' (Griffin, 2003).

10. Biennales often revive a city's spaces and inaugurate new ones: in the Singapore Biennale, religious venues (in tourist areas) were used, in addition to rehabilitated military camps, which were also in proximity to the city's up and coming dining district. The point on installation and site-specific works, more generally, as magnets for travel, was made in Stallabrass (2004: 26). See also Miwon Kwon's critical genealogy of site-specific art's positioning of subjects and identity alongside global capital (Kwon, 2004). However this is not to discredit the complexity of tourism: for instance, New Orlean's Prospect biennale assumed tourism is a matter of economic survival, as the biennale brought a much-needed $30 million in tourism to the impoverished city and generated jobs, yet the question of reviving New Orleans remains troubled, as the city municipality has rehabilitated arts and residential venues while dispossessing the poor who remain in need of housing.

11. For a summary and bibliography of such earlier instances of curating 'otherness', see Tang (2007: 265–6).

12. For Martha Rosler's comments, see Griffin (2003).
13. Stallabrass provides the pithy example of the Havana Biennale giving the Cuban government 'a more lenient and culturally open-minded image by sanctioning dissent within this narrow and delimited frame' (Stallabrass, 2004: 37).
14. Raul Martinez (2009). See also Teresa Margolles' *Universes in Universes*, available at: universes-in universe.org/eng/bien/venice_biennale/2009/ tour/mexico/06_margolles.
15. Chang sees 'the point for holding international exhibitions' as 'learning from the "other"', arguing that the 'diversity' of art practices (and artists) reflected 'the multi-dimensional realities of the world that constantly demand adjustment to the reading of art' informed by the artists' attention to process, as well as their own condition as subjects of 'rapid social transformation, population movement and rich cultural imagining, much of it arising from previously dormant geographical corners' (Chang, 2009: 17).
16. Regarding Gillick's appointment, historian Hans Belting asks 'Is this a kind of staged cosmopolitanism or the result of a now global art world? Can the fine arts only really be understood if they are also anchored in a local context, or has the western art system now become an autonomous international phenomenon?' (Belting, 2008).
17. In the past few years, a number of works have allegorized the relations of states to their subjects, particularly alternative modes of being dependent on statelessness and networked connectivity. See www.biennale.net: *The Discourse, the History and the Future of Internet Pavilion* sponsored by the Venice Biennale 2009 (retrieved: 10 August 2009): 'The Internet is this new cool and free country floating above all the older ones. That's where we go to do many different things, communicate, create, exchange'. See also *Embassy of Piracy* (Venice Biennale 2009 embassyofpiracy.org/) and *Deserto Internet* by Milton Manetas and Rafael Rozendaal (desertointernet.com/) both retrieved 10 August 2009.
18. Curatorial text for the 3rd Guangzhou Triennial 2008 'Farewell to post-colonialism' *Guangzhou Triennial* website: www.gdmoa.org:8088/ zhanlan/threeyear/4/24/3/ (retrieved 15 August 2009).
19. Press circular, '*Farewell to post-colonialism*', Guangzhou Biennale 2008 website (www.gdmoa.org:8088/zhanlan/threeyear/4/24/5/11150. jsp, retrieved 12 August 2009).
20. *Ibid.*, p. 17.
21. *Ibid.*
22. Julian Stallabrass extends Pierre Bourdieu's basic argument regarding art's symbolic production, to argue that art forms a supplement to the dominant system of capitalism, in that free art and free critique can and should be nurtured by capitalism in a neo-liberal world order.

23. Andrea Fraser: '[...] in the past few Whitney Biennales, or the Istanbul biennale, or the Beijing biennale, or Art Basel Miami Beach. What kind of artistic subject is being institutionalized today? Certainly, one thing that we're seeing is the artist as poster girl or boy for the joys of globalization and, with that, whether we like it or not, neoliberalism. It's the most recent formation of the age-old conjunction of artistic and economic freedoms. As we know from Pierre Bourdieu, the freedom from function and use that characterized modernist aesthetics predisposed art to represent and legitimize the freedom from need afforded by wealth. The avant-garde expanded on those freedoms to include the right to social, religious, and legal transgression. In the past twenty or so years, we have added a freedom from place and national cultural traditions as they are transmuted within the global idiom of contemporary art. So, once again, we find that art and artists are predisposed to represent and legitimize the field of power, with its drive toward globalization and deregulation, freedom from local and national constraints, etc. And these homologies are not only functioning at the level of representation and legitimation. Critical discourse aside, artists and curators now figure prominently – in places such as China, very prominently – among the transnational elite.' Anastas *et al.* (2006: 115).
24. See Deutsche (1998) and Bishop (2006).
25. In a post-1973 world order, David Harvey (2005: 156) characterizes the internationalization of the finance system and the relations of capitals between states, in particular the financialization of capital in the US, as that which 'could, from time to time, visit anything from mild to savage bouts of devaluation and accumulation by dispossession on certain sectors or even whole territories'.

References

Altshuler, B. (ed.) 2008. *Salon to Biennale – Exhibitions That Made Art History*, vol. I: 1863–1959. London and New York: Phaidon.

Anastas, R., Bordowitz, G., Fraser, A., Koether, J. and Ligon, G. 2006. 'The artist is a currency', *Grey Room* 24 Summer, 110–25.

Bankowsky, J. 2005. 'Tent community: Jack Bankowsky on art fair art', *Artforum* 1 October.

Basualdo, C. 1999. 'Launching site: an interview with Rosa Martinez', *Artforum* Summer.

Belting, H. 2008. 'Fragrance of difference: spaces for art and cultural diversity', *The Global Art Museum* 20 November (globalartmuseum.de/site/event/72, accessed 10 August 2008).

Bishop, C. 2006. 'The social turn', *Artforum* February, 179–85.

Bourdieu, P. 1993a/2004. 'The field of cultural production, or: the economic world reversed', in P. Bourdieu (ed.), *The Field of Cultural Production: Essays on Art and Literature*. Polity Press, pp. 29–73.

1993b/2004. 'The production of belief' in P. Bourdieu, pp. 71–111.

2005. 'Foreword: revolution and revelation', in A. Alberro (ed.), *Museum Highlights: the Writings of Andrea Fraser*. Cambridge, MA: MIT Press, pp. xiv–xvi.

Bydler, C. 2004. *The Global Artworld Inc. On the Globalization of Contemporary Art*. Uppsala: Acta Universitatis Upsaliensis.

Chang, T. 2009. 'Fare well, the third Guangzhou Triennial', *Guangzhou Triennial Printed Project* 11, 14–17.

Deutsche, R. 1998. *Evictions: Art and Spatial Politics*. Cambridge, MA: MIT Press.

Fraser, A. 2005. 'What's intangible, transitory, mediating, participatory and rendered in the public sphere? Part II', in A. Alberro (ed.), *Museum Highlights: the Writings of Andrea Fraser*. Cambridge, MA: MIT Press, pp. 55–80.

Graw, Isabelle 2010. *High Price: Art Between the Market and Celebrity Culture*. Berlin and New York: Sternberg Press.

Griffin, T. 2003. 'Global tendencies: globalism and large-scale exhibition – panel discussion', *Artforum International*, 1 November.

Harvey, D. 2005. *The New Imperialism*. Oxford University Press.

2006. 'The art of rent: globalization, commodity and the commodification of global culture', *6 Beaver Group*, 27 August (www.16beavergroup. org/mtarchive/archives/001966.php, accessed 31 May 2010).

Higgins, C. 2009. 'United Arab Emirates confronts stereotypes in Venice Biennale debut', *The Guardian*, 4 June (www.guardian.co.uk/artandde sign/2009/jun/04/venice-biennale-united-arab-emirates, accessed 27 June 2009).

Jiménez, C. 2004. 'The Berlin Biennale: a model for anti-biennalization?', *Art Nexus* 53, July–September.

Kwon, M. 2004. *One Place After Another: Site-Specific Art and Locational Identity*. Cambridge, MA: MIT Press.

Leung, S. 2008. 'Can the squatter speak?', *Guangzhou Triennial Printed Project* 11, 40–7.

Liu Ding's Store 2009. *The Utopian Future of Art, Our Reality* (www. liudingstore.com/aContainerofExperience.html, accessed 15 August 2009).

Maharaj, S. 2008. 'Counter creed: quizzing the Guangzhou Triennial 2008 according to James Joyce's "Catechetical Interrogation"', *Guangzhou Triennial Printed Project* 11, 4–10.

Martinez, R. 2009. 'What else could we speak about? Teresa Margolles at the Mexican Pavilion', *Art in America* 9 June (www.artinamericamagazine. com/news-opinion/the-market/2009–06–09/what-else-could-we-speak-about-teresa-margolles-at-the-mexican-pavilion/, accessed 27 June 2009).

Moss, C. 2009. 'A whole new world? On the 53rd Venice Biennale', *Rhizome* 11 June, (www.rhizome.org/editorial/2695, accessed 27 June 2009).

Nadarajan, G. 2006. *Between Production and Exhibition: Medial Arts Biennales*. A lecture at II International Symposium on Art Critics organized by Associació Catalana de Critics d'Art (ACCA) and held at Macba, Barcelona Museum for Contemporary Art, 12 November.

Ross, A. 2007. 'Nice work if you can get it: the mercurial career of creative industries policy', in G. Lovink and N. Rossitor (eds.), *MyCreativity: a Critique of Creative Industries*. Amsterdam: Institute of Network Cultures, pp. 17–41.

Saltz, J. 2005. 'Feeding frenzy: disgusting? Depressing? Or are art fairs the triumph of the corporate avant-garde?', *The Village Voice*, 21 January.

Sassen, S. 1998a. 'Introduction: whose city is it?', in S. Sassen (ed.), *Globalization and its Discontents: Essays on the New Mobility of People and Money*. New York: The New Press, pp. xxiii–xxx.

1998b. 'Toward a feminist analytics of the global economy', in S. Sassen, *Globalization and its Discontents: Essays on the New Mobility of People and Money*. New York: The New Press, pp. 81–109.

Stallabrass, J. 2004. *Art Incorporated: the Story of Contemporary Art*. Oxford University Press.

Stapleton, J. 2005. *Art, Intellectual Property and the Knowledge Economy*. PhD dissertation, Goldsmiths College, University of London.

Stern, M. J., and Seifert, S. C. 2008. 'From creative economy to creative society', *Progressive Planning, The Magazine of Planners Network* 170, Winter 2007, republished in *Social Impact for the Arts* January.

Tang, J. 2007. 'Of biennales and biennalists: Venice, Documenta, Münster', in N. Gane (ed.), *Theory Culture and Society: Annual Review*, pp. 259–72.

Weiss, R. 1997. '6th Havana Biennale', *Art Nexus* 26, October–December.

Wu, C. 2009. 'Biennales without borders?', *New Left Review* 57, May–June, 107–15.

4 | *Staging auctions: enabling exchange values to be contested and established*

CHARLES W. SMITH[1]

Auctions serve a range of different functions, the two most obvious being the pricing and allocation of goods and services. Auctions fulfil these functions in 'tournaments of value', in which both prices and ownership are publicly and openly contested. These contests are generally rich in intense emotionality, expressive gestures, plots and counterplots, dreams, despair, dialogues, repartee, interactions, disclosures, build ups and climaxes. As such, auctions need to be staged to manage physically and normatively the exuberances and contingencies inherent in these pricing and allocation contests. This is done physically by setting and maintaining spatial and temporal boundaries and constraints of the kind discussed in a number of other chapters in this book; it is done normatively by establishing and following various behavioural/ritualistic practices. While these rules, structures, places and times vary from auction to auction depending on a multiplicity of factors, auctions are nearly always a good show.

For social theorists who see social behaviour in general as embodying and revealing dramaturgical features this is not surprising; for them the dramaturgical paradigm is commonly capable of identifying, organizing and explaining facets of behaviour that other paradigms, such as the rational economic man paradigm of neo-classical economic theory, either cannot accommodate or simply ignores. In its most general form, it emphasizes the mutuality of social life and public performances expressed in Shakespeare's line, 'All the world's a stage, and all the men and women merely players'.[2] It conceives of human behaviour as contextual, reflecting and constrained by social expectations, governed more by expressive aims than instrumental tasks, more emotional than rational, and more interactive than self-directed. Perhaps most important, it views social behaviour as requiring the interpretive skills of knowledgeable performers; social life requires not only that social actors comprehend the meaning of the various situations in which they find themselves, but that they are able to renegotiate such meanings with others. Successful performances entail the joint interpretation and modification by performers of scripts and stage directions.

This view has been forwarded and systematically articulated by a number of social scientists, two of the foremost being Erving Goffman (1959, 1975) and Rom Harré (1981). They have analysed the various ways in which everyday activities are structured as performances; the use of costumes and props, anything from a waiter's apron to a sales clerk's pencil; the way some spaces, such as lecture halls, dining rooms and sales floors, function as formal staging areas whereas others, such as teachers' rooms, kitchens and back offices, are used for preparatory activities; teamwork by performers to generate specific impressions for particular audiences, as parents do for children or salespersons for customers; and the way social interactions are organized with beginnings, middles and closings. They have examined broad philosophical issues such as the use of emotions and rhetorical forms, the functions of meaning and inconsistency, and the balance and tensions between individual and communal performances, as well as more limited technical ones such as different uses of lighting, sound and timing.

All these issues pertain to most auctions, where they clarify and illuminate much that might otherwise be overlooked. Auctions, in turn, provide a wealth of empirical evidence that supports and augments the explanatory power of the dramaturgical model. The affinity between auctions and the dramaturgical paradigm is sufficiently strong, in fact, to endow auctions with an explanatory capacity of their own.[3]

In staging any auction, place, setting and props are arranged to reinforce the ambience and sense of community appropriate to the particular auction. These factors convey, among other things, different degrees of affluence, seriousness, glamour, order, separation, formality, tradition and risk. They also put constraints on who can participate. To understand how, it is necessary to be aware of the specific ways in which different auctions are staged and the various factors that favour one form over another.

A number of factors can affect the staging of an auction. One of the most basic is the nature of the item(s) being auctioned. In some cases the items being auctioned make it necessary to bring the auction to where the items are. In most fine art and collectibles auctions, the initial location of the items generally plays little or no role in the location of the actual auction. In these cases, the auction location is more often determined by where buyers are expected to be found. Sometimes this converts into travelling auctions such as those commonly held for rugs and jewellery; more often, it leads to established auction houses in various major cities. Whether the auctions are temporary or permanent, however, their ambience can and does vary considerably.

Sotheby's main New York gallery, for example, is on the Upper East Side in one of the more expensive neighbourhoods of one of the most expensive cities in the world. Limousines and expensive foreign sports cars fill the streets. Most other major art and antiques auction houses are in similar areas. Just to enter one of these galleries is to become part of an upper-class, 'cultured' scene. The young women who commonly serve as receptionists are universally attractive and well-dressed. The patrons are no less well-dressed; in winter, furs abound. Most auctions focused more on folk art and mid-priced collectibles in contrast tend to be located in less expensive neighbourhoods, often with plenty of free parking. The tone is less serious with more women and families present befitting the 'outing' it represents for many in attendance.

The settings within these different auctions also vary. The major art and antique auction houses normally have numerous items on exhibit. The halls are carpeted. The chairs are comfortable and arranged in a manner which calls to mind a music recital or guest lecture sponsored by a prestigious club, or a small theatre. There may even be a few private rooms, which overlook the main auction hall reserved for major buyers and consignors. Folk art and collectible auction halls, in contrast, project a more informal tone. Chairs of varying types are often scattered about; it is also quite common to have food and drink vendors available.

These differences in ambience are not accidental. Each setting is designed to convey a set of particular values, attitudes and expectations. Elegant reserved seats and a formal stage convey the message that a performance of superstars is in process in the central arena. All who participate in or are related to the performance share in the celebrity. The auctioneers and announcers are stars. The items being auctioned are stars. The multi-million dollar bidders are stars. Moreover, you can be a star too. All you have to do is make a bid. The cameras are rolling; the photographers are shooting pictures; the reporters are scurrying around.

There is a deliberate attempt to create an atmosphere that is not only affluent and theatrical in these auction arenas, but also quite detached and distinct from the everyday world. The theatres of Sotheby's and Christie's deliberately have no clocks in view to remind those in attendance of the external world of time and responsibilities. The only numbers one sees are the numbers on the tote boards. Generally there are no windows in the hall to concern people with the weather or the onset of evening. Attendees are requested not to place or receive phones calls within the sales auditoriums. The telephones being used by various staff persons at art and antique auctions are one-way affairs; they allow buyers who cannot be physically present to call in and participate. They are not there to connect anyone inside the auction to the outside world. Cellphone use is discouraged as in any other performance site. The furnishings and the formal seating arrangements serve to underscore the impression that this is a complete and sufficient world unto itself where those present are capable of carrying out the process and determining results independently.

The plush and elegant surroundings, and the presence of attentive and attractive service personnel, further serve to enhance the participants' sense of their own significance and self-sufficiency. Just by attending one of these auctions, it is possible to feel that one has the resources and judgement to make a sizeable purchase. The management of these establishments admits to deliberately fostering this privileged, world-apart atmosphere. 'Hey, this is never, never land, we don't want people worrying about the time' said one vice president. 'When you come in here, you are supposed to leave your everyday concerns at home' said another, 'Do you find any clocks in Vegas?' The very high prices that the items at these auctions bring require a setting of comfort and indeed luxury to encourage expansive bidding. The comparatively high risks involved in purchasing highly priced, 'unique' works of art also require self-confidence and the ability to ignore some of the realities of life.

The settings of country auctions, provincial art and antique auctions, and collectible/estate auctions are more varied. While sales auctions dealing with 'unique' items tend to emphasize the interests of individual participants, these auctions are commonly arranged to enhance the sense of the 'auction' community. From the way items are stacked about the auction hall or tent to the food stand in the back, there is commonly a party/gathering atmosphere that is quite deliberate. Things are often staged to create sub-spaces within the larger auction where smaller groups can congregate and that allow individuals to move about. The greater informality and accessibility of space generates greater participation and involvement.

One common way of structuring space is to assign specific areas for more formal public activities and others for more private preparatory activities. Goffman analyses such differences in terms of his distinction between frontstage and backstage. As applied to auctions, this distinction not only accurately separates the auction proper from supporting practices but also recognizes that particular areas are designated for particular activities. Nearly all auctions, for example, have office space that serves as backstage areas for the auctioneers and is off limits to all others. In addition, many auctions have particular viewing areas where goods to be auctioned can be inspected before the auction. Sometimes, especially with smaller auctions, this space may be the same one where the auction will be held, creating an interesting situation where the same space serves both as backstage and frontstage at different times. Sotheby's and Christie's, in contrast, maintain viewing galleries where the goods are displayed preceding an auction. It is here that buyers inspect goods carefully and record specific pieces of information in their catalogues. It is also time for buyers to determine whether there are any other buyers interested in the items they favour.

There are often secondary front and backstage areas as well. There may not only be a formal frontstage such as the auction floor proper, and a distinct backstage, such as backroom offices, but a backstage area of the frontstage and a frontstage area in the backstage. A quiet corner on the auction floor may serve as a meeting place for two bidders to negotiate a private deal, while the backstage may be used to stage particular happenings, be it the 'discovery' of an 'original' invoice attached to a chest of drawers in the expectation this knowledge will work its way into the auction. The greater the mix of front and backstage areas, the more likely that a given participant may believe that they see something that no one else does, which, in turn, may induce them to act on their own judgement.

However an auction may be staged, it is commonly complemented by particular costumes in the form of specific dress codes for auctioneers and audience. Similarity of dress among the buyers, like the formal dress common to many charity auctions, not only enhances the communal character of an auction but also sets a desired tone. At particular fine art sales at Sotheby's and Christie's, such formal dress is currently reserved for the auction staff. Even when so restricted, the formal attire says this is a special occasion where money isn't a problem and is likely to be spent liberally. In contrast, the work clothes visible at most down-market auctions give just the opposite message: this is a bread and butter business and every penny counts. The particular dress commonly adopted in various folk art auctions serves to authenticate these auctions by introducing a historical and traditional element.

While dress normally serves to eliminate differences among auction participants, it may also be used to accentuate such differences – as seen in the chapter on London Fashion Week (Chapter 10). The clearest example of this is the auctioneers and spotters who often dress in a distinctive manner to set themselves off from bidders and sellers. Specific buyers and sellers, however, may also dress in particular ways to support an image they are trying to project. Some major buyers have affected idiosyncratic outfits from Bermuda shorts and plaid shirts to bright coloured trousers and shirts. Such outfits, however, are nearly always worn either by newcomers unaware of acceptable attire or major players announcing that they are leading actors in the drama. The range of dress in major art and antique auctions tends to be less extreme, but even here any unusual costume will generally belong to an outsider or a major player. (Two or three very casually dressed dealers are normally found at Sotheby's and Christie's.)

Auction dress is as self-conscious and deliberate as any costume in a performance and varies with the play. Many antique dealers who dress casually in slacks and an open shirt for most non-New York auctions automatically put on a jacket and tie for a major New York auction. They will just as consciously remove the jacket and tie for an auction of more modestly priced items even if it is in New York. Participants' sense of appropriate dress is an integral part of all auction environments, though probably less so in each passing year. Such dress not only reflects the ambience of particular auctions but also creates it.

Though settings and costumes play an important part in defining most auctions, they are secondary to the actual performances of the participants, especially that of the lead actor, the auctioneer. The auctioneer, who in nearly all instances is the star of the show, remains the heart of any auction. He or she is the focus of all activity. Figuratively and literally, the auctioneer is at centre stage. In some auctions, he or she is not only the star but also the producer and director. In others, these roles are shared. Even as the star performer, however, what the auctioneer does varies with different types of auctions. Some introduce the items to be sold; others don't. Some recognize all bids; some don't. The one thing they all do and what can therefore be considered the key function of any auctioneer is to request and announce the flow of bids. The common technique for doing this in many auctions is the auction chant.

Nothing symbolizes an auction more than the auction chant. The chant is the theme song of the performance. It is so closely connected with auctions that even a fairly poor rendition by an amateur will normally be sufficient to be recognized. Even auctioneers who do not use a formal singing chant tend to call for bids in a rhythmic manner that has a chant-like quality. Whether or not a formal chant is used, the actual repetition of bids is normally only part of the auctioneer's overall performance. What is more, in most cases where a sophisticated chant is used, very few people are able to understand everything said. All that many people can grasp is the actual bids, and many others cannot even determine those. This is not as disastrous as it might appear since a tote board is normally used, which allows participants to see what the present bid is. Yet the chant, or its equivalent, retains its importance.

The truth is that the importance of the chant does not lie in its role as price monitor. Its major function is rather to orchestrate the auction rhythm. The chant controls the temporal order of an auction, the movement of the bids. Its importance is underscored when we remember the extent to which auctions are ripe with uncertainty and ambiguity. The chant introduces form where it is sorely lacking. It is a basic structure around which other meanings, namely price and allocation, can be built. The key to a good chant is not only to monitor the bidding but also to establish the cadence of the bidding. It does this by controlling the size of bid increases as well as their timing. It manages to take what is a very erratic, disjointed process and meld it into an ongoing, comparatively harmonious process. Like any music, it provides a unifying rhythm or theme. Moreover for those familiar with the rhythm it also reveals where they are in the process. The particular rhythm of the chant and the use of filler, that is, words or sounds used between the actual bids, such as 'give me' or 'right now,' indicate when the auctioneer is about to act one way or another. Like the music in a dramatic movie, tension is built and relieved by the rhythm and its variations.

To a large extent, it is more the sound and cadence of the chant filler that manages to capture attention than its content. Many people can't make out the actual words of the chant even though their meaning manages to be communicated. A good example of this is the filler, 'Will you give more to the buyer?' used by Chris Caldwell and inserted between bids in such a way that one 'feels' the request even if one doesn't hear the words. The whole phrase is said in less than a second in what sounds like about four syllables; 'Willyrgivmr ferdebyr?' Other auctioneers will spice their chants with more clearly heard comments like 'I'm gonner sell her!' or simply 'Let's go!' or 'Right quick!' Fillers, whatever their particular form, are used to move the auction along and participants depend on its rhythms to situate themselves in the process. Only when there are no bids and the auctioneer feels that the present price is unacceptable, will he stop his chant, break the rhythm of the auction, and comment, thereby jostling the players into a new, and hopefully more productive, round of bidding which will be accompanied by a renewal of the chant.

The variable rhythms of a chant are particularly useful because they allow the bidders time to consider what they want to do, while at the same time setting limits on their deliberation. In the case of a tobacco auction, the time limit may be no more than a few seconds; in the case of a thoroughbred racehorse or a ten to twenty thousand dollar antique, the time is more likely to be two to three minutes. With a rare masterpiece or a large estate, the bidding may last for fifteen minutes. The shorter the period of time, the greater the saliency of the bidding practice; the longer the time allowed, the more the significance of the individual buyers. What is central in all cases is that the auctioneer maintains control over the timing and sequence of the bids and keeps potential bidders aware of the process of bids and eventual sale. Like a Greek chorus, or a master of ceremonies, he is responsible for overseeing the auction process and relaying and interpreting it to the audience.

Even when there is no formal chant, which is the case not only at Sotheby's and Christie's but at many country auctions, liquidation auctions and even commodity auctions, the auctioneer's comments, requests for bids and announcements of bids function in a similar way. Prices will be stated and requests for increases will be made periodically, augmented by comments quite similar in content to the fillers of chants. The key fillers are: 'I am going to sell it.'; 'Do I hear any more?'; and the most famous of all, 'Going, going . . .' In some exchange and dealer dominated auctions, the auctioneer may actually address individual buyers by name in making a request for a higher bid. There is an orderliness to the process, however, which is quite similar to that produced by the auction chant.[4]

The performance of the auctioneer, of course, entails more than the chant or call. The chant or call merely serves to bring order to the bidding process. This organizing process, however, is itself only part of a more complex and encompassing orchestrating process. The participants must be managed and given their cues. This is not a major problem in most exchange or dealer only auctions, since here the participants are familiar with their roles and the script. In sales auctions, however, there is a greater need to manage the bidders whose preference and needs might not be commonly known. The auctioneer must try to keep all of the active bidders involved while maintaining a look out for any other bidders who may be interested in becoming active. At exchange and dealer dominated auctions, where the participants are generally all active and known entities, the good auctioneer can focus all his energies on the bidding itself. He may not only note who has the bid at any given moment but urge specific buyers to get back in the bidding or be more aggressive:

250 is the bid, say 275. Come on Lady (to the women who had the bid at 225 and is hesitating) don't lose it for $25. 250!; 275?; 275 anybody? I'm going to sell it. Lady, you stayed with it up to here. One more bid might do it. 275?; 250!; 275? 275! Thank you madam. I have 275; 300?

The task of managing the participants, of course, starts before the bidding even begins. The key to a successful auction is to get all potential bidders actively involved in the process. This is most commonly a problem in sales auctions, especially auctions of medium-priced goods where there are multiple uncertainties regarding the items being sold. (In up-market sales, there may be considerable uncertainty over the price of the items, but the items themselves are generally known.) The auctioneer in these situations must establish a sense of community and trust. The most common strategy for achieving this is through the use of humour and stories. Through laughter and sharing, the auctioneer establishes a general ambience conducive to participation in the bidding. Creating such an ambience often requires a virtuoso performance of an auctioneer.

The auctioneer's performance can range from the benign to the aggressive. Rather than waste time entreating bidders to increase their bids, an auctioneer who feels that the bidders are holding back, especially if they are dealers, may elect to sell certain goods quickly at the low bid offered. This will often serve to galvanize the other bidders to act out of fear that they may end up with nothing while others walk off with bargains. While this strategy often works, it can be expensive for the auctioneer and is generally used only as a last resort. Most auction-eers would much rather activate the bidders by offering them items they cannot ignore.

In sales auctions, where items tend to be more idiosyncratic, it is usually possible to manipulate the order of items offered to maximize interest. The experienced auctioneer begins with enough good things early in the auction to generate some high bids, while keeping back enough good things to ensure that bidders stay around. He or she will also attempt to alternate the type and price of things being sold, and to group items in a manner that will allow the good stuff to carry the bad rather than allowing the bad to bring down the good, much as a master of ceremonies tries to order the various acts of a performance. The outcome of the auction will depend on how successfully these things are done.

These practices are part and parcel of the auctioneer's performance. Although some items may sell themselves, they are more the exception than the rule. It is more often the case, to use the old Madison Avenue line, that people buy the sizzle rather than the steak. Though a good performance by an auctioneer can go a long way towards creating this sizzle, however critical, it is not the whole production. Buyers and sellers must also play their roles. In fact, for many buyers and some sellers, the opportunity to be part of the auction production is the main reason for participating. They are drawn to auctions as amateur thespians are drawn to amateur community theatre groups.

The feeling of being on stage and part of a performance in which you are expected to know and play your part well is widespread among auction goers. It is seldom enough to know what specific things are worth. Many potential buyers admit that they are more nervous about not playing their role properly than the economic consequences of making a poor buy. The classic fear of scratching one's nose at the wrong time and having this taken as a bid arises more from the possi-bility of embarrassment over acting inappropriately than concern with financial loss. Many auction novices admit it is not likely to happen yet cannot avoid the anxiety: 'I would be so humiliated'.

Though some are intimidated by being part of a performance, most regular attendees love the collective venture. It isn't just the glamour and celebrity status associated with the grand sales auctions that attracts them. Neither is it the opportunity for self-expression and the sense of personal power, although these, too, may be attractive. It is rather the

sense of belonging to a creative community that attracts them. As one
amateur auction enthusiast responded when asked what he liked best
about auctions, 'It's being part of the action. You get a chance to put
your two bits in'.

Whatever the feeling, fear of humiliation or exhilaration of being an
active participant, these buyers are caught up in the theatrical tenor of
auctions. To a large extent they are puppets in the auctioneer's production, but most participate willingly and happily, even when they realize
that 'playing their part' is likely to be expensive, as it is in most charity
auctions. It is such pressure that makes auctions such an attractive fund
raising program for many charitable organizations. The wealthy business man who makes a contribution to his Lower East Side Orthodox
synagogue on Purim, by bidding for the right to read or have someone
else read the story of Esther, confronts not only the charitable expectations imposed on the wealthy but also the auction expectations that
'stars' are expected to be the highest bidders. Similar pressures exist in
the black tie Junior League auction dinner, where charitable inclina-
tions are heightened by self-images that must be maintained in the
competitive frenzy of the auction.

While theatrical expectations normally serve, as in charity auctions,
to support aggressive bidding by potential buyers, sometimes, primarily
in exchange and dealer dominated auctions, they serve to constrain
bidding. In part such constraints result from peer pressures rather
than dramatic expectations. There is also a sense, however, that professionals feel that they must try not to become too enthusiastic.
Collectors and amateurs are allowed to go 'wild' and let their emotions
run away with them, but it is somewhat unseemly for a dealer to do so.
As a consequence, many a dealer has dropped out of bidding on an item
that he later wished he had bought, just as many amateurs have bought
things they wish they had stopped bidding on.

There are occasions when even lay buyers may experience constraints
on their enthusiasm that are grounded in the auction script rather than
in either their personal resources or interests. Some buyers, for example,
will fall out of the bidding when they see that they are bidding against a
major buyer, not because they are intimidated – though this is sometimes the reason for such actions, but because it strikes them as inappropriate, as it seemed to a woman at a Sotheby's book auction who
had just made a high bid on a rare book: 'Oh, I hope I am not bidding
against the university. I wouldn't want to do that'. The decision to bid

or not to bid, in fact, more often than not reflects the part and play that bidders perceives themselves to be in.[5]

Not all performances are individual matters. Many require the co-operation of others in a way that might be considered as 'team' playing.[6] Auctioneers and their support staff commonly function as teams. Each acts to complement the other's performance, often by apparently redirecting their attention to each other. A temporarily frustrated auctioneer not able to solicit the bids he wants may break off his chant to ask an apparently unbiased colleague what he thinks of the bidding:

I have 250 thousand, 250. Anyone say 275? 250. 250. Let's go. 275? 275?.... Tom, can you believe only 250 thousand for this?
    To tell you the truth Walt, I can't. It seems we have something really special here. I'm tempted to jump in here myself.
    O. K. Let's see if you were able to wake any of these people up. I have 250. I'll take 260. Thank you! 260. 260 Give me 275, 275?

In some situations, the auctioneer may engage in a similar type of banter with a range of persons including particular buyers or even just inactive members of the audience. The purpose, however, is nearly always the same, namely, to generate some dialogue that will indicate that the present price is too low.

The auctioneer is not the only one to engage others in such team play. Buyers, especially dealers, will do the same thing. While such team play may occur during the auction itself with one yelling to another that he or she is bidding too much, it is more likely to occur before the auction, when in front of the auctioneer or the seller one will indicate to the other that the item is somehow flawed or otherwise really not very good. A number of rug dealers, who often travel in groups, are notorious for coming up to a prospective buyer who is examining a rug and, either singularly or in pairs, indicating to each other in front of the prospective buyer that they don't think much of that particular rug. Such performances often serve to convince an amateur buyer not to bid as high as he would have otherwise, making it possible for a confederate dealer to purchase the rug for less money.

Buyers may also engage in more formal teamwork. The act of forming a buying pool or ring is perhaps the most extreme instance of this. In some cases including most antique and art auctions such pools may be illegal. In other auctions, however, they are permitted. Whether legal or not, there are significant differences in how structured such teams might be. In a fish auction, a buyer with a larger allocation than he wants at a particular price may quite informally make a deal with another buyer nearby him who has lost all or part of his allocation. Similar informal agreements regarding specific items may occur among dealers who run into each other during a preview before an auction. Other rings may be sufficiently established that a member may receive his share of a secondary ring sale even when not present. There are also instances of informal agreements where a successful buyer discovers after purchasing an item that he has a 'partner' and other cases where an inactive bidder discovers he is half owner of an item he never even examined. It may be a horse trainer buying a yearling and bringing in other buyers later, an antique dealer assuming an associate will split the cost of an expensive item, or a rug dealer after the sale claiming part ownership in a particular rug bought by another dealer. Such occurrences often function as plays within plays. The principals and a select number of knowledgeable observers are aware of the sub-drama unfolding, but most participants are not.

It is the teamwork between buyers and sellers that is perhaps the most intriguing as well as the most ethically questionable. At the simplest level, some sellers work out agreements with particular buyers to bid up their goods to a specific level, hoping to induce another buyer to step in at the higher level. If the accomplice ends up owning the item as a result, the seller will normally agree to take it back or give a partial refund. At other times, a buyer and seller may agree to bid against each other without trying to rope in a third buyer. The buyer may be an agent working on a commission who wants the bid to go up so that his commission will be bigger. He may also be a collector who wants to maintain the price of the item.

There are also more complex arrangements in which a buyer and a seller may actually agree to a price before the auction with all money above that price belonging to the buyer. If the buyer ends up with the item, he in effect owns it at the agreed price. If someone else ends up the high bidder, the first buyer receives the surplus over the initially agreed price. Sometimes buyers and sellers will agree to split the surplus over a given price. In this way the buyer will only be paying fifty cents on every dollar he bids above the agreed-upon price, but the seller will still profit if the price keeps going up. As might be expected, most of these arrangements are not looked on with favour by other auction participants, and as such are done secretly. On the other hand, the use of floor bids in literary auctions could be seen as such a public agreement between seller and buyer.

What is relevant about these buyer–seller arrangements in the present context is that they create particular impressions of what is happening in the eyes of the other auction participants. The principals in these cases are often more motivated by calculated self-interest than by social norms, but they are nevertheless keenly aware of the performance aspect of what they are doing as far as others are concerned. The main players in these situations make no attempt to force others to bid one way or another. They are content to create an illusion, which will in turn induce others to act in particular ways. They are practices, like most dramaturgical routines, whose purpose is to generate particular meanings, values and expectations. Where auctions differ from most other performances is in the significant roles played by hope and greed. As one less savoury auctioneer told me, 'Hey, most of the people who come here are motivated by hope and greed. They want to believe what they want to believe. I don't force them to do anything'.

The prominence of hope and greed relate to another similarity between auctions and theatrical performances, namely the high level of emotionality. One of the major assets of the dramaturgical paradigm in comparison to the rational economic man paradigm is its capacity to incorporate expressive aspects of behaviour. Although the model stresses the ways in which settings, situations and roles are defined and interpreted, it also recognizes that how actors perform in given situations will be affected by their emotional state. This is clearly revealed in most auctions where we find not just greed, but fear, hope and even generosity influencing the way people bid. People are emotional as well as thinking actors.

Although all auctions include an expressive component, they vary considerably in its significance. Not surprisingly, it is those auctions that allow for and encourage the greatest degree of individuality, namely sales auctions, which tend to be most subject to emotions. In exchange auctions, the constraint to conform to the consensus of the group limits the possibilities for personal expression. The major emotional outbreaks that do occur are normally in response to an attempt by someone to go against the consensus; they tend to be collective responses. While there is considerably more room in dealer dominated auctions than exchange auctions for individual response, such responses tend to be more cognitive than emotional; participants attempt to determine how ongoing actions modify existing interpretations. It is in the sales auction, where personal taste, self-aggrandizement and individual resources play major roles, that individual passions emerge as relevant. At times, in fact, these emotions may appear to dominate all else, as evidenced by the introduction that John Marion, then head of Sotheby's, received one evening. 'And here is John Marion, the Prince of the Passion Palace!'

The dramatic character of auctions is revealed yet again in the customary presence and importance of the audience, which in most sales auctions (as in the fashion show), is the primary role of most in attendance. They are not there to buy or sell. They are there to observe and to be entertained. Their presence in the drama of the auction and the performance of its participating members is, in turn, acknowledged and used when necessary to move the auction along and generate desired outcomes.

What holds the audience and enables them to be used in this way? At times, the glamour of the scene and the attendees may suffice. There is the thrill of being part of all that money. There is also the vicariously experienced emotional high of the intensive competition among bidders, including the exhilaration of winning and the apprehension of defeat. In most cases, however, people are there to observe a performance and have a story told. The attraction varies with the spectator. For the out-of-towner, the infrequent auction visitor, it is all new. The performance may be in its tenth year but to them it is fresh, fast moving and impressive. For the frequent attendee, the major attraction is the comfort of seeing a familiar production done well. They are interested in seeing who will shine, and if there will be deviations from the script and precedent. The veterans have their eyes open for new big bidders or the very skilled auctioneer who may appear on the horizon. In short, whereas the infrequent observer tends to be immersed in following the plot and keeping all the players in the production separate, the regular is more interested in seeing how the production is being managed and reproduced. And if both observers are pleased, they will break into applause at the proper moment.

It is significant that customers do not clap in department stores or flea markets. Individual buyers and sellers may smile. A passerby or two may nod in response to a particular transaction they have observed. To understand why people clap at auctions, it is necessary to understand why people applaud in the first place.

People applaud a performance that up till then they have not had any opportunity to acknowledge. Their applause underscores the fact that during the performance their silence and lack of engagement in it made them invisible. The actors respond to each other, not to the audience, as they engage in a process of creating a 'reality', though clearly a symbolic one. The audience is 'ignored' because they are not part of this created symbolic reality, and to allow them to interfere during the performance proper would only disrupt the process.[7] It is only when the performance is over or is in recess that applause is considered proper, that is, that the audience can participate by showing their feelings.[8] Through applause, the audience also manages to indicate to all that while they may have been silent through the production, they are part of the production if not the performance proper.

If by definition the audience is not part of the performance, how can they be part of the production? What have they possibly been able to gain – or give – through their attention? A range of vicarious experience is often possible as well as emotional support for the performers. More important, however, is their presence at the creation of another reality, a distinct vision or worldview within which all the behaviour and activity is given meaning. The 'great' performance is one that is capable of generating a 'reality' of particular significance for an audience. Whether it be Shakespeare, a ballet, a magic show, or a professional tennis match, the applause generally acknowledges that the audience has experienced a particular reality through the performance that they could not have experienced without it. Their applause expresses approval and acceptance of what has transpired.

Auctions can function in much the same way. A record sale price for an artistic masterpiece at Sotheby's or an unexpectedly high price for pretty much any unusual object will nearly always be followed by applause. A new 'reality' has been created. Be it a high price for the footstool made for Rock Hudson by Elizabeth Taylor or a record price for an old duck decoy, the audience realizes that they have seen a mundane item transformed into a valuable social object. As in the theatre, the performance by those involved in the auction has secured the audience's approval and acceptance of the new value and meaning given to an item.

To characterize auctions as 'reality' generating processes is to restate the thesis that auctions are primarily processes for dealing with ambiguity and uncertainty by generating not only socially legitimated prices, but also socially generated definitions of goods. Performances are similar 'reality' generating processes. The power of both the theatre and the auction arises from the fact that people depend on such social enterprises to give order and definition to activities that would otherwise be seen as inchoate and meaningless. *The show must go on* because to interrupt the show is to allow the reality and meanings that are dependent for their very existence on the show's performance to crumble. Meanings cannot exist by themselves. They exist only insofar as they are embodied in social practices that are acknowledged and understood by a community. Without the auction there would be no transactions, and without the transactions there would be no attribution of value and meaning to objects whose value and meaning were previously unclear or ambiguous.

There are theatrical elements, beside scripts and roles, which reinforce the dramaturgical imagery; some are present long before the actual sale takes place. Notices and advertisements are sent out. The sponsoring house in most cases will have put together an impressive catalogue that will not only list the items but will attempt to hype the sale as a whole. In many cases there will be a whole array of stories as to how the successful house managed to get the consignment. The extensive publicity for the Andy Warhol auction, which included a $95 catalogue, television appearances by John Marion and extensive previews, was perhaps one of the most extreme examples of this process. The items to be sold are themselves prepared to be shown. Most objects are similarly spruced up unless there is a deliberate attempt to maintain the 'buried treasure' look. Special care is then taken in the way the objects are shown.

Other theatrical practices occur only after the sale has ended; the most striking of these is the auction review. The very fact that such reviews exist underscores the theatrical nature of auctions, especially since they are normally carried in the entertainment or arts and leisure sections of the newspaper rather than the business sections. Such reviews seldom report the prices of all items sold. Specific items are selected; specific participants and the most exciting sales are noted. There is also likely to be some background information as well as some general local colour comments. We are often told who said what and what changes, if any, the auction reflected. It is social rather than economic factors that are noted and stressed and for which the dramaturgical paradigm is ideally suited.

It is these social factors that are embedded in the real world that differentiate auctions from most other theatrical performances. The prices generated in nearly all auctions have wider implications; they can and often do impact on other prices. Similarly, most of the performers remain deeply enmeshed in the everyday world and are motivated by everyday concerns. Auctions make good theatre, but they are also very practical affairs. The ability to reveal the theatrical aspect of everyday life and the practical side of the dramaturgical paradigm is one of the striking strengths of auctions. But auctions, especially when viewed comparatively, reveal more. They tell us where and why difference factors have greater and lesser impact in the way social meanings and values are established.

In the accounts presented above, individual preferences, collective judgements, and past market pricings all play a part in how prices are determined and goods allocated in various different types of auctions. We did not focus, however, on the different weights that these factors play in different types of auctions, which is perhaps where auctions offer us their most valuable lessons into the nature of social reality. That this could be the case is tied to the fact that the three factors in play here, individual preferences, collective judgements and market pricing, mirror the three factors commonly seen to be central to the production/ reproduction of society and social life, namely, human agency, social/ normative structures and existing social practices (See particularly Giddens, 1984). While different social theorists describe and label these three factors differently, most incorporate all three in one way or another. Where they tend to differ is in the weight they give to one or the other, particularly individual agency versus social structures. The splendour of auctions is that they reveal that the weight of these factors vary depending on the situation. More specifically, while all auctions seek to establish consensual values under conditions of uncertainty and ambiguity, they differ in the types of resources they have at their disposal in carrying out their objectives. The value of auctions theoretically is not that they are the 'purest' example of economic behaviour, but rather as a class of improvised alternative forms seeking a similar end they reveal the seams and cracks that allow us to distinguish the discrete elements that contribute to the value determining process.[9]

That different types of auctions make use of different resources in their search for acceptable values is reflected even in the way we commonly refer to different types of auctions. The New York Stock

Exchange, for example, which is, strictly speaking, a double auction, is commonly referred to as a 'stock market' rather than a 'stock auction', which reflects the importance of the transactions themselves.[10] Most bond offerings, in contrast, are referred to as 'bond auctions', which stresses the decision-making role of the large banks that dominate these sales, though secondary sales, which are to smaller investors and more dependent on past transactions, are commonly referred to as the 'bond market'. People enquiring about what happened on a given morning at the Boston Fish Exchange will normally ask about the 'market', given their interest in the actual transactions, while people enquiring about a particular horse sale at Keeneland's will ask about the 'auction', given their interest in the decisions taken by buyers and sellers. Auctions at Sotheby's, on the other hand, are normally referred to as 'sales', emphasizing the importance of the major purchase, while dealers at a wide range of dealer dominated auctions often talk about 'buys', which underscores the significance of acquiring stock for future resale.

The relative emphasis given individual preferences, collective definitions and past and ongoing transactions in determining value relates to other factors including how emotional, how rational, how individualistic, how collective and how predictable the auction is. The fact that no one had any idea how much some movie fan might be willing to bid for the crudely made footstool given to Rock Hudson by Elizabeth Taylor noted earlier explains why hundreds of people at Doyle's burst into applause when it sold for $1,200; it was seen as a highly personal and expressive act deserving of an expressive response. In contrast, the sale of a diamond brooch for over $40,000 in a dealer dominated jewellery auction in a suite at the Waldorf Astoria caused hardly a ripple, because the dealers present expected such a bid as reflecting the collective judgement of what the piece was worth on the wholesale market. The importance of individual desires and tastes in determining values at a Select Sale at Keeneland or Sotheby's also explains why the emotional pitch is often high enough to turn the stomachs of all in attendance, while the high predictability of prices and lack of personal involvement at many exchange auctions often seem to cause buyers and sellers to fall asleep.

The primary reason that different resources, be they individual desires or past transactions, are stressed in determining values in specific auctions is because differing auctions provide us with particular types of information. In most sales auctions, for example, especially the more select ones, little is 'known' about the item – due to the very

idiosyncratic nature of the items offered, and less about past sales since there may never have been any. The only things that can be determined through the auction process are individual likes and dislikes. In contrast, dealer dominated auctions normally handle less idiosyncratic items and have a commonly accepted 'shared wisdom' as to the value range of particular 'types' of items, based both on the experiences of 'professionals' and the views reflected in their professional publications. This consensus will be the most important determinant of value in these auctions as individual preferences are in sales auctions. In most exchange auctions, there is considerable knowledge of both past transactions and other ongoing transactions (that is, the 'market') making such transactions the most important value determining factor.

The emphasis given to individual taste and judgement in sales auctions explains why prices are apt to fluctuate more in such auctions than in others. Comparatively unfettered by collective judgement and previous transactions, prices are able to fluctuate in accordance with the whims and hunches of different bidders. The more idiosyncratic the item, the more subjective can be the bid, though the tastes of even the most egocentric bidder are subject to some forms of financial constraint and various internal checks. Even these restraints, however, are attributes of individuals. To understand most sales auctions, consequently, it is normally necessary to understand the motivations and constraints operating on individual players. In such auctions, psychological/biographical explanations of how value is determined commonly prove most informative.

In dealer dominated auctions, collective judgements are the most important factors determining value. This consensus of opinion is the product of ongoing discussions among experts and commonly formulated in professional journals. Individual members will often have their own opinions, but these are normally dependent on the collective view. Admittedly, a particular individual may, through his or her own bid or action, determine the price of some item at a given time and override the collective judgement. He or she is unlikely, however, to be able to sustain such prices over time. The fact that there are multiples of the items sold through these auctions means that the individual must either have the resources to impose his or her value judgement in all cases, or eventually defer to the collective judgement. A particularly active individual may be successful in redefining this collective wisdom, but it will be the collective wisdom, somewhat modified, which will determine the value.

The situation in an exchange auction is quite different. Here there is a relatively continuous series of transactions, 'a market' in like commodities, which clearly determines both the individual and the collective view. In these situations the public consensus of the moment is subject to the external constraints of ongoing practices, that is, the transactions of the market, in much the same way that individual judgements are subject to the collective view in dealer auctions. The situation is actually somewhat more complex since these past practices themselves incorporate and reflect past expectations and past practices. It is, however, the dominant role of ongoing practices in determining value that distinguishes exchange auctions from other auctions.

Another way of describing the differences between sales, dealer dominated and exchange auctions is to say that definitions of value are rooted in different soil. In sales auctions they are rooted in individual psyches; in dealer auctions, in various publications and face-to-face interactions; and in exchange auctions, in patterns of behavioral practices. These different contexts have their own impact on the way ideas, desires and behaviours are related. We are not surprised when individuals, subject to strong desires, act in a way that we might find irrational. When prices fluctuate erratically and extremely in major professionally populated markets, however, people tend to become anxious.

The weight and effect of values differ according to the contexts in which they are rooted. Evaluations emanating from an individual have less power of persuasion than those that come from a community, and both in turn have less than those that are embodied within behavioural practices. It normally helps an individual to quit smoking if he or she desires to quit, but peer pressure to quit is an even more powerful inhibitor. Nothing helps stop the practice of smoking, however, as much as the act of stopping.

Nevertheless, there are always exceptions. There are times when wanting to stop is the most important thing. There are other times when peer pressure may make one quit even if one didn't want to. Similarly, just not smoking for a period of time may work to 'break the habit' in some cases, but only serve to increase the desire and practice in others. The weight of each factor cannot be accurately predicted for all situations, but generalizations can be made. Although the relative importance of individual preferences, collective wisdom and behavioural practice in determining values varies from situation to situation in everyday life, it is difficult to evaluate each factor except in auctions. In most evaluative situations, group views reflect ongoing practices and individual opinions, individual opinions reflect group views and ongoing practices, and ongoing practices reflect both group and individual opinions. It is only when this interconnected system for determining value breaks down, resulting in the need for a new mechanism to determine value – as occurs in auctions – that we can isolate and examine each factor. What we discover is that there exists a natural priority of social practice over collective opinion and collective opinion over individual preference.[11]

In the end, however, auctions remain shows and as in all shows the stage, where we began this account, remains central. Auction values, in short, whatever other factors may influence them, are also shaped by the meanings associated with their physical settings – in other words, by situational values. Auctioneers consequentially are highly protective of their own space, both spatial and temporal, which is reflected in the way most auctions are scheduled and located. There is a range of auctions, particularly commodity auctions dealing in agricultural goods, where schedules and location are dictated in large measure by the seasonal and geographical character of these goods. Tobacco auctions historically were held in tobacco country. While some cultural items – Amish folk art, confederate memorabilia, Navaho items, early Hollywood movie settings, etc., have similar affinities to particular locations, such items are more the exception than the rule. Similarly, while the clientele of these auctions may, like that of various agricultural auctions, also be located in particular places, the strictures on location are also not as tight. As such scheduling and location tend to require a greater degree of implicit, if not explicit, collaboration with the 'competition'. This is done, however, more in service to their shared clientele. In most other ways the competitive juices run quite strong.

Such competition is to be expected, given that each of these houses claims to be dealing with the most select of select items and there can only be so many such items. Like the buyer who simply must own a particular item, it often appears as if these auction houses simply must have particular consignments. Both Sotheby's and Christie's, for example, will give up part or even all of the seller's commission to acquire a particularly desired consignment, be it a special individual piece or an entire collection. It could be argued that such actions are only good business: you have to get what your customers want. At times, however, it appears that the auction house is mimicking some of its own best clients and is on an ego trip of its own. Such competition between firms may force firms to inflate the estimates they give potential consignors, which, in turn, may force the auction firms to set their reserves high, which can and does influence the values determined in the auction.

What is fascinating about such competition, however, is that it tends, as just noted, to avoid direct spatial/temporal confrontation. Competing houses will attempt to consign the most attractive items, but they will seldom attempt to sell against each other. With what might be labelled the second level art and antique auction houses of New York, Doyle's main sale historically begins on Wednesday morning and Manhattan Gallery's Thursday morning, which leaves Saturday for Tepper's and Lubin's (they're very close to each other). Given the number of auctions that Sotheby's and Christie's ran – up to six a week – it was impossible for them not to overlap. Seldom, however, do they schedule major sales of similar type items for the same time. Here we have a clear example of the type of social discipline that we regularly find in various tournaments of value in which numerous individuals are engaged in pursuing their own self-interests. There is another example of such social discipline in an auction setting that reveals a deeper social interest with which I would like to conclude this account.

Auctions, as we have seen, occur within a rich interpretive and normative social context, which not only constrains what can occur but also makes possible what does occur. Moreover, it is a context that is constantly being reproduced and modified through the auction process. This is the lesson that auctions teach. They do not support a model of human behaviour in which individual rational actors merely seek to maximize their own interests. Rather they support a vision of human behaviour that is inherently social and interpretive, subject to a wide variety of external constraints, yet open to the creative input of individual actors. Nowhere are these factors more vividly documented than in a particular subset of bankruptcy foreclosure auctions, which the community prevents.

These communities don't ignore such auctions. They attend in great numbers. Once there, however, they either refuse to bid or ensure through organized co-operative bidding that all bids are kept so low that it becomes counterproductive for the bank to carry on. Often, many in attendance are themselves in financial distress and could benefit from the bargains that such auctions offer. In preventing such auctions,

these communities are actually continuing to function in the auction spirit. They are deciding to whom the goods belong: the original owner. They are also making judgements over value; namely, that in this particular case, financial value is of secondary importance. Nothing is more in keeping with the social dynamics of auctions than for an auction crowd to chant, 'No auction, no auction!'.

Notes

1. The material in this chapter, while reedited to stand alone, is drawn primarily from Chapters 5 and 7 of Smith (1989). While most of the events depicted occurred in the 1980s, the basic patterns reported have not changed in any significant way. For a condensed overview of different types of auctions, see Smith (1993).
2. *As You Like It*, Act II: scene 7; verses 139–40. The view that life can be seen as a performance pervades Shakespeare's work. For a fascinating discussion of this see Goffman (1975).
3. Economists make similar claims for the explanatory power of auctions, but their claims are based on the assumption that auctions embody and reflect the rational, self-interested, individualistic model of human beings celebrated in neo-classical economic theory. The fact that auctions lend themselves so well to a dramaturgical model, coupled with the many incongruities of the two paradigms, seriously challenges this economic model.
4. The use or non-use of a chant in most cases is a matter of tradition. Chants are used in thoroughbred auctions in the US but are not used in similar auctions in England. Time orchestration provided by a chant in other auctions is managed by a clock or historically by a burning candle. The candle or clock also serves to depersonalize the auction, which given the interpersonal tensions that can arise and the desire to put a business as usual face on the auction, is an additional benefit. Clocks are commonly used to control the declining price sequence of dutch auctions.
5. This particular woman clearly had a specific university in mind. As a knowledgeable collector or agent, she knew who the possible competing buyers were likely to be.
6. See particularly Goffman (1959: 77–105).
7. During some performances, such as a magic show, members of the audience may be included in the show. When this happens, however, they are made part of the process of creating the magician's 'reality'.
8. During a performance, members of the audience may react with 'oohs' and 'aahs', laughter or screams, but the actors are meant to continue their performances as if they did not hear them, though they are allowed to wait sometimes for the audience reaction to subside.

9. The study of 'abnormal' cases is commonly the best way to understand the normal as evidenced in the history of science. I am indebted to Everett Hughes for first making this fact clear to me when I was a graduate student.

10. A double auction is one in which different prices are being offered simultaneously by both buyers and sellers.

11. This ranking is consistent with George Herbert Mead's (1934) theory of mind, i.e., reflexive consciousness, which sees human consciousness as inherently social and grounded in social interaction. Accordingly, ideas and meanings should never be posited in opposition to behaviour. They emerge from behaviour and are grounded in behaviours. Human behaviour, in turn, is itself commonly constrained and formed by meanings and expectations.

References

Giddens, A. 1984. *The Constitution of Society*. Berkeley and Los Angeles: University of California Press.

Goffman, E. 1959. *Presentation of Self in Everyday Life*. Garden City: Anchor Books.

1975. *Frame Analysis*. New York: Harper and Row.

Harré, R. 1981. *Social Being*. Totowa: Rowman and Littlefield.

Mead, G. H. 1934. *Mind, Self and Society*. University of Chicago Press.

Smith, C. W. 1989/1990. *Auctions: the Social Construction of Value*. New York: Free Press and Berkeley: University of California Press.

1993. 'Auctions: from Walras to the real world', in R. Swedberg (ed.), *Explorations in Economic Sociology*. New York: Russell Sage Foundation.

5 | The book fair as a tournament of values

BRIAN MOERAN*

Based on intensive fieldwork at the Frankfurt, London and Tokyo Book Fairs, this chapter describes the role of international book fairs in the publishing industry and analyzes how, by bringing participants together in short-term, face-to-face interaction in a structured environment, they define and reassert the economic, social and symbolic values that constitute the overall field of publishing.[1]

In many respects, international book fairs comply with the criteria set out by Arjun Appadurai (1986: 21) in his seminal discussion of 'tournaments of value' discussed in the Introduction to this book. The criteria that he lays out regarding such tournaments' spatial and temporal removal from the routine of everyday economic life, the status contests engaged in by participants and the relevance of their outcomes for ordinary everyday among them, are all relevant for book fairs. They also fit within Bourdieu's discussion of fields of cultural production with their mechanisms of consecration, and structural homology between creative works, positions, and actual position-taking as participants seek to capitalize on opportunities made available in a specific field (Bourdieu, 1993: 84, 133, 182).

Although Appadurai himself was primarily interested in the Melanesian *kula* ring as an example of a tournament of value, he clearly recognized that 'an agonistic, romantic, individualistic, and gamelike ethos that stands in contrast to the ethos of everyday economic behavior' (Appadurai, 1986: 50) was to be found in contemporary industrialized societies. In answer to his call for 'a fuller examination of the modes of articulation of these "tournament" economies' (*Ibid.*), I myself argued that tournaments of value also included:

The various *haute couture* and *prêt-à-porter* fashion shows held in Paris, London, Milan, New York, and Tokyo; certain types of auction put on with accompanying publicity by Sotheby's, Christie's and other art auctioneers; annual media events such as the Miss World and Miss Universe beauty competitions, the Eurovision Song Contest, the Grammy awards for music, the Oscar awards for those working in the film industry; some art exhibitions and film festivals themselves (in Cannes, Venice, and so on); and, of course, the Nobel prizes. (Moeran (1993: 93))

Some of these examples have since been taken up, sometimes by contributors to this volume. Publications now cover competitions, awards, prizes (Anand and Watson, 2004; Anand and Jones, 2008; Glynn, 2008), fairs (Entwistle and Rocamora, 2006; Skov, 2006; Thompson, 2008) and festivals (Barbato and Mio, 2007; Evans, 2007) in various creative industries. At the same time, the different disciplinary backgrounds of these authors have moved discussion on from 'tournaments of value' to 'field-configuring events' (FCEs) (Lampel and Meyer, 2008). This chapter analyses international book fairs within the context of a perhaps slightly uneasy alliance between these different disciplines, and argues that Appadurai's inspirational ideas need to be taken up in full, rather than merely developed in part as at present.

The publishing industry

Book publishing is the commercial activity of putting books in the public domain (Feather, 2006: 1), and publishing companies are 'content-acquiring and risk-taking organizations oriented towards the production of a particular kind of cultural commodity' (Thompson, 2005: 15). They attract an enormous number of different kinds of authors who want to communicate, and be recognized for, their ideas. One salient feature of the publishing industry *vis-à-vis* other cultural or 'creative' industries (Caves, 2000) is the unparalleled number of new products launched every year: approximately 250,000 new titles in the English language alone, with one million titles in print.

The main difficulties for publishing companies are the acquisition of content and growth. In other words, they have to cultivate authors, on the one hand, and then, in order to publish authors' manuscripts, pay editorial, production and printing costs – not to mention author advances – up front. It is only several months (usually half a year) later that these costs are recouped – and hopefully profits made – through retail sales.[2] Nevertheless, because new products are for the most part untested, income is difficult to determine. Publishing, therefore, involves high-risk decision-making. Without capital, a publisher is

unable to increase the number of titles it publishes every year – which means that it either has to produce a major hit, or somehow raise investment money, in order to grow.

Publishers are more than just intermediaries between authors and readers. They commission manuscripts, and finance their production, marketing, promotion and sales – much in the manner of gallerists in the art world described by Don Thompson (Chapter 2). In the process, they confer authority and add value to authors' works (Clark, 2001: 3). In his excellent study of the academic publishing industry, John Thompson uses three analytical concepts in order to help us understand its organization and structure. These are, firstly, the *publishing cycle*, referring to the (typically four) stages through which a book moves from contracting a manuscript to finished product, by way of pricing and print runs, stock and reprints, and out-of-print decisions. The publishing cycle is divided into two seasons and for most publishers, the front list – that is to say, titles published during the past year – provides the turnover that pays production expenses. Usually, 20 per cent of titles provide about 80 per cent of revenue (Thompson, 2005: 16–20). However, what publishers have to do is to develop a back list: that is, books which continue to sell after their first year. It is these that provide continuous income and so help a publisher to grow (as well as take risks on new titles).

Secondly, there is the *publishing chain* – the interconnecting organizations involved in publishing, selling and distributing books – where each provides a service valued by the others. The publishing chain is thus both supply chain and value chain. Each of the links purportedly adds some value along the line, and intermediaries (like literary agents and book packagers) may be used to create content. The core activity of a publisher is to acquire (and develop) content and build a list; to make a financial investment and be prepared to take a risk; to assess the quality of a text and ensure that it meets certain standards; and sales and marketing (Thompson, 2005: 20–6).

There are five main steps in the supply chain and it is the relationships between parties at each stage that make things work. The first is external, between author and editor, who may well commission up to sixty titles a year. Then there is the internal relationship between editorial and sales and marketing departments within a publishing company as editors try to sell their book ideas and manuscripts, taking into account their suitability for the publisher's list, the author's name, the book's

unique selling point (USP), as well as its front list/back list potential, and so on (Clark, 2001: 85–6; cf. Powell, 1985: 183–5). The third is the relation between marketing and other publishers (to whom the former sells rights), on the one hand, and between marketing and reps and agents (who distribute and place books in retail outlets), on the other. Then, reps and agents liaise with bookstores, booksellers and library suppliers which, finally, have relations with their own customers and libraries respectively.

Thirdly, there is the *publishing field* which consists of 'the structured space of positions in which different publishers, agents and other organizations are located' (Thompson, 2005: 16). In fact, it consists of a number of overlapping (sub-)fields, since different kinds of publishing (textbook, trade, academic and so on) are organized in rather different ways, exhibiting a variety of linguistic, spatial and technological properties.

Thompson argues that publishers possess four kinds of resources: firstly, *economic capital* (consisting of accumulated financial resources); secondly, *human capital* (arising from staff employed and their accumulated knowledge); thirdly, *symbolic capital* (consisting of the accumulated prestige, recognition and respect deriving from publishers acting as cultural intermediaries and arbiters of quality and taste).[3] This helps a publisher to attract, position and promote new books and acquire authors. Symbolic capital therefore underpins relations of trust in the publishing field (Thompson, 2005: 33), although authors themselves develop symbolic capital, too. Finally, publishers accumulate *intellectual capital* (arising from the rights that they own or control). The stock of contracts with authors owned by a publisher 'represents the sum total of rights it possesses over the intellectual content it seeks to acquire, develop and turn into marketable commodities, most commonly books' (Thompson, 2005: 34). Indeed, a publisher's main financial assets exist in its access to and control over the intellectual property rights enshrined in contracts – an issue to which I will return in the conclusion to this chapter.

Book fairs

Book fairs are just one of a number of different events in which different players in the publishing world participate during the course of acquiring content and taking financial risks. They are important nodal points

in the global publishing industry and are located at particular interfaces – type of book (children's, food, travel, etc.), market segment (trade, academic, antiquarian, etc.) and geographical dispersion of the industry (Indian compositors, Hong Kong printers, etc.) – in the value chain (cf. Skov, 2006: 765). As part of its routine sales activities, an academic publisher attends academic conferences, where it meets (prospective) authors and so acquires editorial content, while also making sales; specialist training sessions (in particular for the development of e-systems); librarians' conferences, (where it can tap into library needs and develop, modify and sell its e-tailing platforms); user groups and similar forums (like the Independent Publishers Guild conference), which enables a publisher to share its own knowledge with, and gain knowledge from, other groups in the publishing chain.

International book fairs are extremely important for the light they throw on the publishing industry's organization and structure. Firstly, although held in different parts of the world all the year round, two of the largest international fairs coincide with the *book cycle*: the London Book Fair (LBF) in April, and the Frankfurt Book Fair (FBF) in October, every year. Publishers thus tend to sell their spring lists at fairs held the previous autumn, and their autumn lists at fairs held in the spring (Owen, 2006: 86) (see Figure 5.1).

Secondly, book fairs bring together all members of the *supply and value chains* in the publishing industry, and provide a unique occasion for them to interact face-to-face. They also, thirdly, give a visible structure to the *publishing field*, thereby reinforcing that structure, while making visible the various resources (economic, human, symbolic and intellectual capital) commanded by different publishers in the structured space of positions in which they operate.

The book fair, as we know it today, came into existence soon after the second world war when first Leipzig (1946) and then Frankfurt (1949) reestablished an annual fair the origins of which go back to the twelfth to thirteenth centuries (Flood, 2007; Weidhaas, 2007). Thereafter, there has been a steady increase in the establishment of international book fairs around the world which now form a network or 'cyclical cluster' of fairs (Power and Jansson, 2008). Warsaw (1956) was the first to host a book fair outside Germany, quickly followed by Belgrade and Toronto (1957) and the Bologna children's book fair (1964). In 1972, the London Book Fair was set up, followed by another in Buenos Aires in 1974. The 1980s saw a plethora of fairs, starting with Paris' Salon du

Figure 5.1 London Book Fair at Earls Court, April 2008 (photo: Brian Moeran)

Livre (1981), and followed by places as far apart as Istanbul (1982), Göteborg (1985), Guadalajara (1987) and Tehran (1988). In the 1990s, the net spread to the Middle East and Asia with fairs established in Abu Dhabi (1991), Hong Kong (1990), Tokyo (1994) and Beijing (1995), and in the first decade of the new millennium further book fairs have been started in Bangkok (2003), Bucharest (2006), Cape Town (2006), Thessaloniki (2006), Kuala Lumpur (2008) and Vienna (2008) among other cities. The book fair is now an international event by means of which a city becomes 'a node in the global mosaic and annual timetable' of publishing (Weller, 2008: 111), and the rivalry between fairs found in medieval times still exists today (cf. Flood, 2007: 8).

Of these, the FBF, organized by a subsidiary company of the German Publishers and Booksellers Association, is the largest and most important of all. It takes place in the city's fair grounds (Frankfurter Messe), occupying all twelve halls there, during the second week of October every year (from Wednesday to Sunday). In 2006, it had 7,272 exhibitors, representing 113 countries, showing 382,466 publications, of which 111,913 were new titles. During the fair, there were 2,700 events of one kind or another, covered by 11,000 accredited journalists from

Figure 5.2 Frankfurt Book Fair, October 2009 (photo: Brian Moeran)

66 countries.[4] All in all, the fair was visited by 286,621 people, of whom 183,000 were trade visitors (see Figure 5.2).[5]

Like most other big international book fairs, the FBF is a commercial event and not a festival for writers. It is seen to be *the* most important book fair in the world for international publishing rights, licensing fees and other deals. Like many other book fairs, it is also a critical marketing venue for the launching of new books and industry announcements, and provides an opportunity for participants to conduct their own market research on what is being published by whom. It is participated in by all those in the value supply chain – publishers, agents, booksellers, librarians, academics, illustrators, service providers, film producers, translators, printers, professional and trade associations, artists, authors, antiquarians and software and multimedia suppliers.[6]

A number of these book fairs are organized by international event organizers. The FBF itself has been active in starting book fairs around the world, in places like Abu Dhabi and Cape Town, and almost took over the LBF in 2006 after a disastrous move to the Docklands. Another event organizer is Reed Exhibitions which has a portfolio of more than five hundred trade fairs worldwide, and serves forty-seven key industries ranging from aerospace and aviation to jewellery, by way of energy, oil and gas; electronics and electrical engineering; sports, leisure and health; travel; and books and publishing. It organizes the LBF (and has been doing so since 1986), BookExpo America, BookExpo Canada, the Salon du Livre, the Tokyo International Book Fair and now the Buch Wien fair (Vienna, from 2008), and works closely with trade associations, city authorities and government, or semi-government, organizations (like the British Council, with whom it co-operates to arrange its annual country themes at the LBF).

Although the Frankfurt Buchmesse has been active in helping establish some of these fairs, by no means do all of them follow the structure of the FBF. While some – like the Bologna, London and Guadalajara Book Fairs – have tried to establish themselves as events for international rights, others – like the Warsaw, Beijing and Tehran Book Fairs – are national and cater for local domestic markets, often including the general public. Yet others – like BookExpo America – focus almost exclusively on distribution rights. As a result, publishers and other exhibitors classify the various fairs rather differently, depending on what they are looking for. Generally speaking, however, it is agreed that Frankfurt is number one in terms of internationalism, followed by London, and then either Bologna (for children's books) or Guadalajara (for Spanish rights). The FBF is superior to all other fairs because it has a dedicated trade fair site; the local government has invested in the fair, something that is not true of – say – London; and it is extremely well-organized.

Daily fair activities

So, what goes on at a book fair, and why do people go there? What kinds of activities do they indulge in that makes a book fair a tournament of values? Clearly, book fairs provide exhibitors and visitors with a highly flexible, cost-effective environment where a wide range of sales and marketing objectives can be achieved – from acquiring a potential bestseller to selling film rights, by way of appointing a new sales rep, building brand image, checking up on what competitors are doing, or even selling one's company. Most importantly, fairs provide participants with the opportunity to meet face-to-face and thereby to establish and build customer relations.

Frankfurt gives you a bird's eye view of the publishing world – of who's moved on, who's sold out to whom, and so on. It's all about relationships. Fairs are the only chance for face-to-face interaction, where we can explain all about our company and what we do. People tend to get confused on e-mail.

You also build up friendships with people at fairs, but these may yield no direct business benefits immediately, so they may well pass you on to someone else. As a result, with some people, a lot of post-strategizing goes on. (Naveen Kishore, MD, Seagull Books)

A fair is where you put faces to names. At places like Frankfurt and London you meet new accounts. I've opened up 20 or 30 over the three years I've been with Berg, thanks to the people I've met there. A lot of these orders – now worth £50K a year – may come three months down the line, through friends of friends. Like your Singapore contact tells you about Kinokuniya opening up a new store in Dubai, and orders then come that way. Networking is a crucial aspect of any book fair. (Veruschka Selbach, former sales manager, Berg Publishers)

Book fairs are *hugely* important because a lot of rights business is based on personal contacts, which need to be very long-term so that you become the first port of call when a contact is in search of something. You build up and get to know the tastes of your contacts and therefore to whom to direct a new book's translation rights in Italy or Venezuela, for example. . .

Whatever anyone says, e-mail cannot take the place of book fairs where you have the opportunity to sit down face to face with someone for thirty minutes and have a chat. (Lynette Owen, copyright director, Pearson Education)

So, as part of this two-way communication, fairs also provide participants with information:

Book fairs give you *fresh* news that you'd get on e-mail only one or two months later. You need to *speak* about things with people because talking isn't as heavy as the written word. This is very important when you're negotiating, because partners don't want to write everything down in an e-mail message. To do so is a sign of commitment, and they don't want that. . .yet. So you start negotiations, or start a problem, by *talking*. That is what book fairs are for. (Fanny Thépot, systems manager, Berg Publishers)

There are as many experiences of every book fair as there are people attending it, so that it is impossible to give any one definitive version of what a book fair is and what people do there (Skov, 2006: 773). Some – like publishers – are more or less rooted to their stands, although they may visit other publishers to discuss, for example, a co-publication or distribution possibilities. Others – like rights negotiators – have just a table and four chairs, with wardrobe and coat hangers, to anchor them. Yet others – like reps, distributors and bookstores – have no home base, but are on the move all the time. A final group – including service providers – have their own stands, but also go out to meet publishers at their stands in order to try to sell them their services.

Publishers vary enormously in the number of people they assign to book fairs. Some large companies have dozens of employees meeting potential customers at tables in their spacious stands (where they usually discuss translation, film, media and other rights). Other small, independent publishers may have just one person fielding every enquiry over three to five days. Publishers are more likely, because of costs, to send more employees to their 'home' than to an 'away' fair.

Different personnel generally participate in different kinds of meetings during the fairs, since they bring different sets of expertise and knowledge to negotiations. Thus, a publishing house's managing director (MD) may have half a dozen meetings discussing his company's current and potential distribution abroad, when certain countries have proved problematic in terms of turnover, payments and discounts. He may also discuss co-publishing some of his list's titles with – say – two or three university presses in the US. He will also meet up with publishers from countries like Argentina or Italy interested in his company's list, and wanting to buy rights to a popular journal that he publishes. These foreign publishers will also try to sell translation rights of their own book titles to the MD. The latter also meets companies connected with the supply and archiving of journals for libraries, as well as with companies specializing in data conversion, digital software provision and systems development. Finally, he may well talk to two or three Asian distributors to discuss a particular forthcoming project (like an encyclopaedia). A week after the fair finishes, he will write and distribute to all members of his firm's staff a substantial (nine to ten page) report on his two to three dozen meetings over the three days he is present at the fair, together with instructions on who is to follow up and act on what.

A sales and marketing (S&M) manager is likely to hold up to five dozen meetings over five full days, each scheduled for half an hour, from 9am to at least four in the afternoon. Almost all of these are pre-arranged, although there are usually two or three additional 'drop ins'. An S&M manager focuses primarily on sales and rights, meeting distributors, reps and bookstore managers from all over the world to whom she will try to sell new titles being published that autumn and early the following spring.

During these discussions she may learn all sorts of relevant and irrelevant information – from the potential for sales to fashion school staff and students in Argentina to a Russian wanting to invest in independent publishers, by way of internal politics affecting the appointment and effectiveness of a new director at an American university publisher. She may be confronted with an issue of nudity in a book's illustrations if it is to be sold in Middle Eastern countries. She may negotiate translation rights to a journal with a Slovenian, Brazilian or Bello-Russian publisher. She may also learn of potential remainder deals in the US; the opening of major new bookstores in Bangkok or Dubai; how to take advantage of libraries and their budgets; the issue of supplementary budgets and committee decisions on buying book products over ¥200,000 in Japan; the possibility of sharing with another British academic publisher the cost of hiring a dedicated rep in the US; and the market and focus area for books in Lithuania, along with its distribution system. Again, within a week of the end of the FBF, she will circulate a ten to twelve page report to colleagues.

Although one or two of these meetings can result in on-the-spot sales (sometimes between £5,000–£10,000 worth of books are ordered by a customer), most of them end up with verbal statements of intent about future purchases of titles.[7] It is, therefore, virtually impossible to say exactly how much business is generated during a book fair, although the general consensus is that it *is* generated. Rights, of course, come in packages and it is simple to work out how many titles have been contracted for translation, film, merchandizing and so on and for how much in each instance.[8] However, rights deals are not necessarily signed and sealed at a book fair; they may be agreed beforehand and then announced at the fair.

When it comes to calculating costs and benefits of book fairs, however, sales are rather different from rights. What is interesting is that these are entirely absent from the voluminous statistics published on the websites for Reed Exhibitions and the Frankfurt Buchmesse – primarily because participants find it difficult to quantify what they get out of a book fair. Some orders are placed just before a fair because those concerned know they are going to meet in a week's time. Others come several months after the event. Whichever, trade itself is clearly not marginal. Book fairs provide opportunities for participants to enter into business negotiations with long-term partners, to gain knowledge through market information exchanges and by seeing competitors' stands, and to initiate and sustain social relations (Skov, 2006: 770).

Visibility

A trade fair is similar to a city in the sense that each brings together heterogeneous strangers whose interaction does not depend on a single script. Rather, like the fieldworker, 'multiple actors endowed with individual intentions trace multiple trajectories that interweave to create a spectacle on top of the exhibitors' displays' (Skov, 2006: 773). Still, like a stage play or a fashion fair, book fairs in some respects distract attention from the spectacle they enable. They bring together 'geographically dispersed, socially embedded, culturally diffuse sets of companies on a neutral ground on which they re-enact an internal structure that is abstract and relational' (Skov, 2006: 768). As part of this internal structural reenactment, visibility is a major aim on the part of those exhibiting in and attending book fairs (as we will also see in Entwistle and Rocamora's discussion of London Fashion Week in Chapter 10). It is important in the *timing* and *location* of a fair; in *where* you have a stand; in the *size* of your stand; in your inclusion in the fair *catalogue*; in the *business deals* that you make; and in the *parties* that you put on or attend.

Let us start with timing, location and the framing of a book fair. The two largest international fairs – London and Frankfurt – are timed to coincide with the two publishing seasons starting in March and October. Frankfurt meets this criterion, but London at present does not. April is a little late for publishers to set up deals at the LBF, so that most have been contracted beforehand. If one takes as an example children's books, a local publisher needs five to six months to acquire translation rights, get the book translated, ready for printing, and printed copies in the bookshops by September in time for the Christmas season. By holding the LBF in April, this publishing cycle is severely squeezed.[9]

It was for this reason that in 2006 Reed Exhibitions moved the LBF from Earls Court to a new site, Excel, which it also partly owns, in the Docklands area.[10] While the fair was still small enough to be held in Olympia, which was its site for seventeen years, the timing of March was perfect. However, once the LBF grew too big for Olympia in the early 2000s, a new venue had to be found. Earls Court provided the answer, but it also presented a challenge in that the LBF could *not* be held in March because Earls Court was then the site of the Ideal Home Exhibition, and that particular trade fair had been in existence for well over a hundred years. Its dates were carved in stone.

In order to resolve this issue, Reed Exhibitions proposed that the LBF move to its site in the Docklands. All the big exhibitors agreed and the move was made, with the LBF timed for March again. However, once the fair opened, *every*one began complaining. The Excel site was 'in the middle of nowhere'. Not only did it take 'forever' to get there; there was nowhere pleasant in the vicinity of the fair to wine and dine customers. As a result, Reed had little choice but to move back to Earls Court and hold the LBF in April. The LBF thus shifted both location *and* timing.[11]

All this has to do with visibility in that the LBF is the UK publishing industry's 'home turf':

One reason people wanted to stay at Earls Court had to do with status and visibility. Precisely because it is *their* show on *home ground*, so to speak, UK publishers feel that everything *should* be just right. They are concerned with how they are seen by foreign visitors... and that means having good restaurants and watering holes round and about the fair itself. This was where the Docklands move failed. (Emma Lowe, sales manager, London Book Fair, Reed Exhibitions)

If we move on to stand location and size, where an exhibitor has its stand, and how big or small that stand is, have enormous implications for its visibility in the publishing world (see Figure 5.3). In this respect, book fairs function like 'graphs', in that they chart the relative positions of publishers and other participants in abstract space (Skov, 2006: 768). As Emma Lowe explained:

Our job is to ensure that *every*one *can* be seen. This means that we have to make sure exhibitors don't have long runs of walling, or other things like that, that prevent people being noticed. There's a maximum height, for example. Nothing can be over 4 metres high. And if someone wants to exceed that, they have to go through a lot of administrative procedures that cost both time and money before approval.

The importance of stand location and visibility can be seen in pricing mechanisms, where an aisle stand costs less than a corner stand, which itself costs less than a 'peninsula' stand (fronting three aisles), which costs less than an island stand,[12] and where from four to five different furniture 'sets' or 'packages' are available for rental, with different quality tables and chairs, and additional electric and furnishings at the higher end of a price scale that ranges from €158 to €642 at Frankfurt.[13] Here is Emma Lowe again:

Another aspect to perception is the fact that more and more people are building their own stands at shows. I mean, last year, something like 900 square metres of stand space – that's 6 to 7 per cent of the whole show – was built independently (although when an architect like my husband has a look, he wonders why they couldn't carry out a proper, decent design!). This suggests that appearance and difference are also important. Reed cashes in on providing specially designed sets for foreign exhibitors, like Microsoft, who order in advance and just fly in for the show without having to worry about detail.

Here visibility amounts to a kind of conspicuous consumption, as large, wealthy publishers splash out tens of thousands of pounds on stands which they have had especially designed – something that we also find in the global television markets discussed by Havens in Chapter 6.[14] The single advantage of this expenditure is that exhibitors can then use the same design and equipment in other fairs around the world and so, in the eyes of the regular fairgoer at least, establish a form of 'brand identity'. This backdrop of similarity enabling direct comparison of different firms Lise Skov calls 'the condition of comparability'. She argues that fairs enable publishers to:

Appear free of history, geography and social context; all traces of production are removed from the samples. What is visible at its booth in the fair is only the company's current market position in relation to other companies. Insofar as a company has a reputation, that reputation has to be re-enacted by aid of modular props. Skov (2006: 767)

Stands thus map out power relations among players both within the field of publishing itself, and between publishing and related fields. Not surprisingly, therefore, certain clear preferences are asserted by large publishing companies with regard to *where* they will exhibit, as Emma Lowe explained:

This year (2008), the whole exhibition was planned around Hachette because they were the first to book space with a specific shape and size – three rows back from the main entrance one side of the Main Boulevard. Later Random House came in and wanted a block three rows back, but not on the Main Boulevard opposite Hachette for some reason, but one away. Luckily HarperCollins wanted the free spot opposite Hachette, but we had to consult Hachette about this, of course. And that's a hassle because there are all sorts of subsidiary companies – like Octopus – exhibiting with Hachette, and they all have to be consulted to make sure there are no clashes or anything like that before we get approval for HarperCollins. It took about three weeks to get sorted. It was after that that we could begin to fit together the bits and pieces with other key accounts.

How, then, is space allocated, when it is at such a premium?

We have a points system that we use when allocating space to exhibitors. 50 per cent goes for the number of years someone has been coming to the fair, and 50 per cent for the size of the stand they take. It's very difficult to be fair, but we have to try and this is the only way we can do so. We've asked exhibitors who complain to come up with another method of assessment, but nobody has yet done so successfully. We've got to reward loyalty. So far as exhibitors are concerned, it's not a question of how many books or rights they sell, but how many years they've been seen to be at an exhibition like Frankfurt or London.

Basically it's a question of 'squatters' rights.' The trouble comes when one company decides to expand its space a bit, like Wiley wanting the rest of its block next year. Which means that Murdoch, which occupies that space, will have to move out. Not that they know that yet. And that'll mean I will have to start juggling others around. It's a ripple effect. Some of them are happy to be together – like the promotional people, for example – but others, like the publishing solutions firms – freight forwarding firms like DHL, UPS etc. – really want to be separate.

What is the issue here?

People are afraid of competitors stealing their clients, or stealing a march on them somehow in ideas they come up with. So there's a lot of querying that I have to deal with about 'Where is so-and-so located?' because the person concerned does, or does not, want to be located near so-and-so. There's a lot of diplomacy going on here. I mean, I knew all about the Pearson–Penguin buy-up long before it was officially announced because the new company had to have a stand together and plan floor space and design at the next LBF.

Here we see the reverse side of visibility: invisibility. Companies want to be seen, but only by some and not by others.

SAID BUSINESS SCHOOL
EXECUTIVE EDUCATION LIBRARY

Figure 5.3 Cambridge University Press stand being set up, Frankfurt 2009 (photo: Brian Moeran)

A third aspect of visibility at a book fair is the fair catalogue (or *Official Directory*) which is seen to be a kind of Bible, a *Who's Who* in the publishing world, in which all exhibitors want to be included. The Directory lists all exhibitors in alphabetical order, with each entry including name, stand location, business address, telephone and fax numbers with e-mail address, and an up-to-five-line business description, with up to three names of contact people (who are then listed in a separate Who's Who section in the Directory). It lists the names of all

Figure 5.4 Cambridge University Press party in full swing, Frankfurt 2009
(photo: Brian Moeran)

overseas exhibitors and then classifies all exhibitors under product
categories (computer science, conservation and ecology, cookery/food
and drink/wine, and so on). In this way individuals get at least two
mentions, and exhibitors three (since they are included as individuals'
affiliation in the Who's Who section).

And then, fourthly, there are the business deals made at the fair.
While these can circulate within different segments of the publishing
industry (i.e., trade book deals are soon known among trade book
publishers, and so on), the book fair newspapers disseminate details
of deals – including company acquisitions, book title purchases, auctions and 'pre-empts', film tie-ins, foreign rights deals, industry awards,
e-tailing initiatives and digital innovations – daily throughout the industry as a whole.

Finally, there are the parties. Attendees at book fairs are frequently
invited to one or other of the numerous parties and receptions held at
exhibitor stands – whether to launch a new book, celebrate 100 years in
publishing (Mills & Boone), or just to share their happiness at being

there! These receptions are seen to be very important because they
provide a relaxed environment in which people can meet one another,
exchange information, pick up on gossip and generally show that they
are fully 'paid-up' members of the publishing community. It is important, therefore, that participants in the field of publishing *appear* – that
they see and are seen – for parties mark different categories of 'insiders'
and 'inside status', as both Timothy Havens (Chapter 6), and Joanne
Entwistle and Agnès Rocamora (Chapter 10) note later in this book (see
Figure 5.4).

Conclusion

Economic anthropologists have long been interested in how material
objects are imbued with qualities whose values cannot be reduced to
material necessity or monetary equivalent (Bell and Werner, 2004: xi).
This is the main argument put forward in the introduction to this
volume and taken up in different ways by my fellow contributors.

Values are the very stuff of fairs. A book fair, therefore, is a tournament of *values*, rather than a tournament of value, since there is no
single value held by all the participants with their multiple trajectories at
the FBF, LBF or any other book (or other trade) fair. Rather, as was
pointed out earlier, the field of publishing is characterized by four
kinds of resources. It is in these different forms of economic, social (or
human), symbolic and intellectual capital that different kinds of values –
or worth (Hyde, 1983: 60) – are created, contested and sustained at
book fairs. Participants all cite the cementing of social relations as a
crucial function of the book fair. They also comment on and are affected
by the symbolic dimensions of stand location, stand layout and size,
business deals played up through formal and informal communication
channels and parties attended or heard about. Finally publishers are
concerned to negotiate the intellectual assets – or creativity – of their
authors as business transactions. It is this combination of social, symbolic and appreciative values that is then converted from priceless
'worth' into price, or economic exchange, value. It is this equation
that is first sketched out, then calculated, negotiated and agreed upon
at the book fair.

It is what participants believe the world of publishing to be like and
what they feel they can justifiably demand from that world that is

enacted at every book fair around the world. Social, symbolic and appreciative values can only exist and operate effectively within this web of social relations. Economic value is thus essentially 'negative' in the sense that it can *only* take on meaning in contrast and relation to other values (de Saussure, 1983: 116–8), which may also include the material/technical and utility properties of objects. Together with the other values cited, these constitute a field of values, the contestation and negotiation of which give rise to (commodity exchange) value *per se* (cf. Moeran, 2004: 266–70).

International book fairs – like fashion weeks, Grammy awards and so on – also clearly configure a particular field (of publishing, fashion or music). They do not, however, necessarily do so in identical ways, for each 'tournament of values' tends to emphasize some values at the expense of others. For example, while book fairs exhibit some elements of ritual behaviour, these do not shape field evolution to quite the extent argued, for example, for Oscar awards (Faulkner and Anderson, 1987; Levy, 1987: 269), or for the 'Judgement of Paris' wine tasting competition discussed by Anand later on in this book (Chapter 13). It is true that two literary prizes are announced during the course of the FBF – the Peace Prize of the German Book Trade and the German Book Prize – and the Nobel Prize for Literature also more or less coincides with the holding of this fair, but, generally speaking, major literary prizes are not linked to book fairs. Such prizes privilege particular players and construct prestige hierarchies in the field of publishing. They also have an effect upon fiction sales and future advances and contracts, but such an effect is not as comprehensive as are, perhaps, the Grammy awards or Booker Prize in terms of their influence on commerce, appeal to popular taste and creation of a distinctive new literary category (see also Watson and Anand, 2006; Anand and Jones, 2008).[15]

Nevertheless, in a number of other ways book fairs comply quite closely with Appadurai's definition of a tournament of values. Here, again, symbolic, social and appreciative values come into play. First of all, they are complex periodic events occurring in special places and at special times. They are 'both a ritual and a unique event', a 'show' which has a 'fixed trysting place' set apart in terms of time, place, setting and props (Malinowski, 1922: 85; Baudrillard, 1981: 116; see also Smith's Chapter 4 on auctions). With their sealed-in, windowless structure, their special stand constructions and furnishings, exhibition halls separate the book fair from the outside world. They also, as noted earlier, map out in spatial terms the key agents and institutions (different kinds of publishers, rights sellers, service providers, agents, media) within the field of publishing, and so embody that wider field as they produce, reproduce and legitimate both it and the positions of the players therein (Entwistle and Rocamora, 2006: 736). As with fashion shows, only those already with an acknowledged position in the field of publishing can gain access to fairs such as the FBF or LBF. *Closure* is thus an important aspect of consecration, and is affected by a range of boundaries distinguishing various categories of insider from outsider, and policed by gatekeepers who permit or deny access to the fair.

Thirdly, book fairs serve to define the publishing industry as a *community* (or 'family' as it is often referred to), since they provide an embodied space of practice where visibility and mutual recognition lead to a sense of belonging (Entwistle and Rocamora, 2006: 743, 749). Book fairs involve questions of membership of that community, manage the interpersonal relationships of participants, and to some extent regulate their behaviour (including in-group language and dress codes) (Smith, 1989: 51) during what is a series of performances for other industry 'insiders'.

Finally, although book fairs are removed from the routine of everyday economic life, what goes on there (the selling of rights, the appointment of agents, reps, distributors and so on) has consequences within the more mundane realities of the field of publishing as a whole. Tournaments of values are characterized by the fact that they make use of a 'currency' set apart from money *per se*. This is certainly true of advertising presentations, where the currency at stake is the account (Moeran, 1993: 88–9), and of fashion shows, where the 'collection' forms the currency by which a designer's seasonal output is judged. The 'currency' of book fairs can be said to be the rights stemming from intellectual property assets, since these are the central tokens of value for publishers. Rights are not necessarily subject to laws of supply and demand, since they often depend on personal taste (which is why rights agents spend years and years cultivating personal relations and learning about buyers' tastes). Rights are themselves linked to the status, rank, fame and reputation of both authors and publishing houses, as well as to particular individuals who buy and sell them. Ultimately, however, they depend upon sales.

Copyright – or the right to copy a creative work – is, of course, enshrined in law. But there is more to copyright than its legal and financial repercussions.[16] In his discussion of Mauss's celebrated essay on the gift, Maurice Godelier (2004: 19) distinguishes between selling commodities (which are, as a result, alienable and alienated); giving gift objects (which are inalienable, but alienated); and keeping sacred objects (which thus become inalienable and unalienated). For example, in parts of Melanesia, certain objects (known as *kitoum*) belong to a lineage or individual until launched on a *kula* exchange path and are passed from one recipient to another (as *vaygu'a*). However, such objects continue to belong to the original giver who can, in theory, ask the temporary recipient to return it. In other words, the owner of a *kitoum*-cum-*vaygu'a* cedes the rights of use to enable other gifts to be made, but not ownership as such (Godelier, 2004: 15). So certain valuables are alienated, but remain the inalienable property of the original owner.

The parallel here with copyright is obvious. When an author asserts their moral right to a written work, they imply that creativity involves the immanence of a person (or creator) in a thing (the creative work) – an implication sustained by copyright law (Feather, 2006: 162). In allowing publication of their work, the author assigns the right to copy that work to a publisher for a limited period of time, and the publisher then passes on that right, and associated subsidiary rights (abridgements, adaptations, dramatizations and serializations), to others in the publishing chain. These rights usually revert to the publisher and thence to the author after a stipulated period of time, and remain with the author until fifty years after their death, when the work becomes 'alienable' – in free circulation in the public domain. Copyright is thus something that is given-while-kept (Weiner, 1992). In this respect, the 'selling' of rights at the book fair does not completely separate thing from person, but involves an element of giving, since something of the creator remains in the creative work exchanged. Copyright and other property rights thus occupy 'a wise middle ground between gift and commodity; they manage to honour the desire for individual enrichment and at the same time recognize the needs of the community' (Hyde, 1983: 81 fn).

There is here an irony. In many respects, international book fairs spotlight the sale of rights to creative works. In the process, however, they draw attention away from the fact that neither the author nor the person within the publishing industry most involved in the nurturing of the creative process, the production editor, generally attends book fairs.

Instead, it is those concerned with sales and marketing (plus the occasional commissioning editor) who circulate and deal in the distribution of rights. Given that 'commodities must move between reciprocally independent spheres' (Hyde, 1983: 201), it would seem that the fair is designed to make visible the book as a commodity and to make invisible the given-while-kept inalienability of the book as a gift. It is in the shadow of the gift that the commodity of the book is produced, distributed, sold and read. Under such circumstances, it is not surprising that participants place such high value on social relations at the fair. They are at the heart of gift exchange (Mauss, 1966): it is through exchanges of gifts that spatial proximity (the book fair) becomes social life (the publishing community). As Lewis Hyde (1983: 69) puts it: 'gifts bespeak relationship'.

Notes

*   I would like to thank the Strategic Research Council of Denmark for funding fieldwork trips to Frankfurt, London and Tokyo Book Fairs, plus the research for and writing up of this chapter, as part of ©*reative Encounters*, the socio-economic organization of creative industries. I also owe a great debt of gratitude to Kathryn Earle and Veruschka Selbach of Berg Publishers for allowing me to sit in on their negotiations at the Frankfurt Book Fair in October 2007 and the London Book Fair in April 2008, as well as Bridget Shine of the Independent Publishers Guild (IPG) for accepting me on the IPG stand at the Frankfurt Book Fair in October 2009. This chapter is a revised version of an article by the same title that appeared in the *Journal of the Royal Anthropological Institute* (NS) 16 in the spring issue of 2010.
1. Participant observation was carried out at the 2007 and 2009 Frankfurt, 2008 London and 2009 Tokyo Book Fairs, where I sat in on meetings between Berg Publishers and visiting reps, distributors, publishers and so on over three days (2007 and 2008), as well as man the Independent Publishers Guild stand, and follow United Publishers, a Japanese distributor, 'on the hoof' at Frankfurt for a day (2009). I also visited Reed Exhibitions in Richmond for a day in February 2008 and talked to staff responsible for the London Book Fair. I was then allowed to follow them around the Earls Court venue and observe them coping with the setting up of the Fair the day before it opened. I have also talked to those responsible for setting up the Frankfurt Book Fair.
2. Journals can be an important financial asset to publishers since they provide up-front cash from subscription paid in advance. The introduction

of different payment systems, such as pay-per-view, however, is leading to such income being spread throughout the year.

3. Human and symbolic capital are equivalent to social and symbolic exchange values outlined in the Introduction to this volume.

4. Involvement of the media in trade shows and festivals generally is crucial for both publicity and creation of a positive image of the event in question (Mossberg and Getz, 2006: 321).

5. The fair is open to the general public on Saturday and Sunday only. It is statistics like these which, together with a fair's reputation, are used in a potential participant's evaluation of whether or not to attend the FBF (cf. Berne and García-Uceda, 2008: 567).

6. The only people in the publishing world who for the most part do *not* attend book fairs are editors. Authors, too, generally avoid fairs. As one informant put it: 'Having an author at the LBF would be like giving cows a guided tour of Smithfield'.

7. This is a variation on the art fairs described by Thompson, where purchases are agreed at the fair, but payment is made later in order to avoid local taxes.

8. Owen (2006) gives a detailed rundown of the various terms that can be negotiated, but a basic rule of thumb for the sale of rights in the academic book sector is 10 per cent of a publisher's price, multiplied by print run. However, much depends on a publisher's perception of a foreign market and of how much a buyer can afford to pay (Havens's discussion of television programme rights in Chapter 6).

9. This is why the Bologna Book Fair in March is so important for this particular market sector.

10. Most festivals do not own their event venue (Mossberg and Getz, 2006: 319).

11. Reed has now managed to hire the second exhibition hall at Earls Court, so that space is not quite at such a premium as before and participants appear to be happier.

12. At the FBF, there is a 10 per cent surcharge for a corner stand, 15 per cent surcharge for a peninsula stand, and 20 per cent for an island stand. A peninsula stand must be at least 16 square metres and an island 100 square metres in area.

13. As Skov (2006: 766) points out, 'fairgrounds always carry traces of their own constructedness'.

14. Exhibitors putting up their own stands at Frankfurt have to pay €750 to access the exhibition site from the Thursday before the Fair.

15. Appadurai (1986: 57) has referred to this as 'calculated diversions that might lead to new paths of commodity flow'.

16. I am aware of some of the literature on intellectual property rights published in anthropology, notably by Marilyn Strathern, but will not

be following it up here since my remarks are designed more to initiate further discussion than to act as a full-blown, authoritative account of the meanings of copyright.

References

Anand, N. and Jones, B. 2008. 'Tournament rituals, category dynamics, and field configuration: the case of the Booker Prize', *Journal of Management Studies* 45:6, 1,036–60.

Anand, N. and Watson, M. 2004. 'Tournament rituals in the evolution of fields: the case of the Grammy Awards', *Academy of Management Journal* 47, 59–80.

Appadurai, A. 1986. 'Introduction: commodities and the politics of value', in A. Appadurai (ed.), *The Social Life of Things*. Cambridge University Press, pp. 3–63.

Barbato, M. and Mio, C. 2007. 'Accounting and the development of management control in the cultural sphere: the case of the Venice biennale', *Accounting, Business and Financial History* 17: 187–208.

Baudrillard, J. 1981. *The Political Economy of the Sign*. St. Louis, MO: Telos.

Bell, D. and Werner, C. (eds.) 2004. *Values and Valuables: from the Sacred to the Symbolic*. Walnut Creek, CA: Altamira.

Berne, C. and García-Uceda, M. E. 2008. 'Criteria involved in evaluation of trade shows to visit', *Industrial Marketing Management* 37, 565–79.

Bourdieu, P. 1993. *The Field of Cultural Production: Essays on Art and Literature*. Cambridge: Polity.

Caves, R. 2000. *Creative Industries: Contracts Between Art and Commerce*. Cambridge, MA: Harvard University Press.

Clark, G. 2001. *Inside Book Publishing*. Third edition. London: Routledge.

Entwistle, J. and Rocamora, A. 2006. 'The field of fashion materialized: a study of London Fashion Week', *Sociology* 40:4, 735–51.

Evans, O. 2007. 'Border exchanges: the role of the European film festival', *Journal of Contemporary European Studies* 15, 23–33.

Faulkner, R. and Anderson, A. 1987. 'Short-term projects and emergent careers: evidence from Hollywood', *American Journal of Sociology* 92, 879–909.

Feather, J. 2006 (1988). *A History of British Publishing*. Second edition. London and New York: Routledge.

Flood, J. 2007. '"*Omnium totius orbis emporiorum compendium*": the Frankfurt fair in the early modern period', in R. Myers, M. Harris and G. Mandelbrote (eds.), *Fairs, Markets and the Itinerant Book Trade*. Delaware and London: Oak Knoll Press and the British Library, pp. 1–42.

Glynn, M. 2008. 'Configuring the field of play: how hosting the Olympic games impacts civic community', *Journal of Management Studies* 45:6, 1,117–46.

Godelier, M. 2004. 'What Mauss did not say: things you give, things you sell, and things that must be kept', in C. Werner and D. Bell (eds.), *Values and Valuables: from the Sacred to the Symbolic*.Walnut Creek, CA: Altamira, 3–20.

Hyde, L. 1983 *The Gift: Imagination and the Erotic Life of Property*. New York: Vintage.

Lampel, J. and Meyer, A. 2008. 'Field-configuring events as structuring mechanisms: how conferences, ceremonies, and trade shows constitute new technologies, industries, and markets', *Journal of Management Studies* 45:6, 1,025–35.

Levy, E. 1987. *And the Winner Is ... The History and Politics of the Oscar Awards*. New York: Ungar.

Malinowski, B. 1922. *Argonauts of the Western Pacific*. London: G. Routledge and Sons.

Mauss, M. 1966. *The Gift: Forms and Functions of Exchange in Archaic Societies*. London: Cohen and West.

Moeran, B. 1993. 'A tournament of value: strategies of presentation in Japanese advertising', *Ethnos* 58:1–2, 73–94.

   2004. 'Women's fashion magazines: people, things, and values', in C. Werner and D. Bell (eds.), *Values and Valuables: from the Sacred to the Symbolic*. Walnut Creek, CA: Altamira, 257–81.

Mossberg, L. and Getz, D. 2006. 'Stakeholder influences on the ownership and management of festival brands', *Scandinavian Journal of Hospitality and Tourism* 6:4, 308–26.

Owen, L. 2006 (1991). *Selling Rights*. Fifth edition. London and New York: Routledge.

Powell, W. 1985. *Getting into Print: the Decision-making Process in Scholarly Publishing*. Chicago University Press.

Power, D. and Jansson J., 2008. 'Cyclical clusters in global circuits: overlapping spaces in furniture trade fairs', *Economic Geography* 84:4, 423–48.

de Saussure, F. 1983. *Course in General Linguistics*. London: Duckworth.

Skov, L. 2006. 'The role of trade fairs in the global fashion business', *Current Sociology* 54:5, 764–83.

Smith, C. 1989. *Auctions: the Social Construction of Value*. London: Harvester Wheatsheaf.

Thompson, D. 2008. *The $12 Million Stuffed Shark: the Curious Economics of Contemporary Art and Auction Houses*. London: Aurum.

Thompson, J. 2005. *Books in the Digital Age*. Cambridge: Polity.

Watson, M. and Anand, N. 2006. 'Award ceremony as an arbiter of commerce and canon in the popular music industry', *Popular Music* 25:1, 41–56.

Weidhaas, P. 2007. *A History of the Frankfurt Book Fair*. Toronto: Dundurn.

Weiner, A. 1992. *Inalienable Possessions: the Paradox of Giving-While-Keeping*. Berkeley and Los Angeles: University of California Press.

Weller, S. 2008. 'Beyond "global production networks": Australian Fashion Week's trans-sectoral synergies', *Growth and Change* 39:1, 104–22.

6 | Inventing universal television: restricted access, promotional extravagance, and the distribution of value at global television markets

TIMOTHY HAVENS *

International television programming 'markets' are extravagant events. Unlike the film or animation festivals examined elsewhere in this volume, however, television markets do not spotlight prestigious awards competitions or high-wattage star power; the markets, ostensibly, are all about business.[1] 'We don't call them fairs or festivals', insists a representative of one of the largest markets, 'we call them markets or trade shows' (personal interview, 2002). This insistence on proper terminology reveals a deeper anxiety about the value of the markets, especially the extravagances that are largely responsible for their festival- or fair-like atmosphere.

Television markets are essential to programme trade in two main ways: firstly, they provide unprecedented market intelligence about programming trends and industry developments; secondly, they function, in Brian Moeran's phrase, as 'tournaments of values' (Appadurai, 1986, as well as Chapter 1 by Delacour and Leca and Chapter 13 by Anand), where a range of social and cultural values get transcoded into economic value. Indeed, the very extravagances that worry market organizers are central to these tournaments and, ultimately, to international programme exchange. As perhaps the most business-like of all cultural industry gatherings, international television markets demonstrate just how central extravagance is to the proper functioning of cultural trade, as it creates scarcity in otherwise glutted markets.

The research for this article includes multiple visits to each of the major markets and interviews with thirty-two sales market participants over seven years, including both importers and exporters of programming, as well as market organizers. None of these interviews focused solely on the markets, as my primary research interests lie elsewhere; for this essay, however, I focus only on those interviews that addressed the markets in some way. In addition to these interviews and first-hand observations, I also reviewed trade journal articles about the sales markets from 1999–2009.

Television programme markets

Television markets are extravagant, multiple-day affairs that take place in exotic locations such as the French Riviera or Las Vegas and attract the famous and the powerful of the television business. Comedian Jerry Seinfeld opened the National Association of Television Programming Executives (NATPE) sales market in 2001 and NBC Universal President and Chief Executive Officer (CEO) Jeff Zucker opened the market in 2008. The sale of programme rights is the main activity at the markets, but a range of other activities, including the sale and promotion of programming-related services such as television ratings and rights-tracking software, also take place. In addition, programme producers, technology companies, representatives from other markets and a bevy of journalists also attend. Sales markets are, however, closed events, and the general public cannot gain access.

Most television programmes sold at the markets have been designed with a particular national audience in mind, and are purchased by foreign broadcasters to fill excess airtime. Increasingly, however, international viewers form a *primary* market for television programmes, and a wide variety of business arrangements have developed that allow foreign broadcasters to participate in production decisions about the programmes they import. These arrangements include international co-productions, which are designed from the beginning to air in more than one national market; presales, in which buyers provide upfront money in return for some degree of creative control over the final product; and formatting, where buyers create a wholly new local version of a popular international series, such as the numerous local versions of the reality show *Big Brother*. Negotiations about all of these business arrangements have become common at the sales markets (Havens, 2006).

Sales markets can be divided into three main types: firstly, the global markets: NATPE, Marché International des Programmes de Télévision (MIP-TV, International Television Program Market) and Marché International des Films et des Programmes pour la Télévision, la Vidéo, le Câble et le Satellite (MIPCOM, International Film and Programme Market for TV, Video, Cable and Satellite), where programmes of all genres from all nations get traded; secondly, regional markets, such as the Central European bazaar DISCOP and the Hollywood-dominated Los Angeles Screenings, where local distributors exhibit their wares for international buyers; and thirdly, genre-specific markets that focus on particularly popular international genres such as children's animation, reality shows or documentaries. In this paper, we will focus on global television markets, where the extravagances and rituals of the international television business are most on display.

How television travels

Television distributors rarely produce the programming they sell. Instead, they act essentially as banks, lending money to producers in return for rights. Producers rely on these middlemen, rather than selling their programming themselves, because television production is an expensive business, and many productions, at least in the US, do not turn a profit for their first three years. Except for the major Hollywood studios and the American television networks, which handle distribution internally, few producers have the financial wherewithal to take on such large debts for such long periods of time. Using a distributor or even a series of distributors abroad can help defray these costs. In addition, because distributors spend much of their time keeping up with developments in the international markets, they are capable of getting higher prices and wider distribution than producers, for whom syndication is only a secondary interest. Large distributors can float almost all of the costs of production in exchange for worldwide rights, an arrangement known as 'deficit financing' (Owen and Wildman, 1992). Increasingly, even major programme producers, such as Fox Television Studios, are bypassing deficit financing in favour of international co-production and co-financing arrangements (Flint, 2009). However, for most producers, even these kinds of arrangements require distribution middlemen to find appropriate partners.

　　Most television rights sales involve negotiating a price for a single television programme. Rights agreements typically last from three to five years, and specify what territories and types of distribution (broadcasting, satellite, the Internet) are allowable. After this period, all rights and copies of the programmes revert to the distributor. The pricing of rights is highly elastic, ranging from about $30 per hour in Cuba to more than $2 million per hour in the US (Channel 21, 2009). The reason for these significant differentials is that, despite high production costs, television programming has low *reproduction* costs, because buyers are merely purchasing a copy of the original programme. Prices are negotiated based on a buyer's ability to pay and perceptions about the value of the programming in the buyer's market – a point also noted by Moeran. In contemporary commercial television industries, that 'value' almost always translates into the capacity to attract viewers and, thereby, advertisers.

In addition to individual sales, television rights can be bundled in packages. Packaging tends to be limited to the major Hollywood distributors, which, because they sell television rights to blockbuster movies, can force buyers to take larger packages of less desirable programming as well. Television rights can also be bundled in 'output deals', where buyers agree to purchase all of a distributor's new programmes over a period of time. Again, output deals tend to be limited to Hollywood distributors, and were especially popular in the mid- to late-1990s, when broadcasters across Europe, Asia and Latin America were planning massive expansions of digital channels. These kinds of deals have slowed since 2000, especially with the bankruptcy of the German media giant KirchMedia, which went broke because of expensive output deals and slow adoption rates of digital programming services (Havens, 2006).

In terms of total revenues, the international television wings of the major Hollywood studios (Warner Bros. International Television, CBS Paramount International Television, Sony Pictures Television International, NBC Universal International Television, Disney-ABC International Television, 20th Century Fox International Television and MGM Worldwide Television) continue to dominate global television trade, accounting for nearly 60 per cent of total international sales revenues (Havens, 2006; Waisbord, 2004). However, some television industries such as those in Canada and Australia earn a larger *percentage* of their sales revenues from abroad than do the Hollywood majors. Moreover, syndicators from Europe to Latin American to East Asia are more reliant than ever on foreign sales revenues (Havens, 2006). In 2008, the worldwide trade in television rights topped $30 billion, up from $2.4 billion in 1989 (Meza, 2009; United Nations Educational, Scientific and Cultural Organization (UNESCO), 1989).

Especially on a global scale, television rights are high-risk commodities, in large part because of the unpredictability of audience tastes. As with art works, films and other cultural products discussed in this volume, no reliable methods for predicting the success of an individual television programme exist, and those imperfect methods that do exist, such as screening potential imports for a cross-section of the viewing audience, tend not to be worth the expense. Instead, importers must rely on their 'gut' instincts when purchasing programmes. When it comes to buying *foreign* programmes, difference of culture, audience taste and historical trends among importing and exporting nations – or what media economists call a 'cultural discount' (Hoskins *et al.*, 1997) – all make popularity even more difficult to divine and complicate purchasing decisions even further. While all cultural commodities face this discount to varying degrees, it is particularly high in television trade, due to the deeply local character of most programming. Television has traditionally been an oral medium, which arises from and portrays everyday life, due to its small screen size, moderate image quality, and the domestic nature of its reception in most cultures (Fiske, 1987). Television, therefore, reflects the dialects, rhythms, settings and stories of our immediate day-to-day lives, and these stories are difficult to unmoor from their immediate cultural surroundings. At the same time, it is significantly cheaper to buy programme rights than it is to self-produce one's own programming, and the international markets offer an attractive, low-cost option for most of the world's broadcasters.

In addition to the complications of cultural difference, both distributors and buyers face more practical difficulties enforcing contracts for international programming rights. For distributors, it is time-consuming and expensive to pursue violations of rights agreements, and the ability to sue violators varies by country. Moreover, television formats, such as *Big Brother*, *Survivor* and *Pop Idol*, which are licensed for *remake* in different territories, are not protected by international treaty. Consequently, distributors share 'black lists' of unreliable buyers with one another at the markets. Buyers, meanwhile, typically purchase rights to multiple seasons of an episodic series, based on viewing only one or two episodes. When series change substantially or get unexpectedly cancelled, buyers are often forced to find quick substitutes for their schedules. Buyers expect some form of 'make-good' from distributors under such circumstances. Thus, for sellers seeking reliable buyers and buyers seeking understanding sellers, the market in television rights creates a need for trustworthy partners.

The trade in rights, then, is uniquely dependent on the cultivation of relationships. In the previous chapter, Moeran has argued regarding the publishing industry that the trade in rights emphasizes the importance of relationships, because rights exhibit the characteristics of both commodities and gifts, and the cultivation of relationships is a central component of gift economies. Books fairs mediate this tension between gift and commodity by making 'visible the book as a commodity and [making] invisible the given-while-kept inalienability of the book as a gift'. This inalienability depends to a large degree on the presence of an identifiable author who retains copyright, much as, in gift economies, the identity of the giver influences a gift's value. Perhaps the clearest vestige of this gift economy is the presence of the author's name on a book, which serves as a persistent reminder of who 'gave' us the story. As Moeran puts it, 'something of the creator remains in the creative work exchanged'.

Television, by contrast, is a largely authorless medium, particularly commercial television. Corporations, often distributors, retain copyright to television programmes, and programme producers, who wield the greatest control over the finished programme, have far less visibility, authorial control and name recognition than book authors or film directors (Newcomb and Alley, 1983). In television trade, then, the sales markets are less about deemphasizing the author's inalienable rights to the book, and more about erasing the perceived cultural particularity of the programming by foregrounding the authorial identity of the distributor.

Global sales markets

As the worldwide programming industries have become more integrated over the past twenty-five years (Waisbord, 2004), the sales markets have likewise flourished. Combined, the three major sales markets experienced a jump in attendance of more than 25 per cent between 1992 and 2008.

MIP-TV, held every spring, is the largest global market for television programming. Begun in 1963 as a place for European buyers and American distributors to trade programming, MIP-TV has grown into a truly international event. More than 10,000 programme merchants, representing thousands of companies and more than 100 nations, attend MIP-TV. These numbers have remained quite consistent over the past decade, attesting to the markets' international flavour. In addition, the number of participating companies has increased by approximately 20 per cent over the past ten years, reflecting both the growth in international television trade and the importance of MIP-TV in conducting trade. For many distributors and buyers, MIP-TV is the only international trade show that their organization can afford to attend (Havens, 2003; 2006).

MIP-TV's timing initially served the needs of European buyers, who made programming decisions in early spring for the following autumn. More recently, however, the Hollywood majors have complained about the market's timing, because it comes well after the autumn premieres of their most popular programmes, and precedes the regional Los Angeles Screenings market by only about six weeks, where they screen upcoming series for their most important international buyers.[2] Consequently, the presence of the majors at MIP-TV is less dominant than at some of the other markets. In recent years, the majors have abandoned large sales halls in the Palais in favour of massive sales 'tents' on the beach outside, both cutting their costs and permitting Reed-Midem, the market organizer, to rent the interior sales halls to other distributors.

While the Hollywood majors have sought to economize their costs at MIP-TV, their continued participation demonstrates how important markets are for their global sales operations. In a particularly striking example of this fact, after Disney announced in 1999 that it would no longer attend MIP-TV – in part because it had already secured massive, ten-year output deals with several European buyers – it returned only one year later (Brennan, 2000). Curiously, the majors, who shell out millions of dollars attending the markets, claim to make few important sales there (Brennan, 1999). Thus, they must see benefits other than immediate sales revenues at the markets. As I will argue below, these are the benefits of prestige that accrue from the market's tournament economies.

NATPE was also founded in 1963, as a nationwide American programming trade show. However, the international contingent has grown significantly in recent years. Originally held in New Orleans, NATPE moved permanently to Las Vegas in 2003. The market has also moved all over the calendar, but settled on late January since early 1990 to leave enough time before MIP-TV in March, but also to serve domestic and international buyers making programming decisions for the upcoming autumn. As the domestic US syndication business has dried up since 1996, due to consolidation of ownership in both the syndication and television station businesses, international syndicators have become more visible at NATPE.

As with MIP-TV, the Hollywood majors have significantly changed how they participate at NATPE since 2001, typically abandoning the sales floors for private suites in the nearby hotels, though some of them maintain a presence on the sales floor for their international operations. This type of 'absent presence' is not only a cost-saving device, but also a profound statement of power and prestige, built as much on the distributors' presence *somewhere* at the markets as on their absence from the sales floor. In other words, this absent presence seems to be a more effective business strategy than skipping the market altogether.

Finally MIPCOM, founded in 1985 and sometimes referred to as MIP-TV's younger brother, takes place in Cannes each autumn, and draws participants similar to those at MIP-TV. MIPCOM attendance nearly doubled between 1992 and 2008, paralleling the growth in international television trade over the past twenty years and demonstrating just how important sales markets are for the smooth operation of international sales. MIPCOM is geared more towards American and European programming than MIP-TV because the large Hollywood studios have initial autumn ratings data from the US market to use to lure buyers. Again, the creation of MIPCOM demonstrates the degree to which Western programming and companies dominate international television trade. While the Hollywood majors make most of their deals with larger buyers at the Los Angeles Screenings in May, MIPCOM offers a venue for programming that was not sold at Los Angeles and for buyers who did not attend the Screenings (Mahamdi, 1992; Roxborough and Masters, 2001).

Although sellers and buyers engage in a range of promotional and acquisitions activities throughout the year, beyond the confines of the markets, the markets nevertheless offer unique opportunities. Distributors wine, dine and cajole buyers in extravagant surroundings that demonstrate how successful they are, while buyers seek market intelligence about the newest, hottest series and face-time with large distributors to help secure the broadcast rights to those series: because competition among buyers for certain series is fierce in most markets, the kinds of relationships that get made and renewed at market help significantly in those competitions. That is, every deal is not just about the current sale, but also about past favours and future potential, in addition to the degree of trust among participants. Consequently, the licence fee is only one factor that sellers take into account when deciding whom to licence to. For instance, a buyer at the Hungarian public broadcaster Magyar Televízió recounted how she managed to secure rights to the first season of the

20th Century Fox Television action-drama *24* over her commercial competitors because of her long-term relationship with the distributor, despite the fact that her channel was badly behind the commercial channels in overall ratings (personal interview, 2002).

Programme markets as tournaments of values

Each of the global television markets exhibit a number of the characteristics that Appadurai (1986) has identified as 'tournaments of value', or highly ritualized, transnational exchanges of valuable items whereby participants establish, maintain and lose status. Much like the international book fairs that Moeran has studied, global television markets are 'removed ... from the routine of everyday economic life' of the international syndication business. Likewise, participation in the markets is a privilege, as is participation in the more selective, market-related events that create multiple tournaments at the same market. Only select members of a broadcaster's or distributor's executive team are given the opportunity to attend the markets, most typically high-level programming or sales executives. The markets therefore distinguish participants from their fellow employees, a fact reinforced by the markets' desirable locations.

Programming rights are the 'central tokens of value' at the markets, much like book fairs that Moeran examines in the previous chapter, and the tournaments that take place there work to distribute varying degrees of prestige onto those programme rights. That is, through promotional excess and controlling access to programming, certain programmes get nominated as more valuable than others; in the language of programme merchants, some programmes are more 'universal' than others. Markets control access with various kinds of passes, such as printed invitations to exclusive events or participants' badges, which – as Entwistle and Rocamora describe for London Fashion week in Chapter 10 – identify what they do and where they can go. Access leads to free food and drink, photographs with celebrities and a range of giveaways, as well as the chance to talk business with powerful programming merchants.

The tournaments that take place at the sales markets, then, are mainly about creating the impression that one's programming possesses universal appeal, which is an evaluation based on the perceived appreciative values that are conspicuously on display at the markets. As the introduction to this volume explains, appreciative values are 'primarily, but not exclusively, aesthetic (focusing on such concepts as taste, harmony, creativity, form, style and so on) and emerging from the ways in which cultural products are praised or damned by critics'. Within the television markets, the primary aesthetic concept that appreciates to programming is universality, although a programme's universality is not praised or damned by critics but, rather, by other market participants. This appreciative value arises out of two situational values, or 'the values accruing to an item because of its use in a particular situation which may be temporal or spatial' – specifically restricted access and promotional extravagance, which depend upon the spatial organization of the markets. These two values combine to create the appreciative value of universality.

Restricted access and promotional extravagance as indicators of prestige

Television markets can be conceptualized as a series of levels with diminishing degrees of access (Figure 6.1). On each, multiple levels of access also exist. For instance, some invitations for after-hours events are handed out freely, while others are scarce and coveted. Access accrues as participants navigate the various boundaries within the marketplace that identify particular locations, perks and networks as more valuable than others. These are temporary boundaries that exist only in the marketplace, and the ability to cross them has no real value beyond their walls. Nevertheless, access confers 'social capital' on participants, in particular prestige, which influences such quotidian business decisions as which programmes to purchase, and so confers these cultural products with 'social value'. Access also lends prestige to certain programmes that, by virtue of being housed within restricted sales stands, are marked off as more 'situationally' valuable.

On an individual level, prestige can translate into negotiating power and can also serve individual ambitions: executives with experience in international sales move frequently between companies, and individual prestige in global television is an entrée for such positions. Access also confers prestige on both distribution and broadcasting corporations. For broadcasters, access demonstrates the organization's importance to large distributors, builds and renews relationships, and can also lead to privileged acquisition of highly prized programming.

Figure 6.1 Levels of restricted access at global TV markets

Extravagance, meanwhile, is closely related to access. Extravagance is only achievable at the markets, and only in relation to other participants' promotional efforts. For instance, at MIPCOM 2005, MTV Studios displayed a promotional loop for Carmen Electra's *Aerobic Striptease* on life-size screens near the entryway to the Palais. By contrast, Tokyo Broadcasting System (TBS) placed its logo on the edge of each step on the stairway leading from the entryway to the main sales floor. Both promotions greeted participants immediately after entering the Palais, and the MTV promotion gained a good deal of its extravagance in contrast with the TBS promotion. As mentioned, extravagance is the most immediately obvious trait of every global sales market; it demonstrates to potential buyers and other distributors that one has a track record of success in television distribution. Extravagance extends to advertising on the sales floor, sales booth construction and location, giveaways and perks and invitation-only events. When King World International launched its remake of *Hollywood Squares* at NATPE 1998, for example, it hosted a private concert with Elton John at the New Orleans Superdome, where it introduced the secret celebrity 'centre square', Whoopi Goldberg. As with access, extravagance translates into prestige, though in this case, such prestige is limited to distributors and, indirectly perhaps, to buyers who get to partake of some of the extravagance.

The combination of extravagance and limited access makes a strong statement about the economic value of a distributor's programming. The Hollywood majors, for instance, plaster the marketplace with advertisements for their newest programmes, place ads all over the trade magazines, and promote their exclusive events, but only a fraction of market attendees can actually get access to these programmes and events. Instead, extravagance and limited access create a network of executives within the markets who are likely to have business interests in common, while excluding those who do not. Such cultural processes help create efficiencies in what might otherwise be an unnavigably large pool of potential buyers, sellers and programming. In addition, as we will explore in detail below, these close-knit business networks work together to create industry-wide perceptions about what the hottest, new programming trends are, and what types of programming content are and are not capable of worldwide appeal.

Limited access and tournament networks

Global television markets permit multiple levels of participation, leading to several distinct yet overlapping tournaments of values, by constructing boundaries that only authorized participants may cross. These boundaries include the entryway to the space of the market, various sales floors within the marketplace, restricted areas of sales floors and booths and various parties and events after the markets close each day. Combined, these boundaries construct networks of buyers and sellers of similar calibre who share programming specialities.

At the doorway to the marketplace, participants cross the most important boundary that the sales markets construct, symbolizing their entrance into the culture of global television sales. As we shall see in other chapters discussing fashion fairs and film festivals, only those with proper credentials can cross this threshold, marking the distinction between those who are part of the global television business and those who are not. In Cannes, crowds of curious bystanders milling near the entrances help reinforce this distinction. Some of the clearest examples of promotional excess appear immediately inside the doorway, from billboards promoting new series to costumed characters handing out fliers. The emotional impact of these excesses, especially at the first market I attended, was quite powerful. What I described in my field notes as 'pop culture overload' adds an emotional dimension to the cognitive distinction between those inside and outside the world of global television sales.

Once inside the marketplace, the extravagance and variety of limited-access spaces proliferate. Everywhere, lavish sales 'stands' reach towards the ceiling. Universal Studios built a twenty-foot tall replica of Mount Crumpit from *How the Grinch Stole Christmas* (2000) to house its sales staff at NATPE 2001. Warner Brothers International plastered a whole wing of the Palais de Festival in Cannes with Looney Tunes characters at MIP-TV 1999. MGM had lion cubs on display in a glass cage at NATPE 2001. Commenting on the complexity of preparing the sales floor, one trade show organizer explained, 'It's like building a city' (Pam Smithard, MD of Europe for NATPE).

Venturing further onto the sales floor, one encounters a seemingly endless stream of free giveaways, including large spreads of food and drink and celebrity photo opportunities. At NATPE 2001, executives lined up at the Paramount Studios stand to have their pictures taken with cheerleaders from the now-defunct XFL, a short-lived American football league, and played catch in the long hallway with palm-sized promotional footballs. Some enterprising companies even provide large bags emblazoned with their logos that participants use to carry the armfuls of promotional giveaways.

Large sales stands and promotional giveaways demonstrate a distributor's success, and in a business where success is so highly unpredictable, such extravagances offer some of the only tangible evidence. In addition, limiting access to one's sales stand and sales force provide further evidence of how successful one's programming is.

The Palais in Cannes offers a variety of differently priced and differentially accessible spaces where distributors can set up shop, and each of the spaces communicate different messages about a distributor. At MIP-TV 2004, the Palais was divided into seven primary sales halls, with numerous ways of distinguishing exhibitors within each hall. The largest hall was the main sales floor, which housed nearly 350 sales stands, or about 60 per cent of exhibitors. A wide hallway bisected the main floor, leading from the stairway at the entrance of the Palais at one end to a large, sunny café and bar area at the other end. On either side of the hall stretched thirteen rows of stands, some of which lay near the main hallway and included internationally successful companies such as the Canadian Broadcasting Company and Carsey-Werner International, and some of which hid in barely-accessible nooks. Exhibitors of all stripes rented space here, though the vast majority was small companies with a handful of series, films, or concepts to sell, while many of the buyers were independent redistributors. These tend to be the people who are most dependent upon markets like MIP-TV to conduct sales, as it offers one of the only opportunities for buyers to find new distributors and *vice versa*. During the first few days of each market, the main sales floor is thronged with people, and a frenzied din of voices and video clips fills the air.

The second-largest sales space was the Espace Riviera, which lay up a flight of stairs from the main bar. Nearly one hundred exhibitors set up shop here, including several such as MTV Networks International, Granada International, Paramount and Radio Television Española, that had large reception areas and several meeting rooms. The difference in atmosphere between the Espace Riviera and the main sales room was palpable. Sales stands here ran three or four times larger than the average stand on the main floor, and higher ceilings allowed for much larger exhibitions. More striking, however, was the distinctly different mood of the space, which, while active and crowded, lacked the intensity of the main floor below. In large part, this difference owed to the fact that stands were spaced further apart, which made for more isolated conversations and a more subdued climate.

Nothing prevented participants who were based on the main floor from entering the Espace Riviera, but exhibitors who set up shop there were making a statement that they were successful enough to afford the higher prices of these larger stands: they either had large financial backing or had been successful enough in international sales to 'move up', and they generally expected buyers with larger pocketbooks than those who trolled the main sales floor below. Alexander Charvadze (interview with author, 2004), an international sales representative for TV Channel Russia, which had moved from the main floor to the Espace Riviera beginning in MIP-TV 2004, explained the change as follows: 'Last year, we located on the first floor, and it was not so good … because there's not so big companies. For example, here's Beta Films, who is one of the biggest distributors in Europe, here's Granada. Good neighbors, and so it's good for us'. Obviously, TV Channel Russia's executives believed that their location on the sales floor of the Palais influenced participants' perceptions of their company and the kinds of relationships they were likely to establish at the market.

While a number of exhibitors on the main floor employed receptionists who triaged visitors and controlled access to meeting rooms in the back of the stand, in the Espace Riviera, this practice was widespread, and the size and extravagance of the restricted spaces grew. Several companies here, including CBS International, Paramount and MTV Networks International had large patios overlooking the Mediterranean where participants could escape the rush of the market and relax with free drinks and food. Access to these spaces was determined by personal contact with sales executives, usually through appointments set up months in advance, and getting a meeting simply by showing up at the stand was nearly impossible. By contrast, representatives of most of the exhibitors on the main floor were willing to meet almost immediately on request.

A handful of sales stands belonging to the powerhouses of the global television business, such as 20th Century Fox Television Distribution and Warner Brothers International Television, sat apart from others in their own halls or isolated spaces. For several years, Warner Brothers International Television maintained one of the largest, most visible and least accessible sales stands at MIP-TV and MIPCOM. Located directly above the main entrance, access to the Warner Brothers stand was gained from the second level of the Palais. A mural depicting great moments in the history of filmmaking at Warner Brothers stretched fifty feet across the length of the stand, below which lay two entrances to the sunshine-filled meeting rooms. A large front desk staffed with several receptionists greeted visitors as they came up the escalator to the second level, and two gangplanks guarded by velvet ropes and security guards led over the main Palais entrance below into the sales hall. The 20th Century Fox Television stand encompassed all of Exhibition Hall E, which lay at the top of an unmarked staircase on the third level. Meeting rooms lined the hallway that led from the reception desk to a secluded outdoor patio, and receptionists and security personnel guarded the entrance to the hall.

As mentioned above, since 2004 most of the Hollywood majors have left the main sales halls of the markets, in favour of tents or hotel suites. This move makes them even more inaccessible than they previously were, as buyers must leave the physical space of the sales floor to seek them out. This move not only cuts down on rental costs for the sales stand, but also on the costs of building and decorating the stand. At the same time, the majors retain a good deal of their advertising and promotions on the sales floor, reminding participants of their presence even as their visible presence at the markets recedes.

Finally, on the fourth and fifth levels lay the cheapest sales stands in the Palais, associated with the European Union's MEDIA Program. The MEDIA Program is designed to facilitate the production and region-wide circulation of European-produced audiovisual materials. At the top of the escalator to level four sat a clearinghouse for members of the MEDIA Program, consisting of a reception area and two long racks of fliers for the programming handled through MEDIA. Typically, each company had a representative who attended the sales market and met with interested buyers, though a single representative often worked for several independent producers at once. These companies had sales stands along the hallways that consisted of metal chairs and a TV/VCR hookup, surrounded by a metal cage. Here, companies such as the British Film Institute and the Norwegian Film Institute set up shop. Only buyers interested in specific distributors or those looking for non-commercial and independent programming walked among these stands. In fact, the MIP-TV 2004 'List and Maps of Stands' did not even designate which specific companies were located in the more than thirty stands used by MEDIA Program participants (MIP-TV, 2004).

By marking out clear distinctions among distributors through the layout of the sales floor, markets like MIP-TV facilitate efficient network-ing among those participants who are most likely to have business with one another. Location on the sales floor is one of the primary ways that exhibitors signal to potential buyers the price ranges and varieties of business arrangements they are willing to consider. Many smaller exhib-itors on the main floor, for instance, will gladly meet with and make arrangements with middle-men to represent their programming to buyers in different regions – an arrangement that larger distributors will shun. Restricting access to sales stands adds an allure of desirability to distrib-utors' products, which is critical in an industry where purchasing deci-sions rest largely on hunches. Restricted access gives visible evidence to the claim that one's programming is widely sought-after and commer-cially successful. One commentator writes that 'part of what a station is buying is the promise and grandeur and power of a major syndicator or studio' (Bednarski, 2001: 21). This grandeur, in turn, gets constructed and expressed through the tournament economies of the markets, which utilize access and extravagance as twin indicators of value.

Universal programming as distributor reputation

Distributor reputation articulated through extravagant spending, stand location and size and control of foot traffic, comes to stand in for – or at minimum, complement – programme-based understandings of what is and is not 'universal' in television programming. In other words, distributor reputation agglomerates onto the programming that it carries in its library, working to erase the cultural specificity of the programming through distributor reputation. Again, this is possible because of the authorless nature of television programming and the kinds of tournaments that take place at the markets, through which distributors lay claim to authorship of the programmes they sell and vie for the right to define what constitutes universal programming. By accruing prestige with restricted access and promotional excess, distributors establish their credibility as interpreters of global cultural tastes. Subsequently, the programming they carry takes on an air of that credibility.

Building on the networks that have been constructed at the market, different distributors articulate distinct definitions of what constitutes 'universal' programming. For large distributors and general entertainment broadcasters, who aim at the broadest possible audience segments, universality tends to translate into family- and relationship-based programmes. Consensus on this definition is striking, and reflects the power of a shared business culture to shape the tastes of market participants. Frank Mulder, programme acquisitions director for the Dutch public service broadcasting consortium Nederlandse Omroep Stichting (NOS) explains the popularity of *The Cosby Show* with reference to universality: 'What travels is *Cosby*', he explains. 'It's universal, I mean, it has nothing to do with America. Things that happen in every households, it happens in *Cosby* as well'. Torstren Dewi, commissioner of international co-productions for German commercial broadcaster Prosieben claims: 'I think family problems are the same all over the world'. Marion Edwards, executive vice president of international television at 20th Century Fox International Television, similarly asserts: 'There has to be [some] broader sense of humanity to a show for it to be successful abroad, and some of the shows achieve that … these are like universal issues of family' (personal interview, 1999).

For distributors who deal with different kinds of programming, and buyers seeking to acquire series for particular audience segments, the definitions of universality differ, but the concept itself persists. Maria

Doolan, international co-production manager for Spanish animation house Zinkia, for instance, explains: 'We've tried to incorporate universal values [into their animation] so we are not locked into specific markets', without identifying what those values might be (Esposito, 2004). An executive producer at Canadian animation house, Decode, which specializes in edgy youth and young-adult programming, perhaps strained the boundaries of credulity when she asserted, regarding their animated series *Urban Vermin*: 'We think the combination of sibling rivalry and inner city vermin chaos has universal appeal' (Webdale, 2006). Still, we see distributors employing remarkably similar rhetorical claims to promote their programming: particular kinds of programme content can overcome cultural specificity and succeed in global markets.

In most cases, distributors contrast the supposedly universality of certain kinds of content with national cultural specificity. Mark Kaner, president of 20th Century Fox International Television explains, 'If you have something that is absolutely, totally American, then it is going to be more difficult to sell than something that has a broader, more universal subject matter' (personal interview, 1999). This attempt to accentuate the universal and eliminate the particular in one's programming is a site of struggle among buyers and sellers, which can affect sales. As one representative for BBC Worldwide, which handled international distribution for the Carlton series *Outside Edge*, complained: 'You can tell buyers until you are blue in the face that it's about relationships, not cricket, and they say, "Oh, it's lovely, but it's just too English"'. Obviously, the distributor here believes that 'relationships' are universal, but fails to make sales because buyers focus on different textual elements. In this instance, of course, distributor reputation failed to override content elements, reminding us that reputation does not erase textual elements, but is effectively superimposed over them.

In an authorless medium like television, a distributor's biggest challenge lies in masking *not* the author's copyright and the gift-nature of the commodities in the way that Moeran describes it for the book fair, but rather the perceived cultural specificity of television programming designed for a national or sub-national audience. Distributors' rhetorical efforts to define universality in ways that are beneficial to the programming they carry and to use their own prestige to mark programmes as universally appealing do not eliminate the cultural specificity of the programming. Those efforts do, however, *contribute* to a buyer's overall evaluation of a foreign series.

Gathering intelligence at market

In addition to the prestige that arises from limited access and promotional excess, the markets also serve as a site for gathering intelligence about new programming trends, new technologies and the comings and goings of producers, distributors and broadcasters. In fact, intelligence gathering is perhaps the most commonly recognized function of the markets among industry executives. However, even this seemingly straightforward activity is bound up with the tournaments taking place.

Keeping up with new programming trends is critical for buyers and sellers of television programming, as the business is based on persistent turnover of series, stars and genres. Therefore, importers will pay higher prices for newer rather than older programming, especially programming that picks up on broader cultural trends. Increasingly, these cultural trends come from abroad, as television channels, social networking sites and peer-to-peer video filesharing have made it easier for television fans to seek out new series and genres on their own. Jörg Langer, managing director of T&G Films in Berlin, explains:

I see MIP as a unique instrument for getting an overview of the market situation. What are the trends? What is being internationally produced? More series, singles, docudrama, docusoap? In Germany we have all the trends in the following year, so I get an idea of what we can do. On the other hand, I get an impression of what our competitors are doing. Brown (2001, p. 44)

A recent example of the globalization of programming trends comes from East Asian 'trendy' dramas. Japanese versions of the trendy drama were all the rage among teenagers throughout Asia, Europe and North America in the late 1990s, but this so-called 'J-drama' wave quickly gave way to a 'K-drama' (Korean) wave in the early 2000s, and to 'T-drama' (Taiwanese) and 'H-drama' (Hong Kong) waves more recently (Huat and Iwabuchi, 2008). Any programmer who did not stay abreast of these trends could easily have misjudged the timing of the various waves and bought rights to programmes that were already past their prime.

Market intelligence about programming trends circulates through both official and unofficial channels at the markets: official channels include special issues of trade magazines and publications produced by the market organizers, such as *NATPE Daily* and *MipTV News*, while unofficial channels take the form of sales-floor 'buzz'. Trade journals, in fact, act as a source of much of the informal buzz on the floor, and contribute, in Moeran's phrase, to participants' 'visibility'. During the markets, participants tear through stacks of free journals for the latest information, making the trade journal stands one of the liveliest areas of the market. Debbie Lawrence, managing director of Lippin Group's London office, which handles public relations at the television fairs for several large American and European distributors, explains the importance of trade journal coverage at the fairs plainly: 'To be one of the main distributors of drama [for example] and not to be in the daily drama feature [of the organizer's publication] is seen as a disaster'. In addition to features on distributors, trade journals also publish articles about particular buyers, as well as overviews of current programming trends. Trade journals, then, not only serve as a source for buzz, but also exhibit the same kinds of exclusions and capacity to generate prestige as other aspects of the markets. In other words, the trade journals function as a component of a market's tournaments.

While trade journals serve as official intelligence sources, a good deal of gossip about various broadcasters, distributors, markets and individuals also circulates through the markets. Only occasionally finding its way into official publications, this gossip typically concerns markets, broadcasters and programming at the edges of trade, rather than the centre. One example of this unofficial intelligence comes from pornography trade. While erotica and even softcore pornography proliferate on the sales floor, hardcore pornography is less tolerated. Nevertheless, as a lucrative global programming genre, pornography inevitably does get traded at the major TV sales markets. Rather than showing up in promotional materials, advertisements or trade journals, however, intelligence about who sells pornography, what genres and stars they carry and who is in the market to buy, all travels by word of mouth (anonymous personal interview, 2004).

The example of pornography trade demonstrates the importance of business networks for channelling buzz. While the amount of gossip that 10,000 business executives can generate is probably limitless, only relevant information gets picked up and circulated within specific networks. Executives who specialize in children's animation, for instance, probably have very little need to know which distributors specialize in pornography. These networks, in turn, have previously been established and renewed by the tournaments we have already discussed.

Conclusion

The tournament economies that operate during the global television markets make possible the world trade in television programming. While economic considerations may make foreign syndication attractive to commercial television producers and broadcasters, television remains a highly localized medium. In 1989, the last year during which such data were collected, international trade accounted for about 7 per cent of total television programme spending worldwide (UNESCO, 1989). Almost certainly, that number has increased in the past twenty years, but the fact remains that most of the television in the world never travels beyond its nation of origin.

The programming that does travel is not, as I have argued, somehow of higher quality or more universal in its content, but has rather been anointed as 'universal' by powerful actors in the global television business. This transformation, or transcoding, of a television programme takes place primarily at the markets. Here, a distributor's reputation in global sales lends the allure of universality to programming that otherwise would seem foreign. One of the most interesting examples of this phenomenon can be seen in subtitling versus dubbing practices at the markets. Almost every distributor will translate programme clips into English to screen for potential buyers, but several people I have interviewed suggest that subtitling a programme in English makes buyers think the programme is too foreign, while English dubbing connotes universality. Dubbing, however, requires a much larger time and money investment and, consequently, only comparatively prosperous distributors can afford it. Thus, English dubbing is more than a feature of the programme clips: it is also a demonstration of the distributor's success.

The process of transcoding programming from the local into the universal through distributor reputation can only take place through the kinds of tournaments of values that we witness at the global sales markets. By authorizing certain distributors to articulate what constitutes universal television culture, the tournament economies of the markets create artificial scarcity in international programmes, which is instrumental for any capital market to function properly: that is, goods and services that are abundant, rather than scarce, cannot be bought and sold because people won't pay for them. Internationally traded programmes are, in fact, quite abundant, but distributors use restricted access and promotional extravagance to create the impression that programmes *with universal appeal* are scarce.

The rituals of the programme markets are needed to create scarcity because of the difficulty of predicting viewer preferences, a problem shared by all of the cultural industries. Dubbed the 'nobody knows property' of cultural commodities (Caves, 2000), this difficulty and the uncertainty that it creates for buyers threaten to make trade in television impossible, as the benefits of reduced programming costs associated with importing television might be outweighed by the likelihood of failure. The business relationships that develop at the markets help reduce this likelihood, because they guarantee that buyers will receive future consideration from distributors in the event of catastrophic failure. More profoundly, however, the market tournaments give participants the *impression* of reducing uncertainty by making certain import decisions seem wiser than others.

Notes

* Fieldwork undertaken for this chapter includes interviews with Alexander Charvadze, international sales representative, TV Channel Russia; Kaisa Kriek, program sales manager, Netherlands Public Broadcasting; Debbie Lawrence, managing director, Lippin Group London; Frank Mulder, director of program acquisitions and sales, Netherlands Public Television; Torstren Dewi, commissioner of international co-productions, Prosieben; and Pam Smithard, managing director of Europe, National Association of Television Programming Executives (NATPE). I would like to thank them for their time and trouble.

1. Although television stars do attend the television markets and sit for pictures with participants, such occurrences are side-shows compared to their appearance at film festivals.

2. Moeran also notes a problem with the timing of the London Book Fair and its effect on the market (Chapter 5).

References

Appadurai, A. 1986. 'Introduction: commodities and the politics of value', in A. Appadurai (ed.), *The Social Life of Things*. Cambridge University Press, 3–63.

Bednarski, P. J. 2001. 'The low spark of vegas', *Broadcasting & Cable* 21, 29 January.

Brennan, S. 1999. 'MIP-TV may fall off US A-list: timing and belt tightening reduce studios' interest in Cannes market', *Hollywood Reporter* 357, 30 March, 48.

2000. 'Midseason is in season for MIP-TV buyers', *Hollywood Reporter* 362, 11 April, 54.

Brown, K. 2001. 'Worth the trip to MIP? Producers and distributors weigh-in on the markets in Cannes', *Realscreen*, 1 September, 44–5.

Caves, R. E. 2000. *Creative Industries: Contracts Between Art and Commerce*. Cambridge, MA: Harvard University Press.

Channel 21 2009. 'Program prices map', www.c21media.net/ resources/ index.asp?area=45 (downloaded 24 September 2009).

Esposito, M. 2004. 'Spain's new frontier', *Channel 21*, 26 January, www. c21media.net/features/detail.asp?area=2&article=19037 (downloaded 18 April 2007).

Fiske, John 1987. *Television Culture*. New York and London: Routledge.

Flint, J. 2009. 'Studio's new take on cost-cutting', *Los Angeles Times*, 14 November, http://articles.latimes.com/2009/nov/14/ business/fi-ct-fox14 (downloaded 8 January 2010).

Havens, T. 2003. 'Exhibiting global television: on the business and cultural functions of global television fairs', *Journal of Broadcasting & Electronic Media* 47, 18–36.

2006. *Global Television Marketplace*. London and New York: British Film Institute Publishing.

Hoskins, C., McFadyen, S. and Finn, A. 1997. *Global Television and Film: an Introduction to the Economics of the Business*. New York and Oxford: Oxford University Press.

Huat, B. C., and Iwabuchi, K. 2008. *East Asian Pop Culture: Analysing the Korean Wave*. Hong Kong University Press.

Mahamdi, Y. 1992. 'Television, globalization, and cultural hegemony: the evolution and structure of international television', *Dissertation Abstracts International* 53:04, 977A.

Meza, E. 2009. 'Trade in TV formats explodes', *Variety*, 7 November 2009, www.variety.com/article/VR1118009651.html?categoryid= 2512 &cs=1 (downloaded 18 January 2009).

MIP-TV 2004. *MIPTV and MILIA Guide*. Paris: Reed Midem Organization.

Newcomb, Horace and Alley, Robert S. 1983. *The Producer's Medium: Conversations with Creators of American TV*. Oxford University Press.

Owen, B.M. and Wildman, S.S. 1992. *Video Economics*. Cambridge, MA and London: Harvard University Press.

Roxborough, S. and Masters, C. 2001. 'MIPCOM defies dire forecast', *Hollywood Reporter*, 16 October, http://web.lexis-nexis.com/universe (downloaded 16 October 2003).

UNESCO 1989. *World Communication Report*. Paris: UNESCO.

Waisbord, S. 2004. 'McTV: understanding the global popularity of television formats', *Television & New Media 5*, 359–83.

Webdale, J. 2006. 'Decode breeds vermin for YTV', *Channel 21*, 10 July, www.c21media.net/news/detail.asp?area=4 &article =31200 (downloaded 18 April 2007).

7 Transforming film product identities: the status effects of European premier film festivals, 1996–2005

STEPHEN MEZIAS, JESPER STRANDGAARD
PEDERSEN, JI-HYUN KIM, SILVIYA
SVEJENOVA AND CARMELO MAZZA

One of the most prolific avenues of research in organization theory in recent decades has been the organizational ecology approach (Hannan and Freeman, 1977; Carroll and Hannan, 2004), which views organizations as members of populations and describes the dynamics of those populations. Recent research within that paradigm has focused on the long neglected issue of organizational form, which is central to any conceptualization of organizations as similar enough to be classified into populations (Hannan *et al.*, 2007; Hsu and Hannan, 2005). This has resulted in an ecological conception of identity for both firms and products that differs from past conceptions of identity and advances an understanding of forms in ecological research (Hsu and Hannan, 2005). According to this argument, identity inheres in expectations, assumptions and beliefs held by sets of relatively homogeneous actors called audiences, who can be internal or external to organizations. These beliefs among audience members are conceptualized as codes that constitute the default prescriptions for firms or products – for example identities – as defined by that specific audience (Hannan *et al.*, 2007; Hsu and Hannan, 2005). Interestingly, although higher level – for instance, institutional – processes and occasions for interaction are invoked as mechanisms by which these audiences define and enforce their preferred prescriptions, field-level processes have been largely ignored in this literature. Our study addresses this gap by linking ecological identities, more specifically product identities, with field-level events.

The film industry has been a setting in which some of the first empirical studies of these issues have been conducted (Zuckerman *et al.*, 2003; Hsu, 2006; Hsu *et al.*, 2009). Despite the increasingly global nature of this industry in recent decades, however, these studies have focused exclusively on films produced in the US and the domestic US audience.

We expand the domain of these studies by focusing on a sample of films produced across the globe and premiered at the three major European film festivals, respectively Berlin, Cannes and Venice. We do this not just to expand the application of the ecological conception of identity to new empirical settings, but also because it offers an important opportunity to examine collective processes that affect how audiences define and enforce identities. We share with several other chapters in this volume a focus on how the social processes at collective events, such as trade fairs (Skov and Meier, Chapter 11; Havens, Chapter 6; Moeran Chapter 5), London Fashion Week (Entwistle and Rocamora, Chapter 10), a French art certification establishment (Delacour and Leca, Chapter 1), the annual festival for animation (Rüling, Chapter 8), wine certification events (Anand, Chapter 13; Croidieu, Chapter 12), art biennials (Tang, Chapter 3), and music festivals (Lena, Chapter 9), help to shape markets for particular products. With specific respect to films festivals, Baumann (2001) argued that they played a crucial role in emphasizing artistic status rather than the purely commercial nature of films. In order to separate the role of festivals from the other processes (for example, reviews by critics and amateurs, advertising campaigns, placement into a large number of opening screens, choosing a holiday release and so on), we focus on the premier international film festivals of Berlin, Cannes and Venice. Since premier festivals, by definition, pass judgement on films, via nominations and artistic recognition in the form of awards, prior to their release to the public, they offer an opportunity to study the effect of these field-level judgements of films as precursors to market reception. By contrast, the effect of prizes and other judgements rendered after a film has been released, for instance the Academy Awards or Golden Globe Awards, cannot be seen as precursors to audience reception.

In studying the role of film festivals, we adapt conceptual characterizations of events that organize whole fields of activity (Lampel and Meyer, 2008) to argue that in the market for films, international film festivals are identity-configuring events. According to Lampel and Meyer (2008: 1,025), there has been a paucity of theoretical attention to events like conferences, ceremonies and trade shows, which they call field-configuring events (FCEs).[1] Emphasizing how these events constitute new technologies, industries and markets, Lampel and Meyer (2008: 1,026) linked FCEs with '... ongoing research addressing the growth and evolution of institutional, organizational and professional fields.' Yet, casual observation reveals that even well-developed fields, for example the European film industry in the late twentieth and early twenty-first centuries, continue to hold events that qualify as FCEs. Indeed, the studies in this volume demonstrate the importance of these events in a variety of developed fields, including wine, fashion, art, music, television, animation and books. A key role that these events play in developed fields may be as important occasions for the construction of what Hsu and colleagues (Hsu and Hannan, 2005; Hsu, 2006; Hsu *et al.*, 2009) have called film product identities. As Hsu (2006: 426) argued, the identity of a film forms '... the basis for audiences' expectations of a particular film experience'. Conceptualizing these events as opportunities for the structuring of audience expectations even in established fields offers an opportunity for integrating the concept of FCEs with the ecological concepts of identities and niches. Further, relabelling these occasions as identity-configuring events (ICEs) suggests the possibility of another contribution to understanding the niches occupied by organizations and products. According to Podolny *et al.* (1996: 662), the processes by which status affects niches are endogenous to the population, arising from '... acts of deference between organizations'. This focus on relations between firms has resulted in a rich and valuable literature measuring and emphasizing dyadic relations between firms as a source of status. It is our intent to explore the possibility that ICEs are occasions where status is recognized and officiated, going beyond being a purely dyadic phenomenon. By arguing that field-level events affect status, we intend no slight or refutation of past work treating status as endogenous and based in dyadic relations. Rather, we believe that studying these field-level events and their enactment of status processes sets the stage for future research on how they interact with status processes and dyadic relations endogenous to the population.

Film festivals and the film festival field[2]

Europe appears to be the cradle of the film festival phenomenon (de Valck, 2006), born in the context of the turbulent geopolitical situation in Europe during the 1930s, and the new political order in Europe in the wake of the second world war. The world's first major film festival was founded in Italy under the fascist government and held in Venice in 1932. It thus took just forty years or so from the first public screening in December 1895 by the Lumiere brothers to the founding of the world's first major film festival. However, the way the Venice festival was run soon gave rise to the criticism that films from Italy and Germany were favoured, even though the first festivals had hosted films from several countries. According to Turan (2002): 'in 1937, Jean Renoir's "La Grande Illusion" was denied the top prize because of its pacifist sentiments, and the French decided if you wanted something done right you had to do it yourself' (Turan, 2002: 18; cf. Mazdon, 2007).

This became the birth of what we today know as the Cannes Film Festival. Cannes won out as the preferred site for the film festival after a competition with Biarritz on the Atlantic coast (Turan, 2002; Mazdon, 2007) and was originally scheduled to take place during the first three weeks of September 1939. However, it was cancelled because of the German invasion of Poland on 1 September 1939 and the Cannes film festival did not start up again until 1946 (Turan, 2002: 18–19).

Another early adaptor or 'first mover' within the film festival field was the Moscow International Film Festival (MIFF) which was founded in 1935 and is thus the second oldest film festival in the world, after the Venice Film Festival. MIFF has been redesigned several times – in 1959, 1969 and 1989 – and from 1959 to 1995 it was held every second year in July, alternating location between Karlovy Vary and Moscow. Since 1995, it has been held annually. So prior to the second world war, only three film festivals were established, respectively Venice (1932), Moscow (1935) and Cannes (1939). The other major international film festivals – like Locarno, Karlovy Vary, Berlin and so forth – are a post-war phenomenon dating back to the late 1940s and 1950s (for an overview of early film festivals see Table 7.1).

Harbord (2002) links the creation of European film festivals (as well as other post-war festivals) to European post-war regeneration and rebuilding. Even though film festivals started out as a European phenomenon, they soon proliferated and diffused to other parts of the world (India, 1952; Australia, 1954; South America, 1954; see Table 7.1).

Regulation, accreditation and co-ordination of film festivals

Film festivals are accredited as international film festivals by the International Federation of Film Producers Associations (FIAPF) founded in 1933.[3] This is a global organization representing the interests of the film production communities worldwide with twenty-six national producers' organizations in twenty-three of the world's leading audiovisual-producing countries (FIAPF, 2008: 3). According to its official publicity:

Table 7.1 *Overview of early film festivals*[a]

1932	Venice International Film Festival (Italy)
1935	Moscow International Film Festival (Russia)
1939	Cannes International Film Festival (France)
1946	Karlovy Vary International Film Festival (Czech Republic)
	Locarno International Film Festival (Switzerland)
1951	Berlin International Film Festival – (Germany)
1952	The International Film Festival of India (India)
1953	Donostia–San Sebastian International Film Festival (Spain)
1954	International Short Film Festival Oberhausen (Germany)
	Sydney Film Festival (Australia)
	Mar del Plata International Film Festival (Argentina)
1956	The Times British Film Institute (BFI) London Film Festival (UK)
1958	Bilbao International Festival of Documentary and Short Films (Spain)

[a] This list is based on film festivals accredited by FIAPF (2008). This means, for example, that the Edinburgh International Film Festival in Scotland, established in 1947 and the longest continually running film festival in the world, is not included as it is not accredited by FIAPF.

The FIAPF international film festivals' accreditation system was created as a response to demands from the film industry that a Minimum Standard of quality and reliability be defined for international film festivals: one which international festival organizers must pledge to uphold and apply when they become FIAPF-accredited. FIAPF (2008: 3)

FIAPF 'decided during the Berlin film festival of 1951 that the boom in national and regional film festivals had to be channelled to prevent festival (award) inflation' (de Valck, 2006: 19). Cannes and Venice received immediate FIAPF accreditation (in 1951) and Berlin followed in 1956 (Jacobsen, 2000: 18). According to FIAPF (2008: 4) 'by international film festival, FIAPF, understands an event:

- bringing together films of the world, many of which originate from countries other than the organising country, that are being screened in front of audiences including a significant number of accredited international industry, press and media representatives as well as general public
- taking place for a limited duration of time, once a year or every second year, in a prior defined city.'

FIAPF began its accreditation and classification system with 'competitive film festivals' like Cannes, Venice and Berlin. Over the years the FIAPF classification system was expanded to include more festivals and different categories like 'competitive specialized film festivals', 'non-competitive film festivals' and 'documentary and short film festivals'. In their 2008 catalogue of accredited international feature film festivals FIAPF lists the following twelve film festivals in the category of 'competitive film festivals':

- Berlin International Film Festival (Berlinale)
- Mar del Plata International Film Festival
- Cannes Film Festival
- Shanghai International Film Festival
- Moscow International Film Festival
- Karlovy Vary International Film Festival
- Locarno International Film Festival
- Montreal World Film Festival
- Venice International Film Festival
- Donostia San Sebastian International Film Festival
- Tokyo International Film Festival, and
- Cairo International Film Festival.

Apart from the category of 'competitive film festivals', FIAPF also operates with a distinction between 'competitive specialized film festivals' (twenty-six festivals, among which are included, for example, the Brussels International Festival of Fantastic Film); 'non-competitive film festivals' (six festivals, including the Sydney Film Festival); and 'documentary and short film festivals' (five festivals, including the Tampere International Short Film Festival).

Film festivals as FCEs

The first characteristic of FCEs according to Lampel and Meyer (2008) is that they assemble in one location actors from diverse professional, organizational and geographical backgrounds. The films chosen for exhibition accrue situational value as thousands of participants see them displayed in a particular place, a chosen festival venue and at a particular time, its scheduled screening. All three festivals – Berlin, Cannes and Venice – take place in defined spaces co-located within the confines of the single city for which the festivals are named. Table 7.2 summarizes

Table 7.2 *Diversity of participation in film festivals*

Participation type	Berlin	Cannes	Venice
Total films	382	91	155
World premiers	114	89	80
Percentage of films that are premiers	30	98	93
Total press	4,105	4,376	3,022
Percentage of films that are not local	50	59	39
Total market participants	5,752	10,489	1,632
Total exhibitors	259	534	338

some key numbers illustrating this point from the 2007 editions of the three European film festivals; indeed it is apparent that many films and many world premiers take place at each location during the period of the festival. While Berlin and Venice both had more films on exhibit than Cannes, the proportion of premiers is highest at Cannes, at 98 per cent, while Venice had about 93 per cent of its films as premiers and Berlin less than one-third. Press coverage is extensive at all three festivals, with all having over 3,000 correspondents in attendance. Cannes leads in both total correspondents, at nearly 4,400, and in percentage that are not local, at just under 60 per cent. In terms of total market participants, there is somewhat more variance, with a range from 1,632 at the Venice festival, more than 5,700 at the Berlin festival and nearly 10,500 at Cannes. Cannes also leads in the total number of exhibitors represented, at 534, while Venice attracted 338 exhibitors and Berlin 259. Table 7.2 shows that all three festivals are widely attended and covered events that attract a variety of persons and organizations involved in the global film industry. Considerable social value can be created for products as their producers and distributors interact to create and reinforce the relationships that are at the core of film projects.

All three festivals also have screenings of films, at least some of which are open to persons who are not formal participants in the festivals, as well as numerous other activities that mark the festival as an event that helps to construct the identities of films. At the Berlin Festival, 47 screening facilities with a total seating capacity of 14,398 were used to allow 431,000 persons to watch films included in the festival, and 1,099 screenings of films were conducted specifically to help market films included in the festival. There was a co-production market that included

Figure 7.1 The Croisette at the Cannes Film Festival, 2007 (photo: Jesper Strandgaard Pedersen)

418 participants from 48 countries and a talent campus that included 370 participants from 101 countries. At Cannes, a much smaller number of screening facilities – only 5, with a seating capacity of just 5,300 people – were used to show films to nearly as many persons as at Berlin, 350,000, indicating a much more concentrated viewing experience among participants. More than three-quarters of the exhibitors participating in the Cannes festival, 77 per cent, were not from France. There were also nearly 4,700 distributors and nearly 5,000 producers of films in attendance. Similarly, the Venice Festival brought together a multitude of participants with varied interests in the global film industry. Around 545 distributors and representatives of sales companies or other film buyers attended, and 63 per cent of them were not from Italy; 338 exhibitors, slightly less than half of whom were not from Italy, attended. We believe that the interactions around these screenings, focused as they are on the films and their markets, may create considerable technical value for films, particularly by enhancing the specialized knowledge of participants.

Figure 7.2 The Palais du Festival at Cannes Film Festival, 2007 (photo: Jesper Strandgaard Pedersen)

The second and third characteristics (Lampel and Meyer, 2008) reinforce the importance of these events for the mix of participants in attendance. The fixed duration of less than two weeks as well as the regular occurrence of the festivals, annual in all three cases, delineates the fixed time of the opportunities for configuring product identities, consistent with the second characteristic. Bringing the participants together for a fixed time in a well-defined space – there are numerous formal events in designated festival venues in the case of Cannes, for example The Palais du Festival and along the Croisette – creates opportunities for contact, shop talk, gossip and many other types of information exchange.

Consistent with the third characteristic (Lampel and Meyer, 2008), informal activities like parties, receptions and other types of events offer unstructured opportunities for social interaction (as can be seen in Havens, Chapter 6, and Moeran, Chapter 5). Each festival takes place in its specific host city and at certain designated spaces, offering

Figure 7.3 The red carpet at Potzdammer Platz, Berlin Film Festival, 2008 (photo: Jesper Strandgaard Pedersen)

unstructured opportunities for interaction as people meet at cafés, bars, restaurants and so on during the days and nights of the festivals. In the case of Berlin, for example, the many bars and cafés around Potsdamer Platz are packed with participants during the film festival each year. Again, both the formal and informal opportunities for interaction reinforce the ability of film festivals to create social value.

Of course, the official focus of the festivals is not on the unstructured opportunities for interaction, important as they are. A main draw for participants and a source of shared experiences and information to facilitate the informal interactions are the ceremonial and dramaturgical activities that form the official core of these events – the fourth characteristic described by Lampel and Meyer (2008). Each of the festivals has elaborate opening and closing ceremonies that form official demarcations of the temporal space of the event; in Berlin, for example, Martin Scorsese's film 'Shine a Light' about the rock band the Rolling Stones opened the 2008 edition of the festival.

The principal official events between these time markers include a main competition as well as several ancillary competitions (so-called sidebars) that define a prestige and status ordering for participants and the world to see. Berlin awards a Golden Bear as its main prize for the best film as well as silver bears for a variety of categories, including the jury grand, best director, actor, and actress, outstanding artistic achievement and best film music prizes. Other prizes for various categories, including shorts, generational films and German cinematic perspective, are also presented; there is even an award for culinary depiction. Similarly, Cannes offers a series of prizes and awards, with the Palme d'Or and the Grand Prix being the most prestigious. It also offers prizes for winners of official competitions in the categories of direction, acting and screenwriting, as well as the Vulcain Prize for an artist technician. Also on offer are a variety of special prizes for short films, one from the Cinefondation, and even one for films that are 'out of competition'. Venice offers three main prizes for films, The Golden Lion, The Silver Lion and the Special Jury Prize. Individual achievement is recognized in a variety of ways, including the Coppa Volpi for direction and acting, a Marcello Mastroianni special award for young actors, Osellas for cinematography, a special award for debut films and a lifetime achievement award. Thus, the central value created at these festivals is appreciative or aesthetic value, particularly related to the certification of artistic status that accrues to all films invited for exhibition. In addition, receiving a prize is likely to be an additional source of increased aesthetic value for the films that emerge as winners.

The fifth characteristic clarifies and extends the importance of the prior ones with the observation that FCEs are occasions for information exchange and collective sense-making. Indeed all of the festivals offer the opportunity for master classes and training from well-known and respected film-makers providing young talent (and other people) with knowledge and information on latest trends and suchlike. These might be particularly important opportunities where technical value is created at these festivals in that the knowledge about the professional status and technical skill of various persons distributed in these venues can augment the value of the films with which these highly proficient persons are associated. Together with the official festival information material (programmes and descriptions of the films in competition) special daily editions of film magazines like *Screen*, *Variety* and *The Hollywood Reporter* are also issued at the festival sites, providing critical reaction to the films of the day, opinions and editorials about important events, as well as reviews by a selected panel of film critics. They also provide information about films, stars, exhibitors, producers, distributors and so on, in the same way that we find for book and other fairs.

The sixth characteristic similarly clarifies why these events are important, particularly after the fact: they generate social and reputational resources that can be deployed elsewhere and for other purposes (Lampel and Meyer, 2008). The stars (actors as well as film-makers) are celebrated here through nominations and rewards generating reputations. Homage is given to certain film-makers (dead or alive) for their contribution to film. A special arrangement often called 'shooting star' is trying to promote new talent – young actors on their way up. A multitude of forms of social capital is an important product of these festivals. Of particular interest to our study is the social capital that can be deployed to improve the identity of specific films that are entered in the festivals, increasing their acceptance by audiences.

The effects of identity configuration

Given the strong effects of status found by Podolny *et al.* (1996), we expect the status effects of field-level events that configure film product identities to be substantial. As we have seen above, we believe that film festivals have a variety of activities that can enhance the technical, social, situational, appreciative or aesthetic and functional value of particular films. A first question that arises from this concerns the possibility of status differences among the festivals. While we have demonstrated that all of them share the characteristics of ICE derived from Lampel and Meyer (2008), we did find differences among them. Some have a higher percentage of premiers than others; some are larger than others. While we believe that all of these festivals are equivalents in the sense of offering opportunities for the configuration of product identities, we also believe that there may be status differences among the festivals such that some might offer better opportunities for product identity configuration than others resulting in our first hypothesis: *The effect of the three festivals on film performance will differ.*

One of the most important ways that the festivals configure product identities is by creating among the participants at the festivals shared perceptions and information that are transformed into product performance after the event is over. The diversity of personnel from around the world assembled for a few days in one place allows this. The unstructured and structured activities constitute a concentrated and unparalleled opportunity for information exchange and collective sense-making that generates significant social and reputational resources that can be used to configure product identities. The most enduring manifestations of these effects are the results of the festival competitions. This leads us to expect prize-winning films to have superior product identity to films that do not win – an expectation formulated in our second hypothesis: *Winning a prize will increase the audience for a film.* We also considered the nature of the prizes. Judging from the attention devoted to particular competitions among the films at a given festival, we noted that there seemed to be differences in attention to various competitions and prizes. Specifically, the key prizes for best pictures and directors seemed to receive the most attention. While there was some attention to the key prizes for acting, attention to other prizes was considerably less. Based on these observations, we came up with a third hypothesis about the effects of winning different competitions and prizes: *The films that win best picture and best director prizes will show a greater increase in audience than films that win best actor prizes.*

Finally, combining the implication of status as enacted at film festivals with the prior hypothesis about differences in status across film festivals suggests the possibility that the effects of winning will differ across the three festivals. This leads us to hypothesize that the differences in prestige among the festivals might be reflected in differences among the prizes won at different festivals. In other words, a win at a more prestigious festival might result in a more valuable product identity than a win at a less prestigious festival, as formulated in our fourth hypothesis: *The effects of a win will differ at the three festivals.*

The study

Our sample includes all films that premiered at any of the three major European film festivals, Berlin, Cannes or Venice between 1996 and 2005 and were nominated for any of the major prizes. This yielded a sample of 607 films. In order to carry out a statistical analysis of this sample, we have had to consider dependent, independent and control variables as outlined below.

Firstly, dependent variables: we have used audience size (that is, number of admissions) of twenty-five European countries, listed in Table 7.3, to act as our dependent variable and to operationalize the

Table 7.3 *Countries included in the admissions data*

United Kingdom	Austria	Hungary
Germany	Greece	Slovenia
France	Denmark	Slovakia
Italy	Poland	Lithuania
Spain	Finland	Latvia
Netherlands/	Portugal	Estonia
Luxemburg	Czech Republic	Malta
Sweden	Ireland	Cyprus
Belgium		

level of fitness of the product identities of the films in our sample. It is analogous to the box office gross variable in Hsu *et al.* (2009). Since we collected our dependent variable from multiple countries, counting the number of admissions eliminates the potential effect due to price difference across countries and changes in currency rates over the time frame studied. We use the Lumiere Database (www.Lumiere.obs.coe.int) to collect the number of admissions for our sample films as of mid 2008. We used log of the number of admissions.

Secondly, independent variables: we have considered the Cannes International Film Festival (*Cannes nomination*), Venice International Film Festival (*Venice nomination*) and Berlin International Film Festival (*Berlin nomination*) from 1996 to 2005 as major identity-configuring events. Each of these three independent variables is a dichotomous variable that takes the value of one if a film is nominated for a given film festival and zero otherwise. Since a film submitted to a festival cannot be resubmitted to another festival, these variables are mutually exclusive. Since we only included films premiered and nominated at the festivals, we have to exclude one of the festival variables as our omitted category; we use *Venice nomination* for this purpose. Thus, the effects of *Cannes nomination* and *Berlin nomination* as reported in the estimated models contrast with *Venice nomination*. Significant and positive coefficients would imply that the effect of these festivals on attendance is greater than that of *Venice nomination*. We have also considered whether a film has won prizes and at what festivals and categories to test our second, third and fourth hypotheses, taking into account four award categories: best picture, best actor, best actress and best director awards. A significant effect of winning any of the major awards from a major film festival can be an important event that creates attention from different audience groups. We have created four dichotomous variables that take one if a film has won the given award category and zero otherwise; the names are self-explanatory. To test our second hypothesis, we have added all of these dichotomous variables together to create a variable that is the sum of all wins by a film; the hypothesis is supported if this variable has a significant positive effect. To test our third hypothesis, we have compared the coefficients for variables representing different categories of wins; the hypothesis is supported if the effects of picture and director awards are greater than the effects of actor awards. To test our fourth hypothesis, we have created variables to reflect wins at the different festivals; again, the names are self-explanatory. The hypothesis is supported if the coefficients for wins at different festivals are significantly different from one another.

Thirdly, control variables: following Hsu (2006) and Hsu *et al.* (2009), we have included genre fixed effects to control for possible differences in performance of films based on genres. For example, the size of resource space for action films and documentaries may differ. Given the limited nature of the data and measures, it is not possible to measure the volume of the resource space directly. Following Hsu (2006) and Hsu *et al.* (2009), we use genre fixed effect as a proxy for direct measures of differences in resource spaces of different film products. Thus, we have included the following seventeen genre classifications: action, adventure, animation, comedy, crime, documentary, drama, family, fantasy, horror, musical, mystery, romance, science fiction, thriller, war and western. Since a significant portion of our sample films are non-US films, we have also used 'foreign' as an additional genre. In sum, we used eighteen genre classifications as fixed effects to control for the resource spaces occupied by different film products. We have also controlled for the overall capacity of a film by including the size of its budget in US dollars.[4] Since this variable is skewed on the right side, we have taken the log of this variable (*(Ln) Budget*). We also created a dummy variable to indicate whether the film had a US firm among its producers (*US production*). We intend this variable to capture the effect of major distributors as estimated by Hsu (2006) and Hsu *et al.* (2009).

We have also controlled for different levels of star/director power using the measures developed by Zuckerman *et al.* (2003). We collected the names of the first five actors/actresses who appeared in the casting credits from International Movie Data Base (IMDB). For each of the five actors/actresses, we collect two measures: (1) the natural logarithm of the number of films the actor/actress appeared in prior to the focal film (referred to as *(Ln) No. of films*); and (2) the square root of the highest US box-office revenue of the films collected from (1) (referred to as *(Max. box office)^{1/2}*). According to Zuckerman *et al.* (2003), the *(Ln) No. of films* measure captures how experienced the actor/actress was at the time when the focal film was produced. The *(Max. box office)^{1/2}* measure captures the commercial influence of an actor/actress. We could not use the star power ranking from *Hollywood Reporter*'s Star Power survey (Hsu, 2006; Hsu *et al.*, 2009) because this measure is not available for the full time span of our sample. Having measured the star power of the five principal actors in each film, we needed to convert these into a composite measure for each film. To do this, we followed Hsu *et al.* (2009) and used the maximum as a representative star power value. *(Ln) Star no. of films* is the maximum of the *(Ln) No. of films* values from the five actors/actresses. *(Star max. box office)^{1/2}* is the maximum of the *(Max. box office)^{1/2}* measures of the five. Of the two measures, we used *(Star max. box office)^{1/2}* only because the two measures are highly correlated. Beyond this maximum-based measure, we also ran the model with the average star power measure calculated by the average of *(Ln) No. of films* and *(Max. box office)^{1/2}* of the five actors/actresses. The main results of the study remain the same with this modification.

The director power measure has been easier to construct since there is usually only one director per film. Using the consistent *(Ln) No. of films* measure, we counted the natural logarithm of the number of films directed by the director prior to the focal film. The *(Max. box office)^{1/2}* measure for directors is the square root of the highest US box-office revenue of the films included in the *(Ln) No. of films* measure. Since constructing a composite measure is not necessary, we have used *(Ln) No. of films* to represent the director's experience (*(Ln) Director no. of films*) and *(Max. box office)^{1/2}* for director's commercial influence (*(Director Max. box office)^{1/2}*). For the reason discussed above, we have included *(Ln) Director no. of films* only.

As in Hsu (2006) and Hsu *et al.* (2009), we have controlled for crowding in genres (*Crowding*). Genre crowding for a film is defined by the sum of its genre overlaps with all other films produced in the same year. Since the period of theatrical exhibition is different for each country, we have chosen the production year as a time window in which films exert competitive pressure on other films. While the choice of competitive time window is less fine-grained than that based on the exact period of theatrical exhibition, it is the best alternative given the lack of availability of exhibition period for each country. Following Hsu (2006) and Hsu *et al.* (2009), we have defined genre overlap between two films by the fraction of the total number of genres under which both films are classified. We have also included year fixed effects to control for unobservable variations from year to year.

Results

Tables 7.4 and 7.5 report the maximums, minimums, means, standard deviations and correlations for the theoretical and control variables. Examination of the indicator variables for each of the festivals in Table 7.4 reveals that almost exactly one-third of our films were nominated in each of the festivals; Cannes and Berlin are slightly overrepresented at just over .35 and .34 respectively. The indicator variables for the prize categories reveal that wins were relatively rare; the most common for best picture was just over one film in ten. The variables measuring the total wins per picture reveal a similar rarity of prizes, with the average film receiving less than 0.1 prizes. US co-production was relatively common, with just over a quarter of the films having at least one producer from the US. The reported correlations from Table 7.5 reveal several sets of variables that are highly correlated to each other, but many of them are nested variables or not in the estimation equation together. For example, the total win variables (*Total win Cannes*, *Total win Berlin*, and *Total win Venice*) are not in a same estimation equation with the separate prize win variables (*Best picture*, *Best director*, *Best actor* and *Best actress*). Also, *Total win Cannes* is nested to *Cannes nomination*. These nested relations naturally tend to generate a high level of correlation. Other than these artefacts, we find that correlations among explanatory variables are generally low and should not create multi-collinearity concerns. We verified this by examining variance inflation factors and condition indices for all the models that we estimated; these diagnostics gave no indication of collinearity problems.

In all the reported analyses, we performed ordinary least squares (OLS) regressions. As Hsu (2006) and Hsu *et al.* (2009) observed,

Table 7.4 *Descriptive statistics*

Variable	N	Minimum	Maximum	Mean	Std dev
Cannes nomination	607	0	1	0.353	0.478
Berlin nomination	607	0	1	0.344	0.476
Venice nomination	607	0	1	0.303	0.460
Best picture	607	0	1	0.105	0.307
Best director	607	0	1	0.048	0.213
Best actor	607	0	1	0.056	0.230
Best actress	607	0	1	0.063	0.242
Total win Cannes	607	0	3	0.089	0.348
Total win Berlin	607	0	2	0.104	0.346
Total win Venice	607	0	2	0.079	0.299
(Ln) Budget	607	0	18.198	3.962	7.037
(Star Max. box office)$^{1/2}$	607	0	24.515	6.073	6.074
(Ln) Director no. of films	607	0	4.595	1.838	0.953
US production	607	0	1	0.252	0.435
Niche width	607	0.000	0.847	0.463	0.256
Crowding	607	6.000	100.000	54.560	19.391

Tobit regression is a better estimation method when the values of the dependent variable are censored. Because censored models such as Tobit regressions typically require additional model assumptions (for example, normality), these models are applied only when a meaningful proportion of data sets (for example five per cent or higher) is located at the boundary (Hansen, 2009). Since only a few data points have dependent variable value at zero in our sample, we ran OLS regressions. Supplementary analyses with Tobit regressions yielded the same findings we report below.

Table 7.6 reports the effects of control variables. Not surprisingly, the effect of the log of budget is positive and significant ($p < 0.01$). US production, the variable intended to capture the effect of major distributors (Hsu, 2006; Hsu *et al.*, 2009), is also positive and significant ($p < 0.05$). On the other hand, star and director power measures produced mixed results: while the star power measure (*Star max. box office*$^{1/2}$) is positive and significant ($p < 0.05$), the estimated effect of the director power measure (*(Ln) Director no. of films*) is not significantly different

Table 7.5 Correlations

	1	2	3	4	5	6	7	8	9	10	11	12	13	14
1 Cannes nomination														
2 Berlin nomination	-0.53*													
3 Venice nomination	-0.49*	-0.48*												
4 Best picture	-0.02	0.01	0.01											
5 Best director	0.03	0.00	-0.03	-0.05										
6 Best actor	-0.03	0.03	0.00	0.10*	-0.02									
7 Best actress	-0.03	0.04	-0.01	0.13*	0.01	0.03								
8 Total win Cannes	0.35*	-0.19*	-0.17*	0.39*	0.23*	0.25*	0.31*							
9 Total win Berlin	-0.22*	0.41*	-0.20*	0.33*	0.22*	0.28*	0.34*	-0.08						
10 Total win Venice	-0.20*	-0.19*	0.40*	0.34*	0.12*	0.27*	0.23*	-0.07	-0.08					
11 (Ln) Budget	0.01	0.09*	-0.10*	0.04	0.00	0.06	0.02	0.05	0.07	-0.04				
12 (Star max. box office)$^{1/2}$	-0.05	0.12*	-0.07	-0.07	-0.02	0.11*	0.03	-0.03	0.04	0.00	0.55*			
13 (Ln) Director no. of films	0.07	-0.09*	0.01	-0.05	0.06	-0.12*	-0.13*	-0.04	-0.09*	-0.04	-0.07	0.05		
14 US production	-0.06	0.11*	-0.05	0.00	0.01	0.12*	-0.02	-0.04	0.10*	0.01	0.62*	0.59*	-0.10*	
15 Niche width	0.09*	0.00	-0.09*	0.04	0.03	0.04	-0.01	0.07	0.03	-0.04	0.09*	0.10*	0.11*	0.04
16 Crowding	-0.06	-0.02	0.08*	0.00	-0.01	-0.04	0.04	-0.04	-0.01	0.05	-0.18*	-0.18*	-0.08*	-0.19*

* p < .05.

Table 7.6 *Effects of control variables*

Variable	Parameter estimate	Standard error	t Value	Pr > |t|
Intercept	10.310	0.887	11.620	<.0001
(Ln) Budget	0.067	0.015	4.420	<.0001
(Star max. box office)$^{1/2}$	0.00004537	0.0000179	2.530	0.012
(Ln) Director no. of films	0.086	0.084	1.020	0.307
US production	0.579	0.278	2.080	0.038
Niche width	0.513	1.149	0.450	0.656
Crowding	0.008	0.014	0.600	0.552

Notes:
(1) Genre and year fixed effects are estimated but not reported.
(2) R-square: 0.285.

from zero. This result reflects relative importance of star actors and actresses to the importance of directors. Neither *Niche width* nor *Crowding* is significant. Compared to the findings in Hsu *et al.* (2009) where they found both were negative and significant, these results are surprising. However, we believe there are understandable reasons for these differences in findings. The difference in the effects of *Niche width* might be due to sample differences. In our sample, all the films are premiered at prestigious film festivals or, in our term, identity-configuring events. Hsu *et al.* (2009)'s sample is all the films released in the US during 2002 and 2003, with relatively few being premiered at prestigious festivals. Based on this, we can cautiously infer that the effects of ICEs are strong enough to wash out the negative effects of wide niche. But, to make a more accurate argument, further analyses are required. The difference in the effect of *Crowding* is likely due to the coarseness of our measure. We created our crowding measure using yearly time window while Hsu *et al.* (2009) identified the exact period of theatrical exhibition.

Table 7.7 reports the effects of film festival nominations. As hypothesized in hypothesis 1, the effects of the three festivals on film performance differ. While the effect of *Cannes nomination* on film performance is significantly higher than that of *Venice nomination* (the omitted category) at 5 per cent level of significance, *Berlin nomination* is not significantly different from *Venice nomination*. This supports our first

Table 7.7 *Effects of film festival nominations*

Variable estimate	Parameter	Standard error	t Value	Pr > |t|
Intercept	10.087	0.892	11.310	<.0001
Cannes nomination	0.473	0.197	2.400	0.017
Berlin nomination	0.286	0.196	1.460	0.145
(Ln) Budget	0.064	0.015	4.250	<.0001
(Star max. box office)$^{1/2}$	0.00004565	0.00001786	2.560	0.011
(Ln) Director no. of films	0.083	0.085	0.980	0.326
US production	0.597	0.277	2.150	0.032
Niche width	0.519	1.148	0.450	0.652
Crowding	0.009	0.014	0.620	0.534

Notes:
(1) Genre and year fixed effects are estimated but not reported.
(2) Venice nomination is omitted category.
(3) R-square: 0.292.

hypothesis and enables us to infer that a Cannes nomination has a stronger influence on identity configuration. We further performed the Wald test to see whether the effect of Cannes nomination is significantly stronger than the effect of a Berlin nomination, but cannot reject the null hypothesis that the effects of Cannes and Berlin nominations are the same. However, we ran a supplementary analysis in which we included only the variable for Cannes; in this model, the significant, positive effect of Cannes suggests that this festival has a significantly larger effect on audience than the average effect of the Berlin and Venice festivals. The effects of control variables remain unchanged from Table 7.6. In summary of Table 7.7, the first hypothesis is supported because we find that the effect of nomination at Cannes is significantly stronger than the effect of nomination at Venice.

Table 7.8 reports on the model that introduces the variable measuring the total wins of each film to test our second hypothesis that winning a prize will increase the audience for a film. The variable *Total win* is positive and significant ($p < 0.001$), indicating strong support for the second hypothesis. It is noteworthy that this effect is over and above the positive effects of nomination at Cannes and Berlin, which remain almost identical to what they were in the previous model. Comparison of the coefficients of these variables, which is possible since all of them

Table 7.8 *Effects of total number of wins*

Variable estimate	Parameter	Standard error	t Value	Pr > |t|
Intercept	10.135	0.865	11.710	<.0001
Cannes nomination	0.478	0.191	2.500	0.013
Berlin nomination	0.267	0.190	1.400	0.161
Total win	0.888	0.147	6.050	<.0001
(Ln) Budget	0.059	0.015	3.980	<.0001
(Star max. box office)$^{1/2}$	0.00004682	0.00001733	2.700	0.007
(Ln) Director no. of films	0.138	0.083	1.670	0.096
US production	0.558	0.269	2.070	0.039
Niche width	0.067	1.117	0.060	0.953
Crowding	0.005	0.014	0.340	0.735

Notes:
(1) Genre and year fixed effects are estimated but not reported.
(2) Venice nomination is omitted category.
(3) R-square: 0.335.

are indicator variables, reveals that a win at Cannes is about twice as valuable as the most valuable nomination. This effect is multiplied by the fact that some films won multiple awards. Clearly, winning two or three awards increases the audience appeal of a film far more than simply being nominated to even the most prestigious festival, Cannes. In fact, the difference between these coefficients is significant, and statistical inference reveals that the effect of a win is significantly greater than the effect of a nomination to Cannes.

Table 7.9 reports the effects of prestigious prizes (*Best picture, Best director, Best actor* and *Best actress*). Our third hypothesis suggested that best picture and best director prizes would have stronger influence than best actor or best actress prizes. As expected, the effect of best picture turns out to be positive and significant at 1 per cent significance level. However, unlike what we have hypothesized, the effect of best director prize is not significant. Further, the effects of best actor and best actress are both positive and significant ($p < 0.05$). From this, we can infer that best actor and best actress prizes generated an increase in audience size relative to other films. In a further analysis, we tested whether the effect of *Best picture* is uniquely stronger than the other three prize variables. To do so, we created a new dummy variable named *Other prizes*. This variable takes a value of one if a film won

Table 7.9 *Effects of prestigious prizes*

Variable estimate	Parameter	Standard error	t Value	Pr > |t|
Intercept	10.131	0.867	11.690	<.0001
Cannes nomination	0.490	0.192	2.560	0.011
Berlin nomination	0.271	0.191	1.420	0.156
Best picture	1.140	0.254	4.490	<.0001
Best director	0.473	0.358	1.320	0.187
Best actor	0.824	0.342	2.410	0.016
Best actress	0.803	0.321	2.500	0.013
(Ln) Budget	0.057	0.015	3.880	<.0001
(Star max. box office)$^{1/2}$	0.00004772	0.00001756	2.720	0.007
(Ln) Director no. of films	0.142	0.084	1.690	0.091
US production	0.556	0.271	2.050	0.040
Niche width	0.051	1.120	0.050	0.963
Crowding	0.004	0.014	0.320	0.749

Notes:
(1) Genre and year fixed effects are estimated but not reported.
(2) Venice nomination is omitted category.
(3) R-square: 0.338.

any of best director, best actor or best actress prizes. Table 7.10 reports the result from this analysis. Both *Best picture* and *Other prizes* are positive and significant. To determine the statistical difference of these two coefficients, we performed the Wald test with the hypothesis that there is an equality relationship between these two coefficients. We rejected this hypothesis at 10 per cent significance level and conclude that the effect of *Best picture* is stronger than winning any of the other three prizes.

In Table 7.11, we report the effects of total number of prizes won at each festival. Instead of the prestigious award winning categories, we included the total number of prizes (best picture, best director, best actor and best actress) won by each film at festivals. The effects of these variables are all positive and significant at 1 per cent significance level. Our fourth hypothesis suggested that the effects of total wins may differ by festivals. To test this hypothesis, we performed three sets of Wald tests to see if any of the three pairs of coefficients are significantly different from each other. In these analyses, the null hypotheses were the following: *Total wins Cannes = Total wins Berlin, Total wins*

Table 7.10 *Effects of prestigious prizes (best director, best actor and best actress merged into other prizes)*

Variable estimate	Parameter	Standard error	t Value	Pr > |t|
Intercept	10.159	0.865	11.750	<.0001
Cannes nomination	0.485	0.191	2.530	0.012
Berlin nomination	0.271	0.190	1.420	0.155
Best picture	1.167	0.251	4.650	<.0001
Other prizes	0.710	0.196	3.630	<.0001
(Ln) Budget	0.057	0.015	3.890	<.0001
(Star max. box office)$^{1/2}$	0.00004936	0.00001742	2.830	0.005
(Ln) Director no. of films	0.132	0.083	1.600	0.111
US production	0.553	0.269	2.050	0.040
Niche width	0.012	1.117	0.010	0.991
Crowding	0.004	0.014	0.290	0.775

Notes:
(1) Genre and year fixed effects are estimated but not reported.
(2) Venice nomination is omitted category.
(3) R-square: 0.337.

Table 7.11 *Effects of total number of prizes by festival*

Variable estimate	Parameter	Standard error	t Value	Pr > |t|
Intercept	10.087	0.868	11.620	<.0001
Cannes nomination	0.432	0.212	2.040	0.042
Berlin nomination	0.322	0.216	1.490	0.137
Total win Cannes	1.067	0.236	4.520	<.0001
Total win Berlin	0.699	0.245	2.850	0.005
Total win Venice	0.876	0.280	3.130	0.002
(Ln) Budget	0.058	0.015	3.920	<.0001
(Star max. box office)$^{1/2}$	0.00004677	0.00001736	2.690	0.007
(Ln) Director no. of films	0.140	0.083	1.690	0.091
US production	0.577	0.270	2.140	0.033
Niche width	0.067	1.118	0.060	0.952
Crowding	0.005	0.014	0.390	0.693

Notes:
(1) Genre and year fixed effects are estimated but not reported.
(2) Venice nomination is omitted category.
(3) R-square: 0.336.

Berlin = *Total wins Venice*, and *Total wins Cannes* = *Total wins Venice*. The results suggest that none of the three hypotheses can be rejected. Thus, we conclude that there is no differential effect of the total number of prizes by festivals and reject our fourth hypothesis.

Discussion

From the perspective of our central claim, that film festivals configure product identities in the global film industry, the results of this study are overwhelmingly positive. Winning a prize significantly increases the size of the audience that goes to see a film. In fact, the coefficient indicates that for each prize won, the number of people that see a film increases by about 60 per cent more than the increase that comes with a US partner and almost twice as much as merely being *nominated* at Cannes, the most prestigious of the festivals. There is also significant evidence that these festivals contribute to a status ordering among films. The results indicated that films which are nominated at Cannes receive a much greater increase in audience interest than films that are nominated at Berlin or Venice. In addition, a status ordering among nominated films is created by various competitions. It is clear from our results that films that win a prize receive a significantly greater boost in audience than films that do not win one. A further status ordering is created even among the elite films that win prizes by differences in the prestige of the competitions. Our results show that films that win one of the best picture prizes experience a significantly greater increase in audience than films that win other prizes.

Of course, any empirical study has weaknesses, and ours is no exception. Relative to our desire to claim the importance of the film festivals as ICEs, the biggest weakness is that we studied only films that are nominated to one of the three leading European film festivals. In one sense, this weakness biases our results against the findings we were able to obtain: by examining only nominated films, we can only find effects from identity configuration at film festivals that differ across festivals, between winning and non-winning films, and among prizes of different types. Given that we were able to find effects, one would presume that they would be even more dramatic if we had included films that were not nominated to one of these festivals. In fact, a more telling gauge of the ICEs of nomination to a leading European premier festival would likely be revealed by including non-nominated films in the analysis.

One important extension of this work, therefore, would be to redo the analysis with a matched sample of non-nominated films to demonstrate the generalizability of our findings beyond a sample of films that were nominated.

The non-significance of the control variable to measure the sharpness of the identity of film products, the niche width measure, is also intriguing. As discussed above, perhaps this was the result of sampling only nominated films; future research with a sample that included non-nominated films would allow us to explore this explanation. Perhaps more importantly, a larger sample that more closely resembled the samples used in prior studies might find the negative effect of niche width films that are not entered in the festivals while verifying our finding of no niche width effects for films that are nominated to premier film festivals. Exploring how festival entry shields films from the penalties for not having familiar, narrow, focused identities would be interesting. Examining how broader identities that are less focused and less familiar might be informative in understanding how innovation can occur even in environments where identity pressures enforce conformity.

An interesting route for further exploration of this issue might be to explore the dimensions of uniqueness of film identities. Current studies assume that crossing genre boundaries is a uniformly bad idea from the perspective of creating film identities that will be received well by audiences. However, it is clear from the modern film industry that competition among similar films can reduce audience reception and that some unique films can transform audience perceptions. For example, comic westerns and romantic comedies both have had successes despite the prior clear definition of comedy, westerns and romance films. Exploring how this process has occurred among films nominated to elite European festivals might be a valuable first step in linking the strategic concept of differentiation with the ecological concept of identity. This would have significant potential for advancing our understanding of both strategic management and organization theory.

Notes

1. Other related ways of conceptualizing this phenomenon have been suggested by Appadurai (1986) with his term 'tournament of value', and by Anand and Watson (2004) by their term 'tournament rituals'. This volume includes several studies that examine how the values of products are configured at field-configuring events.

2. When we in the following use the concept film festivals we base our definition and data on the Federation Internationale des Associations de Producteurs de Films (FIAPF; the International Federation of Film Producers Associations).
3. See www.fiapf.org.
4. That is in US dollars and we have fixed effects by year.

References

Baumann, S. 2001. 'Intellectualization and art world development: film in the United States', *American Sociological Review* 66, 404–26.

Carroll, G. and Hannan, M. 2004. *The Demography of Corporations and Industries*. Princeton University Press.

FIAPF 2008. Accredited Festival Directory (L'Annuaire des Festivals Accrédités), www.fiapf.org (accessed 1 September).

Hannan, M. and Freeman, J. 1977. 'The population ecology of organizations', *American Journal of Sociology* 82:5, 929–64.

Hannan, M., Pólos, L. and Carroll, G. 2007. *Logics of Organization Theory: Audiences, Codes, and Ecologies*. Princeton University Press.

Hansen, B. E. 2009. *Econometrics*. University of Wisconsin Press.

Harbord, J. 2002. *Film Cultures*. London: Sage Publications.

Hsu, G. 2006. 'Jacks of all trades and masters of none: audiences' reactions to spanning genres in feature film production', *Administrative Science Quarterly* 51:3, 420–50.

Hsu, G. and Hannan, M. 2005. 'Identities, genres, and organizational forms', *Organization Science* 16:5, 474–90.

Hsu, G., Hannan, M. T. and Koçak, Ö. 2009. 'Multiple category memberships: an integrated theory and two empirical tests', *American Sociological Review* 74:1, 150–69.

Jacobsen, W. 2000. *50 Years International Filmfestspiele Berlin*. Berlin: Filmmuseum Berlin-Deutsche Kinematek and Nicolaische Verlagsbuchhandlung Beuermann GmbH.

Lampel, J. and Meyer, A. 2008. 'Field-configuring events as structuring mechanisms: how conferences, ceremonies, and trade shows constitute new technologies, industries, and markets', *Journal of Management Studies* 45:6, 1,025–35.

Mazdon, L. 2007. 'Transnational "French" cinema: the Cannes Film Festival', *Modern and Contemporary France* 15:1, 9–20.

Podolny, J., Stuart, T. and Hannan, M. 1996. 'Networks, knowledge, and niches: competition in the worldwide semiconductor industry, 1984–1991', *American Journal of Sociology* 102:3, 659–89.

de Valck, M. 2006. *Film Festivals. History and Theory of a European Phenomenon that Became a Global Network*. Unpublished PhD Dissertation, University of Amsterdam.

Turan, K. 2002. *Sundance to Sarajevo – Film Festivals and the World they Made*. Berkeley and Los Angeles, CA: University of California Press.

Zuckerman, E., Kim, T., Ukanwa, K. and von Rittmann, J. 2003. 'Robust identities or nonentities? Typecasting in the feature-film labor market', *American Journal of Sociology*, 108:5, 1,018–74.

8 Event institutionalization and maintenance: the Annecy animation festival 1960–2010

CHARLES-CLEMENS RÜLING

Over the years, I have watched the [Annecy] festival change and grow from a celebration of short independent animation into a big money marketplace where feature films are slowly but surely becoming the star of the show. Major deals are made at MIFA. At first I resented the changes but I have come to accept them. As an industry we do need one major event a year that is all about business. This allows other festivals to retain their character as celebrations of animation as a great form of art.

Denney-Phelps (2009)

This chapter addresses event institutionalization and maintenance in a study of the annual Annecy International Animation Film Festival and the International Animation Film Market (MIFA), a major event in the global animation industry. Since its creation in 1956, this event has evolved from a community-oriented gathering of artistically oriented animation film *auteurs* into a global event featuring aesthetic, techno-logical and business innovations, as well as into a platform for the discovery and recruitment of creative talent. The chapter seeks to high-light the processes that have led to event institutionalization and enabled institutional maintenance. In so doing, it responds to recent calls to study 'mechanisms that serve to prevent dissipation and even-tual deinstitutionalization' (Dacin and Dacin, 2008: 348).

Events which play a role in the configuration of organizational fields by providing arenas for processes of institutionalization and institutional change have recently been conceptualized as 'field-configuring events (FCEs)' (Lampel and Meyer, 2008). While there is growing empirical evidence that such events contribute to the emergence of field-wide institutions and provide institutional entrepreneurs with opportunities to challenge and redefine institutions, little is known about the processes by which such events themselves become institutionalized. A high degree of institutionalization characterizes many of the FCEs presented in the empirical literature, including the Grammy awards (Anand and Watson, 2004), the Booker Prize (Anand and Jones, 2008), the Olympic Games (Glynn, 2008) and the Salon in the nineteenth-century French art field (see Chapter 1 by Delacour and Leca in this volume) – all of which are strongly embedded in systems of norms and regulations, and largely taken for granted by actors within their respective fields.

In order to create a possibility of sustained field-configuring influence, FCEs need to become taken-for-granted moments within the life of organizational fields, and are required to maintain such a status over an extended period in order to prevent or counter functional, political and social deinstitutionalization pressures (Oliver, 1992). The institutionalization of any particular event is related to historical contingencies and industry characteristics (Wu *et al.*, 2003), but also to institutional entrepreneurship and strategic action (Delacour and Leca, 2007). It does not, however, remain stable over time, but tends to erode, so that even highly institutionalized events are not immune to deinstitutionalization (Oliver, 1992; Dacin and Dacin, 2008).

Several examples of the failure of highly central events in different industries suggest a complex interplay of economic, political and institutional forces in the deinstitutionalization of events. For example, in the case of the Leipzig Games Convention, which had held a dominant position as the world's second largest annual event in the video game industry before it had to be drastically rescaled in Spring 2009, deinstitutionalization was triggered by a shift in support of several important industry stakeholders in favour of a newly created rival event. An event's lack of resilience to economic downturn and weak overall community support played a decisive role, too, in the case of the Summer 2009 surprise cancellation of the Berlin Popkomm, one of the largest events in global music production, following a dramatic drop in the number of expected exhibitors.

This analysis of the Annecy event proposes four avenues along which to explore successful event institutionalization and maintenance. Firstly, event institutionalization occurs through several stages of historical development, in which events are related to community building, and community sustaining processes including ecological learning, attribution of status and economic transaction. Secondly, the institutional maintenance of events depends on their ability to manage critical transitions in the co-evolution of an event and its environment. Thirdly, the chapter suggests that symbolic-discursive institutional work plays a particularly important role in the institutional maintenance of events, in particular for events in the creative industries. Fourthly, institutional maintenance is related to an event's role in functioning as a boundary organization.

Theoretical background: FCEs and event roles

Trade fairs, festivals, awards and other forms of transorganizational structures (Anand and Watson, 2004) function as temporary clusters providing 'short-lived hotspots of intense knowledge exchange, network building and idea generation' (Maskell *et al.*, 2006: 997). As such, they have an important influence on the structural and cognitive evolution of organizational fields. FCEs assemble actors around issues, contribute to collective identity and sense making, provide arenas for setting norms and standards and determine positions and orders of value, or values, within a field (Lampel and Meyer, 2008).

FCEs play different roles within different phases of field development (Lampel and Meyer, 2008). During field emergence, they contribute to the creation of a common meaning system by defining standards, practices, vocabularies and positioning the field in relation to entities outside it. Garud (2008), for example, shows how conferences shape technological fields, not only through information exchange but by serving as an arena in which various propositions for technological solutions and standards compete with one other, and McInerney (2008) provides evidence of the role of events in the transformation of relatively loose networks into a cohesive field with an established institutional identity. In more mature fields, FCEs contribute to the replication of dominant field norms and logics, and to the protection and reinforcement of field identity. They function as intermediaries, which play an important role in field dynamics because they 'facilitate or broker exchanges, or [...] collect, organize and evaluate information so as to affect interaction among the "principals"' (Scott, 2010: 13).

Events like 'temporal clusters' (Maskell *et al.*, 2006; Bathelt and Schuldt, 2008) constitute transitory 'ecologies of learning' (Levitt and March, 1988) and play an important role in the creation of global 'knowledge pipelines' between permanent, spatially defined clusters (Maskell *et al.*, 2006). Enabling interfirm learning, they establish an 'ecology of information flows and different forms of interaction [creating] "global buzz"' (Bathelt and Schuldt, 2008: 853). Learning and knowledge exchange constitute communities through the emergence of shared frames of reference and a sense of identity among participants and stakeholders. Events thus serve as spaces of mediation, contributing to the emergence of knowledge through exchanges among participants. They function as 'liminal spaces' and provide border areas that enable interaction among sometimes antagonistic field constituents (Evans, 2007).

In situations of environmental jolts and institutional change, events further play an important role in actors' search processes by functioning as 'solution bazaars', where 'decision makers shop for appropriate solutions and entrepreneurs with solutions [. . .] sell themselves as the best alternative to decision makers' needs' (Sine and David, 2003: 188).

Events also function as tournaments of values, as discussed elsewhere in this volume. As such, they actively contribute to the definition, reproduction and questioning of orders of value within a given field. This they do by setting agendas, defining categories, operating selections, programming, appointing juries, and so on. Different kinds of values in the form of economic, social, symbolic and intellectual capital are attributed, acted upon and contested at events. Award ceremonies and competitions provide the most evident example of gatherings that are constructed around the attribution of values and the construction of status (Anand and Watson, 2004; Rao, 1994), but other forms of events which are less obviously geared towards status construction also serve as social spaces in which values are displayed and processed.

Finally, events provide opportunities for economic transaction. Serving as market places, they foster the interaction of buyers and sellers and provide an environment for economic co-operation. The opportunity to interact with a large number of economic agents reduces transaction costs, and the possibility to compare offers and propositions on the spot contributes to the emergence of a sense of both the adequacy of propositions and the overall developments and directions in which a field is heading. Different types of events – for example, specialized 'vertical' and broad 'horizontal' trade shows – respond to different categories of participants' objectives ranging from transactional (for instance, sales lead generation) to non-transactional goals (for instance, intelligence gathering) (Golapakrishna and Lilien, 1995; Kerin and Cron, 1987). The lower participants' immediate interest in economic transaction, the broader their product interest and the shorter an industry's technology life cycle, the more likely will be the formation of horizontal trade shows catering to that industry (Wu *et al.*, 2003).

The different event roles of community, tournament of values, market and their underlying processes, learning, status and economic transaction are interdependent. An actor's status, for example, orients processes of ecological learning and influences economic transaction. On the other hand, successful economic transactions contribute to the construction of status, and also trigger others' efforts at mimetic learning. Highly institutionalized events play all three roles for different groups of attendees. For example, at the Cannes International Film Festival discussed by Steve Mezias and his co-authors in Chapter 7, the construction of values via the official selection, film critics, jury decisions, and the 'buzz' generated around film makers, actors and films contribute to the market success of films on the adjacent market for distribution rights, and the festival's hierarchy among film critics, materialized in multiple categories and colours of press accreditations, sets overall trends in the coverage of specific films.

In summary, research on FCEs and related areas suggests a need to study how events relate to multiple constituencies, and how they play multiple interrelated roles for their various audiences over time. These issues are particularly important in situations of ongoing changes within an organizational field to which events need to adapt.

Event institutionalization and maintenance

An event, as a particular system of action, can be considered institutionalized when it is taken for granted among field actors, and when it orients actions within a particular field (Scott, 2008; Meyer and Rowan, 1977). This happens when an event structures field participants' interaction and production patterns over time as, for example, in the case of major film festivals, book fairs or academic conferences discussed here. Institutionalization occurs both through a process of gradual evolution over time as interaction patterns are repeated and shared understandings reinforced (Scott, 2010; Berger and Luckmann, 1967), as well as through 'political efforts of actors to accomplish their ends' (DiMaggio, 1988: 13).

Institutionalization, however, is not a stable state, as Delacour and Leca show in their discussion of the art salon, and even highly institutionalized arenas share a natural tendency towards entropy (Zucker, 1988). They therefore require ongoing work directed at institutional maintenance (Zilber, 2009; Lawrence and Suddaby, 2006). While processes of deinstitutionalization have received attention (Oliver, 1992; Dacin and Dacin, 2008), research focusing on institutional maintenance is still relatively scarce. Existing work mainly draws upon research claiming that 'even the most highly institutionalized technologies, structures, practices and rules require the active involvement of individuals and organizations in order to maintain them over time' (Lawrence and Suddaby, 2006: 217). Following this line of argument, Hirsch and Bermiss (2009), for example, analyse strategic decoupling as a strategy leading to the partial preservation of norms of central planning throughout a period of macro institutional change in the Czech Republic, and Zilber (2009) studies institutional maintenance in the travel of institutional stories across social levels.

Lawrence and Suddaby (2006) identify six categories of institutional work aimed at maintaining institutions. The first three categories sustain the regulative elements of institutions: 'enabling work' involves the creation of supportive rules, 'policing' ensures compliance, and 'deterring' establishes coercive barriers. The fourth category, 'valorizing and demonizing', is directed at preserving the normative bases of an institution, and the fifth and sixth categories, 'creating and sustaining institutional myths' and 'embedding the normative foundations of an institution into actors' routine practices' address the cultural-cognitive aspects of institutionalization.

In summary, the study of institutional maintenance should identify and finely analyse those categories of institutional work that can be observed in practice. In the study of events, all categories, regulative, normative and cultural-cognitive, may be salient, and a particular emphasis must be put on the paradoxical impediments of event maintenance sketched out above.

Case study: animation industry characteristics and the Annecy event[1]

The global animation industry is characterized by a multitude of different constituents ranging from animators, animation studios and production companies of all sizes, to multiple distribution channels, policy-makers on regional, national and EU levels, screen writers, licensing agents, animation schools, software and animation services providers and actors from adjacent fields who seek opportunities of convergence including, for example, mobile telecommunication companies. These actors cluster into relatively distinct spheres of creative/artistic work versus technology development versus the business side. Creative talent is often geographically mobile, and people who have been working together on one project go separate ways once the project is over. Finally, the relatively long business cycle from a first demo to a finished film or series demands that all parties involved meet regularly in order to advance their projects and negotiations. Over the past two decades, the entire sector has been marked by rapid technological change and subsequent changes of modes of project organization. Both creative talent and firms in the animation industry are often simultaneously embedded in spatial clusters and global production networks resulting in 'a spatially extended project ecology' (Cole, 2008: 908).

The Annecy festival and market takes place each year in early June in Annecy, a medium-sized city on the shore of Lake Annecy in the French Alps, about 50 kilometres south of Geneva and the Swiss border. The event presents itself as a long-standing showcase of 'the very best in animation', as 'the industry's leading international competitive festival' and as a 'world reference in animation' (www.annecy.org). In 2008, the event gathered 6,700 attendees representing 1,131 firms from 63 countries. A total of 500 films were screened, and 115,000 tickets issued during the festival week. The official selection included 284 films. Out of these, 219 were chosen by several independent juries from among 2,200 or so festival submissions competing in five categories: feature films, short films, commissioned and TV films, and graduation films. In addition to the competitive screenings, the festival also features retrospectives, exhibitions and public evening screenings on a giant screen by the lake. All professional categories in the animation industry are present at the festival.[2] The largest identified group of attendees is comprised of final year animation students and young graduates (approx. 1,800 attendees), followed by animation professionals, that is, mainly animators (approx. 800 attendees), producers (approx. 600 attendees), directors (approx. 500 attendees), animation faculty (approx. 300 attendees) and buyers (approx. 150 attendees).

The Annecy event hosts four distinct sections: (1) the festival competition, retrospectives and artistic programme; (2) the animation film market MIFA, which is dedicated to 'co-producing, buying, selling, financing and distributing animation content across all platforms' (www.annecy.org); (3) the 'Creative Focus', a section dedicated to projects, pitches and recruitment; and (4) a series of professional conferences on a variety of topics ranging from technical innovation to strategic and business issues.

The MIFA animation film market features firms directly situated in the animation value chain (producers, studios, distributors), but also includes providers of animation technology and adjacent services, educational institutions, public policy actors like, for example, the EU Media programme and other organizations representing national animation industries and markets.

The Creative Focus provides an 'exchange forum for animation professionals and young talents' (www.annecy.org), including project competitions and pitch meetings, roundtables, presentations and recruitment sessions for major international animation firms, as well as possibilities to meet a large number of representatives from smaller firms searching for talent and giving advice to young professionals.

Last but not least, the professional conferences aim at creating an 'opportunity to exchange ideas and information and reflect upon current technical, economic and artistic issues' (www.annecy.org) by sharing the experience of highly recognized international speakers.

According to the festival organizers and several independent sources (personal interviews with industry experts and press articles), the Annecy festival is seen by many industry professionals as an important event on the global animation industry agenda. It is the only major event worldwide that brings together participants from all groups of actors, including artistic creation, business and distribution, technology, education and public policy. Virtually all other international events tend to focus on particular groups of attendees like, for example, producers and distributors (MIPCOM: an international film and programme market for TV, video, cable and satellite), intellectual property (New York Licensing Show), TV animation for children (Kidscreen Summit), or computer animation technology (SIGGRAPH annual conferences).

Following Langley's (1999) suggestion of temporal bracketing, I distinguish three phases in the historical development of the event: (1) early development and institutionalization (1956–82); (2) growth, market creation and annualization (1983–2002); and (3) renewal, transaction and brokerage (2003–present).[3] These development phases have been identified through retrospective accounts in the research interviews and corroborated by documentary analysis (event archives and press). Each phase corresponds to a distinct logic of development and a particular set of roles the event plays within the animation field. The transition from one phase to the next typically coincides with a crisis in the event organization.

Early development and institutionalization: Annecy as a community event (1956–82)

The origins of today's event were laid out in Cannes in 1956, when a non-competitive animation week, organized during the Cannes Film Festival, featured more than 100 animated films (many of them classic masterpieces) from all around the world. Two years later, the second Cannes animation week brought together some of the most famous names in animation at that time: Jiri Trnka, Norman McLaren, Alexandre Alexeieff and John Hubley among others. For the third event in 1960, the organizers decided to leave Cannes and transfer the meeting to the city of Annecy. Research interviews and other retrospective sources concur in that both the organizers and the participants of the animation week did not feel comfortable in the 'glittery world' of the Cannes film festival, nor did animation receive the expected exposure there (Teninge, 2000: 74). Furthermore, highly favourable local policy-makers (seduced by the perspective of creating a major festival in Annecy) and a very active local cinema club, which had strong ties with the organizers of the Cannes animation week, created a context in which the organizers decided to move the event to Annecy.

The 1960 Annecy event was the first pure animation film festival ever. It brought together a group of artistically oriented 'auteurs' of animated short films and staged the creation of the Association Internationale du Film d'Animation (ASIFA), an international professional 'group of enthusiastic animation film-makers gathering together to share experiences, exchange information and try to come up with the formula that would promote the art of animation around the world' (Teninge, 2000: 75). From the beginning, ASIFA put a strong emphasis on East–West exchanges and developed a patronage system enabling the worldwide accreditation of animation film festivals. The permanent office of ASIFA was located in Annecy, and the Annecy festival rapidly became the main ASIFA event and host of its general assemblies. Over the first decade, the Annecy festival grew continuously in size and developed into the leading venue among several ASIFA accredited animation festivals in Mamaia, Cambridge and later Cardiff, Zagreb, Ottawa and

Hiroshima. Throughout the entire first phase of festival development, the permanent festival office responsible for all artistic decisions, programming and so on was located in Paris, whereas the local organization was in the hands of the Annecy cinema club. In the 1970s, the Annecy festival was attended every other year by 300–400 artistically oriented international animation film-makers coming to Annecy to exchange and to discover their latest works.

Significant environmental changes occurred in the early 1980s. During this period, privatization of television in many countries and the development of specialized children's channels created a strongly growing market for animated TV series. Selection criteria used by the Paris festival makers, which did not take the new developments into account, were increasingly criticized, and in 1982 two of the main festival stakeholders participating in the festival board, the French National Film Board and the Annecy municipal government pushed towards a separation from the historical organizers in Paris and the recruitment of a new festival director.

Growth, market creation and annualization: towards a showcase event (1983–2003)

Under its new festival director, Annecy moved from an event that defended artistic auteur animation towards showcasing the variety and innovativeness of global animation production including both artistic and commercial films. In retrospect, the 1983 festival board president commented on this decision as follows:

The Film Society and its members were still working as hard as they had always done and the organizers in Paris were still doing their job as well as ever. Yet it was the environment that was changing. I'm talking about audience expectations, the whole scale of production and distribution. The festival was running very smoothly but we were going round in circles. It was becoming a kind of stopgap or refuge for personal animation films and rather academic. It was missing out on the new developments in animation and new types of cinematography. New technology and the new economic situation were passing it by. Pierre Jacquier, quoted by Jean-Luc Xiberras, in Teninge (1997)

The 1983 event proved a milestone in the festival history and the beginning of a new era for the festival. It introduced a new festival director, a new management team, a new festival venue, the newly inaugurated Bonlieu culture centre and a pilot edition of the animation film market. The number of movie theatres had increased from one to six, allowing for a threefold increase of competition screenings together with a large number of tributes, retrospectives and exhibitions. Participation reached a new high of 1,300 accredited professionals. In a 1997 interview, the new festival director recalled the ideas he had held in the early 1980s for the future development of the event:

The idea ... was to integrate all animation techniques, including the much maligned new technologies, into the competition segment. We also began to work on the idea of a film market for an industry that didn't even exist at the time ... What happened at the time was that film-makers would come to Annecy and show their films, but everything stopped there. Jean-Luc Xiberras, in Teninge (1997: 17)

In the following years, competition categories multiplied: TV series, advertising and commissioned film categories entered the general competition in 1983. A specific feature film competition was created in 1985, and a special graduation film prize was created in 1995. The new overall strategy was to create a highly diverse and buoyant 'animation fiesta' (Teninge, 2000). These changes were in line with a strong agenda in early 1980s French cultural and industrial policy to build an internationally competitive French animation sector according to the 'plan image', a strategic plan devised by the French Ministry of Culture (after a 1983 national summit of the animation industry and public administration) in order to revitalize and to develop the French animation industry.

Another highly contested change during the second phase of event development was the decision to move from a biennale to an annual event in 1998. In a contemporary interview, the Annecy festival director outlined the rationale underlying this decision:

It is exactly what I have been trying to do since 1989! Animation has changed so radically since the festival was set up in the early 1960s, that it is simply inevitable. Thirty years ago, it took months, even years to make a short film lasting a few minutes. Nowadays, you can put out a new 13 x 13 minute TV series in just six months. The animation industry needs an annual gathering in Annecy, with an annual competition that can act as a showcase for the latest and greatest in this branch of seventh art. The festival and the market, like animated film-making and the economics of the industry, are inextricably linked. And the rendezvous is in Annecy. Jean-Luc Xiberras, in Teninge (1997: 19)

Other official arguments for creating an annual event included the need to hold the MIFA film market in an annual rhythm, the emergence of American and Asian competitors, the growing number of festival submissions (and thus a very high number of rejections), the need to develop sponsorship loyalty and to further professionalize the festival by ensuring the continuous work of a larger permanent staff – fifteen after the annualization, as opposed to four before.

The move towards an annual event was strongly criticized by parts of the French and international auteur animation community who argued that the Annecy decision would threaten other ASIFA accredited animation festivals that had been taking place in an alternating mode with Annecy. Several animation artists suggested boycotting Annecy, and ASIFA heavily criticized the unilateral decision of the Annecy board arguing that 'Annecy was breaking rules that it had asked ASIFA to set, at a time when Annecy feared competition from other mushrooming festivals, and without regard for the other festivals which had been partners for many years' (Teninge, 2000).

The definition of a convincing programme for the new annual festival and market proved to be a difficult challenge. Artistically oriented critics negatively highlighted the much shorter festival preparation period, the increasing weight of commercial aspects of the festival, and a weakening of the artistic side, the low quality of retrospectives and other festival content. The following comments by Michel Ciment, an influential French film critic, point to some of the problems involved in balancing artistic versus commercial agendas:

Sadly, this new edition hardly makes up for the indulgence of the past. This year, the world's largest animation film festival has been very disappointing . . . Even though MIFA has found its mark and proven its legitimacy, and even though the overall organization of the event was of excellent quality, the artistic dimension of the festival left a lot to be desired . . . (Let us simply express our irritation with the repeated projection at each session of an interminable and annoying clip presenting partners and sponsors.) Ciment (2000; translated by the author)

The event came under additional pressure with the economic downturn hitting the global animation industry in the aftermath of the burst of the Internet bubble and the events of 11 September 2001 in the US.

A significant decline in festival and MIFA attendance from 2001 to 2003 created a sense of crisis among both the festival organizers and major stakeholders, including the French National Film Board. After an external audit, it was decided by the festival board to mandate a new management to reorient the film market.

Renewal, transaction and brokerage: development into an industry event (2003–present)

Since its origins in 1983, the MIFA film market was mainly oriented towards informal encounters and the exchange of project ideas rather than towards co-production and distribution deals (as was the case in established 'pure' film and television markets like MIP-TV or MIPCOM, described in Chapter 6 by Havens). In the context of the 2001–3 crisis, the two alternatives discussed were either to turn around or to discontinue the Annecy film market. Notably the French National Film Board questioned the setup and the organization of MIFA. In Summer 2004, after three years of declining participation and growing pressure from both the National Film Board and the festival board, an external audit concurred with an internal survey of animation professionals: a large number of market participants felt that the market was lacking business opportunities, and few buyers attended MIFA because of a lack of emphasis on sales and transactions. Given the paucity of international buyers (typically representing TV channels), which had not been explicitly targeted in the traditional setup of the Annecy market, the market could not fulfil its function for producers and studios. This questioned the very existence of the Annecy MIFA in the eyes of the National Film Board that put pressure on the organizers to reorient the market part of the event.

The idea of a transaction-oriented reorientation of the market met with some initial inertia within the Annecy organization. According to the new market manager, it was difficult in 2004 and 2005 to gain acceptance within the festival organization for the idea that buyers should be invited to the event. The very idea of paying buyers' travel costs and accommodation was at odds with the widely held belief among the management team that scarce resources should be used only to pay for the travel and attendance of film-makers in the competition.

Another challenge in the context of MIFA renewal was to schedule and position the Annecy event as part of an implicit global 'animation industry event agenda' comprising the most important events during which economic actors meet and advance their collaborative projects. In other words, Annecy was positioned in a *network of fairs*, as discussed by Moeran and Strandgaard Pedersen in the Introduction to this book. In one of the research interviews, the MIFA managers explained the logic of this industry agenda:

The first meeting [for an international co-production] might have taken place in Annecy in June, the partners see each other again at the MIPCOM Junior in October, and eventually sign their project at another event ... We position ourselves on the international event agenda: CartoonForum, a European TV meeting, in September; MIPCOM Junior and MIPCOM in Cannes in October; Kidscreen Summit to meet the Americans in New York in February; CartoonMovie for European feature film pitches in March in Germany; and MIP-TV in Cannes in April. Then there are some regional markets, for example in Hong Kong, to meet the Asian studios that do not come to Cannes. You have to be on the agenda. (Interview with MIFA managers, 25 March 2008; translation by the author.)

Today, the MIFA and festival managers spend an important amount of time visiting other festivals and markets, and meeting studios, buyers, distributors, regional film organizations and so on in order to present the Annecy event, but also in order to sense the development of the industry, and to understand new trends and the evolution of potential market participants' needs and expectations:

There is a need to remain constantly in contact with the industry. For example, in September, we go to the CartoonForum. We do not at all negotiate for MIFA; we just go there and exchange. We listen carefully to understand the ongoing projects – who does what – we shake hands and build relationships. We do not sign any contracts, but it is important to be present in order to be part of the landscape. Those who consider coming to Annecy now have contacts. This is part of the change: being available to optimally respond to their needs. They now have someone to talk to. About the logistics in Annecy, but also beyond – you guys have been to Japan; we are looking for a studio there; do you have an idea whom we could contact? ... By meeting all the players, we know who can be interesting for someone else, and we know who is serious and trustworthy in the industry. (Interview as above.)

A further important instance in the current development phase was a modification of the event's governance structure with the 2006 creation of the *Cité de l'image en mouvement* (CITIA, city of moving images), an *établissement public de coopération culturelle* (public organization for cultural collaboration), which links the Annecy event with regional economic and cultural policy. CITIA is sponsored by the Annecy municipality, the Haute-Savoie department, the Rhône-Alpes region and the French national government. Its aim is to develop cultural, economic and training and research activities related to all aspects of moving images. One of the goals underlying the creation of CITIA was to leverage the festival organization's experience and reputation in order to favour economic development in the Annecy region. CITIA combines its different activities to complete the festival and market events with the idea of becoming a permanent actor in regional economic development.

The current director of CITIA is an experienced former animation producer who is recognized as an expert at the interface between art and business. He and other members of the Annecy event's management participate in panels and expert meetings on cultural policy and frequently act on the selection committees and juries of other animation events. The Annecy organization regularly shares its expertise and knowledge and participates in other events, but systematically refuses any kind of endorsement, labelling or co-inscription of films with other animation events in order to maintain its image of uniqueness.

One of the latest development trends of the Annecy event is to move from a showcase event to being a more active broker within the animation industry. A growing emphasis is put on project competitions, work in progress and the organization of TV and feature pitches around projects endorsed by the Annecy organizers. While the event has traditionally focused on finished work, the new strategy seeks to leverage industry knowledge gathered over the past four decades in order to play a more active brokerage role among field participants.

Project competitions provide a good example of this approach. Here, the Annecy organization selects highly promising projects in early stages and actively puts these projects in contact with other important industry actors. This more active role is in line with a field that is marked by rapid technological development, economic changes and the convergence of various industries (animated film, special effects, computer games, mobile telecommunication and so on). These tend to bring with them new actors who need to rely to some extent on brokers and knowledge hubs in order to find their way through the animation field.

CITIA and the new governance structure allow the festival organization to further professionalize and use both its expertise and its networks to stage other, more specialized events dealing with issues of interest to industry stakeholders. In January 2010, for example, CITIA organized a three-day conference for industry professionals on the issue of convergence between animation and video games. Another example of moving beyond the Annecy event is the development of New Animation Artists' Open World (NAAOW; www.naaow.org), an Internet-based collaborative space for creative talent in the animation industry, designed and managed by the CITIA team.

Over the fifty years since the initial Annecy meeting, the event has grown from a community oriented gathering of artistically oriented animation film-makers into an industry event, which seeks to bring together representatives from all over the global animation value chain, to provide an overview over the latest aesthetic, technological and business developments, to create opportunities for advancing the development of collaborative projects and business transactions, and to recognize a selection of outstanding animation across multiple competition categories.

Discussion: processes of event institutionalization

Institutionalization is sustained by regulative, normative and cultural-cognitive elements (Scott, 2008). Event institutionalization implies that an event becomes a taken-for-granted aspect of organizational life. As a consequence, institutionalization increases an event's stability and influence over time. On the other hand, because of multiple constituencies and conflicting logics involved in organization fields (Friedland and Alford, 1991), event institutionalization can never be complete, and events need to be sustained over time.

During the institutional history of the Annecy event, several moments reveal processes of event institutionalization. A key aspect is the initial role of the event in building and sustaining an international community of artistically oriented animation artists that is clearly separated from the world of live-action cinema and its ritual gatherings, symbolized by the Cannes Film Festival. In the 1960s cold war context, the Annecy event provided opportunities for personal encounters between East and West European animation artists who were unable to meet one another otherwise and who discovered one another's recent work largely at this event. The creation, in strong relationship with Annecy, of ASIFA and the organization of a series of ASIFA accredited film festivals further consolidated the notion that Annecy was at the centre of an emerging animation art world.

The Annecy event plays a role for status construction within the emerging field of artistic animation on two levels. First, being selected for participation in the event is a sign of distinction and acts as a signal that one is part of a distinctive group; and second, the attribution of a prize for the best film presented creates from the very beginning of the festival an additional layer of distinction and artistic (or appreciative) value. Right up to the present day, participating in the official selection represents a very important recognition for animation film-makers. The existence of an independent professional selection jury (see the discussion below), and the rejection of about 90 per cent of all festival submissions, create a sense of personal accomplishment among the selected artists. The notion of distinction is even stronger because short animation films are only very rarely distributed and screened in front of larger audiences. Being selected for the Annecy competition, therefore, provides film-makers with an opportunity to gain visibility by submitting their work to an audience of peers and industry experts.

Finally, the increasing transaction orientation on both the market and in project pitches and recruitment sessions at the 'Creative Focus' provides participants with a sense of participating in an event that might matter for them in both artistic and economic terms. And even though many of the actual transactions occur behind closed doors, the stands, press conferences and official announcements together with several series of more informal breakfast and lunch presentations provide a sense of ongoing business and currently successful animators, studios, formats, styles and so on.

In the recent development of the event, the community aspect has been put once again in the centre of event development. In line with its goal to develop a position as a more active player in the animation industry the Annecy organization itself seeks to become a more central actor in the international animation project, development and career networks. The event organizers' ability to attract multiple, diverse audiences makes it possible to constitute an 'arena for emergence', in which community based knowledge exchange and learning occur.

In conclusion, one could say that Annecy has developed from a strong emphasis on community ties and learning in the 1960s, before adding an emphasis on status in the 1970s and 1980s and on economic transaction since the 1990s. Today, all three event roles co-exist and reinforce each other.

Meta-organizations like ASIFA and strong stakeholders like the French National Film Board have further helped event institutionalization – the former by endorsing the central position of Annecy in the early stages of development; and the latter by providing financial resources, helping the event organization to manage critical transitions (see below) and as a powerful actor subsidizing large parts of the French animation field.

Finally, the relative success of the Annecy event in combining processes of community building and learning with status construction and economic transaction also points to some characteristics of creative industry events in general. While trade fairs have been historically prominent in most areas of economic activity, the emergence of festivals and awards is closely related to specificities of creative industries. High fragmentation, market uncertainty and the importance of the evolution of collective taste, on the one hand, and an emphasis on individual creation, authorship and innovation, on the other, create a demand for temporary spaces of encounter and proximity among industry actors. Within the creative industries, events serve as platforms for collective learning that enable actors to construct and share a sense of the directions of aesthetic and economic evolution. Moreover, creative industry events help reduce uncertainty by attributing value and constructing status within and across areas of creative activity. Through high peer and media exposure they provide privileged entry points for new industry actors as well as a meeting point for friends and colleagues, while they serve at the same time as a means for the reproduction of existing structures of rank and value.

Managing critical transitions

A characteristic of the Annecy event organization is its ability to manage critical transitions to match changes in its environment and to overcome potential deinstitutionalization pressures resulting from misalignment (Oliver, 1992). At several crucial moments, the Annecy event has been able to adapt by redefining its roles within the field and by implementing necessary internal changes in order to keep the event alive. The ability of an organization in charge of an event to develop arrangements that support and enable such change processes (Scott, 2010) provides a major source of institutional maintenance.

Four critical transitions are sketched out in the case study above. The first concerns the decision to move the event from Cannes to Annecy; the second relates to the 1982 relocation of the festival office from Paris to Annecy and the decision to open the festival to the strongly developing genre of TV animation; the third involves the move from a biennial to an annual event in the late 1990s; and the fourth transition occurs around the redefinition of the MIFA in 2004, and is in line with current attempts to move beyond the logic of the 1990s showcase event towards playing a more active role within the animation industry. In all these transitions, the Annecy organization has been able to redefine parts of the event, sometimes against strong public protest and resistance from its prior constituents. Major transitions – for example from social movements into more institutionalized situations ('from the "streets" to the "suites"') – carry with them risks and pitfalls related to different institutional logics and repertoires of action (Scott, 2010: 16). The key question, therefore, is how an event organization manages to design and survive these transitions, all of which (with the exception of the initial move towards Annecy) have involved strong stakeholder pressure (mainly from the French National Film Board) in order to overcome resistance within the existing festival organization and in parts of its audiences.

Another key to event maintenance despite environmental and stakeholder pressures to change can be related to the distinction between core and ancillary aspects of the event (Dacin and Dacin, 2008). From its very beginnings, Annecy's *raison d'être* had been to provide a platform for community building, knowledge exchange and learning and status attribution in relation to high quality animation. By framing the growing TV market of the early 1980s in terms of 'new developments in animation and new types of cinematography' (see the quote from P. Jacquier above), the event could remain loyal to its tradition as a venue dedicated to seeing new things. The institution of independent selection juries – in contradiction with the dominant film festival tradition of relying on a selection by the festival's programmers – further allows the festival to maintain its claim to present high quality animation and shields the festival organizers from possible conflicts of interest and questioning of the selection.

Next to Annecy's ability to manage critical transitions, the history of the event outlined here, the event's positioning as a non-partial platform for engaged exchange around new forms and developments in animation, which is potentially open to even highly peripheral contributions, also allow for continuous flow of micro-transitions by which the event adapts to changing forms and contents of global animation production.

Identity and symbolic-discursive maintenance

Two categories of institutional maintenance work need to be distinguished. The first is concerned with rules and focuses on disciplinary acts in order to secure the regulative and normative foundations of institutions, while the second is concerned with symbols and is directed at 'making sense of the institutional order and reproducing its values and meaning' (Zilber, 2009: 207) in order to maintain the cultural-cognitive elements underlying institutionalization. This distinction strongly resonates with Hirsch's (1997) view of the importance of taken-for-grantedness for institutionalization, and the argument that regulative and normative elements should be considered as pressures on the way to cognitive institutionalization (Phillips and Malhotra, 2008).

Symbolic-discursive maintenance plays a particular role in the Annecy case insofar as cultural organizations tend to be symbol-intensive and to rely heavily on discourse. The discourses sustaining cultural industries are 'multiple, overlapping, and contested' and tend to occur in complex combinations (Lawrence and Phillips, 2002: 439). Discourses visible in the Annecy case study refer to art versus business, tradition versus innovation, and to divergence versus convergence of participants' interests. The dominant organizational discourses addressing these issues in the case seek to integrate these tensions by emphasizing the notion of the 'animation family' and the idea that the identity (and therefore the tradition) of the Annecy event is strongly related to innovation.

Part of the construction of a particular 'Annecy feeling' is the regularly used notion of the 'animation family'. Being the only major industry event, which seeks to bring together actors from the business, technological, creative and policy sides, Annecy constructs itself as a place where the entire animation family, with all its different members, meets. From a critical perspective, one could argue that the family metaphor is strategically used in order to downplay power and status differences among participants. However, many participants interviewed during the 2008 and 2009 Annecy weeks stressed the wide variety of participants and things to see and discuss, and the interest they took in facing up to parts of the field they did not know well before.

In Chapter 1, by Delacour and Leca, we see that deinstitutionalization of the Salon occurs as a result of its inability to embrace innovative propositions. In the Annecy case, the situation is practically the opposite: since its 1983 reorientation, the event has claimed that it serves as a platform for the presentation of high quality animation, independently of the technology, aesthetics, style, medium, narrative approach and so on used for a particular film. This identity related to the selection process and to the social processes enabled by the event – as opposed to an identity that is narrowly tied into particular forms, contents or aesthetics – constitutes an important aspect of event maintenance.

Several other aspects of the event contribute to Annecy's identity as the animation 'family meeting'. Next to the non-competitive curatorial sections including retrospectives, special programmes, conferences, open breakfast and lunch discussions with film-makers, competitions and other formally scheduled events, numerous social events and parties take place that are not formally organized by the Annecy organization (and which resemble the activities of some participants in the television markets discussed by Havens in Chapter 6). The last couple of years have seen first instances of an emerging off-scene including, for the 2010 event, the projection of rejected submissions in the festival's history, which contributes to constructing a specific 'Annecy feeling'.

The family metaphor and the encouragement of a partial appropriation of the Annecy event by the off-festival events represent an instance of cultural-cognitive institutional work (Lawrence and Suddaby, 2006), which is oriented towards creating and sustaining institutional myths, and towards enabling practices of encounters that reinforce the normative construct of an 'animation family'.

Field-level position as a boundary organization

The two final aspects of event institutionalization and maintenance in the Annecy case concern, firstly, the event's position as a form of 'boundary organization' (O'Mahoney and Bechky, 2008), and secondly, the way in which the Annecy event has been able to position and maintain itself on the implicit industry event agenda.

Boundary organizations 'perform tasks that are useful to both sides and involve people from ... communities in their work but play a distinctive role that would be difficult or impossible for organizations in either community to play' (Guston, 2001: 403, quoted in O'Mahoney and Bechky, 2008: 426). They enable links and collaboration between actors that are embedded in environments characterized by different institutional logics. By functioning as boundary organizations, events act as intermediaries and play an important role in stabilizing organizational fields (Scott, 2010), while at the same time, as 'liminal spaces' (Evans, 2007), enabling the emergence of novel constellations of actors. Development and brokerage of network ties and knowledge play an increasingly important role as the animation industry faces rapid aesthetic, technological and economic change and attracts large numbers of new actors. In this situation, Annecy serves as a platform on which different actors can meet and cross – something that normally does not take place at more specialized events oriented exclusively towards economic transactions or technology development.

An important aspect in event institutionalization that is not explicitly addressed in the existing literature on FCEs concerns the position of an event within an overall industry event circuit. While a more detailed analysis of this industry event circuit lies beyond the scope of this paper, it should be noted that the event organizers devote substantial energy to positioning the Annecy event in relation to other events within the animation field. This positioning work involves finding a balance between the use of common, recognized formats (competitions, pitches, conferences and so on), and an emphasis on the specificities of the Annecy festival and market. Annecy seeks to maintain a particular position on the animation industry's 'event agenda' by distinguishing itself from both 'pure' festivals and markets. Relational work and network building with other industry events and festivals, together with a strategy of leveraging industry knowledge, play a further role in helping the Annecy festival and market to maintain and reinforce its position.

Conclusion

This chapter has presented a historical analysis of a major festival and market event in the global animation industry with the goal of discussing institutionalization and maintenance of FCEs. The literature review has brought together existing research on FCEs with a broader consideration of event roles of community based learning, status attribution and economic transaction, and with work on institutionalization, institutional maintenance and deinstitutionalization pressures. The Annecy case study has retraced the development of the festival and market from its origins as a community event towards a global animation marketplace and recent efforts by the event management to leverage the organization's industry experience in order to play a more active role in the animation industry. The discussion section has proposed that we explore the case study in four directions: processes of event institutionalization involving the development of multiple event roles, the event's ability to manage both large-scale critical transitions as well as a continuous flow of micro transitions, strategies of identity and symbolic-discursive maintenance and the position of both the event and the event organization as a boundary organization linking multiple actors and distinct subfields across the global animation industry.

Beyond the concrete discussion of case evidence presented above, this study suggests that we need to develop further our understanding of the multiplicity of partially overlapping organizational fields, and the role of those actors and organizations that serve as intermediaries among multiple groups of actors. A particular emphasis should be put on understanding the emergence and institutionalization of series or 'circuits' of events, which contribute to structuring a field over time. Such an analysis could significantly contribute to the study of the emergence of project firms and 'global knowledge pipelines' (Maskell *et al.*, 2006).

Furthermore, our understanding of institutional maintenance would be advanced by future research engaged in both more fine-grained analysis of local micro-routines and processes that contribute to institutional maintenance, and in developing a better understanding of symbolic-discursive maintenance spanning multiple constituencies. Last, but not least, I have at several points in this chapter referred to specificities of FCEs in the creative industries, but I still feel that we need more systematic comparative studies in order to better understand the specificities of institutional processes at the interfaces between art and business.

Notes

1. The case study presented here is based on fieldwork carried out between Spring 2008 and Summer 2010. The research approach was exploratory, with an initial emphasis on understanding the specificities of the event, its historical development and the role the event plays within the global animation industry. Formal research interviews were carried out with all key actors involved in the management of the event. Participant

observation and informal interviewing of festival attendees, exhibitors and staff took place during June 2008 and 2009 festival weeks. Documentary analysis included all festival-related publications and programmes since 1956 from the festival archive and additional documents from trade journals, internet discussion groups and the French National Film Board. Interpretations concerning the historical development and management practices were on several occasions discussed with key informants and industry experts.

2. Attendance statistics for 2008 according to professional categories have been provided by the Annecy organizers and rely on festival registration data.

3. See Rüling (2009) for a more detailed historical account of the Annecy event.

References

Anand, N. and Jones, B. 2008. 'Tournament rituals, category dynamics, and field configuration: the case of the Booker Prize', *Journal of Management Studies* 45:6, 1,036–60.

Anand, N. and Watson, M. 2004. 'Tournament rituals in the evolution of fields: the case of the Grammy Awards', *Academy of Management Journal* 47, 59–80.

Bathelt, H. and Schuldt, N. 2008. 'Between luminaires and meat grinders: international trade fairs as temporary clusters', *Regional Studies* 42:6, 853–68.

Berger, P. L. and Luckmann, T. 1967. *The Social Construction of Reality*. New York: Doubleday.

Ciment, G. 2000. 'Le festival de film d'animation d'Annecy 2000', *Positif* 480 (http://gciment.free.fr/cafestivalsannecy2000.htm, downloaded 12 May 2008).

Cole, A. 2008. 'Distant neighbors: the new geography of animated film production in Europe', *Regional Studies* 42:6, 891–904.

Dacin, T. M. and Dacin, P. A. 2008. 'Traditions as institutionalized practice: implications for deinstitutionalization', in R. Greenwood, C. Oliver, K. Sahlin and R. Suddaby (eds.), *Handbook of Organizational Institutionalism*. London: Sage, pp. 327–51.

Delacour, H. and Leca, B. 2007. *The Deinstitutionalization of an FCE at the End of the 19th Century in the French Art Field*. Paper presented at the Academy of Management Annual Meeting, Philadelphia.

Denney-Phelps, N. 2009. 'Annecy 2009: life on the animation Riviera', *Animation World Magazine*, 7 July.

DiMaggio, P. 1988. 'Interest and agency in institutional theory', in L. G. Zucker (ed.), *Institutional Patterns and Organizations: Culture and Environment*. Cambridge, MA: Ballinger, p. 3–21.

Evans, O. 2007. 'Border exchanges: the role of the European film festival', *Journal of Contemporary European Studies* 15:1, 23–33.

Friedland, R. and Alford, R. 1991. 'Bringing society back in: symbols, practices, and institutional contradictions', in W. W. Powell and P. DiMaggio (eds.), *The New Institutionalism in Organizational Analysis*. University of Chicago Press, pp. 223–62.

Garud, R. 2008. 'Conferences as venues for the configuration of emerging organizational fields: the case of cochlear implants', *Journal of Management Studies* 45:6, 1,061–88.

Glynn, M. A. 2008. 'Configuring the field of play: how hosting the Olympic Games impacts civic community', *Journal of Management Studies* 45:6, 1,117–46.

Golapakrishna, S. and Lilien, G. L. 1995. 'A three stage model of industrial trade show performance', *Marketing Science* 14, 22–42.

Guston, D. H. 2001. 'Boundary organizations in environmental policy and science: an introduction', *Science, Technology and Human Values* 26, 399–408.

Hirsch, P. M. 1997. 'Sociology without social structure: neo-institutional theory meets brave new word', *American Journal of Sociology* 102, 1,702–23.

Hirsch, P. M. and Bermiss, Y. S. 2009. 'Institutional "dirty" work: preserving institutions through strategic decoupling', in T. B. Lawrence, R. Suddaby and B. Leca (eds.), *Institutional Work: Actors and Agency in Institutional Studies of Organizations*. Cambridge University Press, pp. 262–83.

Kerin, R. and Cron, W. L. 1987. 'Assessing trade show functions and performance: an exploratory study', *Journal of Marketing* 51, 87–94.

Lampel, J. and Meyer, A. D. 2008. 'Guest editors' introduction – field configuring events as structuring mechanisms: how conferences, ceremonies and trade shows constitute new technologies, industries and markets', *Journal of Management Studies* 45:6, 1,025–35.

Langley, A. 1999. 'Strategies for theorizing from process data', *Academy of Management Review* 24:4, 691–710.

Lawrence, T. B. and Phillips, N. 2002. 'Understanding cultural industries', *Journal of Management Inquiry* 11:4, 430–41.

Lawrence, T. B., and Suddaby, R. 2006. 'Institutions and institutional work', in S. R. Clegg, C. Hardy, T. B. Lawrence and W. R. Nord (eds.), *Handbook of Organization Studies*. Second edition. London: Sage, pp. 215–54.

Levitt, B. and March, J. G. 1988. 'Organizational learning', *Annual Review of Sociology* 14, 319–40.

Maskell, P., Bathelt, H. and Malmberg, A. 2006. 'Building global knowledge pipelines: the role of temporary clusters', *European Planning Studies* 14:8, 997–1,013.

McInerney, P.-B. 2008. 'Showdown at Kykuit: field-configuring events as loci for conventionalizing accounts', *Journal of Management Studies* 45:6, 1,089–116.

Meyer, J. W. and Rowan, B. 1977. 'Institutionalized organizations: formal structure as myth and ceremony', *American Journal of Sociology* 83, 340–63.

Oliver, C. 1992. 'The antecedents of deinstitutionalization', *Organization Studies* 13, 563–88.

O'Mahoney, S. and Bechky, B. A. 2008. 'Boundary organizations: enabling collaboration among unexpected allies', *Administrative Science Quarterly* 53, 422–59.

Phillips, N. and Malhotra, N. 2008. 'Taking social construction seriously: extending the discursive approach in institutional theory', in R. Greenwood, C. Oliver, K. Sahlin and R. Suddaby (eds.), *Handbook of Organizational Institutionalism*. London: Sage, 702–20.

Rao, H. 1994. 'The social construction of reputation: certification contests, legitimation, and the survival of organizations in the American automobile industry: 1895–1912', *Strategic Management Journal* 15, 29–44.

Rüling, C. 2009. 'Festivals as field-configuring events: the Annecy International Animated Film Festival and Market', in D. Iordanova and R. Rhyne (eds.), *Film Festival Yearbook 1: The Festival Circuit*. London: Wallflower Press.

Scott, W. R. 2008. *Institutions and Organizations: Ideas and Interests*. Third edition. London: Sage.

  2010. 'Reflections: the past and future of research on institutions and institutional change', *Journal of Change Management* 10:1, 5–21.

Sine, W. D. and David, R. J. 2003. 'Environmental jolts, institutional change, and the creation of entrepreneurial opportunity in the US electric power industry', *Research Policy* 32, 185–207.

Teninge, A. 1997. 'Rendezvous in Annecy: an interview with Jean-Luc Xiberras', *Animation World Magazine* 1:10, 16–19.

  2000. 'The Annecy story: 40 years of celebrating the art of animation', *Animation World Magazine* 5:4, 74–9.

Wu, J., Dasgupta, A. and Lilien, G. L. 2003. *An Empirical Study of Trade Show Formation and Diversity*. ISBM Report no. 4–2003. Institute for the Study of Business Markets, University Park, PA: Pennsylvania State University.

Zilber, T. B. 2009. 'Institutional maintenance as narrative acts', in T. B. Lawrence, R. Suddaby and B. Leca (eds.), *Institutional Work: Actors and Agency in Institutional Studies of Organizations*. Cambridge University Press, pp. 205–35.

    1988. 'Where do institutional patterns come from? Organizations as actors in social systems', in Zucker, L. G. (ed.), *Institutional Patterns and Organizations: Culture and Environment*: Cambridge, MA: Ballinger, pp. 23–52.

9 | Tradition and transformation at the Fan Fair festival

JENNIFER C. LENA*

Fairs and festivals provide a context for the reenactment of institutional arrangements and the negotiation of values within institutional and geographic fields. These arrangements include the spatial and temporal ordering of events, financial management, the provision of lodging, food and entertainment and safety and crowd control, among others. The values participants negotiate are plural and cultural and include material/technical, situational, appreciative and functional aspects of the event. The value orientations of participants rationalize, organize and motivate institutional arrangements, and, in turn, these arrangements reinforce the symbolic meanings that position participants in a relational system (Glynn, 2008: 1,118).

At some festivals and fairs, new relational and symbolic arrangements emerge from the confluence of participants, and therefore have significance for the institutional fields in which they are located. These events can be viewed as tournament rituals, or 'complex periodic events' that 'occur in special times and places' and whose 'forms and outcomes are always consequential for the more mundane realities of power and value in ordinary life' (Appadurai, 1986: 21). According to Durkheim (1965), rituals express and reinforce the cognitive categories that unite communities; tournament rituals serve this purpose within organizational fields (Anand and Jones, 2008: 1,038; see also Chapter 13 by Anand in this volume). Tournament rituals can be found in a variety of contexts, including high art productions (Barbato and Mio, 2007; Evans, 2007; Tang, 2007), sports (Glynn, 2008) and industry events (Havens, 2003; Anand and Watson, 2004; Harrington and Bielby, 2005). Indeed, scholars increasingly address tournaments of value as 'field-configuring events' (FCEs) (Lampel and Meyer, 2008) since they often lead to changing conditions in organizational fields (Anand and Jones, 2008).

In this chapter, I examine the Fan Fair festival in 2001 as an FCE within country music. Fan Fair is an annual country music industry festival that brings together fans, musicians, record labels, broadcast media, advertisers, city officials, business leaders and residents in Nashville, Tennessee. The Country Music Association (CMA), a trade organization formed in 1958 to promote the musical genre, sponsors the festival. Indeed, the official name of the festival is the Country Music Association Festival, or CMA Fest. It has run continuously since 1972 and attracted 191,000 attendees in 2007, making it the longest-running and biggest country music festival in the world.[1]

Festivals like Fan Fair have the potential to create or rearrange symbolic and relational systems in fundamental ways. Importantly, these changes include the symbolic character and traditions that generate the 'look and feel' of the festival (Glynn, 2008). In 2001, the festival was relocated from a fairground outside downtown Nashville to the heart of the downtown tourist corridor. In this chapter, I explore this transition in the spatial location of the festival as an FCE, insofar as it was a moment when festival constituencies crystallized their values through commodity exchange, forged new and collective cognitive categories, and impacted the evolution of the country music field.

The research question framing this study is: 'how – and to what extent – did the festival's physical relocation change symbolic and economic configurations?' The argument proceeds as follows. After introducing the data upon which this project relies, I provide a brief narrative of the festival's history. As I relate, the decision to move the festival from the State Fairgrounds to downtown Nashville was occasioned by a decision in the Mayor's office to rebrand the city and advertise the festival as its 'signature event'. The move had consequences for the scheduling of the festival, including its expansion into more spaces, with more scheduled events and a larger audience. These changing institutional arrangements put pressure on organizers to use more corporate sponsors, who transformed vacant or unmarked spaces into commercial 'zones' for festival activity. These transformations reflect shifting values within the downtown heritage space, and reveal the importance of an emerging (younger and female, middle-class) consumer for country music. The aesthetic tastes of these consumers also drove changes to booking practices at the festival, and I explore this shift in the final section of analysis. I argue that these shifting arrangements and values make the 2001 Fan Fair festival a tournament ritual that had consequences for the city, festival organizers and fans.

Data

This study is based on two summers of fieldwork at the festival, interviews and document analysis by a team of four researchers. The research team logged over 200 hours of participant observation, including all ten festival days in 2006 and 2007, and preliminary research at local music venues and in businesses located within the festival grounds. The present argument relies on 104 formal interviews with municipal and industry leaders, festival organizers, city residents and tourists, completed over the two years, and a material database of artefacts and archival material on the festival.

In 2006, we completed seventeen formal interviews with record label executives and artist representatives, employees at the Country Music Association, the Convention and Visitor's Bureau (CVB), the Mayor's office, the booking agency for the festival and the Convention Center (see Appendix 9.1). The participants were identified through snowball sampling starting with an initial contact who was formerly a record label owner, songwriter and employee of the Country Music Hall of Fame. These formal interviews ranged from twenty minutes to two hours in length. The interview script includes a work and personal history, respondents' memories of and experience with the festival and a series of questions that specifically target their work as it relates to the festival. We also queried subjects concerning a variety of debates central to the festival's history including the relocation of the festival in 2001, its designation as the 'signature event' of Nashville and the dramatic increase in the number of corporate sponsors invited to participate. In the text, the names of all interview subjects have been changed to pseudonyms and their occupational status and titles are stated in such a way as to preserve their anonymity while retaining as much specificity as possible.

In addition to interview and observational data, I created a database of material artefacts including over 200 photographs from the two festival years, biographies and autobiographies of high-visibility respondents, and news articles in the national, local and specialty press, including all CMA 'Close-Up' articles on Fan Fair/CMA Festival from 1973 to 2006.

The end result of the varied data collection efforts has been to provide a social ecology of the festival, one that accounts for the perspectives of city officials, citizens, artists and music industry workers and country

music fans. These data allow me to examine patterns in how participants define the purpose and significance of the festival, to themselves,
the city and the music community.

The transformation of Fan Fair

Country music (or country and western) is a blend of popular musical
forms originally found in the southern US and the Appalachian
Mountains. It has roots in traditional folk, gospel and Celtic music
and evolved rapidly in the 1920s (Peterson, 1997). Originally called
'hillbilly music', the derogatory name was replaced by 'country music'
in the 1940s. Two of the top-selling solo artists of all time, Elvis Presley
(known in his early years as the 'Hillbilly Cat' and featured on the radio
programme *Louisiana Hayride*) and Garth Brooks, are country artists.
The Recording Industry Association of America (RIAA) reported that
country music sales represented 11.9 per cent of the US market in 2008,
making it the second most popular genre after rock (RIAA, 2008).
Country music is now the dominant radio format in the US, with a 42
per cent share of the total market of radio listeners (Haslam, 1999: 293).
This growth is relatively recent: Cusic (1998: 204) reports that the
number of radio stations in the US devoted to country music rose
from 1,534 in 1980 to 2,427 in 1994. Arbitron, Inc. estimates that
77.3 million adults listen to country music radio every week. Four US
cable stations are devoted to the genre: Country Music Television
(CMT) and CMT Pure Country, Rural Free Delivery TV and General
Artist Corporation (GAC). Substantial country music fan scenes exist
across the globe, and major centres of production exist in Canada and
Australia.

The CMA Festival, known as Fan Fair, has its roots in the 'We Shield
Millions' (WSM) Radio Country and Western Disc Jockeys Association
convention. By the mid-1960s, the convention was overrun by hardcore
country fans 'crashing' the event, so the CMA and the Grand Ole Opry
(a well-known country music venue in Nashville) decided to stage a
festival. A board was established with members drawn from the major
and independent labels, the Mayor's office and the CMA. The first Fan
Fair, in 1972, included 5,000 fans, 100 artists, 11 record labels and 100
exhibitors in a four-day event held in downtown Nashville. Attendance
doubled the second year, to 10,000, and hovered around maximum
capacity – 15,000 – until 1981. Existing facilities were strained to the

breaking point, and Nashvillians had lost their patience for the yearly influx of tourists into downtown. In 1981, the festival board decided to move the festival from downtown Nashville to the Tennessee State Fairgrounds, about three miles southwest of the Metro Center (CMA Close-Up, Vol. XIV (6): 1, 4).

The Fairgrounds are a complex of corrugated tin buildings, animal stalls and an auto racetrack perched on a grassless hill in a mixed-use, immigrant neighbourhood. During Fan Fair, most fans lodged on-site, pitching tents or parking recreational vehicles (RVs) in the camp-grounds. Jason Pominville, a highly ranked employee of the CMA, described the Fairgrounds as 'pretty dilapidated' and 'sort of a Frankenstein's monster so far as a facility is concerned'. Looking at photos from the festival from the 1980s, the rural gestalt of both the environment and the visitors is pronounced. Nearly everyone wears country and western gear, and their bodies bear evidence of physical labour and hard living. Record label head Thomas Golisano said of the festival in those years:

It was very old in terms of the demos. It was very adult. I'd say 30s and 40s, and 30s I'm being very kind. So we were nowhere close to being an organized marketing branding machine. It was 'come on down and you can get close to a bunch of artists and sign autographs'.

The buildings that hosted exhibitors (including record companies, indi-vidual artists and their fan clubs) were air conditioned and comfortable in the morning, but because they were not air locked, they would heat up to over 100 degrees by mid-day. Fans complained and artists com-plained, but still the number of tourists, exhibitors and artists grew throughout the 1980s. By the end of the decade, festival organizers had to limit the number of tickets to 25,000 and the festival often sold out as early as February.

In addition to eleven 'label shows', performances included 'theme' shows, like Friday's Bluegrass showcase at the Opry, and a Reunion show of 'old timers' like Ernest Tubb and Roy Acuff, the 'highlight of Fan Fair' (CMA Close-Up, Vol XV: 2). Fan club booths played host to artist visits, when fans could get signatures on publicity photographs, programmes and scraps of paper and clothing. A panel of local bankers awarded cash prizes to the three most attractive and creative Fan Club booths. These booths and the intimate contact fans had with their favourite artists became the hallmark of the festival. Ticket holders followed a schedule in between shows: the Odessa (Texas) Chuck Wagon Gang catered lunch, and most attendees queued to get autographs during the afternoon break.

The festival outgrew the Fairgrounds space by the end of the 1980s, and the appointees on the Mayor's Blue Ribbon Panel strongly suggested that organizers move the festival to downtown Nashville. The city of Nashville offered the festival rent-free use of several of its new downtown facilities including a convention center, a large indoor stadium and the outdoor Riverfront Park. They saw the possibility of expanding the number of daily performances by constructing multiple stages in several locations. The Mayor's office offered to facilitate interaction with city departments involved in the staging of the event, including the provision of police for traffic and security.

The new location for the festival is commonly known as 'Lower Broad' and comprises a roughly 30-square block area from Demonbreun to Church Streets and from 9th Avenue to the Cumberland River. The businesses in this region include honky tonks, restaurants, strip clubs, discos, hotels and country and western clothing stores. All the festival's official events and the majority of Nashville's hospitality industry are located within this zone, accessible during the festival by free bus service provided by the festival organizers.[2]

By 2009, average daily attendance at the festival was 56,000. The festival is now a major revenue generator for the hospitality and entertainment industries in Nashville. According to Thomas Vaneck, a representative of the Convention and Visitors Bureau (CVB), it is 'the largest crowd for the longest period of time of any meeting or group in Nashville on an annual basis', and has brought in over $200 million worth of impact over the last several years. The CVB reported that direct consumer spending at the festival in 2008 was $22 million.[3] For the last several years, the CMA has donated a portion of festival proceeds into the Nashville public school system's music education programmes; funds amounted to over $3.3 million dollars between 2001 and 2009.[4]

The relocation of the festival encouraged the expression of particular (situational) values. The festival moved closer to heritage sites of country music, including the original site of the Grand Ole Opry and the historic honky tonks of Lower Broad. But the new space also offered cosmopolitan comforts, convenience and more profit for the city and private sector. In the following sections, I explore how the institutional arrangements of the festival 'reinforce the symbolic meanings that undergird' the festival community (Glynn, 2008: 1118), and how a city branding initiative influenced the 'look and feel' of the festival.

City values

In 2002, city leaders announced that Nashville would be branded 'Music City, USA'. This decision followed months of discussion within the Chamber of Commerce, city government and the CMA, and the completion of a global survey of perceptions of the town. Fan Fair organizers were asked to contribute to the effort by allowing the festival to be designated the city's 'signature event', and by moving it downtown to the tourist corridor of Lower Broad. Although this move angered some locals who preferred Nashville to be known as the 'Athens of the South', festival organizers saw the potential to expand ticket sales and profits and downtown business owners were eager to increase their potential profits. The Chamber of Commerce capitalized on the festival, using it as a business recruitment tool which one member, Henry Tallinder, claimed 'helped us to land a couple of new corporate headquarters'.

The 'urban branding' (Mommaas, 2002: 34) of Nashville as Music City, USA was a critical decision made by civic leaders. Nashville's rebranding was part of a policy movement towards using cultural communities to 'reaffirm [city] identity/ies; attract and retain their share of cultural industries (and tourists); join the 'competitive city' race and contribute to the design and adaptation of the public realm and consumption in urban society' (Evans, 2001: 14). While some cities turned to 'mega-events' like the Olympics (Glynn, 2008) or the revitalization of urban districts (Dovey and Sandercock, 2002), others relied on festivals, leading some scholars to describe these cities as 'festivalized' spaces (Häusermann and Siebel, 1993; Richards and Wilson, 2004; Quinn, 2005; Hitters, 2007; Richards, 2007; see also Tang's Chapter 3 on 'biennalization').

Festivalization is not without its critics, and Fan Fair's move downtown was not without controversy. Conflict around festivalization stems from the different values held by stakeholders. For example, while Palmer/Rae (2004: 136–7) reported that festivals nurture and reinvigorate local arts (thereby focusing on appreciative values), Dragon Klaic (2007: 203) argued that only modest economic (that is, commodity

exchange) benefits are felt. In Nashville, some downtown business owners complained that festival concessions competed for daytime receipts,
while others felt that the evening and year-round increase in business
outweighed the losses (Appendix 9.1: Pominville; Tallinder; Vanek).
According to those who study festivalization, the fear of elitism may
cause local politicians to 'pressure organizers – subtly or otherwise – to
open these events to the wider public', while elites may have 'a fear of the
"unwashed" taking over town centers' (Waterman, 1998: 68). Nashville
residents had complained for years about the 'dirty, drunk and horny'
tourists, and the move downtown only exacerbated tensions surrounding
the city's dismissal of Nashville's brand as the 'Athens of the South'
(Appendix 9.1: Afinogenov; Hecht; Miller; Pominville; Terry). Finally,
critics of festivalization argue that these events produce formulaic and
bland programming (Evans, 2001; Schuster, 2001; Richards, 2007) that
lacks authentic historical or spatial connections (Hannigan, 2002;
Quinn, 2005).[5]

The question of 'authentic history' is one I take up in the next section
of analysis. Rather than assuming that there is a single history to be told
about Nashville's downtown space, I treat its traditions like any other:
constantly changing as individuals contribute to it through their words
and deeds. In viewing the 2001 Fan Fair festival as a tournament ritual, I
emphasize that 'discourses and practices may undermine some long-
standing cultural meanings, stabilize and give new meanings to others
and subject other elements of local culture to transformative pressures'
(Gotham, 2007: 97). In this case, the creation of new festival spaces
reconfigured traditional places of country music heritage, and revealed
shifting power dynamics within the field of production.

The space of heritage

In 2001, Fan Fair organizers saw an opportunity to expand their profits
by moving the festival downtown. They sacrificed the outdoor, less
costly and more 'rural' environs of the Fairgrounds for an urban,
urbane location in the city centre. The relocation of the festival to
downtown Nashville transformed the 'old' built environment of
Lower Broad into a festivalized space, and produced new circuits of
movement and activity. Festival organizers and corporate sponsors
carved out new spaces of significance and renamed existing places.
These impacts on the built environment redefined a heritage space

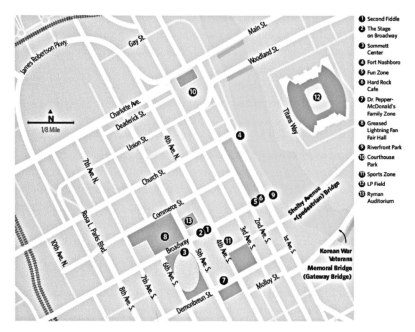

Figure 9.1 CMA festival map, 2009 (available at: www.blueshoenashville.com/cmafestmap.html; downloaded 7 February 2010). Official festival venues include sites 3, 5, 7, 8, 9, 10, 11 and 12

(Johnson, 1999; Light, 2000) for an emerging demographic of country music fans. Transformations within the festival space amount to transformations in notions of heritage.

When scheduling the 2001 festival, organizers decided to block off sections of Lower Broad, clearing the space for pedestrian use. Signs, traffic cones, jersey barriers, fences, police officers and security personnel established the boundaries of this space. Both the downtown businesses (united in an organization called the Downtown Business Partnership) and the festival organizers hired off-duty police officers to serve as roaming security for the space. They travelled on bike and Segway around the area, often stopping to help with medical emergencies, to answer questions and give directions (see Figure 9.1). The space might be conceptualized as a 'festival bubble' to draw a comparison with the 'tourist bubbles' Dennis Judd discovered in his work on urban centres. These core districts have a 'well-defined perimeter [that] separates the tourist space from the rest of the city' and are protected from 'crime, poverty and urban decay', producing spaces that are 'specialized areas ... established as virtual tourist reservations' (Judd, 1999: 36). At Fan Fair, we witnessed many occasions on which security officers, police officers and festival employees relocated homeless citizens outside the perimeter of the festival. Millions of dollars of profit can rest on the ability of the city to provide a safe, clean, problem-free zone for visitors (Figure 9.2).

Fan Fair organizers produced a boundary that differentiated 'country music space' from the rest of the city, and then marked out event areas within the festival environs. These were called 'zones', and in 2009 the six outdoor zones were located in three parks (outside the Hall of Fame, along the riverfront and in front of city hall), in a parking lot and on a blocked off section of Broadway. On a regular day, one might find downtown office workers and tourists eating lunch or relaxing on plastic benches within these parks. During the festival, the spaces are enclosed with fences and filled with tents, trailers, walking paths, restroom facilities, demonstration spaces, food stands and sales tables. Sponsors built concert stages, archery pitches and dog runs. They laid down turf, erected mobile buildings and installed security checkpoints. The largest sponsor of each zone was offered the opportunity to lend their name to the space. For example, the Crisco Family Zone was open to the public and offered music, games and instructional courses for children, while the Chevy Sports Zone was oriented towards the adult fan of professional football, outdoor sports, professional wrestling and National Association for Stock Car Auto Racing (NASCAR).[6]

It was often difficult to distinguish the built environment from the temporary structures associated with the festival. Local businesses including chain restaurants like the Hard Rock Café shared horizon space with the temporary structures and advertising for the festival (see Figure 9.3). These festival tents and RVs offered many of the same services and amenities as local businesses, including seats and respite from the heat in air-conditioned spaces. Visitors described these temporary structures in the same language as they did any other spaces within the festival zones: they were places to rendezvous with family, landmarks to use while orienting oneself, and businesses where you could obtain food, beverages, air conditioning and souvenirs.

Employees of local businesses including the 'Hooters Girls' circulated throughout the crowd, while festival sponsors sold beer and hot wings. Without a critical eye, the 'authentic' commerce of downtown Nashville was indistinguishable from that of the festival.

Figure 9.2 Lower Broadway during 2007 Fan Fair festival (photo: Jennifer C. Lena)

By renaming existing spaces; producing 'meaningful' spaces out of 'empty' ones, like parking lots and building structures within them, the festival and its corporate sponsors produced new spaces out of the old. These competed with Nashville businesses for tourist dollars and attention, and this competition was driven by fans' interest in the entertainment on offer. In the following section, I explore musical programming at the festival in some detail, since the move downtown marked an enormous transition in how audiences spent their time, and transited through this transformed heritage space.

From label to chart: festival booking

The move downtown necessitated the production of multiple, simultaneously operating performance spaces and new booking practices. The expansion of performance venues (from one to four stages) required that festival organizers dispense with a reliance on label rosters and heritage acts and transition to market-driven scheduling. Once festival-goers were forced to choose among competing stages, their tastes were rendered visible and directly influenced future booking decisions. The facilities downtown and changes in booking attracted an emerging

Figure 9.3 Downtown business partnership security officers observe Lower Broadway and the Chevy Sports Zone entrance, CMA Festival, 2006 (photo: Jennifer C. Lena)

audience segment composed of middle-class, white women, and this group increasingly defined the genre's core values.

For twenty-nine years (1972–2001), festival programming was segmented into four, daily 'label shows' punctuated irregularly by 'feature shows'. Fans could expect to see a range of acts representing the artist rosters of all the major and independent labels, in addition to feature shows of bluegrass artists, international artists and the like. Until 2001, slots in the schedule were allocated by CMA personnel and festival organizers in a meeting held with label executives months in advance. Labels were given free rein to decide which of their artists would perform within their spot, and in which order.

But the reduction in size of record label rosters and the expansion of performance facilities at the festival led organizers to replace this programming approach with a system whereby record sales determined artists' placement onto particular stages. In contrast to the 1970s and 1980s, when a label could fill a two-hour showcase with their top-performing artists, label head Golisano argued that 'today you don't have that many acts when you look around to do that. Capital [Records] on its own, you could put Keith Urban and Dierks Bentley in, and then what?' In the 1970s, any major label would have had a roster of between fifteen and twenty artists, while the biggest major now has only eight, according to Country Music Hall of Fame inductee Jochen Hecht.

Starting in 2001, the sub-contracted booking agency responsible for scheduling acts chose to prioritize recent chart performance over other determinants of value. In part, this decision was driven by a shift among fans, who 'don't buy labels, they buy artists', because modern labels have stopped building their brands, according to label head Golisano. Booking agent Joce Thibault explained that all performers on the daytime Riverfront stage had to have had a top 50 single on the Music Row Chart in the previous year or they would not be invited to perform. Paul Gaustad, country music photographer and Nashville celebrity said of the Riverfront stage, 'The hard part is getting on that big stage. Believe me, they fight for it. They really, really want to make it'. Correspondingly, fewer 'catalogue' artists, seasoned performers with membership in the canon of country music, perform at the festival. With respect to the now defunct bluegrass show, booking agent Thibault said:

We used to have a bluegrass show and the crowd would leave in droves, because it's not that people don't like bluegrass, but two hours of it? Bluegrass is really great at [Nashville clubs like] the Bluegrass Inn or the Station Inn or whatever, but people want to come down there, they want to see the stars, they want to hear the music they hear on the radio, stand in the photo line, not a bunch of bluegrass acts.

According to this eyewitness, festivalgoers left bluegrass performances – performances they would enjoy if they were held at other heritage sites – because they didn't reflect their tastes for festival programming. This is an enormously important observation: shifting audiences and tastes accompany shifting programming decisions, and these combine and redefine the festival's connection to its musical heritage.

The country music charts, on which Fan Fair booking began to depend, were dominated by highly produced pop- and rock-influenced songs, like that of American Idol winner Carrie Underwood. This style has earned the genre name, 'new country'. New country performers have few personal connections to rural or working-class lifestyles and instead make reference to middle-class experiences like college attend-ance. Mann (2008: 90) has argued that, 'these new stories reflect not only a profit-minded embrace of urban, middle-class listeners, but the flexibility of a fluid "used to" in the production and reproduction of the country music audience'.

As Mann (2008) suggests, fans of new country are young, wealthy and more likely to be women than men (Strauss, 2002). In the wake of the festival's transformation, organizers began to see changes in the characteristics of the typical Fan Fair attendee – now younger, wealthier and more likely female. According to Tennessean journalist Naomi Snyder, 'the average CMA fan is about thirty-six years old and female, but marketers say the more intense online advertising could attract an even younger demographic with lots of buying power over many more years'. Label owner Tom Golisano says his market research shows: 'it's very female-driven. I think the one thing we've seen over the last couple of years is the sex has shifted from 50/50 to 70/30 in terms of women'. Although former CMA employee and author Toni Lydman argued that this change is an instance of 'the eternal quest for this younger market and this younger audience', most industry experts claimed the trans-formation of the country market in the last twenty years is without precedent.

After 2001, audience members could choose among multiple per-formances at any given time of day (except the evening concerts), and because of this, their tastes were made visible. By shifting towards a competitive stage model, festival organizers rendered audience tastes relevant to booking. Since attendance at heritage events like the blue-grass show was small, these events did not survive the transition down-town in 2001. The relocation of the festival downtown reflected new aesthetic values, those held by a new sub-genre and an emerging audi-ence for country. The increased number of performance slots and the reduction of label rosters shifted festival arrangements from label-driven to market-driven festival booking. The emergent demographic of country consumers had enormous influence over festival practices, both because of their purchasing power and visible preferences. The decline of heritage acts at the festival and the rise of New Country was a direct consequence of the move downtown, and the shift towards a competitive stage model.

Brand alliances and the new country consumer

The move downtown and the expansion of the festival substantially raised the cost of production, and corporate sponsorship was intro-duced to cover these costs. Festival organizers recognized that Fan Fair 'cannot subsist on ticket sales alone because of the logistical require-ments of putting on something like this. It's far more than most people would imagine. The cost of putting it together' (Appendix 9.1: Pominville). The cultivation of particular sponsors reflects the values of Fan Fair attendees, and the value corporations see in brand alliances with country music and the New Country consumer. These values were facilitated by the move of the festival to downtown Nashville, in 2001.

   In 2007, at least fifty-five companies advertised during the festival, up from thirty-five in 2006, 'a sign that companies selling everything from peanut oil to energy drinks are increasingly attracted to the buying potential of tens of thousands of country music lovers' (Snyder, 2007). Jason Pominville, a long-time CMA executive, summarized the situa-tion as follows: 'we've had good fortune in that the event has been interesting to some of corporate America because not only the nature of the event: it's very safe, it's very family-friendly, it's very wholesome, so it fits the imagery for a lot of corporations, as opposed to some of their sponsorship endeavours in recent years that relate to music'. According to the CMA website:

'For CMA these brand alliances have been the backbone of our ability to extend the CMA Music Festival brand, new artist development, media interest, and ultimately increase our ticket sales,' said Tammy Genovese, CMA Chief Operating Officer. 'CMA has worked hard over the past decade to develop an internal organization that is a hybrid between an advertising agency, promotional agency, marketing consultant, PR agency, event production company – and you can add reference library to the mix,' Murray said. 'We provide partners with a wide range of services from grass-root event marketing to helping corporations develop marketing strategies that reach the Country Music fan – whether it be talking to existing customers or expanding to new consumers using the Country Music brand equity and fan base'.[7]

The CMA built a new internal organization, CMA Strategic Marketing, in order to facilitate the expansion of brand alliances required by the move downtown and increased costs. Festival organizers used audience surveys to capture the characteristics of the new country consumer, and provided those to potential sponsors. Organizational actors used their years of experience within the industry to help advertisers translate their brands into the festival context. For some corporate sponsors, this meant the use of images and language associated with country music (for example, hillbilly, down home, boondocks, good ole boys) on scrims and signs; dressing representatives in chequered shirts, jeans, cowboy hats and boots; and decorating spaces with picket fences, turf and corn stalks. For others, this meant emphasizing the urbane sophistication of their brand. ABC daytime television rented a large, indoor space and set up a mock living room, with a mid-century modern design including leatherette furniture and several flat screen televisions (see Figure 9.4). Rather than enforcing a rural gestalt on corporate advertisers, the CMA helped corporate sponsors employ effective hybrid symbols of country's traditions and values.

Within sponsors' spaces, the display of traditional gender norms was striking. For example, Gillette Venus Breeze offered free makeup and shaving consultations for women in a simulated hair salon, decorated entirely in bubblegum pink. In the Chevy Sports Zone, male visitors dominated the space, due to the presence of The Sportsman Channel, NASCAR Busch Series, Hunter Safety System, Mossy Oak, Cutter, Bohning Archer and the Coyote Ugly Saloon. The inclusion of this Saloon, known for its dancing, female bartenders dressed in 'country fashion', points towards the enduring importance of hegemonic masculinity and its expectation of hetero-normativity. Other sponsors – like insurance agents Geico and Allstate, Prilosec OTC and the Norwegian

Figure 9.4 ABC daytime TV booth, 2007 Fan Fair festival (photo: Jennifer C. Lena)

Cruise Line – reflect the increasingly middle class status of festival participants, and their fears, weaknesses and aspirations.

The festival's new institutional arrangements were caused by the increased cost of its downtown location, and this produced alliances between country music and a universe of consumer goods and services. The potential consequences for individual companies and consumers are multiple, but include the reidentification of the genre with norms governing personal and group behaviour. Seen in this way, the connection of commercial brands with country music is not simply a source of differentiation, but also of community, identity and continuity (Mommaas, 2002: 24).

Conclusion

The tournament of value experienced during the 2001 Fan Fair festival was initiated by the festival's move downtown. The relocation of the festival resulted from city leaders' decision to use a policy strategy known as 'festivalization' to build revenue and civic pride. One critique of festivalization is that historic spaces are transformed into commercial districts. Although Nashville always produced commercialized country entertainment, the need to offer festival sponsors branded spaces meant organizers transformed vacant or unmarked spaces into commercial zones for festival activity. At times, this made the festival space and programming indistinguishable from that normally offered in the downtown tourist corridor. The move also occasioned the production of multiple stages and a shift towards market-driven booking. Once fans had to choose how to spend their time, their tastes were rendered visible and both scheduling and advertising practices were transformed in order to cater to and anticipate the desires of the 'New Country' consumer. This group increasingly defines the genre's core values.

I noted earlier that the values Fan Fair participants negotiate are plural and cultural, and wish to review these for the sake of comparison with other chapters in this volume. In 2001, Fan Fair organizers replaced some of the materials used in the execution of the festival, including its location and variety of entertainment, and debates over these changes reflect the *technical* values of participants. Just as a fashion designer selects fabric and design elements that reflect their craftsmanship, festival organizers chose spaces, and designed and scheduled those spaces to reflect an emergent mode of country music craftsmanship. These technical values emerged from and reflect a set of *appreciative* or aesthetic values, present in participants' evaluations of the new festival arrangements. These evaluations emerged during dis-cussions of the festival's music, but were also present in debates about the festival's role in Nashville's rebranding. The choice to dub Fan Fair as Nashville's 'signature event' does not resolve, but rather reflects the multiple values held by festival participants, city government and citi-zens. Some of these identity claims were framed using aesthetic criteria ('the new music isn't *good*') while others reflected *situational* values. Most importantly, the latter included Nashville's significance as a her-itage site for country music fans. The relocation of the festival and its designation as the city's 'signature event' stirred up conflict with those who emphasized Nashville's identity as the 'Athens of the South'. Finally, participants debated *functional* or use aspects of the festival. Just like a dinner plate that is sometimes used as an ashtray, the festival had multiple functions for participants. It was a revenue generator and business recruitment tool for the city, a market expansion and branding opportunity for corporate sponsors, and both a 'family' reunion for country fans and a vacation spot. Although I have provided only the briefest sketch of the multiple values participants negotiate within the event, this should serve to illustrate how a constellation of values that crystallize in the context of a field-configuring event can impact the evolution of a field of production.

Festivals are compelling sites within which to examine field transformation, since they vary in both temporal and spatial design. Fan Fair represents both an emplaced festival, located in the same city for more than twenty years, and a displaced festival, since it was moved by organizers within the city space. This contrast of rootedness and placelessness hints at an important direction for future research on festivals. Just as Glynn (2008) has studied the interaction of the local geographic field with the Olympic Games, scholars might also examine travelling festivals in order to identify the extent to which temporary, while still strongly branded, festivals adapt to local conditions and traditions.

I have argued that the festival shaped relational and symbolic systems in ways that incorporated the character and traditions of the community, but also changed them. I reported that Nashville and festival leaders actively sought to enhance their reputation by staging the event, much as cities use the Olympic Games. As Glynn (2008: 1,137) argues, 'the very act of staging events in local geographic fields tends to imprint particular events with the character and traditions of the host cities'. This is because fields are not configured in a void, but 'constructed by a process of institutional bricolage such that field practices and symbols already sanctioned are appropriated into newly configured communities precipitated by events' (Glynn, 2008: 1,138). Quite clearly, the tournament of values at the 2001 Fan Fair festival produced a newly configured community of new country consumers. Institutional arrangements including festival booking, the attraction of corporate sponsors and the presentation of entertainment were adapted to reflect their (perceived) values. The adaptation of field aesthetics to emerging constituencies is a feature of musical genres known to scholars (Lena and Peterson, 2008), but the role of festivals in these processes remains poorly understood, suggesting one avenue for further study.

For those familiar with the genre, it may initially be difficult to see continuities between the emergent new country values and the traditional imaginary in the genre. Among other obsessions, country music fans are enraptured by tradition. Traditions in country music are many, and they include the accessibility of performers to their fans and an unpretentious demeanour, an appreciation for rural life and physical labour and an accompanying distrust or dislike of 'city folks' and white-collar labour (Peterson, 1997: 6–9). 'Authentic' country artists are white men who maintain relatively conservative views of women's roles in public and private life, as well as 'traditional' family values, faith and tradition, rural life, Christianity, alcohol, death, humour and nostalgia (Mann, 2008). The music valorizes a return to 'simplicity', moral clarity, social stability and cohesion, small-scale community and a 'slow pace', honesty, loyalty and tradition – all of which are usually framed as 'in decline' (Mann, 2008: 87). Almost every scholar of country music notes the association of these values with whiteness (Malone, 1985, 2002; Tosches, 1985; Peterson, 1997; Cantwell, 2003; Fox, 2004; Mann, 2008). Experts describe country fans as having 'the adopted pose of rustics resigned to the march of time' (Mann, 2008: 87), and acting like 'exiles in their own homeland, painfully holding on to closeness in a world that has already deserted them' (Stewart, 1988: 235). It is this last point that bears repeating: the rustic pose is an *adopted* one. The image of country music as local, intimate, folk and anti-commercial is compelling for fans, but at odds with the reality that country music has always been mass produced and commercial (Peterson, 1997). While country music entertainment has maintained what Ellison (1995: xvii) calls a 'distinctly personal tone and a sustained focus on domestic social life', it is also the case that 'the marketing of commercial country music and its trappings fully embrace modernity, the resulting popular culture community functions as an imaginative means for transcending the negative effects of modernity'. This chapter has illuminated one moment in which the field was reorganized to achieve this possibility.

Transformations in fields of production marked by traditionalism pose a particular puzzle: why do participants allow such transformations to occur? In this case, financial advantage united the powerful elements within the field: city, business and festival leaders all sought to profit from the relocation of the festival. The question of how generalizable these results will be depends largely on the extent to which other heritage festivals have stakeholders that benefit from their transformation. Although it may appear unlikely to find a festival in which this is not the case, one should not forget the variety of groups that have arisen to protest encroaching commercialism and technology. Festivals or fairs held by anarchist groups, 'culture-jammers' or survivalists may evolve differently than festivals in profit-driven fields.

Generalizing from this analysis to other festivals and other genres is possible if we consider events and genres as constellations of cultural, social and economic meanings. I have focused here on providing 'glimpses of the ways in which desire and demand, reciprocal sacrifice and power interact to create economic value in specific social situations' (Appadurai, 1986: 4). The festival is a venue for the reenactment of institutional arrangements in a particular field and for the negotiation and affirmation of different values. As a transorganizational structure, a structure that 'allow[s] disparate constituents to become aware of their common concerns, join together, share information, coordinate their actions, shape or subvert agendas, and mutually influence field structuration' (Anand and Jones, 2008: 1,037), the festival unites music fans, producers and artists, city and business leaders and citizens. The festival is a 'medium through which field-cohering interests and issues are identified and sustained' (Anand and Jones, 2008: 1,037).

All festivals should be viewed with an eye to both continuities and discontinuities with a place and a people's history. Such a perspective addresses the ways in which practices and discourses are produced by, and themselves produce, local history, shared experiences and values and institutions. As I have argued, Fan Fair plays an important role in reconfiguring city spaces and economies, but perhaps an even more instrumental role transforming relations within the genre marketplace.

Notes

* The author wishes to acknowledge the research assistance of Sarah Glynn, George Sanders and Jonathan Wynn. This project was made possible through a grant from the Curb Center for Arts, Enterprise and Public Policy at Vanderbilt University, and with support from the Center for Arts and Cultural Policy Studies at Princeton University. Previous versions of this manuscript were presented at Princeton University, the University of Pennsylvania's Urban Ethnography Workshop, the Social Science History Association conference and the American Sociological Association. Comments on earlier drafts were provided by David Grazian, Timothy Vogus, Tammy Smith, Paul DiMaggio, Steven Tepper, Shaul Kelner and Brayden King.

1. See www.cmafest.com/2007/general/press_release_detail.asp?re=649&year= 2007 for the electronic press release; accessed 14 January 2008.
2. The major exception is the Gaylord Opryland Resort which has more than 3,000 rooms (10 per cent of Nashville's total) and is located approximately twelve miles outside downtown Nashville.
3. '2009 CMA music festival attendance up 7.2 percent', www.visitmusiccity. com/media/press_release?id=553, accessed 17 December 2009.
4. 'CMA makes association's largest music education donation to date', 9 December 2009. CMA World.com, www.cmaworld.com/news_publi cations/pr_common/press_detail.asp?re=918&year=2009, accessed 14 December 2009.
5. In contrast, some scholars argue that festivals attract tourist, tourism revenue, and profit for service industries (Peterson, 1973; Hall, 1992), produce positive exposure for the city in the press (Schuster, 2001), and engender citizen pride and self-esteem (Richards and Wilson, 2004).
6. I should note that the names of these zones change from year to year, as sponsors drop out and are replaced by others. The names I use in the text were drawn from 2007, the last year in which data were collected for this project, unless otherwise noted.
7. 'Corporate partners help drive CMA music festival success' www.country music.org/news_publications/pr_common/press_detail.asp?re=648&year= 2007.%20June%2025,%2007, retrieved 5 January 2010.

References

Anand, N. and Jones, B. 2008. 'Tournament rituals, category dynamics, and field configuration: the case of the Booker Prize', *Journal of Management Studies* 45:6, 1,036–60.

Anand, N. and Watson, M. 2004. 'Tournament rituals in the evolution of fields: the case of the Grammy Awards', *Academy of Management Journal* 47, 59–80.

Appadurai, A. 1986. 'Introduction: commodities and the politics of value', in A. Appadurai (ed.), *The Social Life of Things*. Cambridge University Press, pp. 3–63.

Barbato, M. and Mio, C. 2007. 'Accounting and the development of management control in the cultural sphere: the case of the Venice biennale', *Accounting, Business and Financial History* 17, 187–208.

Cantwell, R. 2003. *Bluegrass Breakdown: the Making of the Old Southern Sound*. Urbana, IL: University of Illinois Press.

Country Music Association (CMA) *Close-Up*. Issues from 1971 to 2006.

Festival website 2009. www.cmafest.com/2008/general/press_release_detail. asp?re=733&year=2008 (downloaded 27 February 2009).

Cusic, D. 1998. 'Country green: the money in country music', in C. Tichi (ed.), *Reading Country Music: Steel Guitars, Opry Stars, and Honky Tonk Bars*. Durham, NC: Duke University Press.

Dovey, K. and Sandercock, L. 2002. 'Pleasure, politics, and the "public interest": Melbourne's Riverscape revitalization', *Journal of the American Planning Association* 68:2, 151–64.

Durkheim, E. 1965. *The Elementary Forms of the Religious Life*. New York: Free Press.

Ellison, C. W. 1995. *Country Music Culture: from Hard Times to Heaven*. Jackson, MI: University Press of Mississippi.

Evans, G. 2001. *Cultural Planning: an Urban Renaissance?* London: Routledge.

Evans, O. 2007. 'Border exchanges: the role of the European film festival', *Journal of Contemporary European Studies* 15, 23–33.

Fox, A. A. 2004. 'White trash alchemies of the abject sublime: country as bad music', in C. J. Washburne and M. Derno (eds.), *Bad Music: the Music we Love to Hate*. New York: Routledge, pp. 39–61.

Glynn, M. 2008. 'Configuring the field of play: how hosting the Olympic games impacts civic community', *Journal of Management Studies* 45:6, 1,117–46.

Gotham, K. F. 2007. *Authentic New Orleans: Tourism, Culture, and Race in the Big Easy*. New York University Press.

Hall, C. M. 1992. *Hallmark Tourist Events*. Sydney: John Wiley & Sons Australia, Ltd.

Hannigan, J. 2002. 'Cities as the physical site of the global entertainment economy', in M. Raboy (ed.), *Global Media Policy in the New Millennium*. Luton University Press, pp. 181–98.

Harrington, C. L. and Bielby, D. D. 2005. 'Global television distribution: implications of TV "traveling" for viewers, fans, and texts', *American Behavioral Scientist* 48, 902–20.

Haslam, G. W. 1999. *Workin' Man Blues: Country Music in California*. Berkeley, CA: University of California Press.

Häusermann, H. and Siebel, W. 1993. 'Festivalisierung der stadtpolitik: stadtentwicklung durch grosse projekte', *Leviathan* 13, 7–31.

Havens, T. 2003. 'Exhibiting global television: on the business and cultural functions of global television fairs', *Journal of Broadcasting and Electronic Media* 47:1, 18–35.

Hitters, E. 2007. 'Porto and Rotterdam as European capitals of culture: towards the festivalization of urban cultural policy', in G. Richards (ed.), *Cultural Tourism*. Binghamton, NY: Hawthorne, pp. 281–302.

Johnson, N. C. 1999. 'Framing the past: time, space and the politics of tourism in Ireland', *Political Geography* 18:2, 187–207.

Judd, D. R. 1999. 'Constructing the tourist bubble', in D. R. Judd and S. S. Fainstein (eds.), *The Tourist City.* New Haven, CN: Yale University Press, pp. 35–53.

Klaic, D. 2007. 'Festivaalien turkimisen tärakeydestä', in S. Silvanto (ed.), *Festivalien Helsinasdki.* Helsinki: Helsingin kaupungin tietokeskus/ Heslingin kaupungin kultturiasiainkeskus, pp. 202–05.

Lampel, J. and Meyer, A. 2008. 'Field-configuring events as structuring mechanisms: how conferences, ceremonies, and trade shows constitute new technologies, industries, and markets', *Journal of Management Studies* 45:6, 1,025–35.

Lena, J. C. and Peterson, R. A. 2008. 'Classification as culture: types and trajectories of music genres', *American Sociological Review* 73:5, 697–718.

Light, D. 2000. 'Gazing on communism: heritage tourism and post-communist identities in Germany, Hungary and Romania', *Tourism Geographies* 2:2, 157–76.

Malone, B. C. 1985. *Country Music, USA.* Revised edition. Austin, TX: University of Texas Press.

2002. *Don't Get Above Your Raisin': Country Music and the Southern Working Class.* Urbana, IL: University of Illinois Press.

Mann, G. 2008. 'Why does country music sound white? Race and the voice of nostalgia', *Ethnic and Racial Studies* 31:1, 73–100.

Mommaas, H. 2002. 'City branding: the necessity of socio-cultural goals', in T. Hauben, G. Hauben, G. Ball, E. Ball and E. Brinkman (eds.), *City Branding: Image Building and Building Images.* Rotterdam: NAi Publishers, pp. 32–48.

Palmer/Rae Associates 2004. *European Cities and Capitals of Culture: Study Prepared for the European Commission.* Brussels: Palmer/Rae Associates.

Peterson, R. A. 1973. 'The unnatural history of rock festivals: an instance of media facilitation', *Popular Music and Society* 2:2, 97–123.

1997. *Creating Country Music: Fabricating Authenticity.* University of Chicago Press.

Quinn, B. 2005. 'Changing festival places: insights from Galway', *Social and Cultural Geography* 62, 237–52.

Recording Industry Association of America (RIAA) 2008. 'The RIAA consumer profile', http://riaa.com/keystatistics.php?content_selector=Music ConsumerProfile (downloaded 7 February 2010).

Richards, G. 2007. 'The festivalization of society or the socialization of festivals? The case of Catalunya', in G. Richards (ed.), *Cultural Tourism: Global and Local Perspectives.* Binghamton, NY: Hawthorne Press. pp. 257–80.

Richards, G. and Wilson, J. 2004. 'The impact of cultural events on city image: Rotterdam, cultural capital of Europe 2001', *Urban Studies*, 41:10, 1,931–51.

Schuster, J. M. 2001. 'Ephemera, temporary urbanism, and imaging'. In L. J. Vale and S. B. Warner Jr. (eds.), *Imaging the City: Continuing Struggles and New Directions*. New Brunswick, NJ: Center for Urban Policy Research, State University of New Jersey Press, pp. 361–97.

Snyder, N. 2007. 'Marketers change pitch to reach country fans', *The Tennessean* 9 June.

Stewart, K. 1988. 'Nostalgia – a polemic', *Cultural Anthropology* 3:3, 227–41.

Strauss, N. 2002. 'Music: the country music country radio ignores', *The New York Times* March 24.

Tang, J. 2007. 'Of biennials and biennialists: Venice, Documenta, Munster', *Theory, Culture and Society* 24:7–8, 247–60.

Tosches, N. 1985. *Country: The Twisted Roots of Rock 'n' Roll*. Cambridge, MA: Da Capo Press.

Waterman, S. 1998. 'Carnivals for elites? The cultural politics of music festivals', *Progress in Human Geography* 22, 54–75.

Appendix 9.1: selected interviews

Afinogenov, Maxime: Nashville gossip columnist, former CMA employee.

Campbell, Brian: historian of music and music business, songwriter, high-ranking record label employee, CMA member.

Gaustad, Paul: professional country music industry photographer, Nashville celebrity.

Golisano, Robert: high-ranking employee of international record company with country music offices in Nashville, member of CMA Festival Board.

Hecht, Jochen: singer, former record label head, academic, inductee to the Country Music Hall of Fame.

Lydman, Toni: former high-ranking CMA employee, author.

Miller, Ryan: high-ranking employee of several country music non-profit organizations, national government employee and academic.

Pominville, Jason: high-ranking CMA officer and employee of CMA from the early 1970s to the present.

Roy, Derek: former independent record label head, artist management, songwriter, author, CMA board member.

Spacek, Jerome: country music performer at Honky Tonks.

Tallinder, Henry: former independent record label head, major label executive, academic.

Thibault, Joce: employee of independent booking agency for CMA Festival.

Vanek, Thomas: high-ranking Convention and Visitor's Bureau employee.

10 Between art and commerce: London Fashion Week as trade fair and fashion spectacle

JOANNE ENTWISTLE AND
AGNÈS ROCAMORA*

Traditionally beginning in New York and ending in Paris, 'fashion weeks', also known as the 'collections', showcase the up-coming season's *prêt-à-porter* clothing. Fashion week is an important moment within the life of the industry globally, also acting as a key instrument in 'fashion-branding the city' (Rocamora, 2009: 79–85). As one stop in this international circuit, London Fashion Week (LFW) comprises a large exhibition of designers' work in the manner of a trade show but also, more famously, a series of catwalk shows covered by the world's press. To garner publicity these shows are often spectacular events which involve much more than simply the clothes: they are sensory experiences which invoke moods, sensations and associations around the collection, using particular models, lighting, music and other props. Narratives are created around the various collections presented that help support their branding and add value to the clothes on show. These events, not the trade stands, are what grab press and public attention. Indeed, LFW is a major promotional opportunity for British fashion designers and one way to secure both the attention of the world's press as well as generating actual sales. So, although fashion shows usually make a net loss, showing at LFW can secure important symbolic capital in the form of status accrued through good press coverage, and enable a designer to carve out a visible presence in the fashion world. As described by Aspers (2001) and Entwistle (2009), the cultural value far outweighs any immediate financial gain, although the hope is that the symbolic status accrued will, at some point in time, translate into financial success. Thus, fashion week in general, and LFW in particular, remain situated in an intermediary position between art (Skov *et al.*, 2009) and commerce.

This chapter, based on two separate fieldwork studies, analyses the specific characteristics of LFW as a particular fashion trade fair. While we attended different fashion weeks (during 2002–4), and observed

249

different participants as part of two separate projects (discussed in more detail below), in subsequent discussions we were struck by our remarkably similar observations. We both noted how LFW, in bringing together the key people whose work constitutes the wider field of fashion, mapped out, quite literally in spatial terms, all the key agents and institutions within the field of fashion. These key people include designers, models, journalists and buyers from stores around the world, fashion stylists and celebrities, as well as less important figures, such as fashion students, who exist on the margins of the field.

This led us in the direction of Bourdieu's field theory, which allowed us to capture the role and socio-temporal orchestration of the event. Thus, in this paper we argue that LFW operates as an embodiment of the wider field of fashion: it is an instance of the field of fashion materialized or reified, 'that is to say physically realised or objectified' (Bourdieu, 1993b: 161). In other words, in bringing together the field participants into one spatially and temporally bounded event, LFW renders visible, through its orchestration, wider field characteristics, such as field boundaries, positions, position taking and habitus. This rendering of the field is key to understanding LFW as a critical moment in the life of the field as a whole. In other words, despite its ostensible aim to simply showcase next season's fashionable clothing, we suggest that LFW's main function is to produce, reproduce and legitimate the field of fashion and the positions of those players within it. It is, in this respect, a 'field-configuring event' (FCE). This draws attention to the role of fashion weeks as arenas for the accumulation and consolidation of the value of participants' social, symbolic and economic capitals in what might also be seen as a 'tournament of values'.

After detailing our empirical studies below, we then set out to examine the material realities of this field as realized during LFW, focusing on two critical aspects. These correspond to different spatial dimensions also constituting the main articulations of our paper. We first examine the entire layout of LFW and the way in which borders and boundaries of the field of fashion are made manifest in this setting, particularly the physical barriers that are erected around the event itself in the form of gates, gatekeepers and tickets allowing the field to appear to itself through its materialized enactment. We then move into the more intimate space of the catwalk theatre, where relationships and positions are mapped out, reproduced and legitimated. Here we examine the importance of field participants appearing to one another: the importance of seeing and being seen on the front row. The performances of these participants within this space allows for examination of the ways in which fashion capital and habitus are enacted as part of the performances of these individuals that reproduce field identities and positions in this very public arena.

Methodology

This chapter is based upon fieldwork from two separate projects: an ESRC-funded ethnographic study of womenswear fashion buyers in a major London department store (fieldwork conducted between March and September 2002), and a study of fashion journalism (fieldwork and interviews conducted in 2003). The first study is an ethnography of buying strategies and decisions. Three buying managers were shadowed at store meetings and on buying trips in London, New York, Paris and Milan during the fashion weeks. Fifteen semi-structured interviews with key store people were also conducted. The other study comprises semi-structured interviews with thirty-two journalists, the shadowing of one journalist during LFW (September 2003) and the observation, over the course of one month, of the editorial production of a fashion magazine. The broader aim of both projects is to unpack processes of cultural mediation, interrogating the ways buyers and journalists act as intermediaries between the fields of production and consumption. However, as our chosen methodology of ethnographic interviews and observations demonstrates, the specific embodied and situated logic of fields only becomes apparent during fieldwork, and our discussion highlights this throughout.

Fashion week as trade fair: between commerce and art

Fashion weeks in general share many of the same features as other international trade fairs which are, according to Bathelt and Schuldt (2008: 4): 'characterized by a unique information and communication ecology based on physical co-presence between agents of an industry, technology or value chain from all parts of the world'. They can be thought of as 'temporary clusters' (Bathelt and Schuldt, 2005) where an exchange of information is free-flowing and informal, as much as it is formally orchestrated through the very structure of the fair (stands, displays, shows, screenings, etc). The idea of 'global buzz' (Bathelt and

Schuldt, 2008) captures something of this exchange of information, in the form of 'rumours, recommendations, and speculations', as well as 'strategic information' (Bathelt and Schuldt, 2008: 5). However, it is also similar to 'local buzz' (Bathelt, 2007; Bathelt *et al.*, 2004) and 'industrial atmosphere' (Marshall, 1923), terms that capture the very locatedness of knowledge, and both ideas of 'buzz' are required to understand trade shows in general and fashion shows and LFW in particular. Indeed, as Entwistle argues (forthcoming), fashion information/buzz is a very complex mix of both globally circulating information, in the form of media and press, tacit knowledge worn on the bodies of these globally circulating workers, and very much located in the particular fashion cities. Fashion week, as a major industry event, locates and facilitates the circulation of global and local buzz. Indeed, this is apparent in the very idea of the fashion week's schedule, spread as it is across New York, London, Milan and Paris over four weeks, twice a year, which illustrates both the global circulating and very locally situated nature of fashion knowledge, which historically resides in some cities and not others. While fashion weeks – like the art biennales described in Chapter 3 by Jeannine Tang – are increasingly common in many peripheral cities like Copenhagen or Sydney (Breward and Gilbert, 2006), with more cities introducing such events to upgrade their industries (Skov, 2006) and locate themselves on a global stage, they do depend upon some initial local investment and historical associations with fashion: as we go to press there are fashion weeks planned for Inverness and Scunthorpe in the UK, as well as for Wellesley, Massachusetts and Canton, Ohio in the US.

As Moeran and Strandgaard Pedersen argue in the Introduction to this book, trade shows are spatially and temporally bounded, and the specific ways in which this occurs during LFW we describe below. The spatial formation is, in particular, critical to the reproduction of symbolic and social value, found within the wider field of fashion and hence forms a significant focus in our analysis, as we now discuss.

Boundaries and access

The field of fashion, like all fields, is a system of relations and, as Bourdieu (1996a: 96) observes, 'to think in terms of field is to think relationally'. The field of fashion has its own players, responsible for making, marketing or retailing clothing and these are the players who are brought together at LFW in face-to-face encounters. This wider field of fashion can be mapped out in terms of relations between particular key institutions and agents, the way Bourdieu (1975) himself recognizes in 'Le couturier et sa griffe', where he looks at the structure of the French field of high fashion in the 1970s, focusing more specifically on the relative positions of designers and couture houses. Similarly, the British field of fashion is made up of a hierarchical system of relations between key designers, magazine publications and shops. In the absence of couture houses, British fashion designers jostle for position on the international stage, with many of them securing top positions in French couture houses (for example, John Galliano and later the late Alexander McQueen were both head designers at Givenchy, while Stella McCartney began her international career at Chloé and Phoebe Philo is now the designer for Céline). In the realm of publishing, key institutions are the 'established' players, such as *UK Vogue*, but also 'newcomers', such as *Love* and *Pop*, as well as a new genre of cultural intermediaries: fashion bloggers (Rocamora and Bartlett, forthcoming). In retailing, stores such as Selfridges, Harvey Nichols and Browns dominate the field of high fashion and have contracts to sell exclusive designer ranges. LFW mirrors these hierarchical relations of the wider field of fashion, thereby reproducing them.

Indeed, the first point to note about LFW is that only those players already belonging to the field (that is with an acknowledged position within it) can gain access to the event. In this way, the field of fashion, like all fields, is 'a place wherein some people who fulfil the conditions of access play a particular game from which others are excluded' (Bourdieu, 2000b: 55). This is made particularly visible at LFW. The event is a physically enclosed space that only a select few are allowed to enter, rather than an open-to-the-public exhibition like the 'Ideal Home' or 'Chelsea Flower Show'. The dividing line between inside and outside is not only very strongly drawn but mirrors and reproduces the boundaries that exist around the wider field of fashion. At the time of fieldwork LFW was taking place on the King's Road. In subsequent years it moved to the courtyard of the Victoria and Albert Museum and, more recently, to Somerset House.

In all fields arises the issue as to who belongs to the field, that is, the issue as what constitute its boundaries, 'often invisible' (Bourdieu, 2000b: 53). Such boundaries are 'a stake of struggles' (Bourdieu, 2000b: 42), the struggle to define its legitimate members, here the significant ones being designers, journalists, buyers and other 'producers of the meaning and values of the work' (Bourdieu, 1993a: 37). During LFW the boundaries Bourdieu talks about are rendered visible and materialized in the whole apparatus of gates and gatekeepers that allow or deny entrance to the field and preserve the 'effect of enclosure' (Bourdieu, 2000b: 58) – something also described at length by Havens in Chapter 6, on television programme markets. At the time of fieldwork, on the King's Road, the main boundary that was erected between the inside and outside of the field of fashion as realized during LFW was the long gate supervised by two keepers in uniforms who only let in those armed with a pass. Insiders marched confidently towards the gate while outsiders stood outside.

Through the enactment of these boundaries, clear limits are established between the outside world, the world of 'laity' to borrow Bourdieu's (2000b: 52) analogy, including all the hopefuls waiting outside the tents on the King's Road to catch a glimpse of this world, and that of the 'clercs' (Bourdieu 2000b: 52), or, as the press often calls them, 'fashion-istas'. As Tseëlon (1995: 134) notes:

The temple of fashion though is not open to everyone and only a carefully scrutinised set of fashion editors, photographers, buyers, distinguished clients and celebrities are allowed into the inner sanctuary. Access to such an event and the seating plan draw a political map of social success and a complex web of interests.

The LFW site at the Chelsea Barracks was comprised of two tents; an exhibition hall which housed a larger number of designers on individual stands in the manner of a trade show, and a catwalk theatre, where the spectacular fashion shows that are widely commented on in the press took place. The former was a space for the business of fashion, the latter for the art of fashion. This division between art and commerce mirrors the wider field of fashion, where, as in the field of cultural production more generally (Bourdieu, 1993a), these are separated out and awarded different statuses. This physical separation between the two activities reproduces a critical division within British fashion between fashion as 'art' and fashion as 'rag trade' (McRobbie, 1998). Drawing on Bourdieu, McRobbie notes how 'art' and creativity carry greater value than commerce, which, at least in the context of British fashion, is disavowed by many young designers. LFW, as the biannual event supporting British fashion, reproduces this division from the wider field. The 'creative' and 'artistic' is celebrated through the privileging of the fashion catwalk to the detriment of the 'commercial' exhibition, which receives little press coverage.

Yet, as Bourdieu (1975: 22) argues, the field of fashion is 'situated at an intermediary position between the artistic field and the economic field'. During LFW this position is made clear: while the distinction between art and commerce is translated into the planning of the space discussed above, the commercial dimension of fashion is not hidden, that is, it is not totally disavowed. As Bourdieu (1993a: 75) also observes, 'the disavowal [of the "economy"] is neither a real negation of the "economic" interest which always haunts the most "disinterested" practices, nor a simple "dissimulation" of the mercenary aspects of the practice', and this is made visible during LFW. While commerce is materialized distinctly from the creative process, it nevertheless is shown as complementary to it. During LFW the separation between the two tents, that is the separation between the sub-field of art and the sub-field of commerce is, potentially at least, bridged by the physical movement of fashion players, such as buyers and journalists between the two spaces.

As academics we found ourselves confronting, on a daily basis, the physical boundaries of the field and the separation between 'laity' and 'clercs' (Bourdieu, 2000b: 53) in our status as both insiders and outsiders to the field.[1] We secured access to the event through our claim to be doing research on the fashion industry and through the connections (i.e., social capital, which we discuss below) we had already established with journalists and buyers in the course of our research. This information granted us an entry 'Pass' which meant we could easily move in and out of the physical environment of LFW. However, since our presence in the field was temporary, lasting only for the duration of our research, and since we were not 'industry' insiders, we were acutely aware that we remained outsiders and the fragile nature of our claim to be there was sometimes brought to the fore.

Once inside the site we had to confront yet more boundaries. Our entrance ticket only allowed access to the site and the exhibition tent, but to gain entry to the hallowed arena of the catwalk theatre, passing through the roped area outside the theatre, necessitated negotiating more boundaries to secure tickets to individual shows. With these tickets in short supply, this proved a difficult task. In the case of the journalist's project, most tickets were secured by the journalist being shadowed, although her power arbitrarily to distribute these meant it became important to secure tickets independently as well. In the case of the buyers project, tickets had to be secured independently, since allocations were so few within the store.

Field players in all fields are endowed with different amounts of capital, while different capitals are effective '*in relation* to a particular field' (Bourdieu, 1995: 73). Bourdieu talks about 'specific capital' (1995: 73). We shall call 'fashion capital' the capital specific to the field of fashion. Like all field-related capitals, it is made up of economic and cultural capitals (discussed below) and social and symbolic capitals. In terms of securing access to LFW and fashion shows, social capital is 'what ordinary language calls "connections"' (Bourdieu, 1995: 32). A high value of social capital allows one to move freely within the social network of field participants. In the field of fashion, social capital is essential to the acquisition of tickets to shows (knowing who to contact and how; in our case, the PR agencies of designers, using our research and connections to buyers and journalists). A high degree of social capital buys one access to after-show parties, or to the designers themselves. One's social capital cannot be dissociated from one's symbolic capital – one's status in a field. As Bonnewitz (1998: 43–4) notes, symbolic capital 'is only the credit and authority bestowed on an agent by recognitions and possessions of the three other forms of capital'. The value of one form of capital is therefore highly intertwined with that of the other forms of capital.

Our ability to secure access *without* the aid of the people we were shadowing was an indicator of our ability to find our way into the field; to locate its players and gatekeepers, and mobilize capital. In other words, once inside the show tent, we could potentially increase our capital. To be spotted by buyers and journalists outside a show waiting to go in – holding the precious ticket prominently – or seated in the catwalk theatre itself undoubtedly signalled our social and symbolic capitals and thereby helped lend some weight to our research and our position in the field. Since as researchers we were often made to feel less powerful than the people we were observing, these symbols of our own status helped to maintain our position *vis-à-vis* our informants, indicating that while we might be academics, we had connections.

However, we were excluded from the 'big' shows, such as Julian McDonald's, where tickets were scarce and dependent upon being a known and influential player, that is, someone with a high symbolic capital. Our relative lack of social capital also meant we were excluded from the social events, such as the private 'after show' parties, that run alongside the shows. There are, therefore, even more boundaries within this field: indeed, there are boundaries within boundaries, as Chapter 6 by Havens nicely reveals. The social functions work to exclude everyone but the select few belonging to the 'inner sanctum'. As Tilberi (1998: 397) in her fictionalized account of fashion shows notes, most parties have at least 'three cordoned-off areas for minor, major and middle ranking VIPs [very important persons]'. Lacking sufficient fashion capital to gain entry to this inner sanctum meant that we were clearly positioned as outsiders to these social functions.

The ticket, as suggested above, is one of the main badges of affiliation within this field. By brandishing a ticket for a show, one indicates insider status: it is the material evidence of one's presence in the field of fashion, a visible sign of belongingness for others to see *en route* to the exclusive space of the catwalk theatre. The invitations themselves, in their design and materiality, convey this sense of exclusivity, at once a passport to the elite event of the show but also trophies to display: they are usually highly visible. Often of a large size, too big to be kept in a small bag, some are of high quality, with a design that aims to convey the mood of the collections. The Boyd Spring–Summer 2004 invitation came accompanied by a smiley badge and whistle, both attached to a bright green cord to be wrapped around one's neck.

However, all tickets are not created equally. There are tickets for seats and tickets for standing, and these place allocations mark out and reproduce field positions within the confined arena of the catwalk theatre, as we discuss in more detail below. It is in this way that the theatre itself becomes a microcosm of the entire field. Seat tickets are more valuable and come with a row number. Standing tickets mean waiting in the standing queue. This waiting is a significant activity during the shows to the point that it has become part of the shows themselves. So, while the actual shows last around fifteen minutes, waiting an hour or more for it to start is not unusual. This elaborate orchestration of time mirrors the hierarchies of the world of fashion itself. Only those with the maximum amount of status in the field have the power to keep others waiting and the most notorious of these are celebrities and major dignitaries. Time is critical to the analysis of practice; the temporal structure of practice 'is constitutive of its meaning' (Bourdieu, 1997: 81). As Bourdieu (1997: 106) goes on to observe 'time derives its efficacy from the state of the structure of relations within which it comes into play'.

A hierarchy of time is, in effect, enacted, that conveys the social hierarchies at play in the field of fashion, the expression 'being fashionably late' aptly capturing here the socio-temporal structuring of the field as materialized during LFW. As a commodity capitalized on by the fashion industry to sell the latest fads and the power to be 'ahead of the game', time is also symbolically capitalized on by some fashion players during the collections to signify their high status, that is their dominant position at the head of their field. Moreover, the arrival of particular VIP participants is much like that of royalty: not only do they tend to arrive later, but the show cannot start until they are seated. One young model, discussing his encounters in the fashion industry, described this world as being like a 'medieval court' in its complex social hierarchy – thereby confirming, perhaps, the analogy made in the introduction between medieval tournaments and fairs and festivals. This was very much confirmed by our observations of the organization of each individual show.[2]

As these observations at LFW demonstrate, fields have real material presence and are not abstract entities or disembodied spaces. Events such as the one we observed are opportunities for fields to materialize and reproduce themselves. LFW as a major event, and the more exclusive social functions enacted around it, make manifest the boundaries of the field and mark out clear parameters between the inside and the outside. This has the effect not only of rendering the field an actual space, but also of reproducing the identities of those within and serving to legitimate their positions through the ways in which they appear *as* insiders. It is to the significance of appearing as an insider in the field that we now turn.

Seeing and being seen: on field positions

Visibility and membership

Much debate has taken place about the future of fashion shows (see, for instance, Cartner-Morley, 2003: 3). While shows seem ostensibly about the selling of clothes, in fact they are largely redundant as trade events since they occur too late in the season. Indeed, most of the buying happens beforehand in studios (Cartner-Morley, 2003: 13). As Italian designers Dolce and Gabbana note, 'the product has been sold at least two months beforehand' (cited in Cartner-Morley, 2003: 13). Yet, as Cartner-Morley (2003: 13) observes, it would seem that 'most in the industry remain wedded to the catwalk concept'. When asked 'why fashion shows?' one journalist described them as a 'tradition', while another, referring to the debate about the redundancy of shows, observed that 'there is a definite argument for that. There's no real reason for us to go and look at all this stuff'. However, the shows have remained critical to the work of buyers and journalists. For journalists fashion shows represent news, they constitute stories, while they help buyers to understand the designers' vision. As Entwistle (2009: 134) puts it, shows are not 'a direct sales pitch or a cost-effective means of displaying clothes', but rather dramatic spectacles 'that render[s] an aesthetic environment for the clothes' which serve to 'weave meanings and associations around the clothes, albeit ambiguous ones' that contextualize the collection (Entwistle, 2009: 134). Ultimately, the value of showing is to celebrate and promote the artistic and creative 'vision' for the collection and hence the designer. In other words, the fashion week fashion show is primarily about generating elusive symbolic capital around the designer that, ultimately, may translate into actual economic capital. The late Alexander McQueen and John Galliano, both masters of the spectacular fashion show, are two British designers who have successfully managed this translation: converting the art of the fashion show and the symbolic capital accrued there into commercial success.

Other forms of symbolic capital are also accrued by other players, not just designers, through their participation at fashion shows. By their very presence at LFW, buyers, fashion editors, journalists, bloggers and so on, seek to attend shows not out of economic necessity, but to play their part in the field of fashion – to 'see and be seen', as Moeran also notes of book fairs (Chapter 5) – and enhance their social capital. Kawamura (2004: 62) goes further to suggest that it is through practices such as the collections 'that the particular groups of fashion elites *reproduce themselves.* Organising fashion shows is not only a trade event but also a *cultural event'* (our emphasis). Developing Kawamura's point further, in the remaining part of the paper we detail some of the ways in which fashion shows articulate and reproduce fashion culture. In particular, we suggest that one of the major purposes of the fashion shows is to see and be seen and, by being seen, one's position in the field is reproduced. Thus, the real value of the fashion week event comes not so much from the sales receipts (happy though designers are to have these) but from the exposure they receive from being seen there.

Once part of the ceremonies of consecration of the bourgeoisie (Bourdieu, 1975: 32) fashion shows, we would argue, along with Kawamura, are now important for the consecration of key players and their reproduction in the field of fashion. In a similar vein, Bourdieu (2000b: 66) notes how, in the field of politics, 'an important part of the actions politicians accomplish has no other function than to reproduce the system and to reproduce the politicians by reproducing the system which ensures their reproduction'. In the field of fashion, as in the field of politics, and to paraphrase Bourdieu (2000b: 67) on the latter, many practices are motivated by the desire to reproduce the very system that guarantees the existence of its members. Thus, during fashion shows not only are 'the conditions for the efficacy of the label' produced and reproduced (Bourdieu, 1975: 21), but so are those for the efficacy of the work of fashion participants such as journalists and buyers. During fashion shows creators are created, but so are the roles and positions of the players in the field. Accardo (1995: 32) notes how journalism 'is mainly evaluated against the accumulation of symbolic capital (with the related material advantages), against peer acknowledgement, against public notoriety and social *visibility*'. This process points towards 'the established significance of the collections as social institutions for the controlling elites of global fashion culture' (Gilbert, 2000: 9).

Thus, while Khan (2000: 117) argues that catwalk shows' only purpose is for them '*to be noticed*' by the media and the public more generally, they are also for its participants to be noticed by other participants themselves. As Accardo (1997: 51), drawing on the work of Bourdieu, notes, to have a distinct existence means not only to exist physically but also socially, 'which means *for others*, to be recognised by others, to acquire importance, *visibility*'. It is significant that the most powerful players' presence may actually be in the form of absence: when someone as important as Anna Wintour, the editor of US *Vogue*, decides not to attend, her absence is noted and commented upon by the press: her absence is visible.

This emphasis upon visibility and mutual recognition points to the important way in which LFW facilitates intersubjectivity essential to the maintenance of the field itself. By collecting everyone who is 'anyone' in the field, LFW renders subjects visible to one another and places them in meaningful relation to each other. This visibility produces a sense of 'intercorporeality': as Crossley (2004: 27) observes, 'we belong to each other by belonging to a common *visible* world'. 'Belonging' is important within this particular world, and spatial arrangements of the visual field of fashion encourage this sense of shared belonging and intercorporeality. Belonging is also signalled and reproduced through shared tastes and dress styles: one's whole embodied appearance signals membership of the 'fashion set' – as Smith also notes of auctions in Chapter 4. As visibility is key, we turn to the orchestration of looking in the spatial layout of the fashion show.

The catwalk theatre is a particularly visible realm where identities are created through very visible performances, which in turn constitute part of the way in which struggles in the field are played out. The staging of the catwalk show is a staging of the gaze; the gaze of the participants sitting in the audience, who are at once its object and subject. This gaze contrasts with that of the models, distant and detached, a gaze that does not watch, that is not there to see but only to be seen. As Foucault (1977, 1980) demonstrates, physical space produces particular regimes of looking. However, unlike the panopticon (or indeed, the conventional theatre) the gaze circulates *around* the space rather than emanating from a central point so that all players are both subject and object of the gaze in the game of visibility. This is because the catwalk, or 'runway', stretches out into the audience who sit in a rectangle around it. This relationship of stage to audience allows for the 'struggle for visibility' to be played out between participants who become part of the spectacle as their eyes are directed across the stage to the bodies seated on the other side. In such an auditorium, one becomes keenly aware of being watched in turn, while observing the audience constitutes part of the spectacle and drama of the show. Since the fashion show itself lasts only a matter of minutes, watching the audience take their seats provides the show with much of its drama. Thus, the conventions of seating at the fashion show, sitting opposite other members of the audience, encourage a gaze of mutual recognition as well as being central to the experience of the show as spectacle.[3] Also, again unlike relations within the panopticon, visibility in this arena translates into power: the more powerful bodies are the most visible on the front row.

The seating plan around the catwalk maps out the power relations between players within the field. A field is 'a system of differences' (Accardo, 1997: 45), and its structure 'is a *state* of the power relations among' its players (Bourdieu, 1995: 73). This translates, in the field of fashion as materialized during an event such as LFW, into the physical arrangements of the show itself, where – as we have seen by both Moeran and Havens (Chapters 5 and 6), and as described by Skov (2006: 768–9) – differences are visibly mapped out onto the space itself. The seating arrangement renders in spatial form the different sub-fields of practices within the field, with, for instance, buyers and journalists attributed to different areas: indeed, one journalist, when asked a question about buyers, used space as her reference, stating 'we are here and they're there', while illustrating her idea with a movement of the arm that signalled the distance between two areas of the catwalk theatre, that is two areas of the field of production of fashion. Similarly, photographer Roma Pas (cited in Persson, 2003) notes how 'it's funny that hierarchy can be understood in terms of visual conditions'. He adds that a similar hierarchy informs the placement of photographers:

I met a couple of guys who had the job of placing tape on the podium to mark the best spots for catwalk photographers [...] Within no time the whole surface was covered with crosses of tape and the photographers came and found their spot. I think it's interesting that hierarchy can be seen as a pattern in the most literal way.

While the hierarchical placement of photographers creates a spatial 'pattern' on the floor, the same is true of the rows of seats. One's position within one's respective field of practice is built into the system of rows. On the front row sit the most important participants, such as influential journalists and buyers, dignitaries and celebrities. At the time of fieldwork, these included journalists such as Suzy Menkes from the *International Herald Tribune*, Alexandra Shulman, editor of UK *Vogue*, as well as numerous celebrities. This position on the front row renders their power and influence visible to everyone in the auditorium since, as Pas (cited in Persson, 2003) notes, 'the light from the catwalk shines only on the front row'. Front row participants are, therefore, very much part of the spectacle. Beyond the front row are allocated seats for less important players. The furthest reaches are designated as 'standing', and in this area are those without much power and influence, such as particularly resourceful fashion students. Finally, in terms of the spatialization of the field itself, it is significant that the physical labour of making the clothes, and the less orderly nature of preparing for the performance, is kept 'hidden' backstage. The show preserves the illusion of fashion as art, the product of individual genius and obscures the effort involved (see Skov *et al.*, 2009: 9, 11–12). It thus contributes to the screen which, Bourdieu (1995: 138) argues, is placed in front of the fashion system to allow for its 'magic' to work and its 'ideology of creation' to be reproduced.

Performing (in) the field: fashion habitus and capital

Although the actual publicity machine will render the participants visible beyond the field, to the fashion consuming public, visibility in this often claustrophobic arena is about visibility in relation to one another, impressed upon the participants through the permanent exchange of gaze. This gaze is a scrutinizing one, as Kondo, in her study of race, fashion and theatre, recounts. While waiting in the French Cour Carrée du Louvre for the shows to start she notes (1997: 103):

Never have I seen a gathering of such intimidatingly stylish people. It's not simply what they're wearing and the aplomb and arrogance with which they carry themselves, but the fact that everyone is checking out everyone else. Who's who, who's wearing what, assessed by an audience that knows exactly which designer, what year, the exact price. *We are, I suppose, performing for each other.* (emphasis added)

This idea of performance acted out for knowledgeable others recalls Bourdieu's (2000a: p. 70) comment on the position of men in the Kabyle house whose game of honours, he notes, is 'a sort of theatrical action, accomplished in front of others, informed spectators who know the text and all the stage movements, and are capable of seeing the slightest variations'. In the confined space of the show area, both outside, as Kondo discusses, or inside the theatre at LFW, as in the confined and highly symbolically loaded space of the Kabyle house, one is on display and performs for others. Thus, if seating allocations are central to one's field position, so too is one's appearance which is made visible in this public arena.

To perform effectively within any field one needs to have accumulated the appropriate capital and mastered the field's habitus. These two, while closely linked and within any particular field overlapping, are conceptually distinct from one another. Capital in Bourdieu's sense refers to skills, knowledge and connections, exchanged within the field to establish and reproduce one's position (see, for instance, Bourdieu, 1996b), while habitus refers to deeply embedded, pre-reflexive capacities and competencies that are practical and embodied (Bourdieu, 1997). These two are intertwined and mutually reinforcing: one's capital in any particular field is, in effect, worn on the body, articulated by one's bodily habitus. While all fields are enacted and reproduced through habitus, in fields which are in some way *about* the body (such as the field of fashion, but one could include the fields of dance, acting, or sex work, for instance) the body is placed centre stage. In other words, the field of fashion is one where the appearance of the body is absolutely critical, in contrast to fields where sublimation of the body and its appearance are central, reflecting the demand to 'transcend' the body in order to 'get on' with one's work in organizations (Hearn *et al.*, 1989; Mills and Tancred-Sheriff, 1992) or simply to forget one has a body, as the model of the traditional academic would have it.

Important to the field of fashion, then, is the ability to articulate recognized forms of fashion capital and develop an appropriate fashion habitus so that one's body actually looks like it belongs. We have already looked at symbolic and social capitals in the field of fashion, above. Critically important also is cultural capital. This includes one's knowledge about, for instance, the history of fashion, but also about up-and-coming designers and trends. It also manifests itself in educational credentials in the form, for instance, of an academic title from an institution highly valued in the field. However, significant for the reproduction of one's position in the field (and performance at events such as LFW) are the objectified forms of cultural capital in the guise of clothes and accessories from fashionable and exclusive brands, all highly dependent on one's economic capital.

Over the course of our research both buyers and journalists reiterated the importance of their dress in the conduct of their work. As one buyer put it, 'I feel such pressure to look the part, that sort of inside myself I rebel against it, and don't. And also, I can't afford to. But you do feel massive pressure, especially at the times of fashion shows'. Similarly, one journalist observes that the show is the biggest most traumatic moment especially because I don't have money to buy the bag'. She adds, 'so you know my way is I have to be really clever so I'm going to wear sneakers or you know I just do it my way, I'm not going to wear a cheap copy. You see all these kind of snobbish things go into you'. Finally, bodily demeanour and carriage are also part of one's performance in the field: in the field of fashion examples would include one's weight – a thin, toned body being a fashionable body – and one's bodily ease during an event such as LFW. Kondo (1997: 103) captures something of this habitus in her description of the 'aplomb and arrogance' with which the 'intimidatingly stylish people' of the fashion field put together their appearance. Herself an outsider, her description would suggest she was not quite at ease with this habitus (something that we also found in our fieldwork experience). Indeed, bodily ease is acquired only through prolonged presence in the field and the mastery of its habitus, a mastery made flesh, carried on and by the body and internalized as the proper way to present oneself, and which the buyer and journalist mentioned above express in their use of expressions such as 'I feel such pressure', and 'things go into you'.

This emphasis upon the body in the field is not just articulated through clothing, but is enacted through bodily performances, such as gestures and greetings, that help to make the system of field relations visible and constitute part of the field's habitus. The 'air kiss', in particular, is a very characteristic greeting within the field of fashion. Quite a theatrical act, it is sometimes accompanied by exclamations or greetings, kissing sounds and touching of hands on shoulders or waist. It is also an example of the way in which the body mediates social relations in this field. Two things are accomplished with this kiss. One, the air kiss requires a bodily proximity that signifies proximity between players in the field and, therefore, belonging and membership. In other words, it is a performative gesture that renders visible otherwise abstract field relations and positions, and, in the process, enacts and reproduces one's social capital. When such an air kiss occurred between one of us and two important buyers, while waiting outside the Vivienne Westwood show in Paris, it signalled a significant moment (at the end of the fieldwork). It demonstrated something about our position in the field that we were, at least temporarily, recognized and worthy of public recognition by these important players, visibly signalling we had acquired a certain amount of social capital. Secondly, the air kiss is a bodily expression that renders visible the field's habitus, its 'mother tongue', that is, the 'grammar, rules and exercises' (Bourdieu, 1997: 67) embodied by the fashion players. Since fashion is a practice *about* the body and its presentation (see Skov *et al.*, 2009: 18–20), bodily ease and the ability to display it – 'showing that one is "at home" in the field' inhabited (Bourdieu 1996a: 128) – are an important part of being a player in this field. The air kiss is part of the culture of the field, allowing for performative enactments necessary to the continued presence in the field and field participants.

The 'air kiss' illustrates the performative nature of the habitus and the way in which otherwise intangible qualities of fields are reproduced through embodiment. As Bourdieu (1997: 57) states, 'it is through the capacity for incorporation, which exploits the body's readiness to take seriously the performative magic of the social, that the king, the banker or the priest are hereditary monarchy, financial capitalism or the Church made flesh'. Indeed, fields are reproduced precisely through the specific forms of embodiment demanded by them. This emphasis upon the performative enters into the accounts that buyers and journalists gave of their practice. For example, one fashion journalist observed that during the fashion shows, 'you have to look the part'. The theatrical metaphor draws attention to the performative presence of field participants during the collections and 'the incessant work of (theatrical) representation, through which agents produce and reproduce [...] at least the appearance of conformity to the group's ideal truth of ideal of truth' (Bourdieu, 1998: 142). Another journalist observes how 'appearance becomes very important' as a way of representing 'the editor, publisher and everyone else', in other words, her publication. In short, one's appearance does not simply mediate one's individual position but institutional position as well. Similarly, buyers also stressed the importance of appearance as part of their role as 'ambassadors' for the store. Indeed, not looking the part can have significant implications for one's career trajectory. One buyer noted how winning contracts with the exclusive fashion brands depends upon looking suitably fashionable, since the buyer, in representing what was, in her case, a 'fashion forward' store, has to embody this image to attract the brands on her buying trips. Failure to embody the image could, eventually, cost her her job.

Thus, in the field of fashion, it is critical that one's body articulates fashion capital, position and status in the field. These field-wide demands are felt most acutely during LFW precisely because it materializes or objectifies the field, rendering visible, through the staging of the gaze, field positions, status and power, as discussed above. In sum, these experiences point to the way the body acts as another boundary marker in the field. As these experiences suggest, the boundaries of the body are important for marking out insider and insider status of the field itself: bodies demonstrate they belong, they are 'inside' through their appearance, and this appearance is essential to the reproduction of the key players whose careers depend upon it.

Conclusion

In this paper we have argued that LFW renders visible the boundaries, relational positions and capitals at play in the wider field of fashion. We have discussed the ways in which the boundaries of this event mirror the boundaries of the wider field, allowing access only to those defined as players in the field. Within the event itself, the spatial arrangements also reproduce critical divisions and hierarchies within the field, most notably, the division between art and commerce, and between the different players themselves. The relational positions between players are, however, most visibly reproduced within the confines of the catwalk theatre where hierarchies of time and space are enacted that replicate the power held by different players. As well as making visible the field, LFW is a ceremony of consecration, to quote Bourdieu (2000b: 66) again, 'reproducing the system which ensures their reproduction'. With LFW having little to do with the selling of garments, the shows function to promote the work of designers, as well as the field's players. Although not ostensibly a place of financial exchange or a market in the manner of more traditional fairs, it is a platform for the consolidation of the value of players' economic capital by way of the consolidation of their symbolic capital.

Physical presence, that is, being seen in the field, gives witness to their field membership. It is for this reason that we argue that the presence of the players in the field is a performative one, their appearance, bodily manners, indeed their habitus, being critical to the reproduction of their position within the field. This is reinforced by the orchestration of the gaze, especially within the catwalk theatre, where everyone, but especially the main players on the front row, is subject and object of the gaze of others. Here the body itself is a signifier of field membership.

Throughout this paper, then, we demonstrate the value of Bourdieu's field theory for understanding real institutional settings and their role in the reproduction of the field to which they belong. Fields are not merely abstract spaces of positions but can be seen as embodied spaces of practice. This attention to fields as enacted through material settings puts field theory *in situ* allowing us to reconcile field theory and fieldwork, two key moments in Bourdieu's work, but which he himself does not fully reunite.

Notes

* We are grateful to Don Slater for his helpful feedback on earlier drafts. Dr Entwistle would also like to thank the Economic and Social Research Council (ESRC) for supporting her fieldwork on fashion buyers (grant reference: R000223649). Both authors contributed equally to the paper.

1. When the research was conducted one of us was a London College of Fashion member of staff. While this connection certainly helped in some respects, membership of one of the institutions in the field of fashion does not grant membership to its other institutions. Thus, the researcher was an outsider to the specific institutions of fashion journalism and LFW.
2. Interview data gathered in the course of fieldwork on models in 2001.
3. In this respect, 'the fashion show consists of two performances encased in each other' (Skov *et al.*, 2009: 5).

References

Accardo, A. 1995. *Journalistes au Quotidien*. Paris: Le Mascaret.
  1997. *Introduction à une Sociologie Critique*. Paris: Le Mascaret.
Aspers, P. 2001. *Markets in Fashion: a Phenomenological Approach*. Stockholm: City University Press.
Bathelt, H. 2007. 'Buzz-and-pipeline: toward a knowledge-based multiplier model of clusters', *Geography Compass* 1:6, 1,282–98.
Bathelt, H., Malmberg, A. and Maskell, P. 2004. 'Clusters and knowledge: local buzz, global pipelines and the processes of knowledge creation', *Progress in Human Geography* 28:1, 31–56.
Bathelt, H. and Schuldt, N. 2005. 'Between luminaries and meat grinders: international trade fairs as temporary clusters', *Space: Spatial Aspects Concerning Economic Structures* 6, 1–28.
  2008. 'Temporary face-to-face contact and the ecologies of global and virtual buzz', *Space: Spatial Aspects Concerning Economic Structures* 6:4, 1–23.
Bonnewitz, P. 1998. *Premières Leçons sur la Sociologie de P. Bourdieu*. Paris: Presses Universitaires de France.
Bourdieu, P. 1975. (with Delsaut, Y.) 'Le couturier et sa griffe. Contribution à une théorie de la magie', *Actes de la Recherche en Sciences Sociales* 1, 7–36.
  1993a. *The Field of Cultural Production*. Cambridge: Polity Press.
  1993b. *La Misère du Monde*. Paris: Editions du Seuil.
  1995. *Sociology in Question*. London: Sage.
  1996a. (with Wacquant, L. J. D.) *An Invitation to Reflexive Sociology*. Cambridge: Polity Press.
  1996b. *The Rules of Art*. Cambridge: Polity Press.
  1997. *The Logic of Practice*. Cambridge: Polity Press.
  1998. *Practical Reason*. Stanford California Press.
  2000a. *Esquisse d'une Théorie de la Pratique*. Paris: Points Seuil.
  2000b. *Propos sur le Champ Politique*. Presses Universitaires de Lyon.

Breward, C. and Gilbert, D. 2006. *Fashion's World Cities*. Oxford: Berg.

Cartner-Morley, J. 2003. 'The catwalk, darling? It's so last year', *The Guardian* 13 October, p. 3.

Crossley, N. 2004. 'The circuit trainer's habitus: reflexive body techniques and the sociality of the workout', *Body and Society* 10:1, 37–69.

Entwistle, J. 2009. *The Aesthetic Economy: Markets in Clothing and Fashion Modelling*. Oxford: Berg.

    2010. 'Global Flows, Local Encounters: Spatializing Tacit Aesthetic Knowledge in High Fashion'. volume 8, www.spaces-online.com.

Foucault, M. 1977. *Discipline and Punish*. Harmondsworth: Penguin.

    1980. *Power-knowledge*. Brighton: Harvester Press.

Gilbert, D. 2000. 'Urban outfitting: the city and the spaces of fashion culture', in S. Bruzzi and P. Church-Gibson (eds.), *Fashion Cultures*. London: Routledge, pp. 7–24.

Perint Palmer, G. 2003. *Fashion People*. New York: Assouline.

Hearn, J., Sheppard, D., Tancred, P. and Burrell, G. (eds.) 1989. *Sexuality of Organization*. London: Sage.

Kawamura, Y. 2004. *The Japanese Revolution in Paris Fashion*. Oxford: Berg.

Khan, N. 2000. 'Catwalk politics', in S. Bruzzi and P. Church-Gibson (eds.), *Fashion Cultures*. London: Routledge, pp. 114–27.

Kondo, D. 1997. *About Face: Performing Race in Fashion and in Theater*. New York: Routledge.

Marshall, A. 1923. *Industry and Trade: a Study of Industrial Technique and Business Organization; and of their Influences and on the Conditions of Various Classes and Nations*. London: Macmillan.

McRobbie, A. 1998. *British Fashion Design*. London: Routledge.

Mills, A. J. and Tancred-Sheriff, P. 1992. *Gendering Organizational Analysis*. London: Sage.

Persson, T. 2003. *The Fashion Journalist*. MA dissertation, Central Saint Martins College of Art and Design.

Rocamora, A. 2009. *Fashioning the City: Paris, Fashion and the Media*. London: I. B. Tauris.

Rocamora, A. and Bartlett, D. (forthcoming). 'Fashion blogging: the new fashion journalism', in S. Black (ed.), *The Eco Fashion Handbook*. London: Thames and Hudson.

Skov, L. 2006. 'The role of trade fairs in the global fashion business', *Current Sociology* 54:5, 764–83.

Skov, L., Skjold, E., Moeran B., Larsen, F. and Csaba, F. F. 2009. 'The fashion show as an art form'. *Creative Encounters* Working Paper 12. Copenhagen Business School, October.

Tilberi, L. 1998. *Front Row*. London: Coronet.

Tseëlon, E. 1995. *The Masque of Femininity*. London: Sage.

11 Configuring sustainability at fashion week

LISE SKOV AND JANNE MEIER

In recent years, the principle of sustainability has presented itself as a challenge to the global economic system in general (Jackson, 2009), and to the fashion industry in particular. At first sight, what Orvar Löfgren (2005) has called its 'catwalk economy' – the systematic launching of new collections in the framework of biannual fashion weeks – seems to clash with the long-term orientation of sustainability, as expressed in the United Nations (UN) definition of sustainable development as 'development that meets the needs of the present without compromising the ability of future generations to meet their own needs'.

Even so, the value ascribed to sustainability signifies an ethical turn in business, which has foregrounded the responsibility to address problems related to climate and environment, as well as labour, animal welfare and corporate philanthropy. In association with terms such as organic, eco, green, fair trade and, in company strategy, corporate social responsibility and codes of conduct, sustainability is a figure that is vague enough to gloss over big varieties in definition, stakeholder interest and involvement, and at the same time powerful enough to draw the commitment of many different actors, including consumers, companies and (inter)national organizations. As such we use it as the heading for a new collective value orientation.

This chapter presents an analysis of how European fashion companies represent, commit to and reflect on sustainability, both in strategy and marketing, and in the meetings, sales pitches and informal talks that constitute the so-called buzz of the industry. The analysis is based on participant observation at two European fashion weeks, Berlin and Copenhagen, in the summer of 2009. Data from the fieldwork, which was conducted by Janne Meier, has been analysed against the backdrop of two small but growing bodies of research: firstly, on trade fairs and festivals, and secondly, on sustainable, green and fair fashion. In particular, the analysis builds on Lise Skov's previous research on fashion weeks, fashion shows and trade fairs (2004a, 2004b, 2006; Skov *et al.*,

2009; Melchior *et al.*, 2011), and on ethical issues faced by the fashion industry (Skov, 2008).

The methodological advantage of following a new value parameter's trajectory through the empirical setting of fashion week is that we are able to study change as it unfolds in an organizational field. We conceptualize this as a dual process of externalization – making relative positions visible and fixing value hierarchies – and internalization – ongoing questioning, experimentation and learning of cultural models in different interactional contexts. Theoretically this duality is reflected in the application of two research approaches. From institutional sociology we take the concept of field-configuring events (FCEs), representing what we call externalization. From cognitive anthropology, we take the concept of figured, or narrativized, world: in this latter approach internalization is a key term. The figured world is a collective discursive construction of a cultural world, realized through statements and artefacts, which organize meaning and values in a given field.

The analysis presented in this chapter thus pertains to the genuinely open-ended relationship between industry event and organizational field. Through the study of how the field, or world, is figured by the stories told at the event, we hope to bring out some of the hitherto unrealized analytical potential of the compelling term, field-*configuring* event.

Clashes between fashion and sustainability

We start out with a fieldwork observation to establish a frame of interpretation with regard to the troubled relationship between fashion and sustainability. The opening of the Spring/Summer 2010 Copenhagen Fashion Week, held in August 2009, was marked by a press conference at the city hall, in which sustainability and ethics were high on the agenda. This commitment had been prompted by Nordic Initiative Clean and Ethical (NICE), the Norwegian-led driver behind the formation of a new (regional) Nordic Fashion Association the previous year, and it was paving the way for the fashion events, planned in conjunction with the UN Climate Change Conference COP 15, to be held in Copenhagen a few months later in December 2009. Senior representatives of the Danish Fashion Institute, bio tech company Novozymes and the municipality of Copenhagen jointly endorsed a one-minute film and campaign, entitled 'I do 30'. Consumers were encouraged to save energy by doing their laundry at no warmer than 30 degrees Celsius, and it was stressed that, 'every individual can make a difference'. But the appeal was tempered by Eva Kruse, head of the Danish Fashion Institute, who said, 'Wash at 30. Your clothes will last longer', and added as an afterthought, 'You still have to buy new clothes next year, though. But then you'll have more in your wardrobe'.

In this slip (or was it as statement?), the sustainability logic of prolonged use clashes with the fashion logic of acquiring new things. As is often the case, the former loses out to the latter. It rejects, and in doing so asserts, the industry's association of sustainability with self restraint and dullness, in contrast to the pleasure-seeking ethos of fashion. Indeed it would have been surprising if an event dedicated to next year's shopping for clothes had started out with a warning against its own purpose. It is more striking, perhaps, that it was not one of the Danish fashion companies, or the trade association, the main stakeholders of the event, but a bio tech company, that took centre stage at the official opening. The bio tech industry is not usually seen as a player in the fashion world, but with research and development departments it is well adapted to present 'solutions', unlike the fashion industry, a globalized manufacturing industry invariably stuck with the acknowledged problems of environmental destruction and poor labour conditions.

This reflects the fact that 'hybrid forums' (Callon *et al.*, 2002: 194) such as multi-stakeholder initiatives and network organizations, play an increasing role in business. The principles of sustainability were first applied to issues of environmental impact and technology development, referring to what Moeran (2004) has called production or technical values. But from the middle of the first decade of the twenty-first century the green issue has been enthusiastically adopted by marketing and communication departments (Kleanthous and Peck (2006). The snappy 'I do 30' campaign in an upbeat advertising-like format is typical of consumer politics, with media constraints that are forced to focus on single issues and simple messages (Gabriel and Lang, 2006; Kleanthous and Peck, 2006; Skov, 2008). Even though it is possible to find campaigns that address a wide range of problems such as labour conditions, land use, environmental impact, animal welfare and gender and body images, it is rare to find a holistic approach that recognizes the interrelatedness of the problems, or presents a vision for system change (Bendell and Kleanthous, 2007; Chouinard, 2006; Devinney *et al.*, 2006; Labour Behind the Label, 2006; Model Health Inquiry, 2007).

To be sure, a campaign about washing is well-founded. Each European consumer annually produces over ten kilogrammes of textile waste, and a large proportion of garments are discarded because they have been altered or worn out in the washing machine (Klepp, 2006; 2008). In addition to energy, the use of water and detergent makes clothes washing the largest fashion-induced negative environmental impact from the consumers' perspective (but by no means globally, as cotton farming, which requires extensive use of pesticides and water, is by far the biggest malefactor). Even so, the endorsement of a gentler washing cycle seems a bit too modest an ambition. If consumers begin to look after their clothes better, shouldn't the industry make clothes that are worth looking after? Even optimistic analysts and practitioners who argue that there is genuine potential for economic growth in sustainable development, such as McDonough and Braungart's 'cradle-to-cradle' concept (2002), assert that this depends on a radical rethinking of product development and life cycles. The fact that the fashion industry is directly dependent on consumer demand has been a hindrance to such a radical innovation. Its business innovations have been in the direction of what we call the catwalk economy, the development of variety and fast product turnover, thereby elevating the experience of shopping over that of owning and wearing clothes.

However, this has not made sustainability what, in their Introduction to this book, Moeran and Strandgaard Pedersen call an appreciative value; on the contrary, the industry people we talked to distance themselves from designs that 'look' organic because they consider that aesthetic incompatible with fashion. In their narratives, the value of sustainability cannot enter the plot of a fashion story. Instead sustainability appears as what we call a 'feel-good' value, communicated through hang-tags, booth props, posters, websites and other artefacts that constitute the narratives of fashion marketing. In this respect, it is not visible in the actual clothes, and it is subordinate to the dominant logic of fashion.

Fashion week as field-configuring event

Fashion week, the widely used term for trade fairs in the apparel business, consists of temporally grouped events such as fashion shows, promotions, press conferences and sales exhibitions in several fair grounds. The convention of biannual *defilé* fashion shows was originally established in France during the second world war when all aspects of business, from fabric supplies to visas for visiting buyers, were scarce and rationed (Grumbach, 2006). In the following decades, the bi-annual fashion week cycle caught on internationally as multiple fairs were organized by regional and national garment industries to attract their share of international buyers.

In recent decades the number of fashion weeks worldwide has grown considerably, although the fair's function as a marketplace has become less important – so that this particular instance supports a general tendency noted in the Introduction. The speeding up of product development from two annual collections to near-continuous delivery of new merchandise, known as fast fashion, requires ongoing collaboration between fashion brands and their suppliers. But loss of some of its original purpose has not led to the fair's demise. On the contrary, for the companies that attend fashion week, the opportunity to trade has been joined by, firstly, the opportunity for face-to-face meetings with representatives of partner companies, to consolidate what are otherwise mostly virtual relationships; and secondly, to search for information about new trends, products and business opportunities. The latter, as we have seen in earlier chapters, includes both a programme of seminars with industry experts and visiting the booths of consulting companies, and the informal way of gathering information by 'looking around' and listening to the buzz that spreads rapidly through the fair grounds.

Skov (2006) has conceptualized this as a shift from 'export fairs', which sell local produce to visiting buyers, to 'intermediary fairs', which, detached from the interests of local industry, function as nodal points for multiple stakeholders. It is striking that, while the bi-annual cycle is less functional for garment suppliers and branded fashion companies, it is still strictly followed by the fashion press, which opens each new season with a fashion week report with the prescribed time delays. For example, the fashion weeks studied in this paper, entitled Spring/Summer 2010, were held in the summer of 2009 and reported in the magazines the following year in the March issue, which marks the beginning of the Spring/Summer season.[1] The Fall (Autumn)/ Winter season is instigated by the September issue (appropriately also the title of the 2009 feature-length documentary about American *Vogue* and Anna Wintour, its renowned editor-in-chief). This increasing dominance of marketing, promotion and image creation over trade has been instrumental in giving fashion week such an important role in the catwalk economy.

This function of structuring and ordering is central to the understanding of fashion week as an FCE. As the term is used in psychology or astrology, a configuration is a stable constellation of elements that make up a whole. Fashion week creates a spatial sensory representation of the organizational field, organized according to the themes and industry segments in different fair grounds, and – as we have seen in earlier discussions of book fairs, television markets and London Fashion Week – by relative size and position of exhibitors' booths, fashion show scenes and schedules, seating arrangements, access to invitation cards, fair passes and so on. In addition to this material realization of fashion week, which is fixed as part of the preparation for the event, there are a number of unplanned occurrences, which for regular fair-goers tend to represent its most attractive elements. Which booths attract the most visitors? Who do you encounter by chance on the shuttle bus going from one fair ground to the next? What are people talking about? What is new? This special ability of the fair to make the field structure visible has been conceptualized by Entwistle and Rocamora as 'the field materialized' in a Bourdieu-inspired analysis of London Fashion Week. Based on Goffman (1986), Callon (1998) and White (1981), Skov (2006) has conceptualized trade fairs as framing devices which create 'conditions of comparability' that enable producers to observe and assess one another's relative positions.

In this vein, Skov (2006) proposes to see the fair as a *city*. This definition follows a tradition in urban sociology that goes back to Georg Simmel (1950) and Louis Wirth (1938), and which has more recently been brought into urban anthropology by Ulf Hannerz (1980), where the focus is on how the interaction of strangers gives urban life its characteristic of an overload of sensory stimuli – superficial interaction made necessary by the diversity of people in a compressed space, and the transience of moods and atmospheres. As for the fair, its intensity is only increased by the short duration of the city-like formation, built up and peopled for this brief encounter. The fashion fair thus can be conceptualized as a city in the figured world of fashion. As a get-together of multiple actors with different agendas, and the ensuing multiperspective sense-making, fashion weeks offer participants, however constrained they might be by their positions in the field, an opportunity to negotiate industry-specific stories and meanings while cognitively and narratively linking their own position and understandings to the figured world of fashion.

This metaphor complements the notion of fashion week as a tournament ritual (Anand and Jones, 2008; Appadurai, 1986). Unlike the awards and prize ceremonies discussed elsewhere in this book, fashion week does not produce, as its main outcome, or even as a significant by-product, a formal ranking of actors in the field. Rather, the sense-making that goes on at fashion week is much more complex than, for example, the way the term is used in Anand and Peterson (2000) in their study of the role of music charts in constituting the field of the commercial music industry in the US. Fashion week does not lend itself to a privileged viewpoint, from which the diversity and segmentation of the fashion industry can be condensed into a single hierarchy, even if only for a short duration. There are many, but not unlimited, perspectives, interpretations and comparisons, conducted from different viewpoints.

To be sure, awards are well integrated in the fashion week programme. But the participants in fashion show contests are invariably young designers, such as the eco-fashion contest for ten young designers from Copenhagen and Berlin, 'Next Vision: Bright Green Fashion', which was staged at the 2009 Copenhagen Design Week as a launch for a regional forum for sustainable design. While winning such a contest can be an important distinction in a young designer's *curriculum vitae*, it does not make his or her business fortune. In so far as s/he has a viable company at all, it is such a small business that it cannot handle the steep increase in orders, of the kind expected by award winners in, say, the book publishing or film industries discussed elsewhere in this volume. One effect of this delinking of contest and business is that a competition for 'up-and-coming talent' can be used to promote a range of different purposes, from exploration of a new area to celebrating the creativity of the host city or industry (Skov, 2004a, 2004b).

Seeing fashion week fairs as cities is also different from seeing them as festivals. Following Bakhtin (1993) and Turner (1969), we characterize festivals as a form of anti-structure, alternating from the normal social structure. There are many receptions and parties during the days of the fair, and fashion people in Europe have a distinct preference for champagne and good food. Yet in the midst of all this festivity, networking and positioning can be deadly serious activities. The sense of being there, participating in and observing the spectacle constitute not only a cognitive but also a social experience which can induce an intense feeling of belonging to the fashion industry. In this respect, fashion week is not subversive, but conducive to the way in which business is conducted during the rest of the year. It is the kind of event that combines purposeful involvement and fun, order and disorder at a high level of complexity.

At fashion week, the structure and state of the industry may be grasped with all of one's senses, but the perception is always partial and fragmented, dependent not only on the individual outlook, but also on the interaction of others at any particular moment. In order to do justice to this open-ended, never complete understanding of the event, we wish to supplement the conception of fashion week as an FCE with the notion of *figured worlds*.

Fashion week as figured world

The analytical concept of 'figured worlds' has been developed by cognitive anthropologists Holland and Quinn who have studied the internalization of cultural systems, with special attention paid to the interactional context of learning. Figured worlds are 'socially generated and culturally constructed frames of interpretation in which particular characters and actors are recognized, significances assigned to certain acts and particular outcomes valued over others' (Holland *et al.*, 1998: 52; see also Holland and Quinn, 1987; Holland, 1992). In contrast to the term 'configuration', which refers to outer forms constituting a whole, the verb 'figure' signifies imagination or calculation in an everyday sort of way. This is what Holland *et al.* (1998: 52), refer to when they call a figured world, 'a collectively realized "as if" realm', building on Vygotsky's notion that play and pretend games constitute the most important elements in learning processes. However, culturally figured worlds are not imaginary realms, but rather perceptions of what is real. They are not necessarily expressed in language and never in their entirety, although they organize meaning (Hervik, 2004).

The figured world of fashion 'take[s] shape within, and grant[s] shape to, the co-production of activities, discourses, performances and artefacts' (Holland *et al.*, 1998: 61–2) which make up the fashion week events. It is a narrativized, simplified, culturally modelled world which allows participants to share at least some measure of taken for granted, industry specific 'common sense' interpretation of events and actions, a standard plot against which stories of change and unusual events are told. We have already seen elements of this: for example, the belief that the dynamic of fashion is opposed to and incompatible with sustainability; the perception that the industry is dependent on an exploitative rationality; the distinction between easy-going fashion consumers and decidedly unfashionable political consumers; and the suspicion that consumers, although they might pay lip service to green values, cannot be trusted to pay a premium price for merchandise produced under better conditions. The figured world of fashion comes to life during fashion week through the artefacts, such as press coverage, fair programmes, show schedules and promotional material from exhibitors, which are handed out and eagerly collected. Such artefacts evoke the world in which they are figured and relevant, and serve as instruments both for orientation during the busy days of fashion week and collective remembrance afterwards (Holland *et al.*, 1998: 61–3).

Arjun Appadurai (1986: 48) has pointed to the importance of narratives in business: 'as the institutional and spatial journeys of commodities grow more complex and the alienation of producers, traders, and consumers from one another increases, culturally formed mythologies about commodity flows are likely to emerge'. In his understanding, such narratives compensate for the knowledge that arises from direct interaction. In this vein, story-telling at fashion week is induced both by the ordinary distance and the extra-ordinary proximity between industry actors. (Under these conditions, 'economic markets are caught in a reflexive activity: the actors concerned explicitly question their organization and, based on analysis of their functioning, try to conceive and establish new rules for the game' (Callon *et al.*, 2002: 194).

Once we conceptualize fashion week as an ant's nest with myriad activities and interactions which do not afford any privileged point of view, we cannot claim such a position for ourselves as researchers either. During our fieldwork we participated in press events, seminars, fashion shows and shop openings, visited many of the fair grounds and had numerous informal conversations with a variety of different actors, mostly exhibitors, but also with buyers, press and organizers. Our behaviour as participant observers was not qualitatively different from that of industry people, for whom learning may well be the stated purpose of visiting a fair.

If it makes sense to conceptualize all fair-goers as participant observers, it is because fashion week has this quality of compressing extensive social relations into a single space and time frame. In this respect, our interpretation of fashion week continues a tradition in anthropology starting with Max Gluckman's account of the opening of a bridge across the River Zambezi in Swaziland. The depth of the account, which has made it famous, comes from its being at the same time a detailed ethnographic record of what took place on that particular day and a view into an underlying social structure (Gluckman, 1958). This approach has been conceptualized by Michael Burawoy as the extended case method (Burawoy, 1991; Burawoy *et al.*, 2000), the ethnographic study of a scene of microlevel interaction, selected because it reflects and refracts the macro structures of the wider world. Fashion week is, indeed, such a social frame that makes the structures of the whole field visible, but it does so in the figure of complex human interaction.

The difference in this ethnographic approach from the institutional perspective discussed above is that the former does not limit itself to the pre-scripted ritualistic part of the event. It includes unplanned and unintentional interaction, such as waiting, gossip and chance encounters, which is the inevitable outcome of multiple actors in the same time and space frame. It allows us to explore the intense contrast and interdependence of the carefully planned, highly controlled and orchestrated nature of most major events, and the chaos, excitement and anticipation of spontaneous revelation that the organizers simultaneously convey to the attendees. Our argument is that both ritual and buzz feed into the continuous field configuration that takes place at the event.

Three green industry segments

One of the characteristics of the clothing industry is its segmentation, not only in terms of consumers – men, women, children – and functionalities – work, evening, leisure, sports – but also in terms of price-lining, styles and pace of turnover. Historically only women's outerwear has been designated fashion, but in recent decades the tendency has been to use fashion as a cover term for the whole clothing industry, reflecting the speeded-up product development in areas such as menswear, children's wear, underwear and accessories, that used to be relatively stable. This segmentation has been studied by scholars, like Nancy Green (1997), and Ben Fine and Ellen Leopold (1993), of such non-technologically driven industrial development as exists, but it has also captured the attention of intellectual property scholars who find that, in lieu of copyright protection, market segmentation and continuous launching of novelties provide a protection for product development (Bollier *et al.*, 2010; Löfgren, 2005). Thus, even though the fashion industry is saturated by rip-offs of different degrees, it also offers multiple niches that shelter companies from direct competition. As we shall see, the recent ethical turn has also been used in service of this industry logic.

For some decades, there has been a relatively well-established niche market for sustainable clothes, basics for adults and children, with loose-fitting designs and monochrome marks. They are typically sold in health food or craft stores, rather than in department stores or boutiques. With a few exceptions, such companies do not participate in fashion weeks. Their production is based on value networks that can guarantee commodities and production conditions, certified according to international standards, which require a high level of control down to the make and origin of thread, buttons and elastic band.

In contrast, mainstream fashion companies tend not to adhere to such high standards. The reason for this is that the certified sourcing systems are not geared to large-scale production as they are somewhat irregular, based as they are on natural produce. So, rather than compromise their credibility if they are unable to source, say, the right organic buttons for this year's look, fashion companies reserve full control over their products, in particular the ability to change them from one year to the next. Sustainability is written into company strategy only as a commitment to principles and goals, not to a network of suppliers. In the industry there is a tendency to call this 'green', indicating, perhaps, a flexible commitment. A colour designation is familiar ground for a fashion company, and might indicate that just as colours such as blue or pink can be in fashion some years, so green was in fashion by the end of the first decade of the twenty-first century (Barthes, 2006).

On the basis of our fieldwork we were able to identify three ways in which fashion companies wore the fashionable colour during the period of our research. These three emergent industry segments, which we call 'soft green', 'hardcore green' and 'green luxury', are not yet acknowledged in comprehensive industry analyses, so we are unable to estimate their size and importance. However, it is safe to say that 'soft green', also known as 'light green', is by far the largest. 'Soft green' consists of brands that are securely positioned commercially, mostly use conventional materials and production methods, but set aside a small part of their collection, or a special sub-brand, for ethical initiatives, typically organic cotton. In this segment, sustainability is not a core value, but an extra bonus. Most companies have committed to social responsibility initiatives, but the degree to which they implement them varies greatly. There is an increasing focus on third party auditing and alliances with multi-stakeholder initiatives and non-governmental organizations (NGOs). Some NGOs, notably the Fairtrade Foundation, have adapted to these conditions by certifying producers and companies who only partially live up to fair trade terms, in the belief that the certificate will help secure a solid basis for fair trade business development. An example of 'soft green' is the Danish middle-market brand Jackpot, which has developed the sub-brand Jackpot Organic, with includes relatively few new styles, including a charity t-shirt, in the overall collection. These are foregrounded in marketing, so that at Copenhagen Fashion Week the Jackpot Organic line was the brand's only visible identity, as a selling point for the Jackpot brand's entire collection.

In contrast, in the 'hardcore green' segment, environmental and social responsibility is an integrated part of original brand identity. This is typically only possible for brands that have been founded with a strong green value orientation, such as American outdoor wear brands Patagonia and Dutch jeans brand Kuyichi, discussed later in this chapter. At both Berlin and Copenhagen fashion weeks, this segment was mainly represented by its biggest and best established brands, typically in the 'street and urban wear' section. Smaller hardcore greens tend not to participate in fashion weeks; instead they attend alternative eco-fairs, thus bordering on the alternative clothes market, mentioned above. The Green Area at the PREMIUM trade fair in Berlin tried to break up this long established industry segmentation by creating a fashionable space for brands that want to be clearly identified as green. However, several hardcore green fashion brands, among them the Danish 'The Baand' could be found outside the designated Green Area. They perceived the clash between sustainability and fashion as too great for a small brand to overcome, and did not want to risk their position as a *fashion* brand. In comparison to the soft green, the hardcore green segment is very small. Most people we talked to outside this segment expressed the opinion that hardcore green is not a legitimate part of the fashion industry. It is associated with politically motivated consumers, who are perceived to be old hippies far removed from the proper target market of the fashion industry. In Berlin, however, the alternative fair 'The Key.to' created a space for hardcore greens with a strong fashion identity. This attempt, along with the Green Area at Premium, can be seen as the fair organizer's attempt to brand their event by connecting it to the value of sustainability, reconfigure the fashion field and carve out a niche for hardcore green fashion brands whose targeted consumers are fashion conscious but 'caring'. The subsequent growth of this fair in January 2010 and the events planned there for July 2010 show a consolidation of this sub-field and the success of the move.

The third segment, green luxury, which was visible as an emerging sub-field in Berlin and to a lesser degree in Copenhagen, is aimed at the high end of the market. Most companies in this segment are led by name designers. Green luxury is characterized by valuing quality and style over fast fashion, expressed in a preference for exclusive natural materials and craft-based manufacturing methods. In this respect, it represents a genuine attempt to couple the principle of sustainability with craftsmanship and luxury fashion, and to appeal to what the industry perceives to be a new kind of consumer who combines an ethical concern with fashion sense.

At the two fashion weeks, these green segments stood out against a background of 'business as usual', which made up by far the largest part of exhibitors, mostly small and medium-sized businesses in the price-driven, middle-market segments. When we asked people from such companies how they perceived sustainability as a value parameter in the industry, they drew a line between fashion consumers, whom they perceived to be price and style conscious, and political consumers, who were seen as the antithesis to fashion. They also expressed mistrust of brands that marketed themselves on ethical issues, which they saw as incompatible with the industry's structure and logic, and described them as 'cynical' or 'merciless'. This expressed their realistic, though not enthusiastic, acceptance of the exploitative nature of the fashion industry, while at the same time voicing the belief that fashion would never lead the way to a more sustainable economic system. Furthermore, many exhibitors referred to the economic crisis as a reminder that the fashion industry and its figured world is highly competitive. Many of the business-as-usual brands we talked to saw their staying in business as their main contribution to a sustainable economy because continued relationships with suppliers secured manufacturing jobs, albeit low paid. In this narrative, sustainability is translated into the harsh 'reality' of the industry and the figure of the shop floor worker defies the fashion story.

It was clear that the values of fashion governed each event; sustainability did not enter as an equal value orientation. Hardcore greens expressed their disdain for soft greens who used references to sustainability as a marketing tool. But ultimately, none of the greens we talked to questioned the overall importance of fashion value, the hierarchy or structure of the field of fashion, or indeed sought to subvert it. Instead, they sought to link their brand story to the fashion world master narrative, as a means of advancing or consolidating positions and be recognized as legitimate in the figured world of fashion.

Berlin and Copenhagen (con)figured

In the remainder of this chapter we examine how actors at different levels – municipalities, event managers and fashion brands – are involved, and how the event is configured by both the stabilizing force of planning and controlling and the destabilizing force of movement and emergence. For the municipalities of Berlin and Copenhagen, hosting of a fashion week is an important symbolic statement. For second-tier fashion cities such as these, and indeed for many of the cities that have launched new fashion weeks in the last two decades, it seems particularly important that each fashion week lends its lustre to the whole city (Melchior *et al.*, 2011). However, as we shall see, while officials seek to anchor the events in the surrounding cities, the orientation of the industry players from small fashion brands to fair organizers is, if not completely global, then highly deterritorialized. The public–private partnership between Berlin Partner GmBH and the Senate Department for Economics, Technology and Woman's Issues, which jointly co-ordinate fashion week events, write the following on its website:

Twice a year, Berlin transforms into a national and international fashion metropolis. As part of the Berlin Fashion Week (BFW), buyers, fashion experts and media reps come together to attend glamorous fashion shows and awards ceremonies, to visit trade fairs and to enjoy a variety of exhibitions and off-site events. These two annual fashion weeks contribute significantly to Berlin's economic growth as a major style capital.[2]

We note the explicit link between economic growth potential and a major style capital, a causation which, in spite of its uncertainty, is the central assumption of creative industry policy (Melchior *et al.*, 2011). On the official website for Copenhagen Fashion Week the focus on nation and city branding is stronger:

Danish fashion is known for its unique angle on design, innovation and aesthetics. With a more modern approach to femininity and functionality, expressed in fresh silhouettes, a focus on details and incomparable quality. These are only some of the reasons why more than 50,000 buyers, designers and global press attend Copenhagen Fashion Week twice a year. Of course, the other main attraction is Copenhagen itself. It's a cosy, metropolitan city located by the waterfront, and features an interesting array of design venues, architecture, cultural events, cafés, bars and nightlife.[3]

On the official website, the co-ordinator of Copenhagen Fashion Week, the Danish Fashion Institute, emphasizes the sustainability theme as an image for both city and fashion week. It features a downloadable map of the 'Green Walk', a shopping tour to local shops 'carrying at least one brand with a sustainable profile'.

In his classic study of trade fairs, geographer Allix (1922) has shown how historically fairs have been set apart from host cities, in special fair grounds, governed by exceptional trading regulations. In the case of fashion week, we may add that there is even a special time warp, almost a year ahead of the surrounding city. However, host cities have always used fairs to boost their own images. Most fair grounds and shows can only be accessed by those who have secured entry cards in advance. Sometimes accreditation and control can be tedious (witness earlier comments by Entwistle and Rocamora, Chapter 10).[4] The general public is allowed to participate only in designated events which are usually not attended by industry professionals. In Berlin, the Showroom Meile presented live events with selected fashion designers for Berliners, tourists and business visitors. In Copenhagen, big screens in central squares broadcast the major fashion shows minutes after they had taken place on the catwalk. Likewise, Copenhagen Fashion Weekend – the name indicates the shift from work to leisure – offers a programme of events, mostly related to sales, that are open to the public.

Beneath the tidy official self presentations of the two 'creative cities' are myriad different fair grounds that constitute fashion week in each city. Copenhagen has five separate fairs: Copenhagen International Fashion Fair (CIFF), for commercial middle-to-low market brands, with a large section devoted to children's wear, in the exhibition hall Bella Centre; three fairs for designer fashion – CPH Vision, Terminal 2 and Gallery; and one alternative fair, Unfair, which does not appear in the official programme. The latter four are located in trendy converted industrial spaces in different parts of the city, and, except for Unfair, are connected by a shuttle bus service.

In Berlin, Mercedes Benz Fashion Week Berlin (MBFWB), located in a big white show tent at Bebelplatz on Unter den Linden, acts as a uniting visual symbol for fashion week. Along with four smaller companies, Mercedes Benz has teamed up with the global media company International Management Group (IMG) to organize the major fashion shows, press services and transportation between events. Mercedes Benz is also the co-sponsor of the PREMIUM fair, which takes place at Station-Berlin, an old postal freight depot in Kreutzberg. PREMIUM, one of the first trade fairs to showcase green fashion, featured a special 'Green Area' for brands with an ethical agenda. As mentioned earlier, many brands are ambivalent about being confined to what they perceive to be an 'alternative' market segment, and the fair adapted to that concern in its programme by printing in green ink the names of the green companies that were exhibiting outside the designated area.

In addition, there was also a 'Green Showroom', a small fair for sustainable luxury and life style, located in six suites in the upmarket Hotel Adlon Kempinski. Although not included in the official Berlin Fashion Show website, it received a lot of press attention, as it was sponsored by MBFWB and advertised in their press material. Included in the official programme was also 'The Key.to', a new trade fair for hardcore sustainable fashion and life style, which has established itself, not only as an event organizer, but also as a knowledge centre. The Key.to was located in an old post office in Neukölln, and tried to make up for its distance from the other fair grounds by offering an 'eco-friendly' Toyota-sponsored shuttle service to the street wear fair, Bread & Butter, at Tempelhof Airport. In addition to the fair grounds, established companies may set up private off-site show rooms, where they receive only specially invited buyers and press – much in the manner noted by Havens of global television markets (Chapter 6).[5]

All these fair grounds shape the distinctive landscapes of the two cities' fashion weeks. Organizers put enormous effort into securing easy transportation from one location to another, so that it is possible to participate in the fair without visiting, or getting lost in, the city. This array of different trade fairs, all devoted to specific market segments and flavoured by their location in certain city landmarks and distinctive areas, presents exhibitors with a strategic dilemma of working out which location is most advantageous for them to appear in. As a result of the recent proliferation of fairs, organizers compete for exhibitors, not only at a national but also at an international level. Although they may reject brands that they consider wrong for the image they wish to project, it is relatively easy for exhibitors to relocate to another fashion week. Indeed, the majority of exhibitors we talked to said they were constantly evaluating different fairs in view of their own participation. They invariably expressed willingness to relocate to another country if they felt that it would secure them what they would consider to be a better position in the market.

The best example of fashion weeks' new role as an intermediary hub for a geographically dispersed industry is the move of the street and urbanwear trade fair, Bread & Butter, from Berlin to Barcelona and back again. In 2005, the successful fair had outgrown its facilities in Berlin, and made a controversial move to Barcelona, where it came to be well established. After five years in Barcelona, it was drawn back by the prestigious location of the disused Berlin Tempelhof Airport. Bread & Butter organizers timed their event to start a few days before the official fashion week schedule, in this way forcing less powerful players to realign their programme. The earlier dates gave an advantage to their leading exhibitors, big commercial companies, who could hit the market before potential buyers had spent any of their budgets. However, for small and medium fashion companies, which had adhered to the established fashion calendar, the timing presented an urgent problem because their merchandise had not arrived from the suppliers in time for the fair.

As a recurrent theme in fair participants' stories, Bread & Butter's return to Berlin is an example of how a powerful player can configure a field. In the fragmented fashion industry dominated by small and medium enterprises, a big event organizer can successfully reconfigure the field, even if it is to the temporary disadvantage of the industry players served by the event. In Berlin, commercial price-driven companies welcomed the move, whereas many of the small exhibitors expressed frustration. They saw it as a testament to the power of commercial interests, and the difficulty for smaller companies to compete with the giants. For all exhibitors, however, the move cemented Berlin's status as a fashion city. This, in turn, caused concern in Copenhagen, where Bread & Butter was mentioned as the explanation of declining visitor numbers. Several exhibitors told us that they would skip Copenhagen next time in favour of Berlin, reflecting a general decline in Copenhagen Fashion Week after its international success earlier in the decade.

Bread & Butter exhibition grounds in Tempelhof Airport included the old arrival/departure halls, the hangars and a part of the runway, complete with a concert stage, bars, and a huge variety of entertainment for visitors. The spatial layout of the fair divided exhibitors into areas such as 'Sport & Street', 'Urban Superior', 'Denim Base' and no special measures were taken to identify green brands. However, many soft and hardcore greens were exhibiting at Bread & Butter, where they used the large spaces allocated to each exhibitor to present their commitment with props such as cotton branches, trees, sculptures and a hammock, next to other brands' displays with motor bikes, a boxing ring, and all the fancy dummies and display designs that are seen in a flagship store.

One of the hardcore greens at Bread & Butter was Kuyichi, started in 2000 by the Dutch fair trade NGO Solidaridad. In fact, Kuyichi had secured what was possibly the most visible space right in the middle of the fair. Located under the wide roof of the airport building, its pavilion was designed as a café, serving organic drinks, including 'hemp cocktails'. Next to the entrance was a display of wooden boxes with cotton plants and denim textiles beside posters with information about the environmental consequences of conventional cotton farming. The display also informed the reader that 'Kuyichi was the first jeans brand to make "Pure Denim" out of organic cotton' and that 'by choosing Kuyichi Pure Denim cotton you can have all the benefits of cotton's beauty while minimizing harm to people and the planet while wearing the authentic high quality jeans'. Inside Kuyichi's pavilion, a large crowd was gathered by the bar. In the soft chairs scattered around the room, people were chatting, playing with their mobile phones and relaxing. The walls had displays similar to those by the entrance, with information about living wages and other social issues related to fashion production. At the back of the café, a few steps on both sides of the bar led up to an area with a small collection of

Kuyichi's jeans and large posters about social and environmental responsibility. However, this space was empty of visitors for the full half hour we spent in the pavilion. Obviously, it was not the clothes that attracted people to Kuyichi in spite of the feel good story, framed on the wall, which read:

> *Yes*
> *we love the world*
> *because without it*
> *there would be no denim*
> *and no fashion for that matter.*
> *That's why we take care of the good stuff.*
> *Like the environment*
> *and the farmers*
> *and the workers*
> *you know, the people behind your jeans.*
> *So now you can look good*
> *and feel good at the same time.*
> *That's our story.*
> *And it's true.*

Kuyichi is a reputed character in the figured world of fashion and many other exhibitors in the same segment referred to Kuyichi as proof that it is possible to be cool yet responsible. Its prominent position in the fair seemed to say as much. From its strong position both as a fashion brand and a not-for-profit organization, Kuyichi could indulge in the activist-like rhetoric from which for-profit brands shy away.

The increasing interest in green fashion can therefore be summarized as follows: sustainability has arrived as a new value parameter in the fashion business, but only as supplementary and subordinate to the logic of the catwalk economy. In most cases there is only a weak connection between the growth in green fashion, and positive effects in terms of a more responsible use of natural resources, better working conditions, higher wages, less transportation, healthier models, more durable designs, and all the other ethical issues in the fashion industry. At the same time, the most important effect of green fashion on the organizational field is to make it more complex – by enabling hybrid partnerships between business and NGOs, by increasing industry segmentation and by introducing an ethical question into the actors' self reflection.

Conclusion

In this chapter we have employed fashion week as a methodological device, a lens through which we have been able to view, analyse and interpret a complex and ambivalent industry change. Studying fashion week is a research trick of the trade, in the sense Howard Becker (1998) uses the term, a problem-solving device belonging to a professional culture. In so far as our aim is to understand the intangible underlying structures of organizational fields and narrativized 'as if' worlds, fashion week, along with other trade fairs and industry events, is a social frame that makes such structures visible. What makes fashion week distinctive from other sites of study such as individual companies, magazines or educational institutions – all of which are also involved in the negotiation of green fashion – is that it affords a compressed look at the whole.

We wish to stress that this is not only an optical illusion on the part of the researchers, but a very real social event, which is only brought about at considerable expense and inconvenience on the part of the multiple actors who participate in fashion week to see and be seen. What makes fashion week good to study is thus the same characteristic that ensures industry people's continued participation, even though they no longer need to attend fairs strictly to do business.

As an event that unites participation and signification, we have argued that fashion week can be studied from two complementary theoretical perspectives. The FCE approach focuses on the externalization and projection of the field structure onto tangible forms, whereas the figured world perspective zooms in on the internalization and reflexive activity of the participants through narratives and categorization. Jointly, the two approaches enable us to study both planned and unplanned interaction in the same frame. This, we argue, is an adequate approach to an object of study which is itself characterized by the contrasts between intentional positioning and spontaneity, calculation and fun, tight timetables and chaos, tension and relief, work and party.

The ability of fashion week and other industry events to fix meaning is offset by their regular repetition. Like the frame in an old-fashioned film, fashion week presents a series of stills which freezes perpetual movement that would otherwise only be visible as a blur. In this respect, fashion week enables us to see both stabilization and flux. For industry observers, such as the authors of this chapter, the event's configuration of the field might be more interesting because it allows us the contemplative satisfaction of understanding how social interaction works. For industry participants who populate the figured world of fashion and have learned to look through the framing device of the fair, it is less interesting to understand change as such than to navigate in this world defined by perpetual change. For them the social interaction and ensuing communal stories were more important – as was made evident by the perpetual questions heard throughout fashion week: 'what's new?' and 'who's where?'

Notes

1. Berlin Fashion Week took place from 1 to 5 July 2009, while Copenhagen Fashion Week was held between 4 and 9 August 2009.
2. See www.fashion-week-berlin.com/about-bfw/.
3. See www.copenhagenfashionweek.com/26395/About.
4. We managed to secure press accreditation to most of the fairs after a few email exchanges with the organizers, except for Bread & Butter in Berlin and Copenhagen International Fashion Fair (CIFF). Both fairs are 'strictly' for industry and pride themselves on being serious places of business. A representative from the Bread & Butter press office advised us to get an invitation from an exhibitor. Even so, it was only possible to enter after passing through three security checks. At CIFF, we were allowed to enter with a visitor's pass.
5. Two other fashion related trade fairs, '5 elements.berlin' and 'BOUDOIR', both focusing on lingerie and body wear, took place simultaneously but were not included in the study.

References

Allix, A. 1922. 'The geography of fairs: illustrated by old-world examples', *Geographical Review* 12:4, 532–69.

Anand, N. and B. Jones 2008. 'Tournament rituals, category dynamics, and field configuration: the case of the Booker Prize', *Journal of Management Studies* 45:6, 1,036–60.

Anand N, and Peterson, R. A. 2000. 'When market information constitutes fields: sensemaking of markets in the commercial music field', *Organization Science* 11, 270–84.

Appadurai, A. 1986. 'Introduction: commodities and the politics of value', in A. Appadurai. (ed.), *The Social Life of Things*. Cambridge University Press, pp. 3–63.

Bakhtin, M. M. 1993 (1965/1941). *Rabelais and His World*. Bloomington, IN: Indiana University Press.

Barthes, R. 2006. '"Blue is in fashion this year": a note on research into signifying units in fashion clothing', in R. Barthes (ed.), *The Language of Fashion*. Oxford: Berg, pp. 41–59.

Becker, H. 1998. *Tricks of the Trade: How to Think About Your Research While You're Doing It*. University of Chicago Press.

Bendell, J. and Kleanthous. A. 2007. *Deeper Luxury*. World Wildlife Fund (WWF) UK, www.wwf.org.uk/deeperluxury/report.html.

Bollier, D., Cox, C., Gluck, M., Racine, L., Reed, P. and Sinnreich, A. 2010. *Ready to Share: Fashion and the Ownership of Creativity*. The Norman Lear Centre, University of Southern California (USC) Annenberg.

Burawoy, M. 1991. 'The extended case method', in M. Burawoy et al. *Ethnography Unbound*. Berkeley and Los Angeles: University of California Press.

Burawoy, M. et al. 2000. *Global Ethnography: Forces, Connections and Imaginations in a Postmodern World*. Berkeley and Los Angeles: University of California Press.

Callon, M. 1998. 'The embeddedness of economic markets in economics', in M. Callon (ed.), *The Laws of the Market*. Oxford: Blackwell, pp. 1–57.

Callon, M., Mèadel, C. Rabeharisoa, V. 2002. 'The economy of qualities', *Economy and Society* 31: 2.

Chouinard, Y. 2006. *Let My People Go Surfing: the Education of a Reluctant Businessman*. Harmondsworth: Penguin.

Devinney, T. M., Eckhardt, G. and Belk, R. 2006. *Why Don't Consumers Behave Ethically? The Social Construction of Consumption*. Sydney: Centre for Corporate Change.

Fine, B. and Leopold, E. 1993. *The World of Consumption*. London: Routledge.

Gabriel, Y. and Lang, T. 2006. *The Unmanageable Consumer*. Second edition. London: Sage.

Gluckman, M. 1958 (1940/1942). *Analysis of the Social Situation in Modern Zululand*. Rhodes Livingstone Institute Paper 28. Manchester University Press.

Goffman, E. 1986. *Frame Analysis: an Essay on the Organization of Experience*. Boston, MA: North Eastern University Press.

Green, N. L. 1997. *Ready-to-Wear and Ready-to-Work: a Century of Industry and Immigrants in Paris and New York*. Durham: Duke University Press.

Grumbach, D. 2006. 'Haute couture and ready-to-wear: a recent history', in P. Palmar and D. Grumbach (eds.), *Fashion Show: Paris Style*. Hamburg: Gingko Press, pp. 87–102.

Hannerz, U. 1980. *Exploring the City: Inquiries Toward an Urban Anthropology*. New York: Columbia University Press.

Hervik, P. 2004 'The Danish cultural world of unbridgeable differences', *Ethnos* 69:2, 247–67.

Holland, D. 1992. 'How cultural systems become desire: a case study of American romance', in R. D'Andrade and C. Strauss (eds.), *Human Motives and Cultural Models*. Cambridge University Press.

Holland, D., Lachicotte, W., Skinner, D. and Cain, C. (eds.) 1998. *Identity and Agency in Cultural Worlds*. Cambridge, MA: Harvard University Press.

Holland, D. and Quinn, N. (eds.) 1987. *Cultural Models in Language and Thought*. Cambridge University Press.

Jackson, T. 2009. *Prosperity Without Growth? The Transition to a Sustainable Economy*. Sustainable Development Commission, UK, www.sd-commission.org.uk/publications.php?id=914.

Kleanthous, A. and Peck, J. 2006. *Let Them Eat Cake*. WWF UK, www.wwf.org.uk/news/n_0000002589.asp.

Klepp, I. G. 2006. *Skittentøyets Kulturhistorie: Hvorfor Kvinner Vasker Klær*. Oslo: Novus.

   2008. *Clothes, the Body and Well-being: what Does it Mean to Feel Well-dressed?* National Institute for Consumer Research (SIFO) project note 1. Oslo: SIFO.

Labour Behind the Label 2006. *Who Pays for the Cheap Clothes?* www.labourbehindthelabel.org/images/pdf/low-cost-retailers-070706.pdf.

Löfgren, O. 2005. 'Catwalking and coolhunting: the production of Newness', in O. Löfgren. and R. Willim (eds.), *Magic, Culture and the New Economy*. Oxford: Berg, pp. 57–71.

McDonough, W. and Braungart, M. 2002. *Cradle to Cradle: Remaking the Way We Make Things*. New York: North Point Press.

Melchior, M. R., Skov, L. and Csaba, F. 2011. 'Translating into Danish Fashion'. *Culture Unbound* 3.

Model Health Inquiry 2007. *Fashioning a Healthy Future: the Report on Model Health Inquiry*. British Fashion Council, www.modelhealthinquiry.com/.

Moeran, B. 2004. 'Women's fashion magazines: people, things, and values', in C. Werner and D. Bell (eds.), *Values and Valuables: from the Sacred to the Symbolic*. Walnut Creek, CA: Altamira, pp. 257–81.

Simmel, G. 1950. 'The metropolis and mental life', in K. H. Wolff (ed.), *The Sociology of Georg Simmel*. Glencoes, IL: Free Press.

Skov, L. 2004a. '"Seeing is believing": world fashion and the Hong Kong Young Designers' Contest', *Fashion Theory* 8, 165–94.

2004b. 'Fashion flows – fashion shows: the Asia-Pacific meets in Hong Kong', in K. Iwabuchi and M. Thomas (eds.), *Rogue Flows: Trans-Asian Cultural Traffic*. Hong Kong University Press, pp. 221–47.

2006. 'The role of trade fairs in the global fashion business', *Current Sociology* 54, 764–83.

2008. *Ethics and the Fashion Industry in West Europe*. ©*reative Encounters* Working Paper. Copenhagen Business School.

Skov, L., Skjold, E., Larsen, F., Moeran, B. and Csaba, F. 2009. 'The fashion show as an art form'. ©*reative Encounters* Working Paper 12. Copenhagen Business School.

Turner, V. 1969. 'Liminality and communitas', in V. Turner (ed.), *The Ritual Process: Structure and Antistructure*. Chicago: Transaction Publishers, pp. 94–130.

White, H. 1981. 'Where do markets come from?' *The American Journal of Sociology* 87:3, 517–47.

Wirth, L. 1938. 'Urbanism as a way of life', *American Journal of Sociology* 44, 1–24.

12 | An inconvenient truce: cultural domination and contention after the 1855 Médoc wine classification event

GRÉGOIRE CROIDIEU*

Cultural domination in fields is often thought to favour uniformity, homogeneity and stability at the field level, and conformity and compliance at the actor level. Field domination emerges over time with the stabilization of an unambiguous hierarchy and is associated with an increasing institutionalization, structuration and ordering that occur mostly through the deployment of isomorphic pressures (DiMaggio and Powell, 1983). At the actor level, this process results in conformity to the hierarchy, the alignment of meanings, expectations and behaviour of field members; it tends to increase consensus, decrease ambiguity and inhibit contention and contestation. Conversely, fields without a dominant hierarchy are associated with diversity and heterogeneity at the field level, and contention and contestation at the actor level. This lack of domination results from the distribution of authority sources among multiple legitimate bodies and an overlap of institutional pressures with which to comply. It leads to the co-existence of multiple meanings, expectations and behaviour about what counts in a field; it also tends to increase contention and raise the degree of ambiguity and complexity. In sum, viewed a-historically, the greater the domination there is at a field level, the lower the amount of contention one observes at the actor level.

In this chapter, I challenge this imagery by describing the case of a very hierarchical and stable field that is associated with a great deal of cultural contention at the actor level, and by exploring the case of the Médoc wine field, in the Bordeaux region in the southwest of France. This field has been dominated by a classification of the best wines that was set in 1855 and whose hierarchy has hardly changed since, and yet which has managed to remain powerful. This classification was enacted during the 1855 Universal Exhibition in Paris, which retrospectively became a major field-configuring event (FCE), as it resulted in the clear cultural domination of an unambiguous hierarchy. To study the relationship between field domination and actors' contention, I focus on practices and discourses enacted by various field actors at various points of time after the inception of this 1855 classification. With the emergence and stabilization of such a dominant classification, one would expect from the core tenets of neo-institutional theory that the (possible) heterogeneity in discourses and meanings of the 1855 classification and the emergence of alternative classifications would decrease over time, both between various groups of field members and within these groups. One would also expect that the discursive strategies used to legitimize and to make sense of 1855 would converge, probably around a rationalized and well-theorized myth about what counts in 'good' wine, because this classification becomes increasingly taken-for-granted as a consensual truth.

Although there is some evidence to suggest that this classification does indeed result in cultural domination of the field, contention at the actor level has continued and never really ceased since its inception. In this sense, 1855 has led to an inconvenient truce rather than to a consensual truth. This contention has led to numerous and diverse localized forms of creative cultural contention, as actors have engaged in developing their own alternative classifications. Discursively, field actors are very contentious and creative in making sense of and justifying the social order in which they live, as well as the positions, beliefs, behaviour and values they favour.

This account of concomitant domination and contention matters from a neo-institutional point of view as it challenges frictionless accounts of institutionalization that rest on conformity, compliance and legitimacy at the field level and that discard conflicts, contradictions and power relationships at the actor level (e.g., DiMaggio, 1988; Fligstein, 2001; Seo and Creed, 2002). This nuanced account also raises the issue of an actor-level perspective on institutions that explores logics of attachment to institutions (Powell *et al.*, 2005) and rests on a larger intellectual debate, in which the legacy of Max Weber is divided between a Parsonian reading favouring legitimacy and a more European account grounded in domination (e.g., Clegg *et al.*, 2006).

Médoc is an appropriate setting in which to explore the relationship between domination and contention for three main reasons.[1] Firstly, it offers a clear, tangible and durable case of field domination. Secondly, it unfolds over a long period of time, which allows us to observe whether contention occurs or not. And thirdly, it ties together diverse sets of actors who remain fairly stable over time, thereby enabling a fair comparison between and within group dynamics, as well as enabling us to observe the possible circulation of contention among different sites and actors over time. This case thus makes a contribution to this volume, as well as to the FCE literature in general, by showing how domination does not necessarily repress contention; to field evolution literature by reporting how truces and settlements, even when highly codified and taken-for-granted, can co-exist with contention; and to institutional theory by suggesting how the meaning and expression of rationalized myths evolve over time and among different actors.

FCEs and domination

FCEs such as trade fairs, conferences and festivals, physically constitute fields in a *bounded time-space arena*, and decisively shape field evolution over time (Lampel and Meyer, 2008; see also the Introduction to this volume). They physically constitute fields by gathering periodically and temporarily all the relevant actors who enact the fields through *sense making* and *rituals* (Anand and Watson, 2004), as well as *heightened interaction* (e.g., Garud, 2008; Oliver and Montgomery, 2008), which in turn durably shape fields – such as industries (Anand and Watson, 2004; Garud, 2008; Havens, Chapter 6 in this volume; Rao, 1994), markets (Anand and Jones, 2008), or cities (Glynn, 2008; Rüling, Chapter 8 in this volume) – by providing actors with *opportunities*.

A growing body of the FCE literature points out that events with field-configuring effects are the ones where the formation of a consensus, a settlement or a *truce* – in other words, the domination of a general agreement on the direction to be taken by the field or on its internal hierarchy – is reached among participants. This domination comes about because the truce puts an end to contention among actors over what counts in a field and therefore has field effects. For instance, Garud (2008) narrates how decades of controversy about single and multiple channel devices for cochlear implants were resolved by a single consensus medical conference. By consensually opting for one technology rather than another as the most appropriate, conference participants enabled the dissemination of the selected technology among doctors and patients that then radically affected the treatment of severe cases of deafness and so durably shaped the field.

During this truce-formation process, a double tournament occurs: a *tournament of values*, which is about what counts in a field and is associated with contention over a field's hierarchy, and a *tournament of value*, which organizes field competition along this hierarchy and which is associated with domination (Appadurai, 1986; Moeran, 2010). The dominant perspective is that a tournament of values precedes a tournament of value in time, or the two tournaments co-occur but in different sites that do not collide – as Hélène Delacour and Bernard Leca so ably show in their discussion of the Salon de Peinture (Chapter 1). A truce is then either the moment during which a field shifts from the former to the latter, or the moment during which a spatial segregation excludes contention at the margin of a field and leaves the centre unchallenged.

A truce provides an unambiguous hierarchy, which notably implies that the hierarchy within the field is defined along a value, or set of values, that is well understood and accepted. By defining this hierarchy, a *tournament of value* leads to field isomorphic (normative) pressures to conform and, over time, leads actors to comply and become homogeneous in their evaluating practices (DiMaggio and Powell, 1983). By clarifying the meaning of this hierarchy (and hence its legitimacy), a tournament of value results in lower possibilities for conflict and contention, as its meaning and justification are often theorized and rationalized (Munir, 2005). The durability of this truce rests mostly on the strength of the hierarchy, but also on the alignment of meanings, and justification principles in the fields, with this hierarchy (Rao, 1998; Rao and Kenney, 2008). As a result of this unambiguous hierarchy, cultural contention is low, if not non-existent, and cultural domination reigns with field-configuring effects. What is less known is the situation in which the two tournaments co-occur: that is, one observes both field domination of a hierarchy, and actor-level contention over this hierarchy.

An exploratory model of contentious domination

Where a tournament of value and a tournament of values co-occur on the same site at the same time, I suggest that we use the phrase 'contentious domination' and I want here to develop an exploratory model to describe it.[2] This model stylizes how different sets of actors express themselves over this domination and do, or do not, contend with it over time.

Tournaments of both value and values are about hierarchies and the values attached to them. Therefore, I analyse classificatory practices and discourses that, firstly, deal with hierarchies; secondly, justify, (de-) legitimate and infuse with meaning these hierarchies; and thirdly use discursive strategies of (de-) legitimation that tie these hierarchies to the meanings mobilized by actors. I specifically build on Vaara and Tienari (2008), who distinguish five discursive strategies of legitimation: *normalization*, which aims at justifying a hierarchy by making it appear natural; *authorization*, which legitimizes a hierarchy by referring to a superior authority like a tradition, a law or a person; *rationalization*, referring to the utility of a hierarchy; *moralization*, invoking a specific value attached to a hierarchy; and *narrativization*, which echoes the storytelling of a hierarchy and tries to frame it within its past and its future. I explore these accounts by distinguishing the *field actors' positions* and the evolution of their discourse *over time*.

According to the core tenets of neo-institutional theory (DiMaggio and Powell, 1983; Meyer and Rowan, 1977), one should observe over time the reproduction of the dominant hierarchy by all actors, as well as the emergence of a collective myth about this domination widely shared by actors, and their rationalization of this collective myth. In brief, institutionalization allows contention to occur at the beginning or at the margin, but univocal domination should increasingly prevail (see, for example, Barley and Tolbert, 1997; Colyvas and Powell, 2006; Greenwood *et al.*, 2002; Tolbert and Zucker, 1996).

Fairs and festivals in the wine industry

Trade fairs and festivals are a major part of the 'business life' of the wine industry. Nowadays, one can distinguish four main types of events that structure this business life: trade fairs, wine competitions, wine auctions and wine festivals. Of these, trade fairs occur repeatedly and one can differentiate industry-wide fairs from niche events. The best known industry-wide trade fairs are events such as *Vinexpo* in Bordeaux and Hong Kong, and the *London Wine Fair*. There are also dozens of 'niche' fairs such as the *Salon des Vins Indépendants*, the *Miami Fair*, *Vinitech*, *Vinisud*, *Vinitaly*, *Prowein*, *Wine and Spirits Asia*, and so on. The main activity in these fairs consists of business deals.

A second type of event consists of wine competitions, during which producers and merchants open their wines for tasting in order to get medals, awards and sometimes even ratings. These events include notably *The Sydney Royal Wine Show*, the *Concours des Vins de Paris* (or *Macon*), the *Concours Mondial de Bruxelles*, the *International Wine Challenge* and the *International Wine and Spirit Competition*.

Wine producers and merchants also compete at auctions like the *Vente des Hospices de Beaune* and the *Bernkasteler Ring*. Their interest here is in the media exposure that producers attract by having particular bottles of wine fetching astronomical prices. These auctions also serve the trade by setting a 'gold' standard that serves as a guideline for bidding prices in professional transactions during the rest of the year, as Charles Smith points out in his discussion of the dramaturgical practices of art auctions in Chapter 4.

Finally, there are countless festivals that take place during the course of these fairs or independently. These festivals vary dramatically in size and reputation and aim at promoting countries (for example, the *Israel Wine Festival*), regions (*Salon des Vins de Côte-Rôtie*), grape varieties (*Zinfandel Advocates and Producers Festival*), organic products (*Biodyvin*), lifestyle (*Slow Food and Wine Festival*) and so on. Selling is not necessarily part of such events. Rather, public affluence is the main concern and wine is often associated with food, music, or folklore festivals. These events happen almost everywhere, from Lhasa to Soweto, or Winnipeg to Bangkok.

Most events have been founded recently, occur annually and do not attract much attention on the part of the industry. In the past, universal exhibitions and national and international fairs were sites where wines were displayed alongside other agricultural and manufacture-based products. Although, as we have seen in the Introduction, fairs date back to the middle ages at least; the 1798 Paris national fair is widely seen as the first non-local modern fair, a model that was largely copied during the whole of the nineteenth century in Europe and elsewhere. It was on the basis of this model that the first international fair took place at the Crystal Palace in London in 1851, and inaugurated a whole cycle of universal exhibitions (see Markham, 1998 for an extended account). In the wine industry, the best known fair is the 1855 Universal Exhibition in Paris, because it gave birth to the most famous wine institution of all: the 1855 Médoc wine classification.

The 1855 Universal Exhibition in Paris

The Paris Universal Exhibition in 1855 succeeded that of the Crystal Palace and initiated an era where new nation-states started competing actively in economic terms during succeeding waves of industrialization. Only three months after his 1852 coup, the new Emperor, Napoleon III, created an Imperial Commission charged with organizing the Second Universal Exhibition as part of his desire to display the greatest French achievements in both manufacturing industries and agriculture. Following the creation of this commission and after a somewhat haphazard political process, the Bordeaux Chamber of Commerce was placed by the Gironde organizing committee in charge of gathering the best products, including its common and fine wines.[3]

Bordeaux is both a city and a wine region. As a city, Bordeaux is the main town in the southwest of France and has built its wealth mostly by means of the exploitation of pine trees, wine and sea trade. As a wine region, Bordeaux built a leading position in the world by exporting its *châteaux* and *crûs classés* to every corner of the globe. However, this position rested on a very scattered territory and, among all the diverse Bordeaux wine areas, the Médoc played a key role in structuring this fragmented region, becoming 'the Holy of Holies' (Penning-Rowsell, 1969: 104). Since the eighteenth century, the Bordeaux wine trade has been mostly organized around three professions: the *producers*, who grow the vines and make the wine; the *merchants*, who sometimes blend and age the wine, but mostly just sell it; and the *brokers*, who have institutionally been in charge of negotiating contract terms and prices between merchants and producers. This local and informal system is known as 'the Bordeaux Marketplace' (*La Place de Bordeaux*).

Following designation of the Chamber of Commerce, whose most powerful members were the merchants, a special commission was created for wine. An announcement was released in the press in November 1854 requesting that all producers who intended to display their products should come forward in order to agree on how to proceed. All members of the Bordeaux Marketplace argued over the proper procedures, metrics and valuation method with which to set up this display – ranging from the use of a tasting to the organization of a competition, making use of various rationales that classified wines according to soil, commune, property, proprietor, and so on.

The President of the Chamber of Commerce searched for a way to reconcile these varied and conflicting demands and, after several rounds of negotiations, finally advocated that common wines should be represented at the Exhibition by a chart (that would become a map of communes), and the fine wines by a special classification.

The 1855 Médoc wine classification

The idea of classifying the best wines was not new in Bordeaux: the earliest classifications had already emerged in the seventeenth century (see Table 12.1). Thereafter, several casual wine writers (including John Locke and Thomas Jefferson), wine professionals, administrative bodies, early wine experts and even poets produced a number of classifications, but none of them became dominant until 1855. These 'early' authors proposed various rationales underpinning the structuring of their classifications, shifting historically from region-based to property-based categorizations through soil, parish and commune as alternative solutions (Markham, 1998). Towards the end of the eighteenth century, property-based – or *crû* (translated as growth) – classifications became the norm. These were split into six numbered sub-categories. Market prices (or commodity exchange value), taste (appreciative value) and owner and vineyard reputation (social value) were the dominant means of evaluation used to classify each wine's properties.

The Union of the Wine Brokers of Bordeaux was given the task of completing, at very short notice, the classification of the region's fine wines. Below I have reproduced (most of) the letter that accompanied the 1855 classification (translation by Markham, 1998: 106) and which was sent to the Gironde Chamber of Commerce by the Board of the Bordeaux Union of Brokers on 18 April 1855:

Sirs,

We were honoured to receive your letter of the fifth of this month requesting of us the complete list of classed red wines of the Gironde . . .

In order to satisfy your wishes, we surrounded ourselves with all possible information, and we have the honour to make known to you by the attached table the result of our investigations.

You know as we do, Sirs, how much this classification is a delicate thing and likely to arouse sensitivities; also it was not our thought to draw up an official state of our great wine, but only to submit for your consideration a work whose elements have been drawn from the best sources.

To answer the P.S. in your letter, we consider that in supposing that the First crûs are worth 3,000 francs, the:

Seconds should be priced: 2,500 to 2,700 frs.

Thirds	"	2,100 to 2,400
Fourths	"	1,800 to 2,100
Fifths	"	1,400 to 1,600

We are with respect, Sirs, your most devoted servants.

Among all the classifying rationales, metrics, methods and procedures, the brokers decided to rely on past market prices (that is, on commodity exchange value) and did not necessarily justify all their decisions beyond this price criterion.[4] The final document that they sent included fifty-seven growths from the Médoc region classified according to five categories, the first being the best.[5] More importantly, this classification was never intended to last beyond the Paris Universal Exhibition or to structure the Médoc and Bordeaux wine trade over the following decades and centuries (Coates, 2004; Markham, 1998; Penning-Rowsell, 1969; Roudié, 1988). Yet it has culturally and commercially dominated the whole Médoc wine field until the present day under a single, unambiguous and powerful hierarchy.

Overall, the 1855 classification was presented and accepted at the 1855 Exhibition. It was designed as a truth based on historical market prices and overall did reflect the major trends that had shaped the Médoc wine market over the previous forty years. After more than a 150-year 'reign', this classification has only been modified once: in 1973, Mouton-Rothschild was promoted from second to first class, 'correcting' what many commentators saw as an anomaly that had been present since 1855 (according to prices). This reclassification then may also be seen as a kind of truce.

This stability is particularly remarkable, once it is realized that one classified growth has disappeared, that several others have merged or split, that only two are still in the same hands, and that most of them have changed in vineyard size and shape. Moreover, the classification was never ordered or approved by Napoleon III and it is not clear who has had authority over it. Lastly, few decisions based on prices were justified by the prices themselves: for instance, the overall number of categories; the presence of a few growths that were created or sold by brokers over a very short period of time; and the inclusion of Haut-Brion. In the remainder of this chapter, I will go on to explore how several types of actors commented on and contested this dominant classification, which turned what was supposed to be a consensual truth into an inconvenient truce.

Cultural domination and contention: merchants

The whole paradox surrounding 1855 is that it is undoubtedly a ruling hierarchy that governed the Bordeaux wine field (and some even argue the global wine world) over a period of 150 years, while the classification itself has remained inconvenient and, for some, contentious and contested. By establishing such a fixed hierarchy, it generated a great number of proponents, opponents and commentators. Different merchants, producers and diverse actors commented on it over time, leading to the production of alternative classifications and the invention of different truths at different points in time by means of different discursive strategies.[6]

Historical works suggest that Médoc classifications started in 1647 and have continued until the present day. Table 12.1 shows the distribution over time of the ninety-five Médoc classifications identified. Of these, forty-eight (or about 50 per cent) came into existence after 1855. In other words, in spite of its domination, 1855 did not stop actors from classifying the Médoc wines. Rather, the pace at which such classifications emerged suggests that it has intensified it. These new classifications reflect the fact that contention and contestation over the dominant hierarchy have continued to be present in the field and in a very heterogeneous way, since these post-1855 classifications have rested on multiple logics such as prices, tastings, multiple regions, taste and so on. In other words, different values – commodity exchange, material/technical and appreciative values – have been emphasized by different actors at different times over the years.

The authors/actors proposing these classifications have until very recently constituted a very diverse group. Before 1814, authors were mostly casual writers or administrative bodies. Producers, merchants and publishers of tourist guidebooks joined them during the nineteenth century, while the state became very active in the first part of the twentieth century, notably by regulating (or endorsing) local wine regions. Later, in the 1970s, wine critics emerged and wrote widely about 1855. For their part, the merchants have been overall supporters of the 1855 classification because it has brought stability, visibility and

Table 12.1 *Number of Médoc wine classifications published by historical periods*

Historical period	1647–1814	1815–1852	1853–1885	1886–1920	1921–1929	1930–1956	1957–1973	1974–1982	1983–2006
Number of Médoc classifications	14	29	19	4	2	6	10	1	10

Note: The historical periods stem from historical studies and capture alternatively phases of economic growth and contraction in Bordeaux from 1815 on, 1815–52 being a period of decline.

collective reputation to the whole region, and so made their own activities easier. However, their perception of 1855 has evolved over time and was not a well-organized or rationalized myth that everyone took for granted.

Bordeaux wine merchants were very active in formalizing their professional expertise and, during the nineteenth century, one merchant, Wilhelm Franck, played a major role in structuring the knowledge that merchants needed to trade wines from the Médoc. Between 1824 and 1871, Franck released six editions of a treatise that generations of contemporaneous wine professionals considered the ultimate reference on the topic. In these writings, Franck provides detailed information about winemaking, viticulture, vintages, geographical conditions and so on in the Médoc region. The core of his work is a list, by commune, of all the wine-producing properties of interest to the trade, on the basis of which he proposes a classification of the best wines. Acknowledging the complexity of the task, he refers to an alphabetical ordering and to some external judges to justify his classification in the 1845 and 1853 editions. In the 1860 edition, however, he changed his justification for the Médoc classification in the following manner:

Here comes the most delicate task of our work. The classification of the famous wines, established on consecrated bases, entails some uncertainties for some wines ... *To bring some clarity to these sometimes difficult issues, we can do no better than reproduce the classification drawn up by the Bordeaux Union of Brokers for the 1855 Exhibition* ... It would be an absolute mistake, however, to consider that all the wines not listed in this classification are inferior and without quality. Frank (1860)[7]

This reference to the 1855 classification with its replacement of previous authorizations is the only change made in the introduction. As this editorial decision indicates, 1855 solves the ambiguity and complexity reigning at the time. What is striking is how cautious and moderate the author is and how little he rationalizes and theorizes his arguments. He invokes the 1855 principle, implies it is 'consecrated', but does not discuss it in detail. Interestingly, there is a contradiction in the fact that, while he offers a classification of the best wines, he simultaneously asserts they are no better than the others – implying that the 1855 classification is useless as a justification device. These claims do reflect a constant concern among the Bordeaux wine professionals to keep common and fines wines in the same trade and to prevent any classification from destabilizing what they define as the market order. So 1855 is rationalized and described as useful, though not *that* useful.

This merchant perspective on 1855 is reflected in another professional guide that has become the standard trade reference up to the present day. Since 1850, an independent publishing house, Féret, has issued eighteen editions of a directory of all the Bordeaux wine producers of interest to both merchants and brokers who have regarded its mission and perspective on 1855 in line with the trade. The following excerpt, quoting 1855, remained constant between 1868 (the second edition) and 1881 (the fourth edition):

For the five categories of Great Growths, we have followed literally the latest official document established by the Union of Brokers in 1855. This classification is the basis for most sales in the biggest communes in the Médoc region. It does not result from the personal appreciation of the brokers ... [but] from long observation and calculation of average prices ... The Médoc wine classification dates back to the eighteenth century ... Like all human institutions, it is subject to the laws of time and must necessarily at some stage be rejuvenated ... In 1855, one had to modify the prior classifications ... *this [1855] classification dates back to 1855 and for twenty-five years several changes in the Médoc great growths have required a revision of this work.* (emphasis added)

Again, the tone adopted is quite moderate and the justification for reproducing the classification is at first similar to the arguments developed by Franck, although the authors do mention how the brokers came up with this classification, stressing experience and price, and discarding any appreciative judgement of value. Interestingly, this rationalized authorization strategy rests on a new argument: that of history. 1855 is presented in a moralizing tone as the moment where history 'had' to be made. However, history is not invoked as a legacy to advocate the *status quo* (the consecration effect of time), but as an imperative to change (the degradation effect of time). This argument is developed at length later in the text and rests on the fact that some wines had been improved by their producers, while others had not, or had even declined in quality. Once again, therefore, the 1855 classification was fairly useful up until 1881, but not that much. In the fifth edition, released in 1886, the sentence to which I added my emphasis above disappeared from the text, with the result that there is greater ambiguity and dissonance on what effect history was supposed to play in the classification of Médoc wines. This text, without the contentious sentence, remained unchanged in Féret until the thirteenth edition in 1982.

In that year, this authorization strategy was modified and the authors adopted an approach that mixed rationalization and narrativization. In other words, instead of relying on a few authoritative arguments, they developed a rationalized (with attention to the logical connectors) and detailed account of 1855 to justify its maintenance. To this end, they went into great detail about the history of the 1855 classification, notably by reprinting rare texts about it. This rationalization remains at the level of narrative since the conclusion to this lengthy justification of the stability of 1855 ends up with a 'but moment' that does not lead to the expected conclusion:

But many things have changed since 1855.

… Many properties do not belong to the same families anymore; a few families have disappeared; some properties have been divided; others have had their names modified; a few of them have even disappeared, while new ones have been created from scratch.

It is *also* obvious that growing conditions, viticultural and winemaking techniques, as well as marketing techniques, are not the same as they were in 1855. Cocks (1868: 227; emphasis added)

These lines suggest that the authors are willing to address these changes and to grapple anew with their 'ancient' conception of time as associated with degrading 'human institutions'. However, the conclusion that they drew from their 'but moment' was:

This is why, as in previous editions, we have respected these classifications [talking about the various classes of 1855], *but* in adding sometimes a personal appreciation for some properties whose current quality is, to us, superior to the one acknowledged in 1855. (emphasis added)

In other words, the authors acknowledge the effect of time, but only in part. They do not mention those wines that have declined over time, and only acknowledge those that have improved with a 'personal' appreciative comment. Again, the tone is very cautious and one has the impression that the merchants were concerned about how to preserve both their own and producers' interests by inventing convenient truths justified by authorization, rationalization and narrativization.

Producers' accounts of 1855

Let me now turn to how some producers interpreted 1855. Wine producers were likely to comment on and react to classifications that explicitly or implicitly made a statement about the general quality of their wine. Conflicting interests between merchants and producers historically have been very sharp and resulted in several forms of activism, including publication of *Le Producteur* (1838–41), a journal that aimed to promote the interests of every wine producer and wine-producing commune by diffusing more 'objective' information about the quality of their wines. Later, Armailhacq, a prominent Médoc wine producer, wrote a treatize on viticulture and winemaking in the Médoc region in which he advocated a four-category classification that diverges from the merchants' five-category one (at a time when the 1855 classification was being discussed and enacted):

One used to distinguish four categories for the wine of the Médoc. However, some merchants wanted to have five categories ... even though five categories were not usually admitted. Few people tried to reconcile these views ... M. Franck preferred to distinguish five categories. Since the 1844 sales, it has become apparent that this subdivision should not remain ... We ought to acknowledge, however, that several Bordeaux merchants and brokers want to keep five categories. As we don't pretend to influence public opinion, but only to observe it, we will also conserve the five categories, although it seems natural to us to group together the third and fourth categories, which is especially appropriate as these two subdivisions contain very little wine ... d'Armailhacq (1855: 473–4)

Armailhacq's aim clearly is to delegitimize the merchants' conception of what a classification structure is like and to promote his own classificatory scheme instead. To do this, he adopts several strategies. On the one hand, he appeals to authority by invoking customary words and phrases like 'one used to …' and 'usually'; on the other, he adopts a normalization strategy that refers to what 'seemed to be natural', 'appropriate' and 'not admitted'. He also invokes a moralization strategy by setting up an implicit norm about what 'should' be, and what people 'ought' and 'ought not' to be doing (like 'influencing public opinion'). In these contentious comments, he never makes his point through rationalized demonstration, nor does he speak in detail about what custom requires that one should do.

According to Armailhacq, Médoc wine producers experienced a very difficult period until the 1930s–40s. Despite strong economic growth until the late 1880s, they then suffered from several years of bad vintages, accompanied by three waves of disease and blight that successively hit and destroyed the vineyards (the oïdium crisis in 1852, phylloxera between 1880 and 1910, mildew in the 1880s). These crises had some long-term effects, which were made worse by repeated fraud scandals involving local merchants, and which were followed by the first world war. During this period, very few authors proposed new classifications; nor did they comment on the 1855 one, so that the debate about what constituted the best wines took place for the most part at national and international fairs in London in 1862, Paris in 1867, 1878, 1889 and 1900 and in several other cities like Brussels. At the same time, there were growing concerns among the producers about the merchants' (fraudulent) influence in the trade. Both co-operatives and *appellations contrôlées* systems, as collective means of resistance against the merchants, were discussed before they began spreading in the 1930s. In this context, Robert and André Villepigue, two engineer-agriculturists based in Saint-Emilion, a neighbouring wine area, published a treatise trying to define the basis of an Appellation for Saint-Emilion and sketch a classification:

I think that a classification is useful … Probably, as in every human work, it entails a fair amount of imprecision … I must say that, besides the 1855 classification, only one Bordeaux editor, Féret, tried to do something in this direction. He has published ten consecutive editions of a book, probably paid by subscription and full of eulogistic comments, which only have a relative value. But it does have the merit of existing. My own argument is that it is time to revisit this issue of classification on a new basis that requires the *growing cooperative movement* in Gironde. (Villepigue and Villepigue, 1934: 35–7)[8]

They then raise two questions: who will draw up this new classification, and how will they do so? To answer the first question, they narrate the historical context that authorized the 1855 classification, implying that it rested on some vested interests and on some limited appreciative evaluations. By arguing that 1855 is 'anything but legal' (Villepigue and Villepigue, 1934: 40), they neatly legitimate their own classification. To answer the second one, they distinguish four types of methods:

The first one, used in 1855, I will call the testimonial method … In absolute value, it is only the affirmation of four people … If we wanted to adopt the 1855 method to complete the Gironde classification, nowadays, we need to deal with some angels of impartiality. (Villepigue and Villepigue, 1934: 41–2)

The authors then present three other methods. These are the tasting method led by professionals (where appreciative value is emphasized); the economic method, based on prices and what consumers are willing to pay (commodity exchange value); and the scientific method, based on an analysis of components of the soil, the main predictor of quality (material/technical value). As agriculturists and landowners, they 'logically' favoured the 'scientific' method that they grounded in a larger collectivist ideology (Villepigue and Villepigue, 1934: 46–47). They thus rely on multiple strategies such as authorization and moralization, but mostly use and abuse a rationalization strategy which reflects a process of abstraction weaved into a logical and causal inquiry, similar to theorization (cf. Strang and Meyer, 1993), but which seems to be largely contingent upon the actors' position in the field and the period in which they are writing.

After the second world war, 1855 gained additional interest when it celebrated its centenary at a time when other Bordeaux wine areas, such as Graves and Saint-Emilion, were establishing their own classifications. Among the producers, Alexis Lichine, a Fourth Classified Growth owner, was particularly active in challenging the 1855 order, both by taking part in a commission set to revise 1855 and by writing books and an encyclopaedia that he continued to edit and republish from the late 1950s to the late 1980s. When this was first published, we read:

In 1855 there was a great Exhibition in Paris; the organizers sent to Bordeaux for samples of its best wines, and this set off the local notables on a

classification of their finest growths ... The grading was done by the
Bordeaux brokers ... *The brokers based their judgments on soil, prestige
and prices ... In fact, the old classification no longer tells the whole truth*; and
opinions expressed in the press and elsewhere have proved that even in
Bordeaux uneasiness has, in certain quarters, been steadily increasing –
although the general view was that, while the *ruling of 1855* had its faults,
it was impossible to improve upon it. *At the time of writing*, it is still being
debated and may not be settled for some time. Lichine (1967: 145, emphasis
added)

Lichine presents the 1855 classification in a very factual style, but
literally invents two criteria that the brokers supposedly used then –
soil and prestige – to reflect both his producer's position and the status
of his property. In so doing, he shifts the evaluative criteria from
commodity exchange to technical/material values. His main argument
relies on the assertion that the 1855 order is being contested, and not
only by him. Discursively, the strategies he uses seem to normalize this
contestation and to narrate the factors driving quality and the relationships between them, without clarifying (or rationalizing) exactly how
they interplay. This factual style takes place at a time when a commission was working on a revision and contrasts with earlier more vehe-
ment writing (he described 1855 as 'outmoded'). In 1987, Lichine
republished his encyclopaedia and did not change his comments on
1855, but added the last sentence:

At the time of writing, there is insufficient courage and leadership in Bordeaux
to push through the necessary changes in the obsolete 1855 classification.
More and more the problems inherent in the 1855 are recognized. Lichine
(1967: 127, emphasis added)

One can see how his beliefs, at least partly shaped by his position as
producer, remained fairly constant over time, but how his hopes for
change evolved and how he expresses differently these hopes in slightly
nuanced truths. This narrativization strategy is also present in the
contradiction between the change he described in 1973 and the fact
that he depicts changes as being impossible.

Other field actors

Aside from merchants and producers, other actors expressed their views
on 1855. One group of these consisted of all the tourist guidebook

publishers who flourished in Bordeaux in the 1850s and 1860s, as a result of the development of the railway.[9] Wine was becoming one of Bordeaux's main attractions and those concerned were aiming at:

> ... giving [to a visitor] the most basic understanding of the famous wines of our region. This is the goal of the following table [classification]. If one wishes to further study this subject, one should refer to specialized books, to the *Traité des Vins du Médoc* by Franck [latest editions in 1845/51/53]; or to the *Traité de la Culture de la Vigne*, by M. d'Armailhacq. Lamothe (1856: 15)

These comments and their purpose are very functional and, rather surprisingly, did not refer to local customs or to the 1855 event, as one might have expected in a tourist guidebook, although they quote 'authoritative' sources of that time.

The classification issue was not publicly raised again until the 1960s–70s when a revision commission was created, leading to the sole promotion of Mouton-Rothschild. At that time, the independent profession of wine criticism emerged and critics started writing extensively on Bordeaux, the world leader, commenting on the effects of 1855 on quality and price. Among them, Penning-Rowsell developed a well-regarded expertise in Bordeaux and mostly supported the maintenance of 1855. This British journalist, who later developed some interests in the wine trade and auctions, wrote one of the first books on Bordeaux not written by locals or insiders:

> There are many who say the [1855] classification is irrelevant, meaningless or outdated, it is a factor that has to be taken into consideration in any survey of Bordeaux. That the grading is still a *subject of controversy* is the best demonstration that it still counts for something ...
>
> The origins of the Médoc classification are not clear, but it existed at least a century before 1855 and probably earlier, and the essential point was that class was based on price. It was not the reputation of estate or owner, the size or style of the château which counted, but the hard commercial facts as they existed on the Bordeaux market. Penning-Rowsell (1969: 247, 254–5; emphasis added)

In the late 1960s, the controversy over 1855 grew really intense. Penning-Rowsell described the birth of 1855, before going on to legitimate the classification system by invoking soil as its driving force for permanence (Penning-Rowsell, 1969: 258–61) – thereby following Lichine, but, unlike Lichine, without questioning his supposition.

A decade later, a young American lawyer, Robert Parker Jr, started commenting on and writing about wine and Bordeaux. In 1985, he published a guide in English on Bordeaux, translated into French in 1991, in which he discusses 1855:

> The 1855 Médoc wine classification ... [has] established a rigid hierarchy that, until now, has determined the price of classed wines. However, it happens that, paradoxically, these lists, once created to classify Bordeaux wines according to their quality, are useless to appreciate the true quality of a property. For the consumer, novice or veteran, it should only be of historical interest.
>
> I propose hereafter my classification of the best 152 Bordeaux wines, while adopting the five categories template of 1855. Parker (1991)

Parker is much more radical in his contention and fully dismissed the 1855 classification by discarding price as a means of predicting quality and by introducing a 'new' quality of taste (thereby shifting emphasis from commodity exchange to appreciative value). He does not provide any lengthy rationale for this and implicitly invokes consumerist values.

Several other wine critics, like Hugh Johnson, Clive Coates and Jancis Robinson, have adopted intermediate positions and narrated 1855 in historical terms, developing localized and individual 'truths' to make sense of the permanence of the classification system. Robinson (2008), for instance, authorizes 1855 by creating a direct connection between Napoleon III and the establishment of 1855 as 'a response to a request'. Invoking varying tastings and market prices, Coates (2004), like Parker, offers a new classification, based on just three categories, while developing at great length and in detail the history of Médoc classifications before 1855. David Peppercorn also illustrates very well this increasing trend in 'informed' and sophisticated/narrativized accounts of 1855:

> *It is often said by supporters of the* status quo *that there is no need to revise the old classification, since it was essentially a classification of the soil,* and this is something which does not change. *Unfortunately, this is only a half-truth.* The actual composition of many of the classified growths vineyards has changed, often radically ... Peppercorn (2003: 44–5; emphasis added)

Interestingly, Peppercorn does not fully reject the soil argument but narrates the history of 1855 to make sense of its permanence and the ongoing contestation by calling it a 'half-truth', which then enables him to go on and propose his own classification.

Discussion

This chapter has shown how the enactment of the 1855 classification led to a very stable and unambiguous hierarchy that has dominated the Médoc wine field until the present day. However, this cultural domination is not a story of the diffusion of a consensual truth, but rather one about sense-making of an inconvenient truce. My aim has been to develop a socially constructed view of how an FCE might impact a field and to suggest the role played by material/technical, situational, appreciative and commodity exchange values at various stages according to the various discursive strategies and claims made by the actors concerned. Table 12.2 summarizes the key predictions one would make out of the core tenets of institutional theory (the consensual truth view) and what actors/authors have narrated over time (the inconvenient truce view).

By adopting a historical approach to what an FCE or a tournament of value is, this case study relates to other chapters by Delacour and Leca (Chapter 1), Rüling (Chapter 8) and Anand (Chapter 13), who have similarly made use of historical sources, although it differs from the Annecy animated film festival described by Rüling, which was forced to adapt itself to survive and to keep on exerting field-effects. On the other hand, interesting parallels can be drawn between this chapter and that by Delacour and Leca on the *Salon de Peinture*, especially with regard to the role played by contention in the dynamics of a (cultural) field. Both studies, however, seem to suggest that an FCE benefits from the contradictions between various values, as it both creates contention and attracts attention. In this sense, conflict is not destructive but creative and ritualistically part of the ongoing life of such events (Anand and Watson, 2004). The 1855 case contributes to this line of inquiry by stressing that domination entails a fairly significant amount of actor-level contention that goes beyond simply adopting a rationalized myth and by questioning legitimacy as an appropriate actor-level construct.

This case also informs institutional theory by suggesting how the meaning and expression of rationalized myths evolve over time and among actors. Actors make sense of cultural domination by inventing their individual truths shaped by their values, their field positions and the beliefs that characterize their times. What is shared is not so much a sense of 'what should be' but a sense of 'what is wrong' with the 1855

Table 12.2 *Cultural domination and contention: from a consensual truth to an inconvenient truce*

Field level	Domination as a consensual truth	Domination as an inconvenient truce
Actor level	Little contention, only at the field margin and mostly before the truce	Ongoing and creative contention at the field centre and before, during and after the truce
Hierarchy	A single dominant hierarchy with clear classificatory principles	A single dominant hierarchy with the emergence of competing ones with multiple classificatory principles
Practices	Reproduction of the 1855 classification. The emergence of alternative classifications decreases over time and disappears	Reproduction and creation of alternative classifications, with periods of high rate
Discourses	Homogenization of a collective and individual discourses around a rationalized and well theorized myth (or truth)	Emergence of localized and individual truths to make sense of cultural domination
Rhetorical strategies of legitimation	Convergence towards rationalization. Decoupling	Multiple strategies (rationalization, authorization, normalization, moralization and narrativization). Accounting for decoupling

classification. This finding both suggests that 1855 is a rationalized myth and that coupling is ensured, tightly or loosely, by the invention of individual truths that account for the decoupling and make sense locally. It also illustrates prior theoretical accounts of institutional contradictions that generate reflexivity (Seo and Creed, 2002). However, the contradictions are not *de facto* out there, but rather institutionalized at the actor level. Domination is not then a consensual truth, but an inconvenient truce made of individual truths.

The study clearly calls for additional research. From an empirical point of view, several actors have wondered why this classification has remained in force for so long. Although the narratives do reveal some of the motives of some actors to remain attached to this classification, the chapter does not provide any detailed answer to the question of why they do so. From a theoretical point of view, although this chapter rests on a very large sample of texts that discussed the 1855 classification, the inconvenient truce perspective only suggests that legitimacy and decoupling-based arguments fall short in accounting for the co-existence of actor-level contention within field-level domination. However, this perspective remains descriptive. Mechanisms to explain this co-existence are only assumed and not theorized.

Conclusion

This chapter accounts for an extreme case of stability as the 1855 classification has remained almost unchanged, yet powerful, over 150 years. Reflecting on this long process, one is left wondering about the role played by the truce, or settlement, reached in 1855 in the stabilization of the field (see, for example, Rao, 1998; Rao and Kenney, 2008) and the fact that contention has obviously continued. The new 1855 order seems to have been accepted by varying authors/actors, as it is still ruling, although in the following chapter Anand makes a case for an alternative system. One possible mechanism seems to be that actors have 'accepted' this order by interpreting and making sense of the 1855 event in ways that were often realigned with their interests, beliefs and professional identities. They invented their own truth, which then helped the 1855 truce to remain in force. But cultural production went further than making convenient (hence appropriate and legitimate) a truth that was not. Actors did express their disagreement, in ways that not only simmered from time to time but also blazed. The question then arises: why was this ongoing contestation so innocuous and why were subsequent participants in similar events not able to (re-) negotiate, theorize or impose a new order by channelling this contestation? It is especially puzzling as institutional change in emerging fields is often depicted as coming from contentious actors at the margins (see, for instance, Leblebici *et al.*, 1991) and in mature fields from incumbent actors at the centre (see, for example, Greenwood and Suddaby, 2006; Rao *et al.*, 2003), two situations that have characterized the Médoc wine field over time. These puzzles remain unresolved and call for further inquiry into the dynamics of contention in cultural and political fields.

Notes

* I would like to thank the convenors of the ©reative Encounters workshop
  for which this paper was first written, Brian Moeran and Jesper
  Strandgaard Pedersen, for co-ordinating this volume and for commenting
  on earlier drafts of my work. I am also deeply grateful to Daniel Lawton,
  Dewey Markham Jr., Philippe Roudié, Bruno Boidron, Gilles de Revel, as
  well as to the librarians at the Bordeaux library and at the Gironde archives
  for their help and support. Last, I am indebted to Frédéric Delmar, Mike
  Lounsbury, John Meyer, Philippe Monin, Woody Powell, Eero Vaara and
  Marc Ventresca for continuing to challenge my thinking about 1855.
1. The chapter is part of a larger research project on institutional change and
   persistence in the Bordeaux wine region (1700–2007) which makes use of
   contemporaneous, historical and archival documents. So far, this larger
   project represents fifteen weeks in the Bordeaux region, searching the
   Gironde Department archive, the Bordeaux Library, the Bordeaux library
   Department for old and rare documents, and various private archives.
   During this time, I met several wine professionals, interviewed acknowledged experts such as Dewey Markham, Philippe Roudié and Daniel
   Lawton, attended countless wine tastings, took part in wine sales and a
   wine competition and read extensively local and national (wine) histories
   associated with this period. I also conducted searches at the Bibliothèque
   Nationale de France, the Bodleian Library at Oxford University and the
   Green Library at Stanford University, in order to gain access to rare
   volumes in English and contextual data sources.

   One difficulty has been to generate a full and meaningful population of
   texts. I have relied on three main historical sources to identify these texts,
   the book by Markham (1998) being the most exhaustive source. From
   these three sources, an open-ended snowballing process took place, leading
   from one source to many others. I believe that this open-ended strategy
   enabled me to recreate a full population of texts for the following reasons:
   (1) historical sources are known to be authoritative and comprehensive; (2)
   most texts quote explicitly other texts and indicate their sources, which
   enable us then to identify all the field members who wrote about 1855. As
   a consequence, it is likely that the sampling is unbiased as numerous opponents, proponents and commentators take part in this 'field conversation'.
2. The purpose of this chapter is not to explain contentious domination, but to
   describe it. However, in order to make sense to these descriptions, I find it
   useful to recall that two important factors have been identified in the
   literature to make sense of this situation. Firstly, a stream of research looks
   into *ambiguity* among hierarchies to explain why contentious domination
   might occur (e.g., Stark 2009). This argument often rests on the multiplicity

of hierarchies available to the actors (e.g., Clemens and Cook 1999). Second, a stream of research looks into the *complexity* of evaluation processes as a source of legitimation and delegitimation of hierarchies (e.g., Appadurai, 1986: 42–5; Karpik, 2007; Nelson, 1970).

3. Gironde is the department to which Bordeaux belongs – a department being an administrative geographical unit, similar to a county in England, which structures France and which is governed by a prefect who is the local representative of the State. Prefects were in charge of setting up the local Committees for the 1855 Universal Exhibition.

4. One could argue that giving this task to the brokers implied a price-based classification as their job was to facilitate and record all trans-actions. That said, during their activities, the brokers also tasted all the wines and gave advice to the merchants. As a result, they could also have opted for another rationale such as tasting or immediate market reputation.

5. The Médoc wine region has mostly been producing red wine. However, the 1855 classification document also includes a ranking of white wines from the Sauternes region. Haut-Brion is the only red wine classified as Médoc even though it is not part of the Médoc region. Furthermore, there is a controversy about whether the fifty-seventh growth, Cantemerle, is part of the initial document or not (see Markham, 1998).

6. I refer to the notion of *truth* because I believe that the actors/authors concerned have made sincere 'ontological' claims about the 'right' way to assess the quality of wine and that their writings have tried to unravel what seems to be true for them. In institutional theory, the notion of myth and the logic of good faith are fairly close, although myth is exclusively a collective concept and might para-doxically connote that something is not 'true' for the actors (see Meyer and Rowan, 1977; Frank and Meyer, 2007). Truth is also a word used repeatedly by field actors themselves.

7. Most of the quotations referred to in this chapter have been translated from French by the author.

8. Robert Villepigue also owned a property in Saint-Emilion and was one of the founders and first President of the Co-operative of Saint-Emilion, the first wine co-operative in the whole Bordeaux region.

9. An important group of actors that is not represented here are the brokers but, overall, they hardly interfered in this debate, with the noticeable exception of Guillaume Lawton in 1815. Their intermediary roles might shed some light on this public abstinence.

References

Anand, N. and Jones, B. 2008. 'Tournament rituals, category dynamics, and field configuration: the case of the Booker Prize', *Journal of Management Studies* 45:6, 1,036–60.

Anand, N. and Watson, M. 2004. 'Tournament rituals in the evolution of fields: the case of the Grammy Awards', *Academy of Management Journal* 47, 59–80.

Appadurai, A. 1986. 'Introduction: commodities and the politics of value', in A. Appadurai (ed.), *The Social Life of Things: Commodities in Cultural Perspective*. Cambridge University Press, pp. 3–63.

Barley, S. R. and Tolbert, P. S. 1997. 'Institutionalization and structuration: studying the links between action and institution', *Organization Studies* 18:1, 93–117.

Coates, C. 2004. *The Wines of Bordeaux: Vintages and Tasting Notes 1952–2003*. Berkeley: University of California Press.

Clegg, S. R., Courpasson, D. and Phillips, N. 2006. *Power and Organizations*. London: Sage Publications.

Clemens, E. S. and Cook, J. M. 1999. 'Politics and institutionalism: explaining durability and change', *Annual Review of Sociology* 25, 441–66.

Cocks, C. 1868/1982. *Bordeaux et ses Vins*. Bordeaux: Editions Féret et Fils.

Colyvas, J. and Powell, W. W. 2006. 'Roads to institutionalization: the remaking of boundaries between public and private science', *Research in Organizational Behaviour* 27, 305–53.

d'Armailhacq, A. 1855. *De la Culture des Vignes dans le Médoc*. Bordeaux: Chaurnas.

DiMaggio, P. 1988. 'Interest and agency in institutional theory', in L. G. Zucker (ed.), *Institutional Patterns and Organizations: Culture and Environment*. Pensacola, FL: Ballinger Publishing Co/Harper & Row, pp. 3–21.

DiMaggio, P. and Powell, W. 1983. 'The iron cage revisited: institutional isomorphism and collective rationality in organizational fields', *American Sociological Review* 48, 147–60.

Franck, W. 1860. *Traité sur les Vins du Médoc et les Autres Vins Rouges et Blancs du Département de la Gironde*. Bordeaux: Chaumas.

Frank, D. J. and Meyer, J. W. 2007. 'University expansion and the knowledge society', *Theory and Society* 36, 287–311.

Garud, R. 2008. 'Conferences as venues for the configuration of emerging organizational fields: the case of cochlear implants', *Journal of Management Studies* 45:6, 1,061–88.

Glynn, M. A. 2008. Configuring the field of play: how hosting the Olympic games impacts civic community', *Journal of Management Studies* 45:6, 1,117–46.

Greenwood, R. and Suddaby, R. 2006. 'Institutional entrepreneurship in mature fields: the big five accounting firms', *Academy of Management Journal* 49:1, 27–48.

Greenwood, R., Suddaby, R., and Hinings, C. R. 2002. 'Theorizing change: the role of professional associations in the transformation of institutionalized fields', *Academy of Management Journal* 45:1, 58–80.

Karpik, L. 2007. *L'économie des Singularités*. Paris: Editions Gallimard.

Lamothe, L. 1856. *Nouveau Guide de L'Etranger à Bordeaux*. Bordeaux: Chaumas.

Lampel, J. and Meyer, A. D. 2008. 'Field-configuring events as structuring mechanisms: how conferences, ceremonies, and trade shows constitute new technologies, industries, and markets', *Journal of Management Studies* 45:6, 1,025–35.

Leblebici, H., Salancik, G. R., Copay, A. and King, T. 1991. 'Institutional change and the transformation of interorganizational fields: an organizational history of the US radio broadcasting industry', *Administrative Science Quarterly* 36:3, 333–63.

Lichine, A. 1967/1987. *Encyclopedia of Wines and Spirits*. London: Cassell.

Markham, D. J. 1998. *1855: A History of the Bordeaux Classification*. New York: John Wiley.

Meyer, J. and Rowan, B. 1977. 'Institutionalized organizations: formal structures as myth and ceremony', *American Journal of Sociology* 83:2, 340–63.

Moeran, B. 2010. 'The book fair as a tournament of values', *Journal of the Royal Anthropological Institute (NS)* 16, 138–54.

Munir, K. A. 2005. 'The social construction of events: a study of institutional change in the photographic field', *Organization Studies* 26:1, 93–112.

Nelson, P. 1970. 'Information and consumer behaviour', *Journal of Political Economy* 78:2, 311–29.

Oliver, A. L. and Montgomery, K. 2008. 'Using field-configuring events for sense-making: a cognitive network approach', *Journal of Management Studies* 45:6, 1,147–67.

Parker, R. J. 1991. *Guide Parker des Vins de Bordeaux*. Paris: Editions Solar.

Penning-Rowsell, E. 1969. *The Wines of Bordeaux*. New York: Stein and Day Publishers.

Peppercorn, D. 2003. *Bordeaux*. London: Mitchell Beazley.

Powell, W. W., White, D. R., Koput, K. W. and Owen-Smith, J. 2005. 'Network dynamics and field evolution: the growth of inter-organizational collaboration in the life sciences', *American Journal of Sociology* 110:4, 1,132–205.

Rao, H. 1994. 'The social construction of reputation: certification contests, legitimation, and the survival of organizations in the American automobile industry: 1895–1912', *Strategic Management Journal* 15 (Special Issue: Competitive Organizational Behaviour), 29–44.

1998. 'Caveat emptor: the construction of nonprofit consumer watchdog organizations', *American Journal of Sociology* 103, 912.

Rao, H. and Kenney, M. 2008. 'New forms as settlements', in R. Greenwood, C. Oliver, R. Suddaby and K. Sahlin-Andersson (eds.), *The SAGE Handbook of Organizational Institutionalism*. Thousand Oaks, CA: Sage.

Rao, H., Monin, P. and Durand, R. 2003. 'Institutional change in Toque ville: nouvelle cuisine as an identity movement in French gastronomy', *American Journal of Sociology* 108, 795–843.

Robinson, J. 2008. *The Oxford Companion to Wine*. Third edition. Oxford University Press.

Roudié, P. 1988. *Vignobles et Vignerons du Bordelais (1850–1980)*. University of Bordeaux Press.

Seo, M.-G. and Creed, W. E. D. 2002. 'Institutional contradictions, praxis, and institutional change: a dialectical perspective', *Academy of Management Review* 27:2, 222–47.

Stark, D. 2009. *The Sense of Dissonance: Accounts of Worth in Economic Life*. Princeton University Press.

Strang, D. and Meyer, J. W. 1993. 'Institutional conditions for diffusion', *Theory and Society* 22:4, 487–511.

Tolbert, P. S. and Zucker, L. G. 1996. 'The institutionalization of institutional theory', in S. R. Clegg, C. Hardy and W. R. Nord (eds.), *Handbook of Organization Studies*. Thousand Oaks: CA: Sage.

Vaara, E. and Tienari, J. 2008. 'A discursive perspective on legitimation strategies in MNCs'. *Academy of Management Review* 33:4, 985–93.

Villepigue, R. and Villepigue, A. 1934. *L'aire de Production des Vins de Saint-Emilion avec un Essai de Classement Scientifique de ses Crûs*. Paris: Bureaux de la Revue de Viticulture.

13 | The retrospective use of tournament rituals in field configuration: the case of the 1976 'Judgement of Paris' wine tasting

N. ANAND

In 1976 Paris-based British wine merchant Steven Spurrier organized a wine-tasting event at which French wines were pitted against American ones. The American wines were the surprising winners in the tournament, beating some of the most vaunted French wines. Although this ritual garnered little attention at the time, in intervening years its significance has grown progressively, particularly as the elite dominance of French wines has decreased. For those advocating for the liberating force of globalization in the wine industry, the 'Judgement of Paris' tournament ritual serves as a convenient marker of the shift in the balance of power from the Old World to the New World and from English wine critics to the American Robert Parker. The 'Judgement of Paris' shows how tournament rituals are co-opted retrospectively by forces seeking to reconfigure fields. Using theories of collective memory and social remembering, I show how vested social actors seeking to reconfigure fields co-opt tournament rituals retrospectively. The instance of retrospective utility stands in stark contrast to prospective models of tournament rituals, where institutional entrepreneurs try to shape the unfolding of a field. Thus, ephemeral tournaments that might otherwise have been forgotten have retrospective utility, especially for those shaping the collective memory of the field in order to suit future interests.

Tournament rituals as field-configuration mechanisms

Appadurai (1986: 21) defines tournaments of value as 'complex periodic events that are removed in some culturally well-defined way from the routines of economic life. Participation in them is likely to be both a privilege of those in power and an instrument of status contests among them'. Tournament rituals, a concept derived from this definition, are ceremonial spectacles enacted with periodic regularity in organizational fields and set apart from humdrum everyday routines (Anand and Watson, 2004). Examples of tournament rituals include awards ceremonies such as the Grammy Awards and the Booker Prize.

Tournament rituals are, first and foremost, rituals. Rituals are practical ways for people to deal with specific social and political contexts (Bell, 1992). They can be used agentively to echo existing relationships or to semaphore a vision of alternative arrangements. As Kertzer (1988: 1) states exuberantly: 'Through ritual, aspiring political leaders struggle to assert their right to rule, incumbent power holders seek to bolster their authority and revolutionaries carve out a new basis of political allegiance'. Beyond their direct social and political impact, rituals also have the cognitive effect of reifying the social categories invoked in their enactment (Durkheim, 1965). Tournament rituals are transorganizational structures. Through the enactment of tournament rituals, disparate actors in a field can come together to influence its evolution. Tournament rituals have the potential to dynamically edit and reconfigure the social categories that constitute a field. Studies show that with each repeated enactment, tournament rituals can obliterate pre-existing categories or incorporate new ones. For example, repeated enactments of the Booker Prize ceremony led to the creation of the commercially appealing genre of post-colonial fiction (Anand and Jones, 2008).

According to extant theory, periodic enactment is critical to tournament rituals' ability to influence field configuration. Can a tournament ritual influence field configuration without being enacted repeatedly? The answer is yes. The 'Judgement of Paris' wine-tasting event enacted in 1976 is an interesting case in point. Detailed examination of this case reveals the potential of non-repeating tournament rituals to influence field evolution retrospectively. The case also shows how social and situational factors influence symbolic-exchange and commodity-exchange value.

The 'Judgement of Paris' wine tasting event

The 'Judgement of Paris' wine tasting event was organized in 1976 by Steven Spurrier, a British wine merchant based in Paris. Spurrier's clientele in the early 1970s consisted largely of British and American expatriates living in Paris and he had hired an American, Patricia Gallagher, to help him run wine appreciation seminars. He also worked hard to network with the key figures of the French wine establishment.

When Gallagher told him that various commemorative events were being planned in Paris for the American bicentennial in 1976, the two of them decided to organize a wine-tasting event to celebrate Californian wines. The tasting took place at the Intercontinental Hotel and comprised a set of Californian white and red wines that were compared to corresponding French wines.

Spurrier and Gallagher made separate trips to California to choose wines for the tasting event. Spurrier eventually decided on six white wines (from Chateau Montelena, Freemark Abbey, Spring Mountain, Veedercrest, David Bruce and Chalone) and six reds (from Freemark Abbey, Heitz, Stags' Leap Wine Cellars, Clos Du Val, Mayacamas and Ridge). Bottles for tasting were brought by a group of American wine-makers touring France. Spurrier added a set of renowned French wines for comparison. The four white wines were: Beaune Clos des Mouches Joseph Drouhin, Meursault Charmes Roulot, Puligny-Montrachet les Pucelles Maison Louis Jadot and Bâtard-Montrachet Ramonet-Prudhon. The four reds were Château Montrose, Château Léoville-Las-Cases, Château Mouton Rothschild and Château Haut-Brion.

Spurrier was able to invite a number of well-known figures from the French wine establishment to serve on the tasting panel. This panel included: Pierre Bréjoux (Inspector General of the Appellation d'Origine Contrôlée Board), Pierre Tari (Secretary-General of the Association des Grands Crus Classés), Odette Kahn (Editor of the *Revue du Vin de France* and *Cuisine et Vins de France*), Raymond Oliver (chef proprietor of the Michelin three-star restaurant Le Grand Véfour), Claude Vrinat (owner of the Michelin three-star restaurant Taillevent), Christian Vannequé (head sommelier of the Michelin three-star restaurant La Tour d'Argent) and Aubert de Villaine (co-owner of the Domaine de la Romanée-Conti winery). These individuals had impeccable credentials. The panel also included Claude Dubois-Millot and Michel Dovas. Dubois-Millot was the sales director of GaultMillau, which publishes an influential restaurant guide rivalling the Michelin Guide. Although well known in the French wine field, Dubois-Millot was an inexperienced taster. Dovas taught a wine appreciation course for Spurrier, but was not otherwise well known. Spurrier and Gallagher invited a number of media outlets to send journalists to the event. George Taber, then the Paris correspondent for *Time* magazine, was the only one who bothered to show up.

Spurrier had set up a blind-tasting event, but did not announce the competitive element of the tasting while sending out the invitations and this came as a surprise to the judges. Each judge was given a scorecard to rate the wines. Prior to the tasting, the expectation was that the French wines would easily outscore the Californian ones. However, as the tasting progressed, Taber (2005: 200–1) noted that 'the judges were becoming totally confused as they tasted the white wines. The panel couldn't tell the difference between the French ones and those from California ... At one point Raymond Oliver was certain he had just sipped a French wine, when in fact it was a California one from Freemark Abbey'. When the scores were tallied at the end of the tasting, the wine from Chateau Montelena scored the highest among the whites and the wine from Stags' Leap Wine Cellars scored the highest among the reds. Taber then filed a story for the 7 June issue of *Time* magazine titled 'Judgement of Paris' and announced that 'in Paris, at a formal wine tasting organized by Spurrier, the unthinkable happened: California defeated all Gaul' (Taber, 2005: 213). The 'victory' of the unprepossessing Californian wines over their highly vaunted French counterparts was surprising.

Taber (2005) reports, however, that the reaction to the event from the French media was muted. Panelist Odette Kahn wrote a piece in the *Revue du Vin de France* titled 'On the subject of a "small scandal"', mainly decrying the blind-tasting procedure. Reports in *Le Figaro* and *Le Monde* continued in the same vein. The reaction of the American media was more vigorous. Following Taber's story in *Time* magazine, a number of regional newspapers reported on the event and its results. The retail stock of the 'winning' wines in the competition, predictably, sold out very quickly.

Taber's role in the tournament ritual was a very central one. By his own admission (Taber, 2005: 214), had he not been the sole journalist present, any memory of the event would have been more transient:

If no one from the press had been present, it would have also been much easier for the French and others simply to deny or distort what had happened ... In fact, my major objective in writing this book was to set the record straight once and for all about what transpired that day in Paris.

After its almost accidental, one-off staging, the tournament ritual continues to be commemorated in various ways, mostly with Spurrier's involvement. In 1978, he participated in a recreation of the original blind taste test at the Vintners Club of San Francisco. In 1986, he organized a tenth anniversary blind tasting at the French Culinary

Institute. On 24 March 2006, Spurrier and Patricia Gallagher organized a thirtieth anniversary simultaneous re-enactment in London and Napa (Murphy, 2006). What was common to all of these events was that the best-tasting wine was always a Californian one. It is important to note that the commemorations, though, are just that: they simply do not convey the keen sense of a tournament being played out as the original event did.

The 'Judgement of Paris' as social remembering

The 'Judgement of Paris' event stands in sharp contrast to other tournament rituals that have been studied empirically. It is a ritual frozen in time, enacted just once. It should not be able to command the same field-configuring processes as those tournament rituals that are enacted repeatedly. In prospective tournament rituals such as award ceremonies, institutional entrepreneurs can, with each periodic enactment, marshal social and political process to edit the categorical constitution of a field. Yet the 'Judgement of Paris' ritual itself has had a significant impact in reconfiguring the global wine field, not through active reenactment, but through the ways in which it is commemorated (Connerton, 1989) – through imitative reenactments and retelling of the story by journalists and winemakers themselves. It is a tournament ritual that has had excellent retrospective utility.

Theories of social remembering explore the question of *what* is remembered by *whom* within a given social context (Misztal, 2003) and are useful in examining how 'Judgement of Paris' became a field-reconfiguring event over time. In the pioneering contribution to this theoretical tradition, Halbwachs (1992) coined the term 'collective memory' to refer to the socially constructed nature of remembrance. Halbwachs followed Durkheim in emphasizing that collective memory is a critical aspect of social solidarity. While Durkheim (1965) wrote about the importance of commemorative rituals in establishing a society's link with the past, Halbwachs differed in highlighting the active social processes through which collective memory comes to be framed and the mechanisms through which remembrance is accomplished. He argued that a group's social identity and power determined what a group chose to remember, and indeed a group's ability to remember in a sustained fashion at all. For Halbwach, group identity determines what is chosen to be remembered. Ideally, events that are remembered provide a cherished sense of the past in order to provide an illusion of the group's stability and continuity. As the social power of a group wanes, so does its capacity to enact remembrance mechanisms.

The 'invention of tradition' approach (Hobsbawm, 1983) takes a Marxist rather than functionalist view of social memory. While this approach concurs with that of Halbwachs in viewing collective memory as a means towards establishing and maintaining the social cohesion of groups, what is uniquely highlighted is the identification of agents directly responsible for constructing memories in achieving self-serving political objectives. Hobsbawm views the management of collective remembering as a political response to novel social situations. He speculates that the incidence of collective remembering is higher when there is rapid transformation of existing social patterns, when 'old traditions and their institutional carriers and promulgators no longer prove sufficiently adaptable and flexible, or are otherwise eliminated: in short, when there are sufficiently large and rapid changes on the supply and demand sides' (Hobsbawm, 1983: 4–5). Both Halbwachs and Hobsbawm argue that social agents use the past as a resource to shape current agendas.

Given the constant commemoration of the 'Judgement of Paris' event, it is useful to view it through the lens of social remembrance theories. What, indeed, is the retrospective use to which this ritual has been put, and how has it been implicated in field configuration? We identify three important ways in which the ritual has been retrospectively 'useful': in cohering wine California producers, in symbolically marking large economic shifts in the field, and most importantly, in challenging a dominant and dominating categorical system in the field.

Cohering California wine producers

'Not bad for kids from the sticks' is how Jim Barrett, the owner of Chateau Montela reacted to news of the 'Judgement of Paris' when Taber called him immediately after the event (Taber, 2005: 207). There are two connotations in Barrett's modest reaction. First, there is a sense of plurality of producers ('kids'). Second, that they are the underdogs ('from the sticks'). These connotations suggest that at the time of this tournament ritual, California wine production was a nascent industry with a small set of producers: very much a field in the making. Through the event, rival producers could cognize their collective presence and arrive at a sense of being engaged in a mutual enterprise (White, 1981; DiMaggio and Powell, 1983). A ritual provides a focus of attention for disparate constituents in a field to come together and develop a collective social identity (Anand and Watson, 2004), and, for Californian winemakers, the 'Judgement of Paris' provided this focus.

Our concern here, however, has less to do with the ritual itself and more about how it was remembered. The halo of winning the 'Judgement of Paris' moved from the narrow circle of the producers included in the tournament to California winemakers in general. Robert Mondavi was a notable California producer of that time whose wines were not included in the tasting. Yet in the foreword to Taber's book (2005: xi), Mondavi writes: 'This is a book for every wine lover; it has a history and a very exciting story well told. *And we won!*' (my emphasis). Mondavi thus claims the victory for producers in the tournament as a victory for all California, if not all America. Also, as McCoy (2005: 51) notes, the event had a tremendous impact in boosting the confidence of the humble 'kids from the sticks' who grew increasingly in confidence: 'With the help of American ingenuity and technology, hard work, dedication, and sheer smarts, Americans had made it to the big leagues and humbled those haughty know-it-all Frenchmen. This was an attitude that would last, and last, and last'. This sort of claim defines what it is to be social (Zerubavel, 1997: 91): extended members of a group appropriate a defining event that only a few members have participated in as if it was somehow part of their own past, even when they did not experience the original event themselves. The events experienced by a few members become part of the collective memory of an entire social group.

Viewed from a Durkheimian perspective then, the commemoration of this once-enacted tournament ritual serves the purpose of structuring California wine producers as a coherent group, and in contradistinction to French wine producers. However, this case also addresses a critique of Halbwachs's theorizing. In his scheme, collective identity precedes remembrance; remembrance is the entitlement of established and powerful groups (Misztal, 2003). Here we see the interlocution of identity and remembrance, and how construction of the one occasions that of the other. The tournament acted as a catalyst for California winemakers to take cognizance of each other, to recognize their interdependence and to articulate their distinctive identity (Scott, 1995). Their identity matured through the constant remembrance of the tournament

Symbolizing the shifting moment in the global winemaking field

In examining the 'Judgement of Paris,' there is some support for Hobsbawm's (1983) view that traditions are invented in times of social upheaval: as the economic and material base changes, so does the concomitant symbolic superstructure. The decline of the French Salon and fabrication of the impressionist tradition are attributable, for example, to changes in demographics of both producers and consumers of art (Delacour and Leca, Chapter 1).

The 'Judgement of Paris' event was not, by itself, the pivotal cause for the displacement of France from the centre of the global wine trade. Long-term trends already showed that the relative demand for French wine was shrinking. In the core Old World countries (France, Italy, Spain and Portugal) that were the most significant consumers prior to the 1970s, demand fell by half in just a generation (Taber, 2005). In France alone demand fell by 20 per cent through the 1990s because of changing social mores and strict sanctions on drinking and driving. Between 1990 and 2004, the share of world exports of the core Old World countries declined from 73 per cent to 59 per cent, and that of four New World countries (US, Australia, South Africa and Chile) increased from 4 per cent to 23 per cent. Exports from France declined by over 13 per cent in volume terms (Labys and Cohen, 2006).

Long before the 'Judgement of Paris,' American winemakers were experimenting with innovative agricultural and fermenting processes that started to make their way back to France (Echikson, 2004). Many winemakers in Napa consulted with research scientists based in the Department of Viticulture and Enology in the University of California, Davis, to improve their techniques. Producers such as Gallo of California, Concha y Torro of Chile, and Yellow Tail of Australia had also been pioneering conglomerate-scale business models that included novel techniques of reputation-enhancement through marketing and branding (Benjamin and Podolny, 1999). With the emergence of Robert Parker and other American wine critics increased attention devoted by the latter to California wines literally paid off. While production doubled in the quarter century after the 'Judgement of Paris,' retail value increased fourteen times (Peterson, 2001; Roberts and Reagans, 2007).

In an article in *Business Week* commemorating the twenty-fifth anniversary of the 'Judgement of Paris'. Mike Grgich, maker of the 'winning' Chateau Montelena Chardonnay, remarked: 'My life is divided into two parts – before the Paris tasting and after' (Peterson, 2001). The event allowed producers in the California wine industry to make a claim for 'the day they came of age' both in canonical and commercial terms (cf. Watson and Anand, 2006). This type of anchoring in time is critical for the constitution and sustenance of collective memories (Zerubavel, 1997). Warren Winiarksi, maker of the 'winning' Stags' Leap Wine Cellars Cabernet Sauvignon is quoted in the same *Business Week* article as 'recalling' this as the moment in which his wines were given 'visible endorsement from the [French wine] authorities ... We had people calling us to ask where they could get our wines, both from the trade and among consumers'. The date provides a convenient point for the New World winemakers who were gaining in social and economic power to mark the dawn of a different era and forget about what had happened previously (de Holan and Phillips, 2004).

Challenging a dominant and dominating field classification system

Appadurai (1986: 21) argued that in tournaments of values what is at stake is not 'just status, rank, fame, or reputation of actors, but the disposition of the central tokens of value in the society in question'. Anand and Watson (2004) suggest that 'the central tokens' of an organizational field are the categories that cognitively constitute the field in the minds of its participants. Tournament rituals are profoundly implicated in both the reification and editing of extant categories. The 'Judgement of Paris' event provides another interesting illustration of a tournament ritual associated with challenging a dominant and dominating field classification system: the 1855 classification of quality Bordeaux wines.

The classifications used in the French and American wine industries differ in an important way (Zhao, 2005). French wines are classified primarily by appellation based on geographic origin. The classification of appellation is vertically structured to indicate ascending and descending levels of quality evaluation. French appellation is tied to the concept of *terroir*, which '... encapsulates a tried process, a traditional blend of grapes, a soil, the slope of a valley, and a climate' (Douglas, 1986: 106). American (and other New World) wines, lacking the benefits associated with a tradition of locale, are classified by grape variety, which does not necessarily signify a stratified evaluation of quality.

The most prominent (but no means the only) categorization of the French wine industry is the 1855 classification of Bordeaux wines discussed by Grégoire Croidieu in the previous chapter. The Bordeaux Chamber of Commerce created a classification of winemakers of the area at the behest of Napoleon III for the 1855 *Exposition Universelle de Paris*. The Chamber took into account long-held records of prices commanded by various wineries to put together a hierarchy of *grand crus*, ranging from *premier*(first growth) to *cinquième* (fifth growth). At the time of the classification, there was no implication that it would be in any way enduring, given that there had been various attempts to create a quality listing of Bordeaux wines dating back to at least 1642 (Markham, 1998). However, as Croidieu notes, the 1855 classification has endured with little change, despite changes to the geographic borders of *terroirs* and in techniques of winemaking. What has also persisted is the price premium commanded by the *crus* classified as higher grade, without necessarily a link to the quality of the grapes constituting the wine (Ulin, 1996). The 1855 classification provided a proxy for the mystique, quality and tradition of French winemaking that the dominant Bordeaux establishment sought to continue (Echikson, 2004).

The 'Judgement of Paris' event posed a prominent and forceful challenge to the continuing validity of the 1855 classification. The 1973 Cabernet Sauvignon from Stags' Leap Wine Cellars was given higher scores by the tasting panel than the premier cru 1970 reds of Château Haut-Brion and Château Mouton Rothschild. The event provided the impetus for critics to rate a wine on the merits of what was in the bottle (in other words, appreciative value) rather than what was on the label (social value). The most prominent wine critic to emerge after the 'Judgement of Paris' was Robert M. Parker Jr, who pioneered a novel numeric system to rate the quality of wines. Parker's ratings now hold greater sway than the 1855 classification in the marketplace. As McCoy (2005) notes, the event helped obliterate 'the old approach' to evaluating wine quality: 'the hierarchies of chateaux, the classification of land, the primacy of France, consumption of wine by the upper and upper middle class, the old-fashioned wine merchants purveying advice, the slow ageing of wine in the cellars of the well-to-do, the accepted wisdom ... The time was right for Robert Parker'.

The desecration of the 1855 classification that became possible after the 'Judgement of Paris' has reshaped the global field of wine-making in two important ways (Taber, 2005). Firstly, it is now taken for granted that great wine can be made outside of French *terroir*. Secondly, great winemaking does not necessarily result from long-standing tradition. Both factors favour New World winemakers' claims to excellence. The ultimate impact of the 'Judgement of Paris' tournament ritual, may, then be in the creation and exploitation of the category of New World wine (cf. Anand and Jones, 2008). It is therefore in the collective interest of the New World producers to keep alive the memory of that ritual.

Implications

The 'Judgement of Paris' has three significant implications for theorizing field configuration (Lampel and Meyer, 2008). Firstly, it highlights the importance of social remembrance in field formation. Organizational field theory has matured to include notions of identity and evolution, but, ironically, still lacks a working conceptualization of memory. In this chapter, I have attempted a beginning, and have argued about the ways in which an image of the past is used in ongoing contestation of traditional fields. This raises the question of the extent to which the past can be used as a malleable resource to configure fields (Olick and Robbins, 1998).

Second, the 'Judgement of Paris' demonstrates the retrospective utility of one-off tournament rituals in serving the interests of field-configuring forces. Past theorizing about tournament rituals has largely dealt with the on-going and prospective capacity of tournament rituals: ritual entrepreneurs take a syncopated view of the social context while planning their ritual, and endeavour to change some aspect of the context through symbolic modelling (Collins, 2004; Harrison, 1992). As Anand and Jones (2008: 1,039) note, ritual entrepreneurs are responsive to outcomes from past iterations of ritual performance; they reflexively observe and make any modifications required in order to reflect ongoing changes to social reality or to encode shifts in their own intentions. The faculty of repeated modelling is absent in one-off rituals, but the 'Judgement of Paris' case shows that this need not necessarily lead to diminished power for the purpose of field configuration. Clearly, a closer theoretical examination of the interplay between prospective and retrospective capacities of tournament rituals is warranted.

Finally, the 'Judgement of Paris' reveals how tournament rituals are implicated in the negotiation of the kinds of social, appreciative and even technical values that Brian Moeran and Jesper Strandgaard

Pedersen outlined in the Introduction to this volume. The event has been pivotal for California winemakers to locate themselves in the social space of winemaking *vis-à-vis* the French no longer as subordinate, but as peer or even superior. The persistent tactics of remembrance have been successfully deployed in creating a more favourable appreciative value for California wines. Ultimately, recollections about the event have also influenced the technical value of California wines by exhorting their use of 'new and improved' techniques of winemaking that are now copied on a global scale.

References

Anand, N. and Jones, B. C. 2008. 'Tournament rituals, category dynamics, and field configuration: the case of the Booker prize', *Journal of Management Studies* 45, 1,036–60.

Anand, N. and Watson, M. R. 2004. 'Tournament rituals in the evolution of fields: the case of the Grammy awards', *Academy of Management Journal* 47, 59–80.

Appadurai, A. 1986. 'Introduction: commodities and the politics of value', in A. Appadurai (ed.), *The Social Life of Things*. Cambridge University Press, pp. 3–63.

Bell, C. 1992. *Ritual Theory, Ritual Practice*. Oxford University Press.

Benjamin, B. A. and Podolny, J. M. 1999. 'Status, quality and social order in the California wine industry', *Administrative Science Quarterly* 44: 563–89.

Collins, R. 2004. *Interaction Ritual Chains*. Princeton University Press.

Connerton, P. 1989. *How Societies Remember*. Cambridge University Press.

de Holan, P. M. and Phillips, N. 2004. 'Remembrance of things past? The dynamics of organizational forgetting', *Management Science* 50, 1,603–13.

DiMaggio, P. J. and Powell, W. W. 1983. 'The iron cage revisited: institutional isomorphism and collective rationality in organizational fields', *American Sociological Review* 48, 147–60.

Douglas, M. 1986. *How Institutions Think*. Syracuse University Press.

Durkheim, E. 1965. *The Elementary Forms of Religious Life*. New York: Free Press.

Echikson, W. 2004. *Noble Rot*. New York: W.W. Norton.

Halbwachs, M. 1992. *On Collective Memory*. The University of Chicago Press.

Harrison, S. 1992. 'Ritual as intellectual property', *Man* 27, 225–44.

Hobsbawm, E. 1983. 'Introduction: inventing traditions', in E. Hobsbawm and T. Ranger (eds.), *The Invention of Tradition*. Cambridge University Press, 1–14

Kertzer, D. I. 1988. *Ritual, Politics, and Power*. New Haven, CT: Yale University Press.

Labys, W. C. and Cohen, B. C. 2006. 'Trends versus cycles in global wine export shares', *The Australian Journal of Agricultural and Resource Economics* 50, 527–37.

Lampel, J. and Meyer, A. D. 2008. 'Field configuring events as structuring mechanisms: how conferences, ceremonies, and trade shows constitute new technologies, industries, and markets', *Journal of Management Studies* 45, 1,025–35.

Markham, D. Jr 1998. *1855: A History of the Bordeaux Classification*. New York: Wiley.

McCoy, E. 2005. *The Emperor of Wine: The Rise of Robert M. Parker, Jr. and the Reign of American Taste*. New York: HarperCollins.

Misztal, B. 2003. *Theories of Social Remembering*. Maidenhead: Open University Press.

Murphy, L. 2006. 'California wines beat the French – again!', *San Francisco Chronicle*, 25 May: A1.

Olick, J. K. and Robbins, J. 1998. 'Social memory studies: from "collective memory" to the historical sociology of mnemonic practices', *Annual Review of Sociology* 24, 105–40.

Peterson, T. 2001. 'The day California wines came of age', *Business Week*, 8 May.

Roberts, P. W. and Reagans, R. 2007. 'Critical exposure and price-quality relationships for New World wines in the U.S. market', *Journal of Wine Economics* 2, 56–69.

Scott, W. R. 1995. *Institutions and Organizations*. Thousand Oaks, CA: Sage.

Taber, G. M. 2005. *Judgement of Paris: California vs. France and the Historic 1976 Paris Tasting that Revolutionized Wine*. New York: Scribner.

Ulin, R. C. 1996. *Vintages and Traditions: an Ethnohistory of Southwest French Wine Cooperatives*. Washington: Smithsonian Institution Press.

Watson, M. R. and Anand, N. 2006. 'Award ceremony as an arbiter of commerce and canon in the popular music industry', *Popular Music* 25, 41–56.

White, H. 1981. 'Where do markets come from?', *American Journal of Sociology* 87, 517–47.

Zerubavel, E. 1997. *Social Mindscapes: an Invitation to Cognitive Sociology*. Cambridge, MA: Harvard University Press.

Zhao, W. 2005. 'Understanding classifications: empirical evidence from the American and French wine industries', *Poetics* 33, 179–200.

Afterword: Converting values into other values: fairs and festivals as resource valuation and trading events

JOSEPH LAMPEL

This rich collection of papers on fairs and festivals is a theoretical and empirical exploration of institutions that have thus far been largely ignored by social scientists. They are ignored because their economic role is generally seen as peripheral, and they are ignored because their internal processes, not to mention their relationship to the field in which they are situated, are variously classified as 'field-configuring events' (FCEs) (Lampel and Meyer, 2008), 'tournaments of values' (Moeran, 2010), 'tournament rituals' (Anand, Chapter 13; Anand and Watson, 2004) or 'temporary clusters' (Maskell *et al.*, 2006; Bathelt, and Schuldt, 2008).

A natural response to this state of affairs would be to formulate a definition that stipulates what is meant by 'fairs' and 'festivals'. But this, as the diversity of views in this book show, would be difficult, and would, in any case, divert attention from what is truly important about fairs and festivals: fairs and festivals are sites where social, economic and ideological processes, situated predominately in specialized contexts, interact openly and explicitly. In fairs and festivals the full range of economic, social and symbolic resources are in play; contexts where we can observe economic, social and symbolic resources being valued and converted into each other more directly than in other institutions such as markets or firms where this conversion is indirect or illegitimate.

For researchers fairs and festivals are therefore naturally occurring socio-economic 'laboratories' with two distinguishing features that make them interesting: they are contexts where all resources relevant to the field's strategies are valued in relationship to each other, and they are contexts where actors use resources entrepreneurially to create and obtain other resources that further these strategies. In what follows, I would like to explore both these features using primarily the contributions to this book. My starting point is Moeran and Strandgaard Pedersen's Introduction, which frames and informs many of the subsequent contributions. But building on this Introduction, I would like to develop a view of fairs and festivals as a matrix for entrepreneurial opportunities.

Resource valuation at entry to fairs and festivals

In their opening essay Moeran and Strandgaard Pedersen note that fairs and festivals are essentially events and sites where different kinds of values are produced, negotiated and transacted. The papers in this book persuasively show that values and valuations are central to fairs and festivals, but they also suggest that to explain their institutional durability and effectiveness we must look at values and valuations from a broad perspective that includes a variety of resources that normally fall outside the conventional definition of resources by economists.

Researchers such as Bourdieu (1977, 1997) have done much to draw attention to symbolic and social resources, but other resources such as intellectual (Roos *et al.*, 1998), human (Becker, 1964), moral (Rosenberg, 1990) and relational (Baker *et al.*, 2002), have been added. Of the range of resources that have entered scholarly discussion, symbolic, social and economic resources are singled out for analysis of markets where quality standards are contestable, and where the credibility of producers and intermediaries plays an important role in establishing this value. The markets for creative products display both conditions to an extent that is rarely found elsewhere: not only are quality standards contestable where creative products are concerned, but producers and intermediaries mobilize and use symbolic, social and economic resources to obtain advantageous valuation.

The key distinction that is useful to make when discussing how actors use these resources is between attached and alienable resources (see Moeran, 2010, as well as his Chapter 5 in this volume). Attached resources can be defined as resources that cannot be separated from the identity of the actors that hold them. Attempts to transfer them to others are regarded as illegitimate or at best lead to severe depreciation in value. Alienable resources, on the other hand, are controlled but not embedded in the identity of the actor in such a way as to prevent transfer of control or ownership to others.

When individuals and organizations that produce and deal in creative products set out to use resources they confront two basic problems: firstly, how to value these products as alienable resources; and secondly, how to value attached resources such as reputation, social connections and so on, which are often crucial for obtaining the highest returns for these products. Fairs and festivals are institutions that allow participants to perform both valuation processes. In this respect, they have a significant advantage over alternative institutions such as markets or firms. Furthermore, fairs and festivals have evolved to do both by creating processes that allow participants to capture the value of their resources as 'capital', in the narrow economic sense when it comes to alienable resources, and in the wider social and ideological connotation when referring to attached resources.

The capacity of fairs and festivals to transform alienable and attached resources into capital is consistent with Bourdieu's (1977, 1997) analysis of how actors combine different resources to improve their field position. For Bourdieu, actors have a dual role *vis-à-vis* their resource portfolio. They are investors in as much as they search for opportunities that will yield their resources good returns, and they are entrepreneurs in as much as they adopt and engage in practices that will yield the highest returns once they have decided to pursue these opportunities.

However, to act effectively as investor and as entrepreneur, Bourdiesian actors must know the value of the resources at their disposal, and must have reasonable access to institutions where these resources can be invested, exchanged and converted at preferential rates. Fairs and festivals originally evolved to serve both these needs: merchants and craftsmen converged from the countryside to sell their goods, thereby establishing not only the 'market value' of their products, but also the total value of their capital stock (Verlinden, 1963; Epstein, 1994). But as modern economies developed, this valuation function was more efficiently performed by markets and by supporting institutions such as banks and accounting standards.

The major exception to this gradual replacement of fairs and festivals by markets was in areas of society that produce and trade in 'creative products' such as films, books, music, fashion and television. Success in these fields always depended on a combination of economic, technical, symbolic and social resources. Transformation of these fields into industries in the nineteenth and twentieth centuries gave rise to specialized markets that could efficiently value some of the resources needed to produce and distribute creative products, but the problem of valuing creative products, not to mention valuing attached resources that are often essential for marketing these products, remained essentially unchanged.

The absence of an efficient market mechanism for products and their associated production and distribution resources preserved, and arguably even promoted, the traditional role of fairs and festivals as key industry institutions in these areas. For many individuals and organizations, this has meant a reorientation of activities towards fairs and festivals as a crucial part of their strategy. More specifically, as the papers in this book show, participants in fairs and festivals use these events as an opportunity to value and augment both their alienable and attached resources. They do so in their capacity as investors who possess what they believe to be valuable alienable and attached resources in their possession, and as entrepreneurs seeking to exchange, combine and transform these resources on favourable terms.

Fairs and festivals as investment opportunities

In their introductory essay, Moeran and Strandgaard Pedersen note that fairs and festivals are spatially, temporally and socially bounded. This boundedness runs contrary to modern economic logic, as embodied in the globalization of capital markets for instance, but it is ideally suited for valuation of alienable and attached resources where creative products are concerned.

For example, in their analysis of London Fashion Week, Entwistle and Rocamora (Chapter 10) show how the event's boundaries are used to separate players who belong to the field, or at least have an acknowledged position therein, from others who do not. Borrowing from Bourdieu (2000: 55), they argue that the dividing line between inside and outside the event 'mirrors and reproduces the boundaries that exist around the wider field of fashion'. In practice, however, fields, unlike fashion shows, are not enclosed spaces but territories with ambiguous borders that are shared with other territories. The fields of *haute-couture*, *prêt-à-porter* and mass-market apparel overlap (Waddell, 2004). The fashion show cannot be said to mirror one field, but several, which in practice means that it is not truly a mirror but a restricted arena where those who gain admission manoeuvre to increase their portfolio of economic, social and symbolic resources.

Gaining admission is a crucial point at which the 'base value' of the applicant's portfolio of resources is valued. In some events, there is literally an admission charge, but in just about all fairs and festivals the true boundaries are determined by social and symbolic resources, that is to say, by attached resources, rather than by economic capital alone. There are instances where even attached resources are not sufficient to gain admission without additional valuation of the creative products that participants intend to display and market. In his chapter on art fairs (Chapter 2), Thompson describes the vetting process that takes place before dealers are allowed to participate. Two days before the opening, dealers leave their stands as a committee of vettors inspects each object. The vettors can remove objects that they deem not to have sufficient quality, scarcity or value, or not to be 'show-worthy'. The process, notes Thompson, adds value in 'much the same way as expert appraisal and acceptance by a major auction house' (as shown by Smith in Chapter 4 on auctions).

It is not only works of art that are often kept out of top art fairs, but also dealers. Exclusion of rivals plays an important role in establishing the value of the symbolic resources that accrues to dealers allowed in. In 2009, for instance, 590 dealers applied to exhibit in Maastricht, probably the most prestigious art fair in the world, but only 239 were accorded the privilege.

Selective acceptance is not only used to signal value in general, but also to confer precise meaning on that value. The practice of widely publicizing the ratio of applications to acceptance by organizers of fairs and festivals must be seen in this context as an effort to simultaneously communicate the position of the event in the hierarchy of competing events, as well as validation of the worth of works allowed in. This practice is merely part of a wider process of mutual consecration: the event consecrates the creative product, and the creative product subsequently consecrates the event. In their paper, Mezias *et al.* (Chapter 7) argue that this mutual consecration plays out in European premier film festivals: the festivals configure the identities of the film they consecrate, and the films, in turn, consecrate the festivals by enjoying a more robust box office performance, and perhaps, as Lampel and Shivasharan (2009) show, awards elsewhere.

This mutual consecration, as Delacour and Leca report in their analysis of the *Salon de Peinture* (Chapter 1), can go so far as to allow only medal winners consecrated in previous Salons the right to elect the juries that select art works in the forthcoming Salons. However, this is not without undesirable consequences if the rejected works have alternative sources of valuation, and if these sources mount an effective challenge to the criteria used to make this selection. In the case of the Salon, a rival dealer-critic system used impressionist art that was largely excluded by Salon juries to effectively destroy the legitimacy of the selection process by persuading collectors to shift their acquisitions from the Salon to the galleries. In effect, the collectors' decreasing willingness to pay for works displayed in the Salon at rates commensurate with the Salon's own valuation eventually led to the collapse in the Salon's valuation credibility.

The spatial and temporal structures of valuation in fairs and festivals

Valuation, however, does not stop at the boundaries of fairs and festivals. Once they have crossed the boundaries participants enter the complex process of negotiating the value of alienable resources (more on this later), but they are also intent on further differentiating the value of their attached resources from that of competitors. To facilitate this process, organizers of fairs and festivals partition the event time and space hierarchically. In his chapter on book fairs (Chapter 5), Moeran examines the complex spatial geography that book fair organizers create with the intention of providing publishers with an opportunity to increase their symbolic capital in the field. In his analysis of international television trade shows (Chapter 6), Havens describes in some detail the hierarchy of access that allows participants to increase the value of their attached resources, specifically their reputational and social capital. As he puts it: 'access accrues as participants navigate various boundaries within the marketplace that identify particular locations, perks and networks as more valuable than others'. Entwistle and Rocamora describe similar valuation structures, explicitly noting that 'high value of social capital buys one access to after-show parties, or to the designers themselves'.

Valuation structures are not only spatial; they are also temporal. Obtaining a ticket to the fashion show is only the start of sorting those who are accorded value from those who are not. There is a further distinction between holders of standing and sitting tickets, with the former having to wait for the latter to arrive and take their assigned seat. The distinction not only conveys to the 'fashionistas' the value of their endowed resources, but establishes their value by conveying the same to others in the catwalk theatre.

Fairs and festivals as entrepreneurial arenas

The awareness that reflexive, reciprocal and communal valuation is simultaneously taking place underpins the valuation process in London

Fashion Week, as it does in fairs and festivals more generally. The complex interplay of valuations is also at the heart of these events' internal dynamics. It not only drives behaviour once the participants enter the event space; it also creates a matrix of entrepreneurial opportunities that actors manoeuvre to exploit.

As the chapters in this book show, manoeuvring begins before the event. Participants in fairs and festivals adopt an investor mindset prior to their arrival, with all that this entails: evaluating sums to be spent on facilities, setting up parties while hoping that invitations to very important persons (VIPs) will be accepted and so on and so forth, they quickly turn into entrepreneurs once they enter the event space.

Entrepreneurs in a resource space that consists of alienable and attached resources pursue two parallel but closely related strategies. The first takes advantage of the valuation capacity of fairs and festivals to trade alienable resources on favourable terms. For example, in their chapters on book fairs and international television markets, Moeran (Chapter 5) and Havens (Chapter 6) respectively describe how participants use events to negotiate the value of rights. The second takes advantage of the complex spatial and temporal geographies of fairs and festivals to establish and increase the value of their attached resources. For example, Entwistle and Rocamora note that not only designers with a direct economic stake in the fashion week attend these events, but also buyers, fashion editors, journalists and bloggers. They do not do so out of 'economic necessity', but to increase their social capital by playing 'their part in the field of fashion – to "see" and be seen'.

For designers the game is more complex. As Entwistle and Rocamora (Chapter 10) note, although their collections are usually sold long before the fashion show, they still invest heavily in the event because it generates 'elusive symbolic capital around the designer that, ultimately, may translate into actual economic capital'. In effect, the designers are engaged in a third type of strategy that is central to the role of fairs and festivals: converting alienable into attached resources, and *vice versa*, converting attached into alienable resources. This conversion is institutionalized to some extent by the structure of the fair or festival, as the example of the designers indicates, but not entirely. Fairs and festivals provide both scripted and unscripted opportunities for converting different types of resources into each other. There is the obvious advantage of being able to set up meetings with many more interlocutors than would be economically possible or desirable if each had to be arranged separately during the regular business schedule. During these meetings, as Moeran points out, social capital can be used to obtain rights on favourable terms, but also to generate valuable information that is publicly withheld. Likewise, Havens notes that while the sale of programme rights may be the main activity at the international television market event, social encounters, both planned and unplanned, are crucial for converting attached into alienable resources. Organizations invest heavily in ' promotional extravagance': after-hour events that confer prestige in proportion to the exclusivity of the invited; which they can then convert into resources depending on their ability to navigate the room, schmooze and manage impressions.

The ability to take advantage of these opportunities depends in large part on the mastery of practices that are entailed in what Bourdieu (1997) calls 'habitus': the social, symbolic and cultural codes that are imprinted in the context and in the actor internalizing the context. Actors who enter fairs and festivals confront the habitus that is specific to these events. To operate effectively, they must not only assess and respond to its contours, but internalize the habitus to the point where it is semi-consciously present in action. For example, in his chapter on auctions (Chapter 4), Smith notes the apprehension of many buyers that they will fail to proficiently play their assigned role:

The feeling of being on stage and part of a performance in which you are expected to know and play your part well is widespread among auction goers … Many potential buyers admit that they are more nervous about not playing their role properly than the economic consequences of making a poor buy. The classic fear of scratching one's nose at the wrong time and having this taken as a bid arises more from the possibility of embarrassment over acting inappropriately than concern with financial loss.

To be effective, participants in fairs and festivals must both internalize and distance themselves from the habitus that prevails in fairs and festivals in general, as well as in the specific social and interpersonal contexts that they are likely to encounter within these events. They must fully internalize the habitus to act appropriately, and they must distance themselves sufficiently to act strategically. Not surprisingly, the elaborate rituals common to most fairs and festivals give competent players plenty of scope for accruing social and symbolic capital. Entwistle and Rocamora (Chapter 10) describe how accomplished players in the fashion field use 'air kissing' to confer recognition and establish their own value. As they put it, the air kiss, '. . . signifies proximity between players in the field and, therefore, belonging and membership. In other words, it is a performative gesture that renders visible otherwise abstract field relations and positions, and in the process enacts and reproduces one's social capital'. Air kissing is not only reflexive and reciprocal, but also communal. Nowhere more so than at the Cannes Film Festival, where, to quote a recent *New York Times* article by Dargis (2010): 'Anyone who doubts that the movie industry is still partly a handshake business had only to watch the glad-handing, backslapping and double-cheek air-kissing at the Vanity Fair–Gucci party at the Hôtel du Cap'.

An invitation to an exclusive party at Cannes provides guests with ample opportunities to perform rituals that create and bestow social and symbolic capital. But as Anand (Chapter 13) suggests in his analysis of the wine tasting event that came to be known as the 'Judgement of Paris', the rituals of the event can be used by organizers for their own ends, often without the knowledge of the participants. In this case, Steven Spurrier and Patricia Gallagher inveigled a group of French wine experts to participate in a blind-tasting event, but did not inform them of the competitive element in advance. Caught by the scripted conventions of wine tasting, the group was performatively compelled by their habitus to proceed with the ritual. For the organizers the final tally, which showed American wines as 'better' than their French counter-parts, became a valuable symbolic resource precisely because the judge-ment was rendered by French wine experts with high symbolic capital.

Fairs and festivals as regions of 'predictable unpredictability'

Although fairs and festivals create contexts in which rituals proliferate, it would be a mistake to see them primarily as arenas that choreograph behaviour in the manner of a 'medieval court' – as described by one of Entwistle and Racamora's respondents. Nor would it be correct to see fairs and festivals as events whose primary function is to reproduce the field. If anything, fairs and festivals, in the words of Fernand Braudel (1992: 82), 'interrupt the tight circle of everyday exchange' that struc-ture and routinize value chain relationships. This interruption is partic-ularly crucial in industries where the value chain evolves to serve the efficient transfer of alienable resources, but does so by confining attached resources to specific locations and activities. Fairs and festivals temporarily disrupt established value chain links, allowing actors to congregate in sites where they are not only likely to meet new actors, but also to encounter situations that are unlikely to occur during routine business. Indeed, the very unpredictability of fairs and festivals creates entrepreneurial opportunities to value and convert resources.

However, while actors come to fairs and festivals expecting to profit from the unexpected, they also rely on the events' formal rules, internal geography and rituals, which provide a measure of predictability that facilitates sense-making as well as planning. In effect, fairs and festivals create environments of 'predictable unpredictability' in which experienced participants can bet resources on emerging opportunities within a framework whose principles they can basically master. This is nicely captured by Thompson's explanation (Chapter 2) of why art fairs have become indispensable in spite of their manifest limitations:

Fairs present a terrible physical environment in which to view art; they have been described as 'the best example of seeing art in the worst way'. The work is random and juxtaposed, with no sense of curatorial involvement. The setting and crowds are not conducive to evaluation. The lighting is always excessively bright, to appease safety concerns rather than to aid viewing. But every gallery shows with the same conditions – collectors accept them because they get to see so many new artists, and because at least once every fair, they hope to round a corner and spot a powerful work by someone previously unknown to them.

But the framework in which dealers and collectors function in art fairs, as in all fairs and festivals, is set by organizers who have their own strategic agenda, of which creating contexts that serve the interests of participants and the field is only one part. The location, internal structure and tempo of the event are the means by which this is accomplished. For example, the Annecy animation festival began life in Cannes, but the organizers decided to relocate to Annecy because, to quote Rüling (Chapter 8), they 'did not feel comfortable in the "glittery world" of Cannes'. The London Book Fair moved from Earls Court exhibition centre to the ExCeL exhibition centre in London's Docklands in 2006 to accommodate increasing size and retain a favourable March schedule. The move, however, turned out to be very unpopular, because participants, as Moeran recounts (Chapter 5), complained that it took far too long to get there, and '. . . there was nowhere pleasant in the vicinity of the fair to wine and dine customers'. In response, the organizers moved the fair back to Earls Court, notwithstanding the scheduling disadvantage.

Relocation is often accompanied by internal changes. In her study of Fan Fair, the Nashville country music festival (Chapter 9), Jennifer Lena examines how the organizers combined the relocation of the festival to downtown Nashville with restructuring of the festival programming, moving from 'label shows' selected in co-ordination with record companies, to market-driven scheduling. The change was made possible by greater availability of performance venues during the festival, but also reflected the declining size of record labels and shifts in market demographics. The organizers may have pursued the relocation for reasons of inadequate facilities, but they were clearly mindful of the fact that internal event structure and dynamics in the old location was out of line with the evolution of country music.

Fairs and festivals may reflect the fields in which they are situated, but to retain freedom of manoeuvre they seek a distinctive identity. For events such as the Nashville country music festival and International Television Program Market (MIP-TV), distinct identity is defined primarily by size and visibility relative to other similar events in the field. For others, a distinct identity depends on constructing a legitimacy that is taken for granted by other key players in the field. In the case of the Salon, Delacour and Leca (Chapter 1) show how the Academy successfully constructed a legitimacy endured for more than two centuries. They attribute the legitimacy crisis that fatally undermined the Salon to an inability to respond to new artistic styles, but from another perspective the failure is also strategic: the Academy became a purely defensive enterprise, showing no initiative when faced with a changing environment. By contrast, in his study the Annecy animation festival Rüling (Chapter 8) shows the very opposite: an organization repeatedly taking initiative to reconstruct legitimacy in response to technological, commercial and artistic developments.

In many fairs and festivals, the resources used to construct legitimacy derive primarily from the field. The typical pattern is for leading field players to 'seed' the event using their own symbolic and social capital. In the case of some fairs and festivals, however, the state contributes to legitimacy construction directly and indirectly. This certainly applies to the Salon and the Annecy animation festival mentioned earlier. The Salon benefited directly from the legitimacy conferred on the Academy by the French crown, and Annecy many years later benefited indirectly from the backing of the French Film Board, and from the support of the French state more generally.

The role of the state in assisting the formation of fairs and festivals has been instrumental in pioneering new institutional forms such as the World Fair, which was sponsored and inaugurated by Queen Victoria. For the British Empire in its zenith the World Fair was an opportunity to co-opt images of enlightened progress (Young, 2009). Nashville city leaders, on the other hand, had more modest goals. As Lena notes in her study of the Nashville country music festival, city leaders lent their support to the festival as part of their efforts to brand Nashville as 'Music City, USA'. The biennale, which was launched by the Municipality of Venice in 1895, was later taken over by the Italian Fascist regime for its own ends. But as Tang shows in her study of 'biennalization' as a movement (Chapter 3), in the post-war era state co-optation was based on inclusive internationalism, notwithstanding the fact that the artists that congregated in the event under their national flags were in reality cosmopolitan in residence and outlook.

Conclusion

Fairs and festivals are not merely products of the field in which they are situated, but also organizations that compete for resources against field rivals. Whether one is talking about premier film festivals, art fairs, fashion weeks, or even auction houses, it is clear that these are enterprises that occupy strategic positions. These strategic positions drive behaviour at the organizational level. Thus, it is not difficult to identify dominant oligopolies in many of the industries and fields that are discussed in this book. Nor is it difficult to see some of the key decisions – for example, the decision by the Annecy animation festival organizers to create new prizes and increase the number of categories – as a deliberate move to counter potential challenges to pre-eminence.

A strategic analysis of fairs and festivals is consistent with the field-configuring perspective, but it also ties in with the value-creating perspective that runs through most of the contributions to this book. If we accept that fairs and festivals are events and sites where the values of resources are established, we must likewise accept that value is not absolute but relative to the position occupied by the event. As Mezias *et al.* (Chapter 7) suggest, the symbolic value conferred by winning in a premier film festival is greater than winning in festivals that are not part of the elite group (see also Elsaesser, 2005). Maastricht art fair confers more value on participants and art works because it occupies a dominant position *vis-à-vis* other art fairs. For more than 200 years exhibition in the Salon conferred more symbolic and economic value on art works than any other, but as its strategic position declined so did the value that it conferred.

The internal dynamics of fairs and festivals on a micro scale must therefore be seen in relation to a macro perspective of fairs and festivals at the strategic level. Just as currencies fluctuate in response to the shifting economic position of countries, so does the value conferred on resources by fairs and festivals. By this analogy, a fair or a festival, as we noted earlier, confers a 'base value' on the resources that participants bring with them, but this base value is subject to fluctuations that depend on the position of the event *vis-à-vis* its alternative. For example, an invitation to the Paris, London, New York or Milan fashion weeks generates high valuation of the invitee's symbolic and social resources, whereas an invitation to the dozens of other fashion weeks held throughout the world signifies far lower valuation. More to the point, fashion weeks with lower position in the fashion hierarchy are less restrictive about their invitations, which in turn points to a broader demarcation of where the field's boundaries can be placed. This connects the macro to the micro: for participants in fashion weeks with lower prestige, the name of the game is to move up the hierarchy, not so much because top fashion shows confer membership in the fashion field, but because an invitation to these events certifies the value of resources held.

References

Anand, N. and Watson, M. 2004. 'Tournament rituals in the evolution of fields: the case of the Grammy Awards', *Academy of Management Journal* 47, 59–80.

Baker, G., Gibbons, R. and Murphy, K. J. 2002. 'Relational contracts and the theory of the firm', *The Quarterly Journal of Economics* 117:1 February, 39–84.

Bathelt, H. and Schuldt, N. 2008. 'Between luminaires and meat grinders: international trade fairs as temporary clusters', *Regional Studies* 42:6, 853–68.

Becker, G. S. 1964. *Human Capital: A Theoretical and Empirical Analysis, with Special Reference to Education*. University of Chicago Press.

Bourdieu, P. 1977. *Outline of a Theory of Practice*. Cambridge University Press.

1997. *The Logic of Practice*. Cambridge: Polity Press.

2000. *Propos sur le Champ Politique*. Presses Universitaires de Lyon.

Braudel, F. 1992. *The Wheels of Commerce (Civilization and Capitalism: 15th-18th Century. Volume 2)*. University of California Press.

Dargis, M. 2010. 'At Cannes, the economy is on-screen', *New York Times*, 16 May.

Elsaesser, T. 2005. 'Film festival networks: the new topographies of cinema in Europe', in T. Elsaesser (ed.), *European Cinema: Face to Face with Hollywood*. Amsterdam University Press, pp. 82–107.

Epstein, S. R. 1994. 'Regional fairs, institutional innovation, and economic growth in late medieval Europe', *Economic History Review* 38:3, 459–82.

Lampel, J. and Meyer, A. 2008. 'Field-configuring events as structuring mechanisms: how conferences, ceremonies, and trade shows constitute new technologies, industries, and markets', *Journal of Management Studies* 45:6, 1,025–35.

Lampel, J. and Shivasharan, S. N. 2009. 'Classics foretold? Contemporaneous and retrospective consecration in the UK film industry', *Cultural Trends* 18:3, 239–48.

Maskell, P., Bathelt, H. and Malmberg, A. 2006. 'Building global knowledge pipelines: the role of temporary clusters', *European Planning Studies* 14:8, 997–1,013.

Moeran, B. 2010. 'The book fair as a tournament of values', *Journal of the Royal Anthropological Institute* 16:1, 138–54.

Roos, J., Edvinsson, L. and Roos, G. 1998. *Intellectual Capital: Navigating in the New Business Landscape*. New York University Press.

Rosenberg, N. 1990. 'Adam Smith and the stock of moral capital', *History of Political Economy* 22, 1–18.

Verlinden, C. 1963. 'Markets and Fairs', *Cambridge Economic History of Europe*, Vol. 3. Cambridge University Press.

Waddell, G. 2004. *How Fashion Works: Couture, Ready To Wear and Mass Production*. Oxford: Blackwell Science.

Young, P. 2009. *Globalization and the Great Exhibition: the Victorian New World Order*. Basingstoke: Palgrave Macmillan.

Author index

Subject index